DO METAPHORS DREAM OF LITERAL SLEEP?

DO METAPHORS DREAM OF LITERAL SLEEP?

A Science-Fictional Theory of Representation

SEO-YOUNG CHU

HARVARD UNIVERSITY PRESS

Cambridge, Massachusetts, and London, England

2010

The poem "L'Art 1910" by Ezra Pound, from PERSONAE, is copyright © 1926 by Ezra Pound. It is reprinted by permission of New Directions Publishing Corp. Additional credits appear before the index.

Library of Congress Cataloging-in-Publication Data
Chu, Seo-Young, 1978–
    Do metaphors dream of literal sleep? : a science-fictional theory of representation / Seo-Young Chu.
        p.   cm.
    Includes bibliographical references and index.
    ISBN 978-0-674-05517-9 (alk. paper)
    1. Science fiction, American—20th century—History and criticism.   2. Literature and technology—United States—History—20th century.   3. Literature and society—United States—History—20th century.   4. Literary form.   I. Title.
    PS374.S35C49   2010
    813'.0876209—dc22   2010014760

To my parents

Contents

DO METAPHORS DREAM OF LITERAL SLEEP?

Introduction: Lyric Mimesis

Traditionally science fiction (SF) has been understood as a genre whose objects of representation are hypothetical if not outright imaginary. *The Oxford English Dictionary (OED)* defines science fiction as "imaginative fiction based on postulated scientific discoveries or spectacular environmental changes, freq. set in the future or on other planets and involving space or time travel." The *Cambridge Advanced Learner's Dictionary* defines SF as "books, films or cartoons about an imagined future, especially about space travel or other planets." *A Glossary of Literary Terms* defines SF as the portrayal of "an imagined reality that is radically different in its nature and functioning from the world of our ordinary experience" (Abrams, 278).[1] *American Heritage* defines SF as a "literary or cinematic genre in which fantasy, typically based on speculative scientific discoveries or developments, environmental changes, space travel, or life on other planets, forms part of the plot or background." *Brave New Words: The Oxford Dictionary of Science Fiction* defines SF as "a genre (of literature, film, etc.) in which the setting differs from our own world (e.g., by the invention of new technology, through contact with aliens, by having a different history, etc.), and in which the difference is based on extrapolations made from one or more changes or suppositions."

Practitioners and theorists of science fiction have characterized it in ways that are consonant with the term's denotations. Joanna Russ has identified SF as a discourse whose "subject matter does not exist" ("Speculations," 16). Philip K. Dick has likewise stressed the counterfactual nature of SF, arguing in "My Definition" that a work of science fiction must portray "events that could not occur in our society—or in any known society present or past" (99). In *The Dreams Our Stuff Is Made Of,* Thomas Disch insinuates a dichotomy between works of SF and truthful statements about reality: "America is a nation of liars, and for that reason science fiction has a special claim to be our national literature, as the art form best adapted to telling the lies we like to hear" (15). In *Structural Fabulation,* Robert Scholes characterizes science fiction as a "modern body of fictional works" that "accepts or pretends to accept a cognitive responsibility to imagine what is not yet apparent or existent, and to examine this in some systematic way" (102). And in *Metamorphoses of Science Fiction,* Darko Suvin offers what has become perhaps the most influential definition of SF ever devised: science fiction, according to Suvin, is an art form that achieves the effect of "cognitive estrangement" by way of "an imaginative framework alternative to the author's empirical environment" (8).

In each of these comments, science fiction is portrayed as a genre that operates beyond (or even counter to) mimesis.[2] By "mimesis," I simply mean "the representation or imitation of the real world in (a work of) art" *(OED),* and in using this definition I accept as a postulate the capacity of language to reflect a reality ontologically prior to representation. (To borrow a phrase from *Structural Fabulation:* I have faith in the transcribability of things.)[3] My use of so uncomplicated a definition of "mimesis" in this book is deliberate. I am mindful that mimesis has a complicated history extending as far back as Plato (who is generally thought to have judged mimetic art as a counterfeit of reality and reality as a counterfeit of Truth) and still actively unfolding in the twenty-first century (as evidenced, for example, in the 2002 book *The Aesthetics of Mimesis* by Stephen Halliwell, who argues that Plato's judgment of mimesis was more nuanced and less pejorative than is generally thought to be the case).[4] Over the centuries, the idea of mimesis has undergone countless permutations and revisions by thinkers as diverse as Adorno, Aristotle, Erich Auerbach, Barthes, Derrida, René Girard, Goethe, Kathryn Hume, Rousseau, and Michael Taussig. Although this history has informed my own thinking on mimesis, it is ultimately incommensurate with the theoretical project of this book. Positing the simplest possible conception of mimesis as an axiom, I approach mimesis not from the familiar context of its long and contentious past but from a context more alien and futuristic: science fiction.

Do Metaphors Dream of Literal Sleep? proposes a science-fictional theory of mimesis. What does it mean for something to elude representation? What makes some referents less susceptible than other referents to representation?

What does it take for an elusive referent to become available for representation? As I hope to show, there are vibrant advantages to a science-fictional approach to these questions. Through its prolific abundance in today's global culture and its otherworldly relevance to matters of the world, science fiction presents itself as an intriguingly convenient resource for generating new perspectives on an ancient topic. The discourses that already encompass science fiction and make it what we perceive it to be—for example, telekinesis, robots, time travel, superpowers, and other items from the repertory of science-fictional motifs; the virtual nonexistence of science-fiction poetry; etymological resonances of the term "science fiction"; the cultural aura of iconic films such as *2001: A Space Odyssey*, as well as the blockbuster influence of franchises such as Star Wars—together comprise a rich supply of aesthetic and philosophical materials from which to construct a suitable framework for thinking experimentally and productively about the representation of reality.

One material that I have found particularly vital to constructing a science-fictional theory of representation is the pervasive characterization (cited a few paragraphs ago) of science fiction as a genre that operates beyond mimesis.[5] Transposing this paradigm—discovering how it works from the other side—yields a strikingly viable paradigm for reconceptualizing mimesis, science fiction, and the relationship between them. *Do Metaphors Dream* is an argument for such a reconceptualization. Science fiction, I hope to demonstrate, operates fully within the realm of mimesis. The objects of science-fictional representation, while impossible to represent in a straightforward manner, are absolutely real. My reconceptualization of science fiction can be understood, more specifically, as Suvin's definition turned inside out. Instead of conceptualizing science fiction as a nonmimetic discourse that achieves the effect of cognitive estrangement through "an imaginative framework," I conceptualize science fiction as a mimetic discourse whose objects of representation are nonimaginary yet cognitively estranging.

Cognitively Estranging Referents

As a concept both integral to my argument and far from self-evident, the "cognitively estranging referent" requires some exposition in these introductory pages. What exactly does it mean for a referent, an object of representation, to be "cognitively estranging"? To answer this question, we must first ask what Suvin himself means when he calls science fiction the "literature of cognitive estrangement" (4). In Suvin's exact words, science fiction is "a literary genre whose necessary and sufficient conditions are the presence and interaction of estrangement and cognition, and whose main formal device is an imaginative framework alternative to the author's empirical environment" (7–8, emphasis deleted). According to Suvin, the presence of estrangement, which "differentiates SF from the 'realistic' literary mainstream," is determined by settings and characters that are *"radically or at least significantly different from empirical times, places, and characters* of 'mimetic' or 'naturalist' fiction" (8, viii, emphasis in original). The presence of cognition, which differentiates SF "not only from myth, but also from the folk (fairy) tale and the fantasy," is determined by the plausibility of the scenario depicted: the settings and characters, while estranging, should nonetheless be "perceived as *not impossible* within the cognitive (cosmological and anthropological) norms of the author's epoch" (8, viii, emphasis in original). In *Critical Theory and Science Fiction* (2000), Carl Freedman provides a valuable gloss on Suvin's definition. Freedman expands on the relationship of cognition to estrangement in the following way.

> Science fiction is determined by the *dialectic* between estrangement and cognition. The first term refers to the creation of an alternative fictional world that, by refusing to take our mundane environment for granted, implicitly or explicitly performs an estranging critical interrogation of the latter. But the *critical* character of the interrogation is guaranteed by the operation of cognition, which enables the science-fictional text to account rationally for its imagined world and for the connections as well as the disconnections of the latter to our own empirical world. If the dialectic is flattened out to mere cognition, then the result is "realistic" or mundane fiction, which can cognitively account for its imaginings but performs no estrangement; if the dialectic is flattened out to mere estrangement (or, it might be argued, pseudo-estrangement), then the result is fantasy, which estranges, or appears to estrange, but in an irrationalist, theoretically illegitimate way. (16–17, emphasis in original)

Freedman goes on to suggest that science fiction (or what he calls the science-fiction tendency) may be a precondition for representation itself: "Owing to the character of representation as a nontransparent process that necessarily involves not only similarity but *difference* between representation and the 'referent' of the latter, an irreducible degree of alterity and estrangement is bound to obtain even in the case of the most 'realistic' fiction imaginable" (21). In other words, to the extent that all representation is in some measure nontransparent—to the extent that it is impossible to establish full mimetic correspondence between referent and representational text—the process of representation is always characterized in some measure by the same dialectic that defines SF, namely, the dialectic between cognition and estrangement. While I agree that the dialectic between cognition and estrangement is essential to SF, I locate this dialectic not in the formal apparatus of a given SF text but in the object or phenomenon that the SF text seeks accurately to represent. Whereas Freedman characterizes representation as a "nontransparent" process that necessarily involves dissimilitude between referent and representational text, I characterize representation as a *translucent* process that necessarily involves greater similitude than dissimilitude between referent and representational text. Furthermore, whereas Freedman identifies realism as the product of a "flattened" dialectic between estrangement and cognition, I identify realism as a form of representation whose intrinsic "flatness"—unlike the intrinsic multidimensionality of science fiction—is unequal to the dynamic complexity that distinguishes the cognitively estranging referent. (I also differ with Suvin's and Freedman's characterization of fantasy as the product of the flattening of the dialectic between cognition and estrangement to mere estrangement. As I will soon explain, fantasy is a type of science-fictional mimesis whose cognitively estranging referent is the prodigious working of the imagination itself.)

To appreciate the dynamic complexity that distinguishes the cognitively estranging referent, let us consider the cognitively estranging referent as an object of wonder.[6] Wonder, as Philip Fisher observes in *Wonder, the Rainbow, and the Aesthetics of Rare Experiences*, is "the middle condition between an unawakened intellect and a systematic knowledge so complete that there no longer exists anything unexpected"; it is "a horizon-effect of the known, the unknown, and the unknowable" (81, 58). Objects completely unknowable (objects with respect to which our intellects remain completely "unawakened") are merely estranging. Objects completely knowable (objects with respect to which our knowledge is "so complete that there no longer exists anything unexpected") are merely accessible to cognition. But objects of wonder (objects that produce in us "a horizon-effect of the known, the unknown, and the unknowable") are cognitively estranging. These are the objects represented in science fiction. A successful work of SF is one whose wondrous effect on its reader/viewer/listener reproduces the wondrous qualities of the object or phenomenon that the work of science fiction mimetically represents.

To be sure, objects completely knowable and objects completely unknowable constitute hypothetical extremes: all objects are cognitively estranging to some extent. As Daniel Albright observes in *Representation and the Imagination,* even something as solid and seemingly unproblematic as a low-tech writing utensil will resist the writer's efforts to comprehend it as veridically as possible:

> The more closely I attend to my pencil, the more obscure it grows; if I assigned myself to write a page, a chapter, about my pencil I would increasingly have to lie or plagiarize. Or, if sheer truthfulness were my goal, I would have to write in a more and more attenuated and obtuse manner about my incomprehension and nescience; that is, the more concrete a representation I attempt, the more I am driven to either fantasy or abstraction. (61)

To create a perfect representation of the pencil—to represent the pencil in all its unmediated pencilness—is impossible. But anyone who attempts this impossible task is ultimately uninterested in creating a mimetic representation of the pencil. Rather, he or she is interested in testing the limits of mimesis and exposing the measure of unrepresentability (however minor this measure may be) inherent in all referents. What matters most to such an artist is not the pencil as an object of representation but the physicality of the artistic medium. As Albright puts it: "The urge to do away with convention and technique, the urge to seize and display something real beyond artifice, will lead to increasing preoccupation with the purely conventional and technical aspects of art" (12). Meanwhile, the writer tasked with producing a recognizably mimetic representation of the pencil might accomplish the task with a single sentence: "The pencil is 15.4 centimeters long, 7.2 millimeters in diameter, made of cedar wood and graphite, and painted yellow."

The difference between the representability of the pencil and the representability of any other referent is a difference in degree. Picture a spectrum whose two limits are "referents wholly accessible to cognition" and "wholly estranging referents." One end of the spectrum is populated by concrete objects highly susceptible to understanding and amenable to representation. These include softballs, paintbrushes, oak leaves, dimes, apple blossoms, almonds, and pencils of the kind discussed above. Realism and naturalism are extremely capable of representing such objects. The other end of the spectrum is occupied by referents virtually unknowable, referents that all but defy human language and comprehension. These include the infinitely remote future, the infinitely remote past, and whatever lies on the other side of death. Mimetic accounts of such referents exist nowhere—not even in science fiction.

Of particular interest to me is the rich and complicated area at the center of the spectrum. Located here are objects of full-blown wonder, objects that (to use Fisher's words) evoke "the middle condition between an unawakened intellect and a systematic knowledge so complete that there no longer exists anything unexpected." Neither totally knowable nor totally unknowable, such cognitively estranging referents encompass the sublime (e.g., outer space), virtual entities (cyberspace), realities imperceptible to the human brain (the fourth dimension), phenomena whose historical contexts have not yet been fully realized (robot rights), and events so overwhelming that they escape immediate experience (shell shock). Although impossible to assess empirically—cyberspace cannot be weighed on a scale; a traumatic experience cannot be quantified in units of time—these referents can, have, and do become available for representation in SF. Accordingly, SF is distinguished by its capacity to perform the massively complex representational and epistemological work necessary to render cognitively estranging referents available both for representation and for understanding. Realism, by contrast, is distinguished by the alacrity with which it can imitate certain kinds of objects, objects such as almonds and nickels, objects themselves distinguished by the alacrity with which they offer themselves up to flat description.

Yet to differentiate between science fiction and realism in this manner is misleading. As I suggested earlier, all representation is to some degree science-fictional because all reality is to some degree cognitively estranging. What most people call "realism"—what some critics call "mundane fiction"—is actually a "weak" or low-intensity variety of science fiction, one that requires relatively little energy to accomplish its representational task insofar as its referents (e.g., softballs) are readily susceptible to representation. Conversely, what most people call "science fiction" is actually a high-intensity variety of realism, one that requires astronomical levels of energy to accomplish its representational task insofar as its referents (e.g., cyberspace) elaborately defy straightforward representation. In this book, "realism" designates low-intensity mimesis, while "science fiction" designates high-intensity mimesis. Realism and science fiction, then, exist on a continuum parallel to the above-mentioned continuum where every object of representation has its place—from shoelaces, dimes, and oak leaves to cyberspace, trauma, black holes, and financial derivatives.

Although the distance between realism and SF may be vast enough for the difference in degree to amount to a difference in kind, the distance will never be so vast as to render "science fiction" and "realism" each other's antonym. There is no such thing as the opposite of science fiction. Likewise, there is no such thing as the opposite of realism.

Since the extent to which a referent challenges representation may be liable to fluctuation, the continuum of referents and the continuum of representational modes are capable of changing over time. For example, under certain cultural and political conditions, a referent previously thought of as extremely cognitively estranging (e.g., romantic desire between two women) may cease to estrange and instead become the kind of referent more at home in low-intensity SF (realism) than in high-intensity SF (SF "proper"). Consequently, the science-fictional status of a text—the status of a text as a mimetic representation of a highly cognitively estranging phenomenon—may vary with circumstance. A work of SF can even help to bring about its own obsolescence by causing its referent to grow more accessible to cognition and thereby less estranging. (Chapter 2, "Cyberspace in the 1990s," addresses this very issue.) Furthermore, the act of analyzing a cognitively estranging referent has the potential to modify that referent's status as cognitively estranging, whether through elucidation, through unwitting obfuscation, or through some other means difficult to predict. In writing this book, I have sought to explain as exactly as possible the cognitively estranging nature of each referent without demystifying or mystifying either the referent in question or the intricate process (itself a cognitively estranging phenomenon) by which the referent becomes available for representation in a work of science fiction.

The phrase "a work of science fiction," I should clarify, is not meant to posit the existence of texts in which science-fiction representation is sustained at the same level of intensity from beginning to end. Hardly any mimetic text refers exclusively to a single referent. A science-fiction text may refer to various referents of varying levels of susceptibility to representation. Indeed, almost all "works of SF" (i.e., works likely to be found in the "Science Fiction" section of a bookstore) do contain elements of "realism"/low-intensity SF. For instance, Octavia Butler's time-travel narrative *Kindred* (1979) contains a brief account of a red-brick house comparable to accounts of houses we might find in realist novels. In *Kindred*, however, the red-brick house is a stray moment of realism that happens to be included in a text whose predominant referent (the trauma of American slavery) challenges straightforward representation, and whose predominant representational task (performed here by the SF narrative of time travel) could not be accomplished by low-intensity representation. A "work of science fiction" is a text in which high-intensity mimesis predominates. A "work of realism" is a text in which low-intensity mimesis predominates.

If the difference between science fiction and realism corresponds to the difference in the levels of intensity needed to render their referents available for representation, then the differences among various types of SF correspond to the various types of cognitively estranging referents that require high-intensity representation. Genres often classified as both nonmimetic and non-SF are actually varieties of science fiction that correspond mimetically to specific types of cognitively estranging referents. *Surrealism*, for example, is a type of science-fictional mimesis whose cognitively estranging referent is the phenomenon of dreaming. *Utopianism* is a type of science-fictional mimesis whose cognitively estranging referent is the ideal polity. *Detective fiction* is a type of science-fictional mimesis whose cognitively estranging referent is the mystery of ratiocination. *Gothic/horror* is a type of science-fictional mimesis whose cognitively estranging referent is the occulted-yet-irrepressible unconscious. *Slipstream*—a relatively young subgenre that has emerged over the past several decades, with prominent examples including Don DeLillo's 1985 novel *White Noise*, the 1998 film *The Truman Show*, and Ed Park's 2008 novel *Personal Days*—is a type of science-fictional mimesis whose cognitively estranging referent is the partially virtual reality of living in a mainstream hypermediated and rendered half-surreal by technology.[7] *Fantasy* is a type of science-fictional mimesis whose cognitively estranging referent is the prodigious working of the human imagination. *Magical realism* is a type of science-fictional mimesis whose cognitively estranging referent is the hybrid nature of realities lived in postcolonial spaces such as modern India and Latin America. And *young adult supernatural fiction* (e.g., the Harry Potter books and films) is a type of science-fictional mimesis whose cognitively estranging referent is adolescent subjectivity.

Insofar as these various types of referents are not identically cognitively estranging, certain types of science fiction sit more closely than others do to the realism (low-intensity) end of the spectrum. For example, insofar as the process of ratiocination is slightly less cognitively estranging than the working of the imagination, the genre of detective fiction is more "realistic" than the genre of fantasy. However, the differences in the degrees to which these various types of referents challenge representation are sufficiently minor to keep the types of SF enumerated above (surrealism, gothic, etc.) appreciably distinct from realism proper. What unites these types of SF—what differentiates them from realism proper—is their capacity to generate mimetic accounts of aspects of reality that defy straightforward representation.

A Lyric Theory of Science Fiction;
A Science-Fictional Theory of the Lyric

It might seem paradoxical to identify science fiction as a referential mode of discourse whose referents defy literal representation. But as I am about to explain, science fiction is powered by *lyric* or *poetic* forces—I use those two terms interchangeably[8]—that allow SF to transcend the literal/figurative dichotomy.

Figurative language occupies a special place in science fiction. Occurrences of figurative language in SF texts and contexts have an interesting tendency to elicit literal interpretation almost as a matter of course, especially among readers well versed in SF. Samuel Delany has famously characterized SF as a "play of codic conventions" that program the reader of SF to apply literal understanding to potentially metaphorical phrases—"Her world exploded" is one of several memorable examples that Delany invokes to illustrate his point—where a reader more accustomed to a different set of interpretive protocols might apply no literal understanding at all ("The Semiology of Silence," 27). Along similar lines, Ursula Le Guin has theorized that devotees of SF are conditioned to take for granted the literality of potentially metaphorical phrases such as Delany's "Her world exploded" and Le Guin's own "He was absorbed in the landscape" ("Introduction" to *The Norton Book of SF*, 30–31). These insights call to mind Tzvetan Todorov's remarks in *The Fantastic* (1970) concerning the dynamic between fantastic literature and the relationship of literal to figurative: "The supernatural often appears," Todorov notes, "because we take a figurative sense literally" (76–77).

Like Delany, Le Guin, and Todorov, I am struck by the propensity of SF readers to anticipate (even if subliminally) the literalization of metaphors in their favorite stories and novels. What separates the insights of Le Guin, Delany, and Todorov from my own observations is a discrepancy in the magnitude of importance that they and I respectively attach to the literalization of lyric figures in science fiction. Whereas Le Guin and Delany suggest that SF enthusiasts are predisposed to expect the literalization of metaphors from SF, I subscribe to a more extreme position: lyric figures are systematically literalized, substantiated, and consolidated in science fiction as ontological features of narrative worlds. For example, *apostrophe*—a lyric trope whereby a speaker addresses an absent or inanimate person as though the "you" were alive and attendant—is routinely literalized in SF as *telepathy*, whereby a speaker addresses an absent person who is actually alive, mentally present, and capable of listening to the speaker without the aid of telephones or even ears. *Synesthesia*—the poetic description of one kind of sensory experience via words that ordinarily describe another—is routinely literalized in SF as a *paranormal sensorium*, for example, the mutant anemone who hears photons as music in J. G. Ballard's 1962 story "The Voices of Time." *Personification*—a lyric figure whereby an abstraction or inanimate object is characterized as if endowed with human attributes—is routinely literalized in SF as the *animation of a humanoid artifact*, with examples ranging from the imprinting of the robot child in the 2001 film *A.I.* to the moments in Richard Powers's 1995 novel *Galatea 2.2* when an artificial personality named Helen evinces a sentience growing daily more and more human.

Beyond literalizing individual lyric figures, science fiction as a whole constitutes a literalization of *catachresis*, defined by the *New Princeton Encyclopedia of Poetry and Poetics* as "the misapplication of a word, especially to produce a strained or mixed metaphor" (172).[9] Known also as the metaphysical conceit, catachresis has legendarily been characterized by Samuel Johnson as a "combination of dissimilar images" whereby "the most heterogeneous ideas are yoked by violence together" (348). (An oft-cited example comes from John Donne's "Valediction: Forbidding Mourning," which incongruously likens a pair of separated lovers to the legs of a compass.) Johnson would likely have applied these same words to SF, where instances of literalized catachresis abound. Here are just a few: Dr. Jekyll and Mr. Hyde (two incongruous selves—one morally upright, the other depraved—yoked by violence together within one person); "The Mortal Immortal" (Mary Shelley's 1833 short story, whose protagonist struggles with the predicament of having been born mortal but granted immortality as a youth); *The Female Man* (Joanna Russ's 1975 novel, which explores the catachrestic yoking together of "opposite" sexes); *The Peace War* (Vernor Vinge's 1984 novel, in which world peace is enforced by a mega-weapon designed to neutralize military instruments); *TV Garden* (a 1974 installation piece by Nam June Paik in which high-tech monitors bloom startlingly amidst natural flora); and steampunk (a late-twentieth-century/early-twenty-first-century breed of SF that revels in such anachronistic spectacles as a steam-powered wood-and-brass laptop surrounded by Victorian décor). Indeed, the term "science fiction" is itself a metaphysical conceit. Tellingly, SF is called neither "scientific fiction" nor "fictional science"—phrases in which a noun is modified by an adjective—but "science fiction," a phrase that violently yokes together two heterogeneous nouns while leaving both terms unmodified. Every science-fiction world is a metaphysical conceit literalized as ontological fact within a narrative universe.

To characterize science fiction as a lyric discourse, as I have just done, may seem even more counterintuitive than my earlier characterization of SF as a mimetic discourse. Science-fictioneers and non-science-fictioneers alike are apt to think of SF in narrative terms. Poems rarely show up on syllabi for courses on science fiction.[10] Poems are absent, too, from the majority of SF anthologies. (Most of the anthologies in which SF poems do appear are dedicated exclusively to SF verse: e.g., the 1969 anthology *Holding Your Eight Hands;* the 1984 anthology *Burning with a Vision;* and the annual Rhysling anthologies, composed of poems nominated for the Rhysling Award, given annually since 1978 to the best long and short SF poems of the year, chosen by members of the Science Fiction Poetry Association.) Wikipedia's entry for "science fiction" covers a range of media (television, film, novels, radio, comics, theater) but makes no mention of poetry. Furthermore, "lyric," "poem," "poetry," and "verse" are nowhere to be found in the indexes to the following important field-shaping monographs, surveys, and essay collections on science fiction (listed here in chronological order): *Science Fiction: History, Science, Vision* (1977) by Robert Scholes and Eric Rabkin; *Metamorphoses of Science Fiction* (1979) by Darko Suvin; *Alien Encounters: Anatomy of Science Fiction* (1981) by Mark Rose; *Terminal Identity* (1993) by Scott Bukatman; *Science Fiction before 1900* (1994) by Paul Alkon; *Reading by Starlight: Postmodern Science Fiction* (1995) by Damien Broderick; *The Dreams Our Stuff Is Made Of* (1998) by Thomas Disch; *Critical Theory and Science Fiction* (2000) by Carl Freedman; *Science Fiction Culture* (2000) by Camille Bacon-Smith; *Genre Fission* (2000) by Marleen Barr; *Science Fiction* (2000) by Adam Roberts; *Learning from Other Worlds* (2001), edited by Patrick Parrinder; *Edging into the Future* (2002), edited by Veronica Hollinger and Joan Gordon; *Imaginary Communities* (2002) by Phillip Wegner; *Science Fiction after 1900* (2002) by Brooks Landon; *Science Fiction, Canonization, Marginalization, and the Academy* (2002), edited by George Edgar Slusser and Gary Westfahl; *The Cambridge Companion to Science Fiction* (2003), edited by Edward James and Farah Mendlesohn; *Speculations on Speculation* (2005), edited by James Gunn and Matthew Candelaria; *Science Fiction* (2005) by Roger Luckhurst; *A Companion to Science Fiction* (2005), edited by David Seed; *The History of Science Fiction* (2005) by Adam Roberts; *Archaeologies of the Future* (2005) by Fredric Jameson; *Colonialism and the Emergence of Science Fiction* (2008) by John Rieder; *The Seven Beauties of Science Fiction* (2008) by Istvan Csicsery-Ronay Jr.; *The Science Fiction Handbook* (2009), edited by Keith Booker and Anne-Marie Thomas; and *The Routledge Companion to Science Fiction* (2009), edited by Mark Bould, Andrew Butler, Adam Roberts, and Sherryl Vint.[11] (A notable exception: *Anatomy of Wonder* includes Steve Eng's essay "The Speculative Muse: An Introduction to Science Fiction Poetry," which provides a helpful overview of SF verse.) Equally astonishing is the fact that literary reference books explicitly label SF as a nonlyrical genre. *The Oxford Concise Dictionary of Literary Terms* classifies SF as a "branch of prose fiction" (230). Likewise, *A Glossary of Literary Terms* classifies SF as a set of "novels and short stories" (278). Such classifications are plainly contradicted by the verifiable existence of SF verse by poets such as Diane Ackerman, Suzette Haden Elgin (founder of the Science Fiction Poetry Association and author of *The Science Fiction Poetry Handbook*), Robert Frazier, Cathy Park Hong, Andrew Joron, and Frederick Turner.

As the preceding paragraph indicates, the SF canon of writing is dominated by prose. Furthermore, SF prose is dominantly perceived as void of lyricism—a perception voiced by Robert Scholes when he remarks that "it is fair to say that much SF is written in journeyman's prose, serviceable but inelegant" (*Structural Fabulation*, 48). Yet to deem SF categorically prosaic is to overlook an important lyric presence discernible not just in SF poems but in SF movies, novels, comics, and myriad other kinds of SF production. I hereby submit a theory that might initially sound implausible but will, I hope, have become more convincing by the end of this introduction. Science fiction and lyric poetry are joined inseparably by rich affinities.[12] The qualities that (either individually or in some combination) make a work of science fiction "science-fictional" tend to coincide with the qualities that (either individually or in some combination) make a lyric poem "lyrical." The coincidence lies in more than a shared intensity of figurative language. What makes a lyric poem "lyrical" is a constellation of interrelated attributes that have characterized Anglophone poetry from the Renaissance (if not earlier) to the present. Lyric poetry is frequently soliloquy-like. Lyric voices speak from beyond ordinary time. Lyric poems are inhabited by situations and tableaux transcending ordinary temporality. Lyric descriptions are charged with depictive intensity. Lyric poetry is musically expressive. Lyric poems evoke heightened and eccentric states of consciousness. These statements (each of which I will expand on shortly) are true of SF as well. SF is frequently soliloquy-like. SF voices speak from beyond ordinary time. Works of SF are inhabited by situations and tableaux transcending ordinary temporality. SF descriptions are charged with depictive intensity. SF is musically expressive. And works of SF evoke heightened and eccentric states of consciousness.

Each of the statements above can be supported by copious examples from a huge variety of SF texts. To gather, analyze, and place in meaningful order some of this staggering wealth of bibliographic evidence will constitute much of my work below. The evidence is organized taxonomically to reveal the systematic nature of lyric's omnipresence in science fiction. In amassing this evidence and assembling this taxonomy, I have tried to make the collection of examples as comprehensive as possible. The SF texts encompass film, concept art, drama, short stories, novels, and more. Chronologically they span four centuries. Authors range from those established in the "Western canon" (e.g., Swift, Shelley, Orwell) to those not yet firmly established in the "SF canon" (e.g., Ted Chiang, Nalo Hopkinson). They include both writers of "hard" (scientifically rigorous) SF (e.g., Greg Bear, Arthur Clarke) and writers of "soft" SF (e.g., Bradbury, Atwood). Moreover, the authors include not only prose stylists celebrated for their lyrical writing (e.g., Delany, Gibson, Cunningham) but also writers who are not often considered lyrical stylists (e.g., Niven, Asimov). Despite my attempts at inclusiveness, the catalogue remains grievously incomplete. Certain types of media—for example, radio, television, video games—are underrepresented. Also, most of the authors are Anglophone, with Verne, Lem, and Zamyatin among the few exceptions. A project such as this would have a better chance of succeeding as a truly encyclopedic compilation if it existed online as a database to which contributors from all over the world could add updated information and new entries.

Nevertheless, by launching even a partial exploration of the pervasiveness of lyric attributes in narrative science fiction, we can at least begin to appreciate how and why science fiction is capable of performing its representational task. As I hope to demonstrate, only a narrative form thoroughly powered by lyricism possesses enough torque—enough twisting force, enough *verse* (from "vertere," Latin for "to turn")—to convert an elusive referent into an object available for representation. Only a form in which poetic *tropes* (from "tropos," Greek for "turn") are systematically turned into narrative literalities can accommodate referents ordinarily averse to representation. By literalizing poetic figures, science fiction transcends the literal/figurative dichotomy. In transcending the literal/figurative dichotomy, science fiction provides a representational home for referents that are themselves neither purely literal nor purely figurative in nature. To this crucial knotwork of logic I will return in a later section.

Science-Fictional Soliloquists

To open an investigation of the rich symmetries between poetry and science fiction, let us visit that set of texts where both poetry and science fiction are explicitly present: science-fiction poems. When we ask ourselves what makes a science-fiction poem science-fictional, and when we then ask ourselves what makes this same science-fiction poem lyrical, we are bound to realize that what makes the poem lyrical is also what makes it science-fictional.

Consider, for example, the following lines from Ruth Fainlight's 1969 poem "A Report," anthologized in *Holding Your Eight Hands.*

> For the first ten years I fell
> Through enormous space and did not pass one star.
> . . .
> Somewhere early on I died.
> In the emptiness of my metalled suit
> God fell with me.
> Then I left such thoughts behind
> Or above, or below, me
> Lost awareness of God and time simultaneously
> And approached the first star.
> But my suit did not burn, so I kept falling.
>
> How many stars, how many light-years later
> When I first knew nothing would be my salvation?
> Nothing and nothing, outside and inside:
> The same fabric of thoughts and metal suit.
> Through expanding instants,
> Perhaps an aeon, I had my last idea.
> I was not moving. Stars fled from me
> And dragged space with them.
> My vacant suit could be the home of God
> Whose welded seams might last forever.

What is most science-fictional about this poem (aside from the spacesuit) is the otherworldly voice of the lyric speaker. "Somewhere early on I died," she recalls, her voice reaching us from outside the limits of human experience: "Stars fled from me/And dragged space with them." For the reader of this poem, such words constitute a source of awe. What does it mean for stars to drag space in their wake? How can someone who died long ago speak as though still alive? Yet the awe we feel is absent from the astronaut's voice. For her, the phenomenon of awe is an obsolete notion. Light-years beyond death, she has superseded human time. Aeons beyond her "last idea," she has become part of the nothingness of eternity. The absence of awe from her voice escalates the reader's own sense of awe.

The astronaut's science-fictional voice would be out of place in the world of realist fiction. In Austen's *Emma* (1816), for instance, all voices emanate from people who reside on earth, people whose living bodies exist in a domain where time can be measured in minutes, hours, days, months, etc. Yet the science-fictional voice of Fainlight's star-lost astronaut is at home in the universe of lyric poetry. Lyric speakers often address the reader from beyond the realm of human chronology. The following poem by Emily Dickinson is exemplary of the timeless quality of the lyric "I":

> I felt a Funeral, in my Brain,
> And Mourners, to and fro
> Kept treading—treading—till it seemed
> That Sense was breaking through—
>
> And when they all were seated,
> A Service, like a Drum—
> Kept beating—beating—till I thought
> My Mind was going numb—
>
> And then I heard them lift a Box
> And creak across my Soul
> With those same Boots of Lead, again,
> Then Space—began to toll,
>
> As all the Heavens were a Bell,
> And Being, but an Ear,
> And I, and Silence, some strange Race
> Wrecked, solitary, here—

> And then a Plank in Reason, broke,
> And I dropped down, and down—
> And hit a World, at every plunge,
> And Finished knowing—then—

Like Fainlight's astronaut, who speaks from beyond human life, the lyric "I" in Dickinson's poem speaks from a dimension where human time is nonexistent. No clock could gauge the "breaking through" of sense, the mysterious "toll" of "Space," the feeling of a funeral in the brain. Not only do the speakers in both poems address us from outside the scope of temporality, but both address us from outside the scope of earthly knowledge. Where "Being" is "but an Ear," where "stars" have "dragged space" in their wake, human understanding has no access. Indeed, the voice that says "I fell/Through enormous space" and long ago "had my last idea" is indistinguishable from the voice that says "I dropped down, and down—/And hit a World, at every plunge, /And Finished knowing—then." Such a voice originates in a state of unthinkable loneliness, a loneliness that we human readers are unequipped to conceptualize, a state of consciousness that cannot be shared with our own. Dislocated from the human race, the speaker in both poems has instead joined what Dickinson calls the "strange Race" of "Silence"—a race consisting of one member alone.

"A Report" illustrates a number of important connections between science fiction and poetry. First, there is something soliloquy-like about both SF and lyric. "All poetry is of the nature of soliloquy," John Stuart Mill famously observed in his 1833 essay "What Is Poetry?": "The peculiarity of poetry appears to us to lie in the poet's utter unconsciousness of a listener. Poetry is feeling confessing itself to itself in moments of solitude, and embodying itself in symbols which are the nearest possible representations of the feeling in the exact shape in which it exists in the poet's mind" (1055). More recently, Sharon Cameron has elaborated on Mill's observation: the lyric, Cameron writes in *Lyric Time* (1979), "must attend to no more than one (its own) speaking voice. This fact makes the self in the lyric unitary, and gives it the illusion of alone holding sway over the universe, there being, for all practical purposes, no one else, nothing else, to inhabit it" (119). Unlike the typical novel, which Bakhtin has identified as a dialogical form characterized by the plurality of speech types (*Moby-Dick*, for example, includes zoology, maritime adventure, historiography), the lyric speaks in the solitary voice of introspection. "A Report" and "I Felt a Funeral" are two poems in which the soliloquy-likeness of poetry is particularly noticeable. But the unselfconscious voice of the solitary lyric speaker can be heard in poems generally—from Wordsworth's 1804 poem "I Wandered Lonely as a Cloud" (whose speaker invokes "that inward eye / Which is the bliss of solitude") to Anne Sexton's 1972 poem "The Ambition Bird" (whose speaker talks to herself at 3:15 A.M.). Even in poems that acknowledge a "you," the effect is of soliloquy insofar as the addressee is typically framed as absent or dead. By using apostrophe, by addressing someone who is conspicuously missing, the speaker calls attention to her aloneness. Thus, poems such as Elizabeth Bishop's "One Art"—"Even losing you (the joking voice, a gesture / I love) I shan't have lied. It's evident / the art of losing's not too hard to master"—might as well be soliloquies.

Mill's and Cameron's remarks on poetry and soliloquy are readily applicable to science fiction. This is not to say that all works of SF center on soliloquists, nor is it to suggest that narratives must exclude dialogue to qualify as science fiction. Yet it is worth noting that many emotionally significant moments in SF narratives are moments of soliloquy-like narration. These are moments that readers of poetry would identify as expressions of lyric subjectivity, moments that readers of SF would identify as soulful characterization, and moments that I identify as expressions of states of consciousness simultaneously science-fictional and lyric. Doomed to soliloquy by apocalyptic circumstances, SF characters frequently, and lyrically, reveal their innermost thoughts and feelings while alone or unselfconscious of a listener. In many cases, the soliloquist is the lone survivor of a planetary disaster; he or she has no choice but to soliloquize. Mary Shelley's 1826 novel *The Last Man* is narrated by the last human alive on a postapocalyptic earth. So is M. P. Shiel's novel *The Purple Cloud* (1930), whose narrator—the only person to have survived a global chemical disaster[13]—keeps a journal although "no eye can ever read it" (9). In the epilogue to Karel Čapek's play *R.U.R.* (1921), Alquist, the sole human in a world overrun by robots, gazes out the window and soliloquizes: "Night again! Are the stars still there? What is the use of stars when there are no human beings?" (51). Harlan Ellison's story "I Have No Mouth, and I Must Scream" (1967) is told from the perspective of a man stranded inside a supercomputer that has massacred the rest of humankind and kept him alone alive for the purpose of torturing him. Anne Alstein, one of the few women remaining in a world ravaged by femicide, records her lonely final thoughts—"I guess nobody will ever read this" (31)—before killing herself on the last page of "The Screwfly Solution," a 1977 story by James Tiptree (real name: Alice Sheldon).

Other characters are condemned to soliloquy by circumstances less apocalyptic than the ones cited above but no less stirring. In Octavia Butler's *Parable of the Sower* (1993), the heroine, who secretly suffers from a syndrome that causes her to feel other people's pain, tells the story through soliloquy-like diary entries. Daniel Keyes's *Flowers for Algernon* (1966) is narrated by the hauntingly lonely and unselfconscious voice of Charlie Gordon, an experimental subject who chronicles both his transformation from a cognitively disabled janitor to an alienated superhuman genius and the agonizing experience of reverting to his original mental state. During the climax of Shelley's *Frankenstein,* the unnamed creature delivers a moving soliloquy—"he seemed to forget my presence," Walton observes—while beholding the corpse of his creator (219). In "The Voices of Time," Ballard illustrates the consciousness of a mutant sea anemone as a third-person soliloquy, luminous, dreamlike, and full of enigmatic yearning. Toward the end of *Blade Runner,* the android Roy suddenly turns aside and soliloquizes—"I watched sea beams glitter in the darkness . . ."—before falling silent and dying. Throughout the "star gate" sequence of Kubrick's *2001: A Space Odyssey* (1968), the ever-evolving expression of wonder in Bowman's eyes can be understood as a kind of visual soliloquy, a reflection of his desolate journey through alien wildernesses as he ascends to a higher form of sentience. By the end of Jonathan Swift's satire *Gulliver's Travels* (1726/1735), the narrator has been transmogrified by his adventures abroad into a creature of seclusion: exiled by his beloved Houyhnhnms, and unspeakably revolted by the company of other humans (including his wife and children), Gulliver spends hours each day in a stable "conversing" with his horses in a manner reminiscent more of soliloquy than of conversation.

Lyric Time in Science Fiction

There is a second important connection between science fiction and poetry: both resound with voices that speak from beyond time. In realism (low-intensity SF), the narrator speaks from a world where it is possible to tell what time it is, what year, and so on. In lyric poems, by contrast, the lyric "I" speaks from beyond linear temporality. Both "A Report" and "I Felt a Funeral" emit voices speaking from out of time: somehow the "I" reaches us from beyond death, from beyond that ghostly horizon no living person has crossed. Yet such a voice (the strangely timeless voice of the mislaid cosmonaut; the strangely timeless voice of the funereal brain) can be heard even in poems where the

"I" is unequivocally alive and earthbound. Lyric voices, as a rule, speak from beyond ordinary time. The lyric inhabits its own mysterious time zone, a zone where the soliloquy-likeness of lyric speech is (not coincidentally) utterly at home. As Cameron explains in *Lyric Time,* the lyric "enjoys an independence from authorial interruption (those breaks in the action that remind us all action inevitably ends), and it is free as well from the speech and thought of other characters" (207). Liberated from the company of others and from intrusive reminders that *tempus fugit,* the lyric "I" transcends the chronologic order dictated by social calendars and eventful timelines. Thus the "I" is left alone to soliloquize in a "stasis of perception" where "present tense" fuses with the ineffable "presence" that, "distinguished from action or story, will bring them to a halt" (71, 207).

Jonathan Culler approaches the same enigma of lyric time through a category of voice slightly different from soliloquy: apostrophe. The lyric, Culler remarks in *The Pursuit of Signs,* "is characteristically the triumph of the apostrophic." According to Culler, the "O thou" of apostrophe "resists narrative because its *now* is not a moment in a temporal sequence" but an out-of-sequence "now" that is "scarcely understood" and fascinatingly "difficult to think" (149, 152). If the lyric, as Culler contends, is distinguished by apostrophe, and if the out-of-sequence and scarcely thinkable *"now"* of apostrophic temporality is innately resistant to narrative, then it follows syllogistically that lyric temporality is an out-of-sequence and scarcely thinkable *"now"* that resists linear narration. As Culler elaborates, lyric temporality "might be called a timeless present" but is more accurately "the set of all moments at which writing can say *'now'*" (149). Lyric "temporality" is no more "temporal" than Percy Bysshe Shelley's "Oh hear!" (one of multiple invocations in his "Ode to the West Wind") is grammatically indicative in mood.

What Cameron designates as lyric time, and what Culler characterizes as the narrative-resistant and difficult-to-think *"now"* of lyric invocation, can be approached from a third angle as an effect achieved by the poet's use of the simple present tense. As George Wright has shown in "The Lyric Present," the simple present is the grammatical tense most characteristic of poetry. Paradoxically, the simple present—for example, "I walk"—is almost never used in spoken English to indicate simple present-tense action. "The action described," Wright explains, "may be habitual *(I walk nights),* future *(I walk there tomorrow),* conditional *(If I walk six miles in two hours),* true in general *(I walk on my hind legs),* or ceremonial *(I walk about this town where I was born),* yet in all such examples the action described need not be taking place at this moment" (563).

Unlike the present progressive, which situates the action in a palpable context of "now" (for example, "I'm eating dinner—may I call you back later?"), the simple present is fraught with multiple temporal features: timelessness, duration, pastlikeness, futurity. In using this tense without specifying the time of action, poets locate their poetry in what Wright describes as "a realm outside our normal conscious time world" (565).

A prominent example of the lyric tense is Wallace Stevens's "Of Mere Being."

> The palm at the end of the mind,
> Beyond the last thought, *rises*
> In the bronze decor,
>
> A gold-feathered bird
> *Sings* in the palm, without human meaning,
> Without human feeling, a foreign song.
>
> You know then that it is not the reason
> That makes us happy or unhappy.
> The bird *sings*. Its feathers *shine*.
>
> The palm *stands* on the edge of space.
> The wind *moves* slowly in the branches.
> The bird's fire-fangled feathers *dangle* down.

What is the temporal framework in which the "gold-feathered bird / Sings in the palm"? If we had been told that "the gold-feathered bird *is singing* in the palm," we would recognize that the bird is in the midst of performing an action unfolding through time in a linear manner. However, the use of the simple present obfuscates the temporal status of the bird's singing. It may be that the bird is singing a melody whose notes are unfolding through linear time—a melody that began at a specific point on the temporal continuum and will end at a different specific point on the same continuum. But perhaps, alternatively, the bird habitually "sings in the palm" all the time; that is, the bird is singing the same general song over and over again. Or perhaps "A gold-feathered bird / Sings" constitutes a truth as universal as "Humans live and die." That there is more than one possibility suggests that the bird is singing in a place beyond the world of human temporality—and indeed we are told that the bird sings "without human meaning, / Without human feeling, a foreign song."

What, moreover, is the temporal framework in which the "wind *moves* slowly in the branches"? Is it the case that the wind perpetually "moves slowly in the branches" of the palm tree? Or is the slow movement of the wind here an isolated meteorological incident? If the movement of the leaves of the tree by the wind is a rare occurrence of finite duration, does the wind's movement in the tree indicate that something unusual and important is about to take place? The simple present allows all potential scenarios to coexist, lending a strangely eternal quality to the movement of the wind, as if the tree stands in an exceptional time-space where somehow it is possible for the wind to move slowly in the tree's branches for the last, first, and only time—repeatedly. And indeed we are told that the palm tree exists not in terrestrial, weather-bound reality but "on the edge of space" and "at the end of the mind."

"Of Mere Being" is only one of many poems in which the simple present evokes lyric time. The lyric tense is found in poems across centuries and literary movements. It recurs in poems from the British Renaissance: "Weary with toil, I *haste* me to my bed" (Shakespeare, "Sonnet 27," 1609); "With Nectar pure his oozy Lock's he *laves*" (Milton, "Lycidas," 1637); "Ripe apples *drop* about my head" (Marvell, "The Garden," 1681). Furthermore, the lyric tense can be found in Romantic poetry: "The hapless Soldier's sigh/ *Runs* in blood down Palace walls" (Blake, "London," 1794); "thy plaintive anthem *fades*/ Past the near meadows" (Keats, "Ode to a Nightingale," 1819); "I *fall* upon the thorns of life! I *bleed!*" (Shelley, "Ode to the West Wind," 1820). The lyric tense can also be found in Victorian poetry: "The wrinkled sea beneath him *crawls;* / He *watches* from his mountain walls,/ And like a thunderbolt he *falls*" (Tennyson, "The Eagle," 1851); "You *hear* the grating roar/ Of pebbles which the waves *draw* back, and *fling,*/ At their return, up the high strand,/ *Begin,* and *cease,* and then again *begin*" (Arnold, "Dover Beach," 1867). So, too, can the lyric tense be found in nineteenth-century American poetry: "A sprig, with its flower, I *break*" (Whitman, "When Lilacs Last in the Door-yard Bloom'd," 1865); "The Clock *Strikes* One/ That Just Struck Two" (Dickinson, 1883). The lyric tense can be found, moreover, in modernist poems: "Slowly our ghosts *drag* home" (Wilfred Owen, "Exposure," 1918); "Thunder *blossoms* gorgeously above our heads" (Jean Toomer, "Storm Ending," 1922); "the/ moon *rattles* like a fragment of angry candy" (Cummings, "the Cambridge ladies who live in furnished souls," 1923); "The unpurged images of day *recede*" (Yeats, "Byzantium," 1932). And the simple present recurs throughout contemporary poetry: "The Ladies *look,* / In horror, behind a substantial citizeness/ Whose trains *clank* out across her swollen heart" (Gwendolyn Brooks, "The Lovers of the Poor," 1960); "Their smiles *catch* onto my skin, little smiling hooks" (Plath, "Tulips," 1961); "The child *draws* another inscrutable house" (Bishop, "Sestina," 1965); "We *circle* silently/about the wreck" (Adrienne Rich, "Diving into the Wreck," 1972); "My hand *veers* in the thin air" (N. Scott Momaday, "The Eagle-Feather Fan," 1976); "Two chrysanthemums/*touch* in the middle of the lake/and *drift* apart" (Cathy Song, "Girl Powdering Her Neck," 1983); "The huge hum *soaks* up into the dusk" (Jorie Graham, "What the End Is For," 1987); "Now as I *watch* the progress of the plague,/The friends surrounding me *fall sick, grow thin,*/And *drop away*" (Thom Gunn, "The Missing," 1992); "as they do/almost every day at this hour,/impregnable metal containers *dissolve* in the sky" (Stephen Burt, "Dulles Access Road," 2007). Hasting, laving, dropping, and so on are actions that take place not in the temporal world but in some kind of eternity— the eternity where the gold-feathered bird sings; an eternity neither mappable by calendars nor recordable by chronometers. As Wright puts it, the actions "seem suspended, removed from the successiveness of our ordinary time levels, neither past, present, nor future, neither single nor repeated, but of a different dimension entirely" (565). Thus the voice of the lyric simple present addresses us from beyond ordinary time.

Science fiction operates in this lyric grammar. My purpose in positing this claim is not to stipulate the lyric present as a required feature of SF but instead to call attention to an arresting fact: the lyric present, even in prose narratives composed mostly in the past tense, often accompanies archetypically science-fiction moments such as narrations of virtual reality, apocalypse, abrupt disembodiment, and prophecy. In some sense, the lyric tense can be understood as a grammar in which are compressed the many hundreds of tense formations—among them: the Future Semi-Conditionally Modified Subinverted Plagal Past Subjunctive Intentional—delineated in Dr. Dan Streetmentioner's "Time Traveller's Handbook of 1001 Tense Formations" in Douglas Adams's 1980 novel *The Restaurant at the End of the Universe.* In another sense, the lyric tense can be understood as a grammatical counterpart to the "novum," a philosophical concept used by Ernst Bloch to signify the periodic irruption of timeless newness into the continuum of history. Suvin famously adapted Bloch's mystical concept of the novum into a literary principle, invoking Bloch's terminology to designate the element of novelty (e.g., time machinery) that differentiates a science-fiction text from a realist text. Whether understood as a grammatical counterpart to the novum or as a compressed version of the Time Traveler's 1,001 verb formations, the simple present is as much a science-fictional tense as it is a lyric one. What follows is a taxonomic discussion of the use of the lyric present to narrate quintessentially SF moments.

The simple present is the tense in which accounts of virtual reality often and even regularly occur. It is the tense in which the narrator of Richard Powers's *Plowing the Dark* (2000) describes a virtual reality laboratory: "This room *spreads* under the stilled clock"; "Your eyes *adjust* to the light of this hypothetical" (3, 400). It is the tense in which the heroine of William Gibson's 1988 novel *Mona Lisa Overdrive* experiences visions induced by cybernetic voodoo entities: "Angie *watches* the evolution of machine intelligence. . . . Fragile, short-lived tubes *compact* themselves, *become* transistors; circuits *integrate*, *compact* themselves into silicon" (256). It is the tense in which the narrator of Neal Stephenson's *Snow Crash* (1992) depicts a theatrical spectacle in virtual reality: "The column of light *begins* to flow up and down and resolve itself into a human form" (457). And it is the tense in which the narrator of Gibson's 1982 short story "Burning Chrome" describes the artificial environment of cyberspace: "Ice walls *flick* away like supersonic butterflies made of shade. . . . The matrix *folds* itself around me like an origami trick" (177, 188).

The simple present is also used to narrate apocalypse and postapocalypse. It is the tense in which the hero of E. M. Forster's futuristic story "The Machine Stops" (1909) predicts the cataclysmic end to the technology-saturated dystopia in which he lives: "The machine *stops*." It is the tense in which the narrator of Margaret Atwood's 2003 novel *Oryx and Crake* describes the postcatastrophic existence of Jimmy/Snowman, the only surviving member of a human race extinguished by biomedical experiments gone wrong: "He *looks* at his watch. . . . It *shows* him: zero hour" (3); "'Now I'm alone,' he *says* out loud" (10); "Get me out! he *hears* himself thinking" (45). It is the tense in which the narrator of Ray Bradbury's *Fahrenheit 451* registers the belated impact of an instantaneous nuclear war that explodes into narrative consciousness toward the novel's end: "Now, a full three seconds, all of the time in history, before the bombs struck, the enemy ships themselves were gone half around the visible world, like bullets in which a savage islander might not believe because they were invisible; yet the heart is suddenly shattered, the body *falls* in separate motions, and the blood is astonished to be freed on the air; the brain *squanders* its few precious memories and, puzzled, *dies*" (158).

Moreover, the simple present is a tense favored by humans gifted/burdened with visionary insight and foresight. It is the tense in which the coma victim in Ted Chiang's "Understand" (1991) narrates the surreal effects of a drug that has regenerated damaged neurons in his brain: "fearful symmetry *surrounds* me. . . . Lines of force *twist* and *elongate* between people, objects, institutions, ideas" (75, 77). It is the tense in which the narrator of Octavia Butler's 1993 *Parable of the Sower* recounts a dream that foreshadows the future: "The fire *spreads*. I *drift* into it. It *blazes* up around me" (4). It is the tense in which the narrator of Sherman Alexie's novel *Flight* (2007), an orphaned Native American teenager living in 2007, relates his journeys across time through the bodies of various figures in American history, among them a nineteenth-century Indian tracker named Gus who leads a military attack against a group of Native Americans: "Gus *remembers*—and I *remember*—what he saw when he came upon those slaughtered white settlers"; "Gus's eyes *water* at the memory. My eyes *water*"; "I *scream* as I *lead* one hundred soldiers down the hill into the Indian camp" (86, 87). It is the tense in which the protagonist of Delany's epic *Dhalgren* (1975) illustrates his perception of the past: "It continually *fragments* on the terrible and vivid ephemera of now" (10). It is the tense in which the prophetic musician in K. S. Robinson's *Memory of Whiteness* (1985) encounters the phantasmagorical essence of music: "My hands *fly* about the control booth, my feet, elbows, forehead, all playing, while the essential I *floats* out of the body to observe and to listen, astonished to rapture" (26–27).

In addition to being favored by visionary humans, the simple present is favored by otherworldly nonhumans. It is the tense in which a vaporous Martian life-form narrates its encounter with humans in Bradbury's "The One Who Waits" (1949): "Three objects *bend* over the well mouth, and my coolness *rises* to the objects" (631). It is the tense in which the "ice-shapes" speak in Ursula Le Guin's *Left Hand of Darkness* (1969): "I *bleed*"; "I *weep*" (237). It is the tense in which a disembodied "noncorpum" in David Mitchell's novel *Ghostwritten* (1999) narrates his detention in a mysterious yurt populated by the ghosts of animals and humans apparently waiting to be reincarnated: "One of them *coughs*. . . . A swan *inspects* the ground. . . . Tallow candles *spit* and *hiss*. . . . The monk in a saffron robe *sighs*. . . . The swan *spreads* its wings and *flies* up through the roof" (182). It is the tense in which the supernatural Dr. Manhattan experiences and narrates temporality in the graphic novel *Watchmen*: "Two hours into my future, I *observe* meteorites from a glass balcony, thinking about my father. Twelve seconds into my past, I *open* my fingers" (chapter 4, page 2).

Furthermore, the simple present is the tense used to narrate liminal and transformative states between human and other-than-human. It is the tense in which the posthumous voice of Poe's Valdemar ("The Facts in the Case of M. Valdemar") communicates while his not-yet-dead body is still under the influence of animal magnetism: "I *say* to you that I am dead!" (203). It is the tense in which Yagharek narrates his physical transformation from bird-human into complete human at the end of China Miéville's *Perdido Street Station* (2000): "My fingers *close* and *clutch* at the stiff shafts and oiled fibers on my cheeks and I *snap* my beak shut so I will not cry out, and I *begin* to pull" (621). It is the tense in which Canopean alien emissary Johor, the protagonist of Doris Lessing's 1979 novel *Shikasta,* narrates the moment of conception in which he is incarnated into an embryonic human form destined to be born and named George Sherban: "The terrible miasmas of Shikasta *close* around me and I *send* this report with my last conscious impulse" (210). It is the tense in which the narrator of Greg Bear's 1985 novel *Blood Music* narrates the process whereby the human consciousness of Michael Bernard is assimilated into the posthuman consciousness shared by microscopic biological computers in his flesh: "The cells *pulse, separate, contract* according to the rush of fluid"; "He *feels* the dizzying spiral of recursion" (218, 220). It is the tense in which the narrator of Atwood's 1986 feminist dystopian novel *The Handmaid's Tale* experiences the condition of having been dehumanized from a freethinking woman in late twentieth-century America to a reproductive slave in the fundamentalist patriarchy of Gilead. Deprived of human rights, valued solely for her ovaries and uterus, Atwood's handmaid spends her "free" time confined to her bedroom, haunted by memories of long-lost family members—"they *fade,* though I *stretch* out my arms towards them, they *slip* away from me" (193)—and numbed by compulsory inactivity into a state of unendurable expectance: "I *wait* for the day to unroll, for the earth to turn, according to the round face of the implacable clock. The geometrical days, which *go* around and around, smoothly and oiled. Sweat already on my upper lip, I *wait,* for the arrival of the inevitable egg" (200).

The lyric tense is heard even in works of SF that do not technically feature the simple present. It can be heard in Vonnegut's *Slaughterhouse-Five* (1969), which tells the story of a man who is perpetually becoming "unstuck in time." It can be heard in Russ's *Female Man,* a novel that addresses the reader through the gaps between alternate histories. It can be heard in Olaf Stapledon's *Last and First Men,* whose narrator is "one of the Last Men" communicating to us telepathically from two billion years into the future. It can be heard in the "archaic voices" of the constellations that "sing across the millennia" in "The Voices of Time" (97). It can be heard in Octavia Butler's novel *Kindred* through the narration of Dana, a twentieth-century African American woman who is mysteriously transported back in time to save the life of one of her ancestors, a white slave owner living in the nineteenth century. It can be heard in Jack London's *Before Adam* (1907), narrated by a prehistoric man who shares awareness with one of his remote descendents, an American living in the 1900s. It can be heard in Wells's *Time Machine* (1898) through the narration of the Time Traveler, whose anachronistic voice speaks from beyond the scale of human history. It can be heard in John Crowley's futuristic elegiac novel *Engine Summer* (1979), whose first-person narrator—a man dead for centuries—is revived for a spell of time as a file of his consciousness is played by the mind of a living person whose unconscious body serves as an instrument for the dead man's haunting voice. It can be heard in Robert Heinlein's 1959 story "All You Zombies," which recounts the life of an intersex person who via time travel turns out to be his/her own mother, father, and offspring. Finally, the lyric tense can be heard in Harlan Ellison's "I Have No Mouth, and I Must Scream," whose narrator is trapped inside the timeless subjectivity of a supercomputer named AM: "AM has been having fun for some time, accelerating and retarding my time sense. I will say the word now. Now. It took me ten months to say now" (189). Like the voice of the lyric simple present, each of these science-fiction voices speaks from a dimension beyond ordinary time.

Not only do SF and poetry share timeless voices, but both are filled with images, situations, and tableaux that occur beyond ordinary temporality. Examples in poetry include Wordsworth's "spots of time"; the frozen timepiece that cryptically reads "degreeless noon" in Dickinson's "A clock stopped"; the "forever young" human figures on Keats's Grecian urn; the gold-enameled bird who sings of the "artifice of eternity" in Yeats's "Sailing to Byzantium"; and the fire-fangled feathers that dangle down in Stevens's poem. Such images would be out of place in the world of realism. Yet they are at home in science fiction, itself filled with situations that transcend or defy human categories of time.

There are numerous ways in which a science-fiction narrative may withstand or manipulate our assumptions about temporality. A situation may evoke timelessness by dismantling our culturally shaped expectations about how it feels (or ought to feel) to experience time's passage: in Ballard's "Chronopolis" (1960), for instance, mutilated clocks are everywhere on display in a city where telling time has been illegal for thirty-seven years. Along similar lines, a science-fiction narrative may elicit temporal disorientation by disturbing our conception of human lifetimes as commensurable, uninterrupted, and uniform in the rate at which life is being lived. In *Aliens* (1986), Ripley, a young woman who has just been revived after fifty-seven years of suspended animation, gazes mournfully at a recent photograph of her daughter, who died two years before at the age of sixty-six.

Other SF narratives explicitly disrupt our Earth-bound circadian perception of time. A subtle instance can be found in Delany's *Dhalgren*, where two moons appear simultaneously in the skies above the American city of Bellona, imbuing the streets with "double-lit mist" (96) and bewildering the city-dwellers' sense of nighttime. A less subtle example can be found in Larry Niven's Ringworld novels, which are set on a massive artificial sun-encircling ringlike structure approximately one million miles wide and 600 million miles in circumference. From the ring's constant rotation, centrifugal force generates artificial gravity. The ringworld's inner surface—the sunlit side of the ring—is equivalent in area to three million Earth-sized planets. On the ringworld, there is no such thing as sunrise or sunset (as there would be on a spherical world). Instead there is a separate smaller concentric ring composed of evenly spaced "shadow squares" whose own steady revolution around the sun casts the effects of a night/day cycle on the inner surface of the ringworld. Yet the simulation is imperfect. During the day, the sun is always at high noon. During the night, an observer looking skyward from her own shadow-squared location on the ringworld sees an unthinkably vast celestial arch patterned with "daylit rectangles" alternating with rectangles of darkness (*Ringworld Engineers*, 88).

Furthermore, SF is filled with narrative situations that literalize and externalize the discrepancy between "objective" time and time as perceived by individual subjectivities. In Greg Egan's novel *Diaspora* (1998), "tau" are units of "internal time" with "real time" equivalents: one tau of internal time corresponds to one millisecond of real time ("Glossary," 387). In Frank Herbert's novel *Dune* (1965), Jessica imbibes a powerful chemical that removes her from the flow of time and allows her to perceive the vibratory dance of molecular structures (355). In Dick's "The Minority Report" (1956), mutant "precogs," endowed with prophetic foresight and hence employed to prevent crime, sit inside a maze of wires connected to machines that transcribe their every syllable recounting perceived futurities. In Joe Haldeman's *The Forever War* (1974), a soldier leaves Earth for an interstellar expedition and, due to time dilation, returns after a matter of months to find an Earth left almost unrecognizable by the passage of decades.

Closely related to the category of SF narrative timelessness just discussed is the SF narrative situation in which déjà vu—the subjective impression that an experience being lived for the first time might somehow actually be a reliving—turns out to be not illusion but fact. In *The Matrix*, Neo believes that he is afflicted by temporary déjà vu after he sees a strangely familiar black cat walk past him for what seems like the second time; but soon he learns that he had in fact both lived and relived the moment of seeing the black cat, and that such déjà vu is symptomatic of a glitch in the reality-generating system. Toward the end of Orson Scott Card's 1985 fable *Ender's Game*, an ex-soldier stumbles upon a Delphic structure that telepathic aliens—aliens whose race he annihilated in war long ago—had constructed out of images from his own dreams in the weeks before their annihilation (318–319). In Dan Simmons's novel *Hyperion* (1989), enormous artificial structures called "Time Tombs" are driven chronologically backward by "time tides," the pull of which is undergone empirically by one visitor to the Tombs as "waves of *déjà vu* tugging at every cell of his body" (164).

Simmons's *Hyperion* also belongs to the category of SF narratives that appeal overtly to the notion of lyric time. Parts of the novel are set on the fictional planet Hyperion (named, as the novel is, after Keats's poem), where a remote sylvan plateau is home to exactly seventy mysterious childlike creatures (they call themselves the "Three Score and Ten") who share the fate of the figures in Keats's "Ode on a Grecian Urn": they are incapable of dying, of growing old, or of leaving the confines of their eerily unchanging pastoral environment. Another example of a science-fiction narrative that appeals overtly to lyric time can be found in Shiel's *The Purple Cloud* (1930), where a mysterious vapor not only kills but also instantly embalms the body of each person it touches—including a poet who dies caught, immortalized, in the act of writing a poem (87). In "No, No, Not Rogov!" (1959) by Cordwainer Smith,[14] a Russian scientist develops a telepathic espionage device that unexpectedly paralyzes his mind so that he gazes forever onto a scene over 10,000 years into the future and powerfully reminiscent of Yeats's "Sailing to Byzantium": "The golden shape on the golden steps executed shimmering intricacies of meaning. The body was gold and still human. The body was a woman, but more than a woman. On the golden steps, in the golden light, she trembled and fluttered like a bird gone mad" (3). In Ballard's 1966 novel *The Crystal World*, a steady depletion of time from the solar system transmogrifies Earth into a space of growing timelessness where the dreamlike tension of which Shelley wrote in his poem *Adonais*—tension between the "white radiance of Eternity" and "Life, like a dome of many-coloured glass"— systematically infects all matter: one character awakes to discover his arm "encased in a mass of crystalline spurs" inside of which the fingers are "out-lined in a maze of rainbows," just as the world around him is frozen with "crystalline trees" and "the jeweled casements of the leaves overhead, fused into a lattice of prisms" through which sunlight shines "in a thousand rain-bows" (177, 93). Delany's 1966 novella *Empire Star* is structured through and through by lyric temporality. As James Holden has remarked, the site mentioned in the novella's title—a site where "the temporal present joins the spatial past . . . with the possible future, and they get totally mixed up"—is a lyric allusion to the "still point" in Eliot's *Four Quartets*, where "Time present and time past/Are both perhaps present in time future, /And time future contained in time past" (*Conceptual Breakthrough*, 44).

Finally there are SF narratives that evoke lyric timelessness through a poetics of anachronism whereby disparate chronological eras are somehow juxtaposed, brought into ghostly superimposition, or compelled to hover in one another's vicinity. In the concluding scenes of *2001*, a suddenly aged Bow-man, having undergone a voyage transcending space and time, finds himself bedridden in a suite furnished with Louis XVI–style décor yet transfused with artificial fluorescence. In Isaac Asimov's story "The Ugly Little Boy" (1958), scientists abduct a Neanderthal child from the remote past and imprison him inside a high-tech "Stasis bubble" where "time as we know it doesn't exist" (260). In H. P. Lovecraft's 1931 novella *At the Mountains of Madness*, a team of explorers in the Antarctic exhume the remains of a civilization that apparently died out eons ago but whose fossilized artwork has "its closest analogue in certain grotesque conceptions of the most daring futurists" of the twentieth century (54). Steven Spielberg's *A.I.* is filled with anachronistic tableaux, wondrous and strangely moving: a spellbound robot child sitting for 2,000 years inside a watercraft at the bottom of the Atlantic Ocean amid the sub-merged ruins of New York City; a frozen earthscape reminiscent of the Ice Age yet populated by superadvanced robots whose luminous metallic bodies resemble the modernist sculptures of Giacometti; a woman, dead for millennia, revived for a single day. In Roger Zelazny's 1967 novel *Lord of Light*, humans in the far future apply sophisticated technologies (biofeedback, electronic mind transfer, nuclear weaponry) to graft ancient Hindu avatars, mythic beliefs, and supernatural attributes onto their technologically enhanced and multiply bodied lives, resulting in a pantheon of anachronistic deities whose ancient superpowers are fueled by futuristic technologies, and whose archaic mannerisms intricately belie high-tech sensibilities. A similar situation exists in Sheri Tepper's novel *The Gate to Women's Country* (1988), where citizens of a postapocalyptic matriarchy in twenty-third-century America religiously incorporate classical Greek tragedies and myths into the cultural fabric of their eugenicist ecotopia. The book-cover artwork that David Pelham created for several 1970s Penguin editions of Ballard's science fiction evokes a poetics of anachronism by depicting new technological artifacts already submerged in barren postapocalyptic wastelands: the cover art for Penguin's 1977 reissue of *The Four-Dimensional Nightmare*, for example, depicts a still-functioning multimonitor device half-buried at an angle in an otherwise empty desert that looks ominously radioactive.[15] *The Land That Time Forgot* (1918) by Edgar Rice Burroughs is set on a mysterious island where temporal epochs coexist on a continuum—"parklike forest," "eucalyptus and acacia," and primeval "tree ferns" intermingle "as though two distinct periods of geologic time had overlapped" (39)—and different species of humans are separated not by millennia but by miles, with humankind "evolving" from the prehistoric southern end of the island to the posthistoric northern end. A comparable situation can be found in Philip José Farmer's Riverworld novels (1960s–1980s), in which billions of humans encompassing nearly every individual ever born, from prehistoric time to the twenty-first century, and including historical figures from sundry chronological eras (among them Aphra Behn, Li Po, Cyrano de Bergerac, and Mark Twain), find themselves resurrected simultaneously on a strange planet whose entire surface consists of one astonishingly long meandering valley through which a single river runs continuously along a densely mazelike path. Lastly, the enigmatic monolith in *2001* serves as an exemplary image of timelessness—not only by exemplifying eternal geometric perfection (in the novel, Clarke describes the monolith's proportions as corresponding precisely to the squares of the first three integers), but also by synchronizing the ancient with the new (the monolith is over three million years old yet looks as if it has just been created) and by juxtaposing the apelike Moon-Watcher (prehistoric humankind) with the sublime Star-Child (humankind's posthistoric future).

Verbal Intensity

It is no accident that timeless images in SF novels and stories are typically described with lyric intensity. Both poetry and narrative SF feature highly vivid descriptions. Here one might raise the objection that the realist novel features vivid descriptions, and indeed realist novels contain accumulations of finely observed detail and concrete specificity. But the descriptiveness of a realist novel cannot possibly be as intense as the descriptiveness of a lyric poem. The reason is simple: lyric poems are physically smaller than novels. The smaller the textual space, the higher the density of imagery must be. Consider, for example, the sensory density of Ezra Pound's two-line Imagist poem "L'Art 1910":

> Green arsenic smeared on an egg-white cloth,
> Crushed strawberries! Come, let us feast our eyes.

Pound's critique of post-Impressionist art is rich in synesthesia: "feast our eyes" suggests at once an orifice and an eyeball, while color (green, white, red) is associated with touch (the messy texture of crushed strawberries) as well as taste and smell (strawberries, eggs, toxic arsenic). What results from such synesthesia, as Daniel Albright has observed in *Quantum Poetics* (1997), is a powerfully vivid and succinct image of revulsion: "It is as if the feasting eye were a little mouth, profoundly disgusted by the raspberries and strawberries that it saw/swallowed" (147). Such sensuous compression of imagery occurs not just in Imagist poems but throughout poetry in general—from Elizabeth Bishop's deceptively ekphrastic poem "The Map" ("These peninsulas take the water between thumb and finger/like women feeling for the smoothness of yard-goods") to Keats's luxuriant "Ode to a Nightingale" ("The coming musk-rose, full of dewy wine,/The murmurous haunt of flies on summer eves").

Science-fiction novels are compelled to use description of the same intensity that we find in lyric poetry—not, however, because the SF novel is constricted in size, but because the work of description is extraordinarily difficult when the thing described does not belong to our everyday world. The work of verbal description is difficult to begin with: as Elaine Scarry observes in *Dreaming by the Book* (1999), "verbal art, especially narrative, is almost bereft of any sensuous content," and it is despite this absence of any actual sensuous content that the novelist manages to create images that "somehow *do* acquire the vivacity of perceptual objects" (5). But if the work of realistic prose is difficult, then the work of SF prose is even more so. For it is not just despite the nonsensory content of verbal art *but also* despite the unfamiliar nature of the thing described that the SF prose stylist manages to create images that acquire the vivacity of perceptual objects. A description of a familiar real-life object such as a fork need not be extremely vivid for the reader to visualize the object being described: the reader already has a sense of how a fork looks and feels. But a description of an unfamiliar entity—or, more precisely, the verbal creation of a science-fictional entity—*does* need to be extremely vivid for the reader to visualize what is described. Consider the following passage from *The Time Machine.*

> I saw that, quite near, what I had taken to be a reddish mass of rock was moving slowly towards me. Then I saw the thing was really a monstrous crab-like creature. Can you imagine a crab as large as yonder table, with its many legs moving slowly and uncertainly, its big claws swaying, its long antennae, like carters' whips, waving and feeling, and its stalked eyes gleaming at you on either side of its metallic front? Its back was corrugated and ornamented with ungainly bosses, and a greenish incrustation blotched it here and there. I could see the many palps of its complicated mouth flickering and feeling as it moved. (146)

The Time Traveler's question—"Can you imagine . . . ?"—is a heightened version of the appeal to the reader's imagination that we find in realist novels. "When we say 'Emily Brontë describes Catherine's face,'" Scarry points out, "we might also say 'Brontë gives us a set of instructions for how to imagine or construct Catherine's face'" (6). Similarly, when we say "Wells describes the futuristic crab," we might also say "Wells gives us a set of instructions for how to imagine or construct the futuristic crab." Unlike Brontë, however, Wells must make his instructions as vivid as possible for the reader to begin to know how to perceive the futuristic crab. To this end, Wells uses multiple rhetorical strategies to instill his crab with the vivacity of a perceptual object. Modifiers accrete and coagulate at a tempo suggestive of the creature's advance toward the Time Traveler as well as of the increasingly concrete accumulation of the Time Traveler's sensory impressions of the creature. At nearly regular intervals throughout the description, Wells inserts a distinctive verbal cluster composed of two words from the same part of speech and paired explicitly by the conjunction "and": "slowly and uncertainly" (adverb), "waving and feeling" (present active participle), "corrugated and ornamented" (past participles, both containing four syllables identically accented), "flickering and feeling" (alliterative present active participles). This potentially hypnotic rhythm, however, is disrupted repeatedly by diction calculated to sensitize the reader's nerves. The adjectives "reddish" and "greenish," for instance, are subtly livelier than their abstracter counterparts ("red," "green"). Other nuances further animate the description. The fleshiness implied by "palps" is an unsettlingly palpable divergence from the hard surface implied by "metallic," "corrugated," and "incrustation." And the vagueness of the "many" repeated in "many legs" and "many palps" disturbingly suggests that the creature's legs and palps are so profuse that their exact numbers cannot be determined.

Wells is not alone among SF writers in his use of descriptive intensity. Vivid verbal creations thrive in SF. Below are close readings of ten such verbal creations, divided into two categories: SF environments and SF bodies. As the samples show, there is no one method of achieving descriptive intensity. A science-fiction description may pullulate with plush and freakish particularities. It may detain the reader in a state of sensory deprivation so charged with mathematical abstraction that the description assumes hallucinatory verve. It may operate diachronically, attaining its effect through the gradual unfolding of many details over time. It may operate in a nonlinear manner, inviting the reader's eye to absorb the jumbled impressions contained in jumbled clauses as simultaneously as possible. It may abduct a familiar icon from its native context and leave it stranded in an ill-fitting frame. It may concentrate a few odd details into slightly eccentric focus. It may backlight a phantom. It may presuppose the atrophy of one sensory organ while kaleidoscopically fusing those that remain.

Yet in whichever way a science-fiction description achieves intensity, it does so artfully. Earlier I cited Scholes's claim that "much SF is written in journeyman's prose, serviceable but inelegant." The following readings challenge the attitude exemplified in such a remark. Far from "inelegant," the prose that I am about to explore is aesthetically compelling, charged with lyricism, and proof that there is an art to science-fiction description. To say that SF prose can be more than "serviceable," however, is not to say that such prose cannot be fully serviceable as well. The aesthetic impact of each description below is wrought by the same poetic apparatus on which SF relies to execute its representational function. Objects of description in SF are *not* the cognitively estranging referents to which works of SF mimetically refer. Rather, they are examples of the units of the SF medium through which cognitively estranging referents become available for representation—a process that I will discuss at more length toward the end of this chapter.

Five Science-Fiction Environments

(1) "Imagine, if you can, a small room, hexagonal in shape, like the cell of a bee," Forster writes in the first sentence of "The Machine Stops," opening his description with an injunction almost identical to Wells's "Can you imagine . . . ?" "It is lighted neither by window nor by lamp," Forster goes on to write, his words vibrating with the subsonic hint that something is subtly amiss,

> . . . yet it is filled with a soft radiance. There are no apertures for ventilation, yet the air is fresh. There are no musical instruments, and yet, at the moment that my meditation opens, this room is throbbing with melodious sounds. An armchair is in the centre, by its side a reading-desk—that is all the furniture. And in the armchair there sits a swaddled lump of flesh—a woman, about five feet high, with a face as white as a fungus. It is to her that the little room belongs. (91)

Like a timed-release drug, the vividness of this described environment is controlled to deliver an evenly sustained effect. The initial injunction to "Imagine" is automatically tempered by the subordinate clause "if you can," itself retroactively adjusted by the unchallengingly imaginable details that we have been challenged to imagine: "a small room, hexagonal in shape." The next three sentences generate descriptive intensity by way of a parallelism designed to build tension gradually in the reader's perception of the environment described. In particular, the structure paralleled in all three sentences ("X itself is absent, and yet X makes its absent presence felt through its effects") suspensefully builds tension between the felt presence of certain effects in this environment (soft radiance, fresh air, throbbing melodious sounds) and the absence of the expected physical sources of such effects in the same environment (window, lamp, apertures for ventilation, musical instruments). By the time the parallelism has run its three-sentence course, we are alert to the possibility that we may be entering a science-fictional world where causes and consequences operate independently of each other, where primary origins have been displaced by secondary freestanding outcomes, where superficial appearances constitute the substance of reality. Our suspicions continue to grow through the remaining sentences, from which we learn that the hexagonal room contains the following solid objects: armchair, reading-desk, swaddled lump of flesh. That this last object is subsequently identified as "a woman, about five feet high, with a face as white as a fungus" does nothing to change our impression of the "swaddled lump of flesh" as an inert object. Until the reader has proceeded to the story's third paragraph (where the woman does begin to demonstrate signs of life), the armchair may as well be occupied by a corpse, itself a physical cause (body) that no longer functions to generate its expected effect (life).

(2) At the beginning of a chapter near the end of William Gibson's 1984 novel *Neuromancer*, the protagonist awakes to find himself in a feverishly limned virtual environment:

> His vision crawled with ghost hieroglyphs, translucent lines of symbols ar-
> ranging themselves against the neutral backdrop of the bunker wall. He
> looked at the backs of his hands, saw faint neon molecules crawling be-
> neath the skin, ordered by the unknowable code. He raised his right hand
> and moved it experimentally. It left a faint, fading trail of strobed afterim-
> ages. (241)

These sentences generate an immediate and enduring impression. When parsed, however, the vividness of the impression might appear groundless. The description is almost empty of sensuous content. The nouns ("vision," "hieroglyphs," "symbols," "backdrop," "wall," "molecules," "code," "hand," "trail," "afterimages") appeal not to the actively living senses (the way, say, "incrustation" and "palps" do in Wells's description of the crab) but rather to a disembodied mind that only distantly remembers what it was like to be connected to a physical body. Similarly, the adjectives and adverbs ("ghost," "translucent," "neutral," "faint," "neon," "unknowable," "right," "faint" again, "fading," "strobed") are of a consistency so diaphanous that its decimal form, relative to the zero of total abstraction, would hover around 0.0000020507. The lone potentially bright detail here—"neon"—is deactivated by the modifier "faint" ("faint neon" is virtually oxymoronic) and by the fact that the color is left unspecified (neon ___?). From start to end, the description is dimly suffused with a barely lucent monochrome. Why, then, does the description bristle with strange liveliness? The beginning of the answer lies in the verb that Gibson polyptotonically repeats to invoke the creepy actions of the spectral objects perceived in virtual reality: "vision *crawled* with ghost hieroglyphs"; "faint neon molecules *crawling* beneath the skin." Normally we associate the action of crawling with insects and other miniscule entities that are disquietingly intrusive but tolerable from a safe distance. To read, then, of ghostly autonomous buglike things crawling visibly *within* the surface of the protagonist's body—not only subcutaneously but (eerier still) inside the organs of vision themselves—is to feel one's own flesh crawling with ghosts all the more alarmingly tangible because ghosts have no flesh. Gibson's description of virtual reality is alive not with sensuous presences but with disembodied (and therefore unsettling) activity prickling at the reader's nerves. We have already experienced the protagonist's reaction to his surroundings when we learn, in the first sentence of the subsequent paragraph, that the "hair stood up along his arms and at the back of his neck" (241).

(3) Of the many remarkable environments described in Greg Egan's 1998 novel *Diaspora*, the environment that I recollect most vividly is the "sixteen-dimensional slice of a thousand-dimensional frequency space" (246) that appears in chapter 11 ("Wang's Carpets"). In the paragraphs below, two scientists, Paolo and Karpal, investigate the newly discovered thousand-dimensional frequency space:

> They moved away from the swimming coral, into a swarm of something like jellyfish: floppy hyperspheres waving wispy tendrils (each one of them more substantial than Paolo). Tiny jewel-like creatures darted among them. Paolo was just beginning to notice that nothing moved here like a solid object drifting through normal space; motion seemed to entail a shimmering deformation at the leading hypersurface, a visible process of disassembly and reconstruction.
>
> Karpal led him on through the secret ocean. There were helical worms, coiled together in groups of indeterminate number—each single creature breaking up into a dozen or more wriggling slivers, and then recombining . . . although not always from the same parts. There were dazzling multicolored stemless flowers, intricate hypercones of "gossamer-thin" fifteen-dimensional petals—each one a hypnotic fractal labyrinth of crevices and capillaries. (247)

The challenge in describing a hyperspatial environment is to create instructions enabling the reader to visualize shapes that human brains are unequipped to visualize (other than imperfectly by analogy). What does a fifteen-dimensional petal look like? Yet this is a question that Egan himself has anticipated and answered in advance. Specifically, he has answered the question poetically, by incorporating the fifteen-dimensional petal (which I ought not to have plucked from its context a few moments ago) into a much more elaborate composite image: "There were dazzling multicolored stemless flowers, intricate hypercones of 'gossamer-thin' fifteen-dimensional petals—each one a hypnotic fractal labyrinth of crevices and capillaries." Instead of giving us a precise delineation of a fifteen-dimensional petal, this sentence gives us a lively impression of the fifteen-dimensional petal as one vital part of a multi-faceted entity that transcends the sum of its parts as vibrantly as each of its parts transcends, in turn, the sum of its own endlessly divisible components. The preponderance of polysyllabic words in this sentence aurally conveys the sense that the flowers themselves are, if not strictly sesquipedalian, then poly-morphous and composed elaborately of myriad concatenations of smaller parts, parts such as the gossamer-thin fifteen-dimensional petals, themselves composed of infinitely reducible and infinitely elaborate components such as the "hypnotic fractal labyrinth of crevices and capillaries." The manifold af-fixes ("multi-" in "multicolored," "-less" in "stemless," "hyper-" in "hypercones") and hyphenated words ("gossamer-thin," "fifteen-dimensional") multiply the impression of compositeness. Together such rhetorical strategies bring to life the hyphenated mathematic-biologic creatures—helical worms; floppy hyperspheres—inhabiting this verdant alien ecosystem.

(4) Stanislaw Lem's 1961 novel *Solaris* is set on a planet whose sole native life form is the oceanic entity that covers the planetary surface. Unfathomable, ever-mutating, apparently sentient, and talented at reading minds, the ocean taunts its human visitors with personifications of their most repressed memo-ries. It also provides Lem with numerous occasions for spectacular descriptions of science-fictional environments—or, more precisely, spectacular descriptions of science-fictional environmental *events,* for the ocean in *Solaris* is less a passive setting and more a dynamic environmental force perpetually staging architec-tonic performances that mystify, enchant, and sometimes kill the human re-searchers who study the planet's behavior. Among the many types of oceanic performances classified by researchers are "tree-mountains," "fungoids," and "symmetriads" (111). Here is an excerpt from a much longer description (Lem's account of each type of performance often goes on for pages) narrating the birth, life, and death of a "symmetriad":

> The effects of light on a symmetriad are especially striking during the blue day and the red sunset. The planet appears to be giving birth to a twin that increases in volume from one moment to the next. The immense flaming globe has scarcely reached its maximum expansion above the ocean when it bursts at the summit and cracks vertically. It is not breaking up; this is the second phase, which goes under the clumsy name of the "floral calyx phase"

and lasts only a few seconds. The membranous arches soaring into the sky now fold inwards and merge to produce a thick-set trunk enclosing a scene of teeming activity. At the center of the trunk, . . . a process of polycrystal-lization on a giant scale erects an axis commonly referred to as the 'back-bone,' a term which I consider ill-chosen. The mind-bending architecture of this central pillar is held in place by vertical shafts of a gelatinous, almost liquid consistency, constantly gushing upwards out of wide crevasses. Meanwhile, the entire trunk is surrounded by a belt of snowy foam, seeth-ing with great bubbles of gas, and the whole process is accompanied by a perpetual dull roar of sound. From the center towards the periphery, pow-erful buttresses spin out and are coated with streams of ductile matter ris-ing out of the ocean depths. Simultaneously the gelatinous geysers are converted into mobile columns that proceed to extrude tendrils that reach out in clusters towards points rigorously predetermined by the over-all dy-namics of the entire structure: they call to mind the gills of an embryo, except that they are revolving at fantastic speed and ooze trickles of pinkish "blood" and a dark green secretion. (117–118)

In this strenuously kinetic account of the transformation of raw essence into the raw essence of transformation, formlessness and form coexist in incessant mutual tension. Distilled to a series of actions, the description becomes a catalogue of phrases each centering on a present participle: the planet birthing a twin globe → the twin globe swelling in magnitude → the globe reaching its maximum expansion → the maximal globe bursting → the burst globe cracking vertically into arches → the arches soaring into the sky → the arches folding inward → the folded arches merging to produce a thick-set trunk → the trunk enclosing a scene of teeming activity → a process of crys-tallization erecting an axis → vertical shafts gushing upwards → a belt of snowy foam seething with bubbles → buttresses from center to periphery spinning out → streams of ductile matter rising out of the ocean → geysers being converted into columns → columns extruding tendrils → tendrils reaching out in clusters → clusters revolving at fantastic speed → clusters ooz-ing trickles. As this catalogue of actions suggests, Lem's symmetriad behaves like a fantasia of proprioception designed to elicit the reader's kinesthetic re-action to sublime variations on metamorphosis: upsurge, fragmentation, tor-sion, outflow, ramification. Yet the catalogue does not adequately capture the way in which the description engages the senses of vision, touch, and (to a limited extent) hearing. Such sensory information in the above passage can itself be parsed into catalogues, with each item listed in order of evocation.

Colors: blue → red → snowy white → pinkish → dark green. Textures: membranous → crystallized → gelatinous → liquid → foam-like → bubbling →
ductile → extrusive → texture reminiscent of the gills of an embryo. Shapes:
globe → vertical crack → floral calyx → arches → trunk → crystals → pillar →
vertical shafts → crevasse → bubbles → buttress → streams → geysers →
columns → tendrils. Sound: "a perpetual dull roar" heard throughout the
entire process.

(5) The environments analyzed thus far have been either unnerving (Forster,
Gibson) or sublime (Egan, Lem). But SF environments can be peaceful and
lovely, too. In *Engine Summer*, John Crowley describes a terrestrial orchard of
mysterious rotund organisms not indigenous to Earth, organisms from which
humans harvest a pleasantly mind-affecting psychedelic substance called
"bread":

> Imagine a pile of bubbles as large as a tree, the big bubbles on the bottom
> as large as yourself, the small ones at the top smaller than your head, than
> your hand, trailing off in an undulating tip; a great irregular pile of spheres,
> seeming as insubstantial as bubbles, but the weight of them great enough to
> press down the bottom bubbles into elliptical sacks. And imagine them not
> clear and glassy like soap bubbles, but translucent, the upper sunside of
> them a pale rose color, the undersides shading into blue-green at the bot-
> tom. And then imagine as many of these piles of bubbles as fir trees in a
> grove, all leaning gently, bulging and bouncing as in a solemn dance, the
> ground around them stained colors by the afternoon sun striking through
> their translucence. (394)

As with Wells's crab and Forster's hexagonal room, Crowley's verbal creation
opens with the injunction to "Imagine." Yet Crowley's "Imagine" has an overt
instructional exactness missing from the verbal creations of Wells and Forster.
Explicitly oriented to the scale of the human body, Crowley's description follows
a sequence. It begins by supplying information about the various sizes—relative
to various human body parts—of the bubbles in a single "pile": the large bubbles on the bottom are the size of one human body; the small bubbles at the
top are smaller than one human head; and so on. Only after the description
has oriented the reader to the object's size and scale does it go on to add details
concerning mass and silhouette: the pile as a whole, we are told, is "irregular"
in shape, and the bubbles are weighty enough to squeeze the sub-structural
bubbles into elliptical sacks. Having addressed size, scale, shape, and mass, the
description proceeds to details concerning texture and color: the bubbles, we

learn, are not glass-clear but semitransparent and iridescently blue-green and rosy-pink. Finally, the description dilates the scope of the reader's attention to encompass much more than a single pile of bubbles: the reader is instructed to imagine "as many of these piles of bubbles as fir trees in a grove" interacting with one another, gently dancing in concert, and collectively amounting to a milieu delimited horizontally by the ground and by the afternoon sky. As an object of description, the bubble-trees have the potential to destabilize the reader's attention—for example, the bubbles appear insubstantial but are actually heavy—but the step-by-step procedure that Crowley follows in developing his descriptive instructions effectively stabilizes the bubbles and allows them to remain vivid and intact in our minds.

Five Science-Fiction Bodies

(1) China Miéville's steampunk novel *Perdido Street Station* swarms with science-fictional bodies, but one body in particular has infested the tissues of my brain and cannot be excised: Motley, a monstrous entity who has modified his original body into a "garden of multifarious limbs, a walking patchwork of organic forms" (581). The reader's first encounter with Motley occurs in a scene that culminates in the following tour de force:

> Scraps of skin and fur and feathers swung as he moved; tiny limbs clutched; eyes rolled from obscure niches; antlers and protrusions of bone jutted precariously; feelers twitched and mouths glistened. Many-coloured skeins of skin collided. A cloven hoof thumped gently against the wood floor. Tides of flesh washed against each other in violent currents. Muscles tethered by alien tendons to alien bones worked together in uneasy truce, in slow, tense motion. Scales gleamed. Fins quivered. Wings fluttered brokenly. Insect claws folded and unfolded. (38)

As if under the spell of poetic blazon, Miéville itemizes the features of Motley's miscellaneous physique. But whereas a conventional blazon might itemize a desirable woman's pearl-like teeth, starry eyes, and so on, Miéville's blazon itemizes body parts that resemble neither jewelry nor the heavens but the still-living remnants of some deranged taxidermist's rampage: scraps of fur, feathers, limbs, eyes rolling from obscure niches, antlers, protrusions of bone, feelers, cloven hoof, scales, fins, wings, insect claws, etc. Parataxis predominates, vivifying the impression of a body whose loosely interconnected parts are equal in status and disobedient to any unifying logic of subordination. The most conspicuous unit of description is a blunt independent clause corresponding to a corporal feature: "Scales gleamed"; "Fins quivered"; and so on. However, not every descriptive unit succeeds entirely in containing the body part(s) that it describes. In several cases—for example, "Muscles tethered by alien tendons to alien bones worked together in uneasy truce, in slow, tense motion"—the described body parts threaten to overflow the constraints of their receptacles in a manner reminiscent of poetic enjambment (the overflow of a syntactic unit from one line of verse to the next). Wayward and unruly, inexplicably leashed together into an ongoing crime scene, the scattered pieces of Motley's body seem to live on the centrifugal brink of lashing out and exploding apart.

(2) Near the beginning of Joe Haldeman's novel *The Forever War,* a human soldier recounts his first close-up encounter with an enemy alien:

> He had two arms and two legs, but his waist was so small you could encompass it with both hands. Under the tiny waist was a large horseshoe-shaped pelvic structure nearly a meter wide, from which dangled two long skinny legs with no apparent knee joint. Above that waist his body swelled out again, to a chest no smaller than the huge pelvis. His arms looked surprisingly human, except that they were too long and undermuscled. There were too many fingers on his hands. Shoulderless, neckless. His head was a nightmarish growth that swelled like a goiter from his massive chest. Two eyes that looked like clusters of fish eggs, a bundle of tassels instead of a nose, and a rigidly open hole that might have been a mouth sitting low down where his Adam's apple should have been. (64)

At first sight, this body seems human and familiar enough: "He had two arms and two legs." But the reader is soon alerted to the body's deviations from the human norm as the narrator himself, growing more aware of the contours of the alien's physique, notices aberrations in proportion (a waist "so small you could encompass it with both hands"; a "pelvic structure nearly a meter wide"; arms "too long"; "a chest no smaller than the huge pelvis"), aberrations in shape ("horseshoe-shaped pelvic structure"; "no apparent knee joint"; upper torso both "shoulderless" and "neckless"), and aberrations in quantity of limbs ("too many fingers"). These increasingly nonanthropomorphic details culminate in the narrator's graphic xenophobic account of the alien's "nightmarish" visage: eyes resembling "clusters of fish eggs"; a "bundle of tassels" where a nose would be if the face were human; "a rigidly open hole that might have been a mouth." What makes this countenance so disturbing to the anthropocentric reader is its physiognomic illegibility. Each major facial feature has been replaced with something repellently opaque. If eyes are proverbial windows to the soul, what kind of soul resides behind two clusters of fish eggs? Is it possible for a bundle of tassels to respire? How does a "rigidly open hole" smile, frown, or indicate expression at all?

(3) A memorable passage in Charles Stross's novel *Singularity Sky* (2003) is Stross's description of the automated process whereby "Critics"—sentient entities of distantly terrestrial descent—are redownloaded into bodily existence after years of dormancy in cryogenic storage:

> Strange emulsions stirred within some of the bubbles, a boiling soup of nanomachine-catalyzed chemical reactions. Other bubbles faded to black, soaking up sunlight with near-total efficiency. A steady stream of tanks drifted toward the foam on chaotic orbits, ejecta from the mining plants in the outer system. Within the bubbles, incarnate life congealed, cells assembled by machine rather than the natural cycle of mitosis and differentiation. Thousands of seconds passed, an aeon to the productive assemblers: skeletons appeared, first as lacy outlines and then as baroque coral outcroppings afloat in the central placentory bubbles. Blood, tissues, teeth, and organs began to congeal in place as the nano-assemblers pumped synthetic enzymes, DNA, ribosomes, and other cellular machinery into the lipid vesicles that were due to become living cells.
> Presently, the Critics' bodies began to twitch. (42–43)

In a manner similar to time-lapse photography, this description provides an accelerated version of a process that takes several hours within the real time of the novel's universe. Stross's description can be anatomized into a series of film frames. In the first frame, a boiling chemical soup bubbles with emulsions and globules tinted various shades of black. In the second frame, cellular machineries—still translucent—gelatinize within the frothy matrix. In the third frame, foam surrounds the lacy outlines of skeletal configurations. In the fourth frame, the skeletons—now solidified—resemble baroque coral outcroppings afloat in an effervescent sea. In the fifth frame, the skeletons are embellished here and there with teeth, blood, and organs in various phases of materialization. When this sequence of frames is played through the mind at the speed of reading, the result is a spasmodic impression of fitful growth, disjointed coagulation, and paroxysmal animation reminiscent of time-lapse photography. The spasms culminate in the verb that Stross uses to illustrate the newly formed organisms' physical movements: "Presently, the Critics' bodies began to *twitch*."

The impression of convulsive disjointedness persists well beyond the moment of the Critics' corporealization. In a much later scene, a human named Burya is jolted by the abrupt appearance of a Critic (he has never encountered one before) that Stross describes as "hairless and pink and larger-than-human-sized, with stubby legs and paws and little pink eyes—and four huge, yellowing tusks, like the incisors of a rat the size of an elephant" (142). Stross's use of polysyndeton ("and" is repeated five times) heightens the sense of disjointedness by exposing the conjunctions (joints) of the sentence, conjunctions that expose in turn the sentence's paratactic syntax. Such syntax, in turn, calls attention to the paratactic arrangement of the creature's body. The Critic's features—hairlessness, pinkness, larger-than-human-sized-ness, stubby legs, paws, little pink eyes, huge yellowing tusks—hardly seem to fit together as parts of a larger organic unity. Even the Critic's elocution as it addresses Burya is disjointed and incoherent: "Talk. We. Must." Unsurprisingly, Burya's initial response is to think he must be hallucinating: *"I haven't been sleeping enough"* (142).

(4) Bodies being gestated are recurrent objects of science-fictional description. In Robert Sawyer's novel *Calculating God* (2000), the narrator describes the emerging phenotype of an embryonic new life-form incubating in an artificial matrix, its genotype an unprecedented amalgamation of hereditary information from three distinct species (one human and the other two extraterrestrial). During the first several months, the fetus undergoes a wildly exaggerated version of the process whereby ontogeny seems to recapitulate phylogeny:

> It was incredible—like watching the Cambrian explosion play out in front of my own eyes, a hundred different body plans tried and discarded. Radial symmetry, quadrilateral symmetry, bilateral symmetry. Spiracles and gills and lungs and other things none of us recognized. Tails and appendages unnamed, compound eyes and eyestalks, segmented bodies and contiguous ones.

Unlike the gestated bodies in *Singularity Sky*, the gestated body above is described not diachronically frame by frame but synchronically as a nonlinear chaos of details—the better to convey the riotous and disorderly nature of the fetus's experimentation with myriad morphological possibilities. We subsequently learn that after months of experimentation the fetus resolves on a body plan unlike that of human, Forhilnor, or Wreed:

The fetus's body consisted of a horseshoe-shaped tube, girdled by a hoop of material from which six limbs depended. There was an internal skeleton, visibly forming through the translucent material of the body, but it was made not of smooth bone but rather of bundles of braided material. (332)

Here is a set of clues suggesting how the reader might visualize the emerging phenotype. These verbal cues, when followed closely with pen in hand on paper, result in an intriguing diagram resembling a blueprint for synthesizing an avant-garde sculpture. Due to the sparseness of concrete data in this description, the several details present—in particular, the horseshoe-shaped tube, the hoop of material from which six limbs depend, and the bundles of braided material—magnetize the reader's scrutiny and acquire a measure of vividness by virtue of their scarcity. Were it not for this acquired vividness, and were it not for the trial-and-error frenzy contextualizing Sawyer's account of the chosen body plan, the "horseshoe-shaped tube," the "hoop of material from which six limbs depended," and the "bundles of braided material" might come across as inert artifacts haphazardly heaped together. But because of the stark rarity of details cited and the preceding whirl of prolific experimentation, the images are charged with intentionality: both Sawyer and the fetus itself have selected these specific features out of countless possibilities, and our awareness of this design instills the features—however random they might seem to us—with a living sense of purpose.

(5) In *Specimen Days* (2005), Michael Cunningham creates a verbal portrait of a hybrid infant whose father (named Emory—hence the "Emoryish" nose) is human and whose mother is Nadian (a sentient lizardlike alien species):

The baby's skin was the color of a celery stalk. She (it was a she) had the big, round Nadian eyes and the agitated Nadian nostrils, but in her the eyes were a creamy coffee brown and the nose an Emoryish minibeak upon which the nostrils perched like sea urchins on a sliver of rock. She had ears, perfectly human but dwarfed, like tiny shells. Atop her smooth green head stood a silky fury of fine white-gold hair. (311)

Lingering over pigments and textures redolent of modernist juxtapositions, Cunningham creates a lyrical account of the young Nadian-human hybrid. This is the kind of description that makes the reader long to translate the words into a different medium, only to realize that something vital would be lost in the translation. I actually tried to translate Cunningham's description into a multimedia collage. Noticing the absence of primary colors in this passage—each hue evoked is a soft, pale tint—I used pastels to establish the baby's yellowish-greenish skin and beige-brownish eyes. I attached marine fossils to the pastel surface to signal the baby's nostrils ("like sea urchins") and ears ("like tiny shells"). And I fashioned wild tufts of delicate lustrous metallic threading for the baby's "fine white-gold hair." The resulting brico-lage, however, was less than the sum of its parts, just as the original descrip-tion is more than the sum of its words. It matters, for example, that the baby's skin is not only pale yellowish-green but specifically "the color of a celery stalk," and that the baby's eyes are not only pale brown but specifically the color of "creamy coffee." The odd clash between the mild taste of celery and the bracing aroma of coffee molecules (complicated by the heavy milkiness of cream)—intersecting orthogonally with the visual softness of pastel green blended with pastel brown—is vital to the portrait's synthetic, synesthetic, science-fictional appeal. The same can be said of other details in the portrait, for example, the description of the baby's hair not only as white-gold in color but also as actively standing in a silky fury. The specific energy communi-cated by the word "fury" in this context would be difficult to communicate nonverbally.

Before I leave "Verbal Intensity," let me acknowledge that there is nothing inevitable about the duality of the scheme that organizes the close readings above. I might have added other classificatory groups (e.g., science-fictional artifacts). Moreover, the twofold scheme that I ended up using admits some ambiguity: the sentient ocean in *Solaris*, for instance, is both a science-fictional environment and a science-fictional body. Indeed, SF writers are fond of lavishing descriptive attention on things categorically ambiguous. A number of examples are worth mentioning here as a way of concluding this subsection.

Arthur Clarke devotes several passages of his novel *Rendezvous with Rama* to describing alien objects that transcend distinctions between flora and fauna, between organism and machine. Of one such object, Clarke gives the following explicitly indecisive account: "The petals were brightly colored tubes about five centimeters long; there were at least fifty in each bloom, and they glittered with such metallic blues, violets, and greens that they seemed more like the wings of a butterfly than anything in the vegetable kingdom" (159).

H. P. Lovecraft likewise has a penchant for describing borderline alien entities, though his descriptions are less clinical than Clarke's and more sensational and viscidly impressionistic. In Lovecraft's 1931 novella *At the Mountains of Madness*, scientists exploring the ruins of an Antarctic city, haunted by rumors of an ancient man-made substance "able to mock and reflect all forms and organs and processes," are stunned and appalled to confront such rumors literally substantiated in the appearance of a massive colloidal larviform gel hideously riddled with watchful orbs and capable of locomotion: "It was a terrible, indescribable thing vaster than any subway train—a shapeless congeries of protoplasmic bubbles, faintly self-luminous, and with myriads of temporary eyes forming and un-forming as pustules of greenish light all over the tunnel-filling front" (91, 97).

Ray Bradbury's *Martian Chronicles* features a similarly many-eyed and insectile (albeit not-as-gelatinous) vehicle of transportation: "It was a machine like a jade-green insect, a praying mantis, delicately rushing through the cold air, indistinct, countless green diamonds winking over its body, and red jewels that glittered with multifaceted eyes. Its six legs fell upon the ancient highway with the sounds of a sparse rain" (81).

Not all ambiguous objects of SF description are reminiscent of insects. In *Consider Phlebas* (1987), in a passage describing the "glittering" psychedelic multimedia costumes worn by "tall humanoids," Iain M. Banks blurs the line between humanoid and costume such that the reader cannot always tell where the humanoid ends and the costume begins, or whether the creature is the glittering artifact and the costume is the living organism: "from a network of fine, golden-colored tubes branching all around their bright red and dark purple faces, tiny puffs of incandescent gas pulsed out, wreathing their semi-scaled necks and naked shoulders, and trailing and dimming behind them in a fiery orange glow," while their "cloaks, flowing out behind as though hardly heavier than the air through which they moved, flickered with the image of an alien face, each cloak showing part of one huge moving image, as though a projector overhead was focused on the capes of the moving group" (203).

These objects of science-fictional description, it bears reiterating, are not the cognitively estranging referents to which works of science fiction mimetically refer. Rather, they are instances of the units of the science-fictional medium (what I will later call *science-fictionemes*) through which cognitively estranging referents become available for representation.

Musicality

The images cited above for the most part emphasize vision and touch, but those are not the only senses engaged by science fiction. SF shares with poetry an engagement with the aural faculty. In ancient Greece, the lyric was a song for accompaniment on the lyre, and to this day the lyric—a form characterized by acoustical devices such as meter and rhyme—vibrantly reflects its musical origins. As Northrop Frye has put it, the "babble" at the root of "melos" (music) is vital to lyric poetry (*Anatomy of Criticism*, 275).

While SF may not have originated as song, musical "babble" thrives as much in SF as in poetry. Science fiction teems with aural and onomatopoetic signifiers. In Wells's *War of the Worlds*, aliens announce their own deaths with an eerie "sobbing alternation of two notes, 'Ulla, ulla, ulla, ulla,' keeping on perpetually" (140). In Delany's *Triton* (1976), language in the year 2112 includes incantatory syllable-chains such as "mimimomomizolalilamialom-uelamironoriminos" (2). In *Snow Crash*, the human race is threatened by a virus that reduces its victims' speech to babble reminiscent of the "do re mi fa so la ti do" of solfege: "ma la ge zen ba dam gal nun ka aria su sun a an da," one victim declares (119). In Rudy Rucker's 2007 novel *Postsingular*, a metanovelist named Thuy makes heavy use of onomatopoeia while recounting her recent encounter with an other-dimensional grated portal where, for a moment, she literally lost her head: "Right away the grating dices my head into bouillon cubes—*dzeeent*—one voice apiece. Zoom in on them and you can hear the little voices are choruses too—*aum aum aum*—the grills buzzsaw me more, my cells sing good-bye, I'm subatomic—*fweee*—as above so below, my fragments live in tide pools by an unknown sea—*wheenk*" (186). In *The First Men in the Moon*, Wells invokes the sounds of alien landscapes and unfamiliar technologies with echoic words like "zuzzoo" (9, 12, 23), "phoo-whizz" (170), "chid chid chid" (127, 128), and "chuzz-zz-zz-zz" (134). In Russell Hoban's 1980 novel *Riddley Walker*, descendants of humans who survived a long-ago nuclear apocalypse speak an English language that has eroded almost beyond recognition, a musical and evocative English-like language forever verging on sound poetry, as in the following incantatory lines that mythologize nuclear fission: "Owt uv thay 2 peaces uv the Littl Shynin Man the Addom thayr cum shyningnes in wayvs in spredin circels. Wivverin & wayverin & humin with a hy soun. Lytin up the dark wud" (32). By contrast, in Paul Auster's dystopian novel *In the Country of Last Things*, set in a city where "entire categories of objects" are constantly vanishing, the word for each object retains its shape but loses meaning over time and eventually turns into musical noise: "Little by little, the words become only sounds, a random collection of glottals and fricatives, a storm of whirling phonemes, and finally the whole thing just collapses into gibberish. The word 'flowerpot' will make no more sense to you than the word 'splandigo'" (89).

Many science-fiction texts invoke the mystifying "sound" of science by innovating strangely gorgeous pseudotechnical abracadabra. The best-known SF neologism—"cyberspace"—is no longer a strictly SF term: introduced by cyberpunk author William Gibson in his 1984 novel *Neuromancer*, "cyberspace" quickly entered both scientific terminology and the global vernacular in a process that I discuss in "Cyberspace in the 1990s." A slightly less famous example of SF "jargon" is "positronic," a nonscientific word whose "delightful science-fiction sound" compelled the person who coined it, Isaac Asimov, to use the adjective to describe artificial intelligence in his stories and novels ("Cybernetic Organism," 464). (For citations, see the entry "positronic" in Jeff Prucher's *Brave New Words*, 151.) "Ansible" is another term whose science-fictional aural effect belies its lack of real-life scientific meaning. Introduced by Le Guin in her 1966 novel *Rocannon's World* and her 1974 novel *The Dispossessed*, "ansible" denotes a hypothetical device capable of superluminal communication; her neologism has since been adopted by other SF authors, including Orson Scott Card, Dan Simmons, and Vernor Vinge. (For citations, see "ansible" in *Brave New Words*, 7–8.) Yet another well-known example of science-fiction lingo is "noocytes," a word that Vergil Ulam—the fictional biotechnologist at the heart of Greg Bear's 1985 novel *Blood Music*—invents as a name for the sentient biological computers that he has synthesized from his own lymphocytes: "I looked all around—dictionaries, textbooks, everywhere. Then it just popped into my head. 'Noocytes.' From the Greek word for mind, 'noos.' Noocytes. Sounds kind of ominous, doesn't it?" (84). Just as the word "buzz" onomatopoetically "sounds like" buzzing, so too do words such as "noocytes," "positronic," and "ansible" onomatopoetically "sound like" science. This principle of onomatopoeia is at once thematized, satirized, and lovingly implemented in Lem's *Futurological Congress* (1971), parts of which are set in a world saturated with scientific-sounding jabberwocky zestfully evocative but largely empty of meaning: "benignimizers"; "psychemized" (76); "psychedelicatessen" (80); "synthecs" (85); "sonnetol," "rhapsodine" (91); "torturometry" (103); "interflorentrix" (111); "psycholocalizers" (113); "pharmacocracy" (118);

"optimistizine," "seraphinil" (119); "nazarine anointium," "obliterine" (121); "microtroshm," "obstetronics" (122); "selfthrong proliferox" (124); "superneomascons" (133); "retrotemporox" (134).

Music lives not only in the texture of SF prose but also in the structure of SF texts. Works of science fiction are often constructed like musical fantasias, variations on sets of themes driven by contrapuntal or fugal elaboration. The chapters of Stapledon's *Last and First Men* are variations on the trauma of World War I. Similarly, the chapters of Haldeman's *Forever War* are variations on the trauma of Vietnam. Russ's *Female Man* is a feminist fugue in which the voices of four versions of one woman—Joanna, Jeannine, Janet, Jael—play with and against one another. Darren Aronofsky's cinematic poem *The Fountain* (2006) uses three thematically interrelated storylines set in three disparate contexts (sixteenth-century Meso-America; twenty-first-century North America; a twenty-sixth-century starship ascending toward a mysterious interstellar cloud) to orchestrate evolving variations on the human aspiration to transcend mortality. *The Sonatas of Saint Francis* by Michael Joyce, Andrea Morris, Carolyn Guyer, and Matthew Hanlon (2000) is a hypertext structured like a musical fantasia. *2001: A Space Odyssey* is a four-part fugue that explores permutations of thematic fragments both visual (the iconic monolith) and auditory (the opening chords of Strauss's *Thus Spake Zarathustra*). *The Memory of Whiteness* is divided into sections explicitly named after musical techniques such as "inversion," "retrogradation," "interpolation," and "retrograde inversion."

At the level of content and imagery, too, music has a prominent place in science fiction. According to *The Encyclopedia of Science Fiction*, edited by John Clute and Peter Nicholls, music is of all the arts the one most commonly featured in SF texts (844). Dystopian narratives, for instance, frequently rely on music to establish dissonant atmospheres. In Huxley's *Brave New World*, citizens of the World State are mentally conditioned by synthetic music machines that generate plangent litanies ("Ford, Ford, Ford . . .") and haunting "Solidarity Hymns" (52–55). In Orwell's *1984*, telescreens radiate patriotic hymns, military music, and "hate songs" about Oceania's enemies. In Forster's "The Machine Stops," the subterranean air is polluted with computer-generated melodies that entropically grow decreasingly melodic over time. In Jonathan Lethem's hard-boiled dystopic *Gun, with Occasional Music* (1994), news is broadcast through evocative nonverbal melodies: "Violins were stabbing their way through the choral arrangements in a series of ascending runs that never resolved, never peaked, just faded away and were replaced by more of the same. It was the sound of trouble, something private and tragic; suicide, or murder, rather than a political event" (3). In Lovecraft's fiction, the sound of eerie musical piping is often a signal (to narrator and reader alike) that we are in the vicinity (or midst) of a territory haunted by hostile not-quite-human beings.

Music is also an occasion for SF authors to fabricate strangely gorgeous instruments of musical expression. Delany's *Nova* (1968) features the sensory syrynx, a musical technology capable of affecting human vision, smell, and taste. Alastair Reynolds's *Revelation Space* (2000) features a similar instrument called a teeconax: "Disturbingly liquid sounds emanated from the girl's cortex, amplified by the instrument and then modulated by the pressure of her fingers on its complex, spectrally coloured touch-sensitive fretboard. Her music toiled up staircase-like ragas, then splintered into nerve-shredding atonal passages" (108). In *We Can Build You* (1972) by Philip K. Dick, musical contraptions such as the "Hammerstein Mood Organ" directly stimulate the brain. Robinson's *The Memory of Whiteness* features a fantastically intricate apparatus spanning eleven meters and consisting of "all the world's soundmakers hanging like fruit in a giant glass tree," including a "cloud of violas," a "broken staircase of trombones," and a "spiral of organ pipes" (14, 60). In Rucker's *Postsingular,* an otherworldly harp—ancient, sentient, telepathic—vibrates with luminous hyperdimensional strings that, if strummed to the "Lost Chord," can unfold the eighth dimension and thereby endow everything on Earth with unlimited memory and omnividence. As Rucker's sentient harp demonstrates, not all SF musical instruments are inanimate. In the 1997 film *The Fifth Element,* an alien diva uses her voice-box to imitate a spectrum of sounds, from keyboard synthesizers to near-ultrasonic frequencies. In *Darwin's Radio* by Greg Bear, members of a new human subspecies vocalize coo-whistling noises that sound ethereal and electronic: one child amuses herself by vocalizing "two different notes at once, splitting one note away, raising and lowering it," producing an effect "uncannily like two theremins arguing" (516).

Elsewhere in science fiction, music—especially song—indicates the presence of subjectivity in places where we might not expect it. The main character of Anne McCaffrey's novel *The Ship Who Sang* (1961) is an emotionally sentient titanium spacecraft named Helva whose gift for singing is what humanizes and endears her to other characters in the story and to the reader as

well. Geoff Ryman's *Child Garden* (1989) revolves around the human heroine's abiding love for Rolfa, a genetically engineered polar bear shunned by
most of society due to her passionate genius for opera and her achingly exquisite mezzo. In Theodore Sturgeon's 1953 novel *More Than Human*, a teenager,
secluded since birth from the outside world and from her own inner world,
inexplicably beings to sing when she awakens to the unfamiliar sensation of
connecting telepathically with a stranger who happens to be nearby: despite
the fact that she "had never been told of music," her singing possesses "strange
and effortless fluctuations in pitch from an instrument unbound by the diatonic scale, freely phrased" (7). "No Woman Born," a 1944 short story by
C. L. Moore, centers on a singer whose body was burned in a fire and replaced with a golden shell through which her voice sings even more euphoni-
cally than it did before the tragedy. In David Brin's *Startide Rising* (1983),
earthlings find themselves marooned on a planet on which a subterranean
metallo-organic life-form sings a "claustrophilic song, in praise of rough hard
stone and flowing metal" (356, 408). In *2001*, the computer HAL memorably
intones "Daisy Bell" as he dies, and alien intelligences evoke their presence
through a hauntingly dissonant chorus of nebulous, unearthly voices. In Vonnegut's 1959 novel *The Sirens of Titan*, Mercury "sings like a crystal goblet"—
the planet can "hold a single note in the song for as long as an Earthling
millennium"—and through this song nourishes its inhabitants: diaphanous
skin-like creatures that cling to cave walls, feed on musical vibrations, and
respond to the melody by arranging themselves unconsciously into a "dazzling pattern of jonquil-yellow and vivid aquamarine diamonds" (187, 190).

As some of the examples above suggest, music in SF often accompanies
cosmic awe. In *On Wings of Song* (1979) by Thomas Disch, the act of singing
allows humans to break free from their earthbound bodies and fly in astral
ecstasy. In Asimov's "Escape!" (1945), astronauts undergoing interstellar
travel are astounded to hear an inexplicable "piercing shriek of a hundred million ghosts of a hundred million soprano voices" (198). Clark Ashton Smith's
short story "The City of Singing Flame" (1931) revolves around a fountain of
fire that emanates "the light of remote worlds and stars translated into sound"
(237). In Stapledon's 1937 novel *Star Maker*, the narrator learns from a vision
that space itself originated as an evolutionary novelty in a primitive universe
whose structure was not spatial but musical: "The creatures in this 'musical'
cosmos could approach one another or retreat and finally vanish out of ear-
shot. In passing 'sideways' they traveled through continuously changing tonal

environments. In a subsequent cosmos this 'sideways' motion of the creatures was enriched with true spatial experience" (417). In *Close Encounters of the Third Kind* (1977), starshipped aliens communicate with humans through a wondrous five-note diatonic theme. In Mary Doria Russell's novel *Children of God* (1998), three sentient species—humans and the extraterrestrial Runa and Jana'ata—are finally united, after decades of interspecies strife, by their mutual enrapturement at the discovery of "God's music": gorgeous and weird harmonies corresponding to the DNA sequences of all three species "played together" (426).

Beyond the fact that SF texts are musical in sound, structure, theme, and imagery, many works of SF are works of music. A few examples in chronological order: the ethereal "Neptune" movement of Gustav Holst's 1920 *Planets Suite;* Bernard Herrman's score for *The Day the Earth Stood Still* (1951), which made pioneering use of the theremin; the electronic soundtrack that Bebe and Louis Barron created for Fred Wilcox's film *Forbidden Planet* (1956); *Atlas Eclipticalis* (1961), John Cage's first orchestral work; the eerie and disturbing micropolyphonic textures in György Ligeti's *Atmosphères* (1961), *Requiem* (1963–1965), and *Lux Aeterna* (1966), whose slowly shifting dissonances transfuse crucial scenes in the film *2001: A Space Odyssey* (1968); the pop rock song "Space Oddity" (1969), written and sung by David Bowie; Wendy Carlos's ominous "Timesteps" (1970), composed largely as a musical counterpart to the dystopia portrayed in Anthony Burgess's 1962 novel *A Clockwork Orange; Einstein on the Beach* (1976), an opera scored by Philip Glass and inspired by the special and general theories of relativity; the haunting, unforgettable melodies and aural moodscapes created by Vangelis for the 1982 film *Blade Runner;* the space-themed hard bop and funk of Afrofuturists such as Sun Ra and George Clinton; Tod Machover's 1987 opera *VALIS*, based on Philip Dick's 1981 novel of the same name; Kenji Kawai's "Making of Cyborg," a mystical chorus from the soundtrack to the 1996 Japanese anime film *Ghost in the Shell;* the futuristic electronica of Radiohead's 2000 album *Kid A;* the ambient mathscapes of Boards of Canada's 2002 album *Geogaddi.*

Heightened and Eccentric States of Subjectivity

The overwhelming presence of music in science fiction is hardly surprising when one considers the fact that both music and SF refer to phenomena that can neither be photographed nor represented in straightforward prose. Both music and SF, moreover, appeal to our emotions and moods with rousing speed. (Such speed, by definition, cannot attend the process of rendering a cognitively estranging referent available for representation.) As K. S. Robinson has observed, "Music moves directly from the inner ear to the lower brain stem, where our emotional lives are generated" (*The Memory of Whiteness*, 109), and one may say the same thing about SF (just as one may say the same thing about poetry), which kindles such heightened and primal states of subjectivity as wonder, alertness to the uncanny, and what Wordsworth called the "spontaneous overflow of powerful feelings." The states of subjectivity that SF has the power to ignite are not only extraordinary in degree ("heightened" and "primal" states) but also extraordinary in quality and configuration. Like poetry, which Shelley defined in his "A Defence of Poetry" as an artform that "awakens and enlarges the mind itself by rendering it the receptacle of a thousand unapprehended combinations of thought" (786–787), science fiction awakens and enlarges the mind by charging it with myriad unapprehended combinations of ideas and feelings.

Whether the states of subjectivity incited by science fiction are unusual in quality or in degree, the power of science fiction to incite eccentric and extreme states of subjectivity is often considered one of its essential features. Istvan Csicsery-Ronay Jr. writes eloquently in his 2008 book *The Seven Beauties of Science Fiction* about the science-fictional sublime ("a complex recoil and recuperation of self-consciousness coping with phenomena suddenly perceived to be too great to be comprehended") and the science-fictional grotesque ("the realization that objects that appear to be familiar and under control are actually undergoing surprising transformations, conflating disparate elements not observed elsewhere in the world") as two of SF's major aesthetic pleasures (146). Fredric Jameson has characterized science fiction as an art form that sensitizes the mind to history in unfamiliar ways, arguing that SF makes us conscious of the present as the past of some unexpected future rather than as the future of a past.[16] And the titles of many SF magazines (*Amazing Stories, Thrilling Wonder Stories*, and *Startling Stories)* implicitly define science fiction as a phenomenon that performs strange effects ("amazing," "thrilling," "startling") on the reader's consciousness.

Furthermore, just as poems often thematize the heightened and eccentric states of subjectivity that they instill in the reader—George Herbert, for instance, praises the exalted state of consciousness brought about by prayer; Whitman rhapsodizes about the cosmic experience of sharing an emotion with people not yet born—works of science fiction regularly take as their subject heightened or eccentric states of knowledge and emotion. In "Lyric Time in Science Fiction," I discussed some of the ways in which SF scenarios such as time travel and suspended animation can result in complexly science-fictional emotions such as nostalgia for the future and nonillusory déjà vu. Below I discuss five additional categories of science-fictional subjectivity. The list is not exhaustive: it omits, for example, Earthsickness, cosmic serenity, and alien xenophobia. Still, the categories below cover an array of science-fiction moods and emotions, from extraordinary intersubjectivity to reality-altering revelations.

Extraordinary Intersubjectivity

In ordinary life, as in realism, we routinely encounter varieties of intersubjectivity such as common sense and sympathy for friends. In science fiction, the varieties of intersubjectivity are more drastic and eccentric in configuration. The protagonist of Butler's *Parable of the Sower* suffers from excruciating "hyperempathy," a condition that causes her literally to suffer others' physical pain. Computer programmers jacked into cyberspace mutually experience an ecstatic "consensual hallucination" in Gibson's *Neuromancer*. Humans in Dick's *Do Androids Dream of Electric Sheep?* religiously use household "empathy boxes" enabling them to experience physical and spiritual "fusion" with all other individuals in the world who happen also to be using their empathy boxes at the moment. In Robert Heinlein's *Stranger in a Strange Land* (1961), the Martian human Michael Valentine teaches humans on Earth a sort of unutterably intense rapport called "grokking": " 'Grok' means to understand so thoroughly that the observer becomes a part of the observed—to merge, blend, intermarry, lose identity in group experience" (213–214). In the short story "Voices," from Walter Mosley's 2001 collection *Futureland*, brain tissue from a deceased young girl is grafted onto atrophied sections of an elderly man's brain, resulting in a state of conjoined subjectivities (alive and dead, old and young, male and female) within a single body. In "A Work of Art" (1956) by James Blish, Richard Strauss finds his consciousness reanimated in the year 2161, his mind incorporated into a volunteer's living body by a "mind sculptor" who successfully reenacts Strauss's musical genius for a single performance after which the "sculpture" (Strauss's reanimated consciousness) is desculpted and the volunteer's body recovers its "own" mind. In Cory Doctorow's 2003 novel *Down and Out in the Magic Kingdom,* the narrator, while test-experiencing a newly renovated Hall of Presidents in twenty-second-century Disney World, is stunned by "flash-baked sense-impressions, rich and detailed," of being Abraham Lincoln: "I pulled up my HUD and switched on guest access. Tim pointed a finger at the terminal and my brain was suffused with the essence of Lincoln: every nuance of his speech, the painstakingly researched movement tics, his warts and beard and topcoat. It almost felt like I *was* Lincoln, for a moment, and then it passed. But I could still taste the lingering coppery flavor of cannon-fire and chewing tobacco." In Nancy Kress's novel *Beggars in Spain,* superintelligent humans who excogitate in substrings and cross-hatching patterns construct an externalized intersubjective artifact in the form of a revolving holographic sphere embodying a philosophical argument: "A sudden three-dimensional graphic appeared on the screen, a complex globe made of strings of words looped and crossed and balanced, each word or phrase an idea that connected to the next, the whole thing color-coded in ways that emphasized the stresses and balances and trade-offs in meaning from concepts that opposed or reinforced or modified each other. The globe lingered, rotating slowly" (389). During a crucial scene in Octavia Butler's 1989 novel *Imago,* an alien induces temporary delirium in its child by injecting its body with generations of inherited memory (692–693). As this collection of examples suggests, characters in SF are just as likely to telepathize, hyperempathize, and transpathize as they are to sympathize with one another.

The Eerie State of Subjectivity That Results from Knowing Objectively That One Is Somehow Other Than Uniquely Identical to Oneself

As the following examples show, there are many variations on this particular state of subjectivity. In the opening pages of Richard Morgan's novel *Altered Carbon* (2002), the narrator, who has moments ago woken up to find himself in a new "sleeve" (body), relates his discombobulation on seeing a stranger gaze back from his own mirror reflection: "It's like pulling an image out of the depths of an autostereogram. For the first couple of moments all you can see is someone else looking at you through a window frame. Then, like a shift in focus, you feel yourself float rapidly up behind the mask and adhere to its inside with a shock that's almost tactile" (12). Toward the end of Greg Bear's *Blood Music,* a girl named Suzy, one of the last humans remaining on a posthuman Earth, experiences the uneasy sensation of being ontologically photo-copied by family members who have already been nanotechnologically up-graded: "For a dizzy moment, she was in two places at once. She was with them—they had taken her away, and even now she spoke to her mother and brothers," and then suddenly "the feeling passed" (264), leaving her alone again. In chapter 14 of Kazuo Ishiguro's novel *Never Let Me Go* (2005), a co-terie of human clones, having glimpsed a woman whose mannerisms and ap-pearance suggest that she might be the "original" from whom one of them was "copied," furtively pursue the elusive woman through an unfamiliar streetscape while eluding the potentially duplicitous motives that haunt them in their pursuit. In Egan's *Diaspora*, in which each citizen of a virtual polis on Earth has been cloned 1,000 times and strewn across millions of cubic light-years for the purpose of exploring the universe, an emotional quandary arises when a clone named Orlando informs his son Paolo (also a clone) that the Orlando who had remained on Earth committed suicide fifty years after the clones had been launched into space. "How was he supposed to mourn a dis-tant version of Orlando, in the presence of the one he thought of as real?" Paolo wonders to himself. "Death of one clone was a strange half-death, a hard thing to come to terms with. *His Earth-self had lost a father; his father had lost an Earth-self.* What exactly did that mean to him?" (240; italics added to call attention to the way in which antimetabole formalizes the self-reflexive structure of Paolo's emotional predicament). A cybernetic character named M.Million struggles with similarly perplexing sorrow in Gene Wolfe's story "The Fifth Head of Cerberus." He attempts to explain to his great-grand-clone the procedure that long ago replaced his original body with a mechanical simu-lacrum: "Call me, call the person simulated, at least, your great-grandfather. He—I—am dead. In order to achieve simulation, it is necessary to examine the cells of the brain, layer by layer, with a beam of accelerated particles. . . ." But in the midst of his explanation, M.Million suddenly breaks down. "I am sorry," he confesses; "I was told, a very long time ago, just before the opera-tion, that my simulation—this—would be capable of emotion in certain cir-cumstances. Until today I had always thought they lied" (56).

The Feeling of Becoming Either More Human or Less Human

Science fiction is filled with situations in which superhuman or nonhuman en-tities undergo palpably humanizing experiences whereby they feel themselves growing more human (which may mean growing less superhuman) than they were before. Toward the end of Kress's *Beggars in Spain*, Leisha Camden, a superhuman genetically wired to exist without sleep, is astounded to find herself dreaming for the first time in her life when she is subjected to a bleeding-edge art form that uses holographic projection and hypnagogic recitation of Hopkins's poem "Spring and Fall" (303–305). In Cunningham's *Specimen Days*, a soul-searching robot named Simon is unexpectedly overcome with perplexing human feelings of yearning, delight, and nostalgic awareness of the ephemerality of life as he watches newfound friends splash in a pond: "This was a new sensation. . . . It was something that moved through his circuits, like shutdown but not quite; a floatier sensation, vaguely ticklish; an inner unmooring" (286). In *Return of the Jedi* (1983), the hitherto inhuman cyborg Darth Vader, stirred by the sight of his son Luke being tortured by Palpatine, is retransformed into a human father named Anakin Skywalker: he saves Luke's life and expresses a final wish to see his son face-to-face before succumbing to mortality: "Luke . . . help me take this mask off. . . . Just for once . . . let me . . . look on you with my *own* eyes." Near the end of "Mongolia," the fifth narrative in David Mitchell's ten-narrative novel *Ghostwritten* (1999), an immortal *noncorpum* that has spent most of its conscious life transmigrating freely through an endless succession of human hosts finds itself grappling with the decision of whether to fuse permanently with the newborn body of a Mongolian infant who will otherwise die. "I considered my future as a *noncorpum*," the narrator recounts: "Nowhere in the world would be closed to me," and "I would never grow old." Then "I looked down at the feeble day-old body in front of me, her metabolism dimming, minute by minute. Life expectancy in Central Asia is forty-three, and falling" (195). We learn of the *noncorpum*'s decision in the narrative's concluding sentence, a sentence that leaves the reader spellbound in the lyric present: "Inside, my wail, screamed from the hollows of my eighteen-hour-old lungs, *fills* the ger" (195, emphasis added).

If science fiction is filled with moments when superhuman or nonhuman entities undergo palpably humanizing experiences, the converse is also true. Science fiction is filled with occasions when a human undergoes the experience of turning into someone/something superhuman or nonhuman. Many obvious examples can be found in superhero lore—for example, the moment when Peter Parker (pre-Spiderman) finds himself endowed with superpowers by a radioactive spider bite—but not all such moments are superhero related.

In Stevenson's *Dr. Jekyll and Mr. Hyde,* the human Jekyll imbibes a potion catalyzing his corporeal and spiritual conversion into the not-quite-human Hyde: initially suffering "racking pangs," Jekyll soon detects in his feelings "something indescribably new and, from its very novelty, incredibly sweet"— and before long it is Hyde, not Jekyll, basking in "disordered sensual images" and "a solution of the bonds of obligation." In Bear's *Blood Music,* a scientist colonized by intelligent microscopic cells undergoes the alienating sensation of "crossing an interface" as he ceases to exist as a human self while his consciousness is "encoded" into sentient patterns of information composing what was once his physical body (217). In Alastair Reynolds's *Revelation Space,* human visitors to "Juggler" worlds—planet-sized oceans alive with diffusive biochemical perception—are neurally transmogrified during their visits: "Humans swimming in the Juggler-infested ocean were able to enter rapport states with the organism, as Juggler micro-tendrils filtered temporarily into the human neocortex, establishing quasi-synaptic links between the swimmers' minds and the rest of the ocean"; afterward, some swimmers "made startling breakthroughs in mathematics," with neurological tests revealing unmistakable yet unquantifiable alterations to the human brain (101–102). At the end of Tiptree's "Slow Music" (1977), the protagonist, one of the last humans alive, experiences a mix of human anguish and unhuman calm as he finally joins the alien river of light for which so many others of his race have already deserted Earth. Although "mortal grief fought the invading transcendence," his flesh began "to attenuate, to dematerialize out into the great current of sentience that flowed on its mysterious purposes among the stars" (503–504). Like the lyric speaker of Yeats's "Sailing to Byzantium," Tiptree's character surrenders to the science-fiction desire—the lyric desire—to be extracted out of nature and gathered into the artifice of eternity.

Sublime Sensory Excess

Sensory hyperstimulation is virtually ubiquitous in science fiction. The examples below are so overloaded with sense data that each must be given its own paragraph.

Near the conclusion of Alfred Bester's proto-cyberpunk novel *The Stars My Destination* (1956), Gully Foyle's nervous system is "twisted and short-circuited" by an explosive substance that leaves him "trapped in the kaleidoscope of his own cross-senses": "Smell was touch"; "the feel of glass cloyed his palate like over-rich pastry"; "A distant clatter of steps came to his eyes in soft patterns of vertical borealis streamers" rendered on the page as concrete shape poetry (235, 237).

In Miéville's *Perdido Street Station*, humans are hunted by monstrous moth-like organisms whose hideously gorgeous hypersensory wings—"the rippl*ing* tide of colors unfolded like anemones, a gentle, uncanny unfurl*ing* of en-thrall*ing* shades"—hypnotize victim's minds into similarly ongoing states of unfurling dreaming, a "mutat*ing* mass of the undermind" seemingly endlessly ending in a blur of "-ing" (413, italics added to each suffix "-ing").

In Smith's "The City of Singing Flame," the narrator's senses are transfig-ured by interdimensional travel: "The world on which I now gazed was a vast arabesque of unfamiliar forms and bewildering hues from another spectrum than the one to which our eyes are habituated. It swirled before my dizzy eyes like a labyrinth of gigantic jewels, with interweaving rays and tangled lustres" (250).

In Ballard's "The Voices of Time," the mutant anemone perceives activities happening outside its laboratory tank in lushly textured novas of synesthetic awareness: "A figure moved, adjusting the flow through its mouth. As it stepped across the floor its feet threw off vivid bursts of color, its hands racing along the benches conjured up a dazzling chiaroscuro, balls of blue and violet light that exploded fleetingly in the darkness like miniature star-shells" (95).

Toward the end of Yevgeny Zamyatin's dystopia *We* (written 1920–1921), the narrator, having crossed the "Green Wall" enclosing the monochromatic One State and entered the natural world for the first time, is awestruck and sent into a state of exuberant lyric perception: "The sun . . . this was not our sun, evenly diffused over the mirror-smooth surface of our pavements. These were living fragments, continually shifting spots, which dazed the eyes and made the head reel. And the trees, like candles—rising up into the sky itself; like spiders crouching on the earth with gnarled paws; like mute green foun-tains" (154–155).

In Nalo Hopkinson's story "Ganger (Ball Lightning)" (2000), a Senstim sex toy—a diaphanous human-sized and human-shaped wetsuit engineered to amplify the sensitivity of the wearer's skin—unexpectedly comes to electri-fied life and emerges from a closet to find its owner immersed in a bathtub where it virtually electrocutes her, sending shockwaves of unspeakable sensa-tion opalescing across her nervous system: the wetsuit "leaned over the water and dabbed at her clutching toes. Pop-crackle sound. The jolt sent her leg flailing like a dying fish. Pleasure crackled along her leg, painfully intense. Her knee throbbed and tingled, ached sweetly. Her thigh muscles shuddered as though they would tear free" (237).

In the wake of an inexplicably psychedelic trip though "vast converging planes of a slippery-looking substance" and "unknown, alien light in which yellow, carmine, and indigo were madly and inextricably blended," the main character of Lovecraft's story "The Dreams in the Witch House" (1933) finds himself in a lavishly appointed dreamscape comprising a "jungle of outlandish, incredible peaks, balanced planes, domes, minarets, horizontal disks poised on pinnacles, and numberless forms of still greater wildness—some of stone and some of metal—which glittered gorgeously in the mixed, almost blistering glare from a poly-chromatic sky" (313–314).

Mary Doria Russell's novel *The Sparrow* (1996) turns on critical moments of sensory extravagance, including the moment when an extraterrestrial poet named Hlavin Kitheri, who is gifted with an exquisite faculty of smell, opens a flask containing exotic fragrances from Earth and is overwhelmed and intoxicated by odors that to him are as otherworldly as they are earthy to humans: chocolate, basil, tarragon, vanilla, and (most crucially) human sweat—"tenuous odor of volatile short-chain carbons, the saline memorial of an alien ocean"—from the fingers of Emilio Sandoz, a man whom Kitheri does not yet know but will eventually destroy for reasons tracing back to this fateful olfactory encounter (277).

Jules Verne's novel *20,000 Leagues under the Sea* (1870), whose narrator is repeatedly enthralled by subaqueous spectacles such as cities of coral and the ruins of Atlantis, seems at times to vibrate with the intensity of the narrator's sensations, as when he describes an underwater scene of heightened iridescence resulting from the refraction of morning sunlight through the ocean and its prismatic effect on the ocean's floor: "The sun's rays hit the surface of the waves at a fairly oblique angle," he recounts, "and when this light came in contact with flowers, rocks, buds, seashells, and polyps, the edges of these objects were shaded with all seven hues of the solar spectrum," supersaturating the eyes with a "riot of rainbow tints," a "kaleidoscope of red, green, yellow, orange, violet, indigo, and blue" (part I, chapter 16).

The texts cited above are verbal, but any discussion of sensory extravagance in SF must include at least brief mention of "concept art"—a type of visual illustration designed to convey a specific mood, atmosphere, or style of environment, often commissioned for use in video games and SF movies. The overpowering displays of visual information even in two-dimensional works of SF concept art—for example, the photorealistic panoramas of otherworldly settings that can be found in the portfolios of Daniel Dociu, Cecil Kim, and James Paick—are so voluminous in detail, elaborate in configuration, and conspicuously vast in scope, that viewers find their own amazement incorporated in advance into the artwork's themes. Consider Paick's "Sky Port." Backdropped by unearthly clouds aloft mountains intricately etched with pale-gold crisscrossing, a massive aerial cityscape dominates the picture's foreground. The floating edifices comprising the city are miscellaneous in shape—from voluptuously oblong to vertical, lank, and endlessly storied. Here and there, edifices are linked by soaring arched bridges, diagonal ramps, gantry-like shafts in which staircases or elevators (or both) zigzag along intricate scaffolding, and pipelines vanishing and materializing through drifting layers of radiant mist. Together these interconnected structures encompass a sprawling network of façades, alternately opaque and translucent, encasing a concatenation of indoor provinces to which the viewer is provided glimpsing access: towering factories, inverted terraces of aquamarine bioluminescence, miles of jammed traffic receding in the distance, hill-slopes textured by glittering streets. From the city's balconied underside, mysterious tapered columns dangle at perpendicular angles, like icicles or tentacles. The landscape far below the aerial city is itself densely boulevarded and populated with metropolitan arrangements of light. In between the two cityscapes (aerial and landbound) hover several balloon-like entities, gigantic and peculiarly honeycombed, whose roots barely touch the ground, as well as a constellation of airborne vehicles, each vehicle reminiscent of both pterodactyl and starfish. "Sky Port" may be physically two-dimensional, but—much like James Cameron's dramatically immersive alien epic movie *Avatar* (2009)—it is three-dimensional in effect, submerging the viewer in a system of vistas and mazes brimming with details.

An Epiphany, a Revelation, So Implosive or Intense
That It Virtually Alters the Nature of Reality

Toward the end of *The Matrix* (1999), Neo's vision of reality is magically revolutionized when, instead of perceiving his surroundings as a world of physical surfaces, he perceives a moving current of luminous green numeric code following geometric patterns. In Jane Yolen's 1996 story "Sister Emily's Lightship," a fictional Dickinson has an otherworldly encounter that creates "a sudden rip in the fabric of her world" and inspires "a lifetime of poems" (279, 283). In Delany's novel *Babel-17,* the "headlong compactness" of an alien language called "Babel-17" (a language in which "I" does not exist) colonizes and restructures the language-user's mind as it is being learned, awakening one of its users to a universe of enhanced perceptions, "a flexible matrix of analytical possibilities," delineated in the book through an eccentric typographical layout: stanzas of italicized prose (each stanza corresponding to an isolated moment of interstitial alertness) float like rectangular islands in an unparagraphed stream-of-telepathic-third-person-consciousness narrative spanning several pages (140–144). At the end of Walter Miller's *Canticle for Leibowitz* (1959), a monk near death in the wake of a nuclear blast is inexplicably shown a revelation that leaves his knowledge of reality forever transubstantiated: as he lies dying, he is astonished to encounter "primal innocence" in the form of "Rachel," the "second" head (childlike, smiling, mysterious) of a two-headed mutant human whose "first" head (a fretful elderly woman named Mrs. Grales, who had made a confession to him just before the explosion) has been rendered comatose by the same blast that has mystifyingly brought to sudden life the heretofore inanimate Rachel, who gives the monk his final sacraments before he dies (336). In Clarke's *2001: A Space Odyssey,* Bowman undergoes a Dickinsonian experience in which sense literally breaks through: "He had been hanging above a large, flat rectangle, eight hundred feet long and two hundred wide, made of something that looked as solid as rock. But now it seemed to be receding from him. . . . 'The thing's hollow—it goes on forever—and—oh my God!—it's full of stars!'" (254).

An Absent Omnipresence

If lyric, as I have been arguing, is so prevalent in science fiction, then why do so many discussions of SF exclude poetry?

There are three ways of answering this question.

The first answer: those who read, write, study, and teach poetry tend not to overlap with those who read, write, study, and teach science fiction. As I have already mentioned, discussions of poetry are nearly absent from monographs, surveys, anthologies, and collections of essays on SF. The converse is also true: discussions of SF are nearly absent from monographs, anthologies, surveys, and collections of essays on lyric poetry. One aim of *Do Metaphors Dream of Literal*

Sleep? is to promote dialogue between those who study poetry and those who study science fiction.

The second answer: protocols/preconceptions surrounding poetry and protocols/preconceptions surrounding science fiction have evolved along disparate tracks. Several generalizations are in order here. The lyric is considered high art, and lyric poems are treated (rightly so) as worthy of formal appreciation and analysis. Science fiction, by contrast, is mostly considered subaesthetic pop-cultural entertainment. Rarely are SF novels, stories, and films treated as sophisticated works of compelling art. More often they are treated as pulp commodities to be consumed rather than appreciated seriously. These differing attitudes toward poetry and SF can be explained in part by historical circumstances. The lyric is an immemorially ancient institution and practice. Accordingly, it inspires reverence, even in those unfamiliar with poetry. Science fiction, meanwhile, is an institution and a practice whose very name originated (in the 1920s) in the context of lurid magazine publications literally made of pulp. Accordingly, science fiction tends to inspire less reverence than derision or apathy in those unfamiliar with it. The differing attitudes toward poetry and SF can be explained not just by their respective histories but also by formal attributes intrinsic to each discourse. In *The Fantastic,* Todorov articulates a perspective representative of an outlook shared by many when he claims that poetic images are to be read solely "on the level of the verbal chain they constitute, not even on that of their reference. The poetic image is a combination of words, not of things, and it is pointless, even harmful, to translate this combination into sensory terms" (60). In Todorov's view, the necessity of reading poetic images solely as incantatory chains of signifiers (rather than as referential descriptions) renders the protocols for reading poetry incompatible with the protocols for reading fantastic narratives. Todorov goes so far as to claim that the two sets of protocols are mutually hostile: "Poetic reading constitutes a danger for the fantastic," he warns. "If as we read a text we reject all representation" and consider "each sentence as a pure semantic combination"—which is how Todorov idealizes the process of reading poetry—then "the fantastic could not appear: for the fantastic requires, it will be recalled, a reaction to events as they occur in the world evoked. For this reason, the fantastic can subsist only within fiction; poetry cannot be fantastic" (60). By contrast, I prefer to see no reason why readers should be forbidden to read poems as more than incantatory combinations of words. To be prohibited from reading poems as referential descriptions is to be deprived of revelatory aesthetic experiences. For example, many of Dickinson's poems, when approached as more than "pure semantic combinations," reveal an astonishing science-fiction cosmos where clocks are afflicted with timelessness, mathematical diagrams glow across night skies, and the specter of postapocalypse haunts every other mindscape. However, I agree with Todorov's assertion that the lyric entails certain kinds of reading while precluding other kinds. Due to its compressed size, the lyric is much more spatial than temporal in its proportions. In general, spatial forms such as two-dimensional photographs are limited in their representational capacity. A photograph may suffice as a mimetic account of a simple concrete object, but photography is unfit for the task of representing cognitively estranging phenomena such as cyberspace. The process through which a cognitively estranging referent becomes available for representation is a massively complicated one that requires ample time and ample space. Unlike the lyric, the novel is capable of prolongating along axes both temporal and spatial. This may be one reason why SF writers tend to write novels rather than poems.

The third and least obvious answer: lyric qualities are so prevalent in science fiction, so thoroughly characteristic of SF, that their collective presence need not take the physical form of verse to make itself felt to the reader of SF narratives. By "lyric qualities," I have in mind not just musicality, soliloquy-likeness, lyric time, etc., but also—more broadly—the lyric *"turn"* that subsumes as its subcategories lyric time, soliloquy-likeness, descriptive intensity, musicality, and eccentric/heightened perception. As Northrop Frye has remarked, "the lyric *turns away*, not merely from ordinary space and time, but from the kind of language we use in coping with ordinary experience" ("Approaching the Lyric," 34, emphasis added), and it is equally true that science fiction *turns away* from ordinary space and time and from the kind of language we use in coping with ordinary experience. The existing canon of SF may consist mostly of prose, but the straightforwardness of prose ("prose" derives etymologically from "prosum," Latin for straightforward) is absent from science fiction. Just as verse constitutes a turn away from prose ("verse," as noted earlier, comes from the Latin verb "vertere," to turn), and just as poetic tropes constitute a turn from literal to figurative meaning ("trope" comes from "tropos," Greek for "turn"), science fiction constitutes a *turn away* from familiar reality. The organism *turned* by mutation into something else; the wormhole twisting and *turning* through universes; the mind-*turning* realization that "reality" is actually a computer-generated simulation; the moment when an inanimate robot *turns* into a living person: each of these science fictions is literally a trope, a verse, a deviation in narrative space-time and consciousness. The "turn" that defines verse is so deeply implanted in SF that *science-fiction verse* nearly amounts to a redundancy. Paradoxically, then, the omnipresence of lyric poetry in SF narrative is an *absent* presence. This paradox explains why SF authors tend to write novels and stories as opposed to poems, and it explains why the study of SF in lyric terms remains largely unexplored territory—one that I hope to open up to investigation.

An intriguing epiphenomenon of the paradoxically absent omnipresence of lyric in narrative science fiction is the prevalence of lyric intertexts and paratexts in SF novels and short stories. Paratexts and intertexts are themselves paradoxical spaces: a book's title, for instance, is at once central to the book and overtly peripheral; an intertextual allusion is neither fully here nor exclusively there yet definitely present in both texts simultaneously. Such paradoxical textual spaces are frequently the same places where the absent presence of lyric manifests itself most explicitly in narrative SF. Titles of SF narratives, for example, often allude intertextually to specific poems. To cite a few cases: the title of Philip José Farmer's 1971 novel *To Your Scattered Bodies Go* echoes a line from one of Donne's Holy Sonnets; the title of Iain M. Banks's 1987 novel *Consider Phlebas* echoes a line from *The Waste Land;* the title of Simmons's Hyperion tetralogy echoes the title of Keats's unfinished epic; the title of Bradbury's short story "There Will Come Soft Rains" echoes Sara Teasdale's poem of the same name. Moments of verse also erupt intertextually *within* many SF narratives. In David Brin's novel *Startide Rising,* sentient dolphins, biologically uplifted by humans, communicate in haiku-shaped thoughts. In Cunningham's *Specimen Days,* soulful androids compulsively recite lines by Whitman and Dickinson. This latter poet, it is worth noting, appears intertextually as a science-fiction figure in a growing sub-subset of narrative SF. In Yolen's 1996 story "Sister Emily's Lightship," set in nineteenth-century Amherst, a fictional Dickinson has a mystifying nocturnal encounter with an extraterrestrial life-form that leaves Dickinson forever mind-altered and launches decades of otherworldly creativity. In Joyce Carol Oates's 2006 story "EDickinsonRepliLuxe," a childless suburban couple purchases a robot designed to simulate Dickinson's personality—with heartbreaking results. In the 1999 film *Being John Malkovich,* an early hint to the viewer that the world in the film is not quite normal takes the form of a giant building-sized Dickinson marionette reciting her own poetry in a televised broadcast. In a 1997 short-story-disguised-as-a-scholarly-article by Connie Willis entitled "'The Soul Selects Her Own Society': Invasion and Repulsion: A Chronological Reinterpretation of Two of Emily Dickinson's Poems: A Wellsian Perspective," the narrator fancifully speculates that Martians invading Earth around the turn of the century inadvertently disturbed Dickinson (d. 1886) from her slumber in the grave, thereby angering the dead poet and provoking her to relay admonitions in verse to the Martian invaders. Severely injured by Dickinson's weapons of slant-rhyme, the Martians (Willis conjectures) hastily retreated from Earth before suffering further casualties. What exactly makes Dickinson an attractive figure to writers of SF? My guess is that there is something enticingly science-fictional about Dickinson's idiosyncratic sensibilities. Dickinson's poems are so hyperbolically lyrical, so acute in their lyricism, that they virtually self-literalize into recognizable science fiction.

The absent omnipresence of lyric in SF narrative is precisely what accounts for the representational work that SF is capable of performing. Only a narrative discourse powered through and through by lyricism possesses enough *torque*—enough *twisting force,* enough *verse*—to *convert* referents ordinarily *averse* to representation into referents accessible to representation. Just as the "turn" that defines poetry is so deeply implanted in SF that "science-fiction verse" approaches redundancy, lyric figures and devices (apostrophe, synesthesia, the simple present, etc.) are so thoroughly and systematically literalized as features of SF narrative worlds that SF cannot be understood as *narrative* without concurrently being understood as *lyric.* Hence the moment when a humanoid robot comes alive is not only a narrative event but also a spatiotemporal *trope*—a *twist,* a *turn,* in space-time—charged with the lyric energies of personification. Within the narrative universe of SF, the literal and the metaphoric share ontological status. As a figurative discourse whose grammatical mood is indicative, SF can provide a representational home for referents that are themselves neither purely literal nor purely figurative in nature.

My claim here about the representational powers of SF is a corollary to an argument that Elaine Scarry makes about the verbal arts in *Dreaming by the Book.* The verbal arts, Scarry writes,

> are at once counterfactual and counterfictional. Like the daydream, the verbal arts are counterfactual: both the daydream and the poem bring into being things not previously existing in the world. But the verbal arts are

also counterfictional, displacing the ordinary attributes of imagining—its faintness, two-dimensionality, fleetingness, and dependence on volitional labor—with the vivacity, solidity, persistence, and givenness of the perceptible world. (38)

In science fiction, the features of verbal art are heightened and reinforced. Not only is SF at once counterfactual and counterfictional, but it is also at once *counterliteral* and *counterfigurative*. Like the metaphor, SF is counterliteral: both metaphor and SF bring into imagined existence things nonexistent in the world of literal facts. (For example, the X-Men movies and comics bring into imagined existence globalization-as-a-mutagen-transforming-the-human-species.) But SF is also counterfigurative, displacing the ordinary attributes of figurative language—its weightlessness, virtuality, as-if-ness, dependence on cognitive labor—with the vivacity, solidity, persistence, and givenness that characterize the perceptible world of literal facts. (Thus, in the X-Men cosmos, globalization is literally a mutagen physically transforming the human body into a new kind of organism capable, for instance, of occupying diverse localities on the globe simultaneously.) As a result of this counterfigurative literalization, the cognitively estranging referent becomes substantiated into something kinesthetically recognizable that makes immediate sense to our tendons, muscles, nerves. By empowering SF to operate beyond the opposition between the counterfigurative and the counterliteral—by allowing lyric figures in SF to operate on a literal level without losing their figurative power—the absent omnipresence of lyric enables SF to represent objects and phenomena normally averse to representation.

Five Cognitively Estranging Referents and Over Fifteen Science-Fictionemes

Science-fictional environments, creatures, and artifacts are not the imaginary referents that most people understand them to be. They are mediums of representation constituted by literalized poetic figures of speech. The basic unit of SF—what one might call a *"science-fictioneme"*—is a literalized figure of speech (or system of literalized figures of speech) through which a cognitively estranging referent becomes available for representation. Each chapter of *Do Metaphors Dream* examines one cognitively estranging referent and its corresponding *science-fictionemes.* Starting with cognitively estranging "spaces," proceeding to cognitively estranging "experiences," and ending with a cognitively estranging ethical category, I study numerous ways in which SF has overcome the formidable challenge of representing cognitively estranging phenomena— not just in texts readily identifiable as SF (e.g., writings by Asimov, Dick, Vonnegut) but also in texts seldom considered SF (e.g., travel writing, Korean American memoir).

CHAPTER I: "THE GLOBALIZED WORLD." The global is more cognitively estranging than the local. In the realm of the local, "What time is it?" and "Where am I?" have simple answers. In the global realm, the answers are more complex. For the Texan jetlagged in Jilin, the hotel clock may read 1 A.M. while daylight jams her every nerve. Members of a chatroom may reside in cities as geographically far-flung as Lima, Oslo, and Harare, while their on-line selves are separated by inches. The realm of the global, then, is a dynamic space where the literal distance between two points (distance measured objectively) and the figurative distance between the same two points (distance as subjectively perceived) regularly conflict. "The Globalized World" explores SF's capacity to accommodate representations of this dynamic space. The texts discussed—from Octavia Butler's Xenogenesis Series (1987–1989) to *The Calcutta Chromosome* (1995) by Amitav Ghosh—literalize global tropes as narrative situations; in doing so, they integrate literal and figurative aspects of the globalized world. For example, we often say that globalization collapses distance. But we rarely stop to imagine this metaphor as a concrete reality. In our minds, the distance remains uncollapsed and the global referent stays beyond the purview of representation. In SF, however, we find this metaphorical collapse of distance literalized and brought to life: we might, for instance, find someone using teleportation to occupy multiple places simultaneously. Through such scenarios, globalization-related paradoxes such as "closer apart" become perceivable kinesthetically; they assume proportions that our muscles and nerves can easily recognize.

- Cognitively estranging referent: the globalized world
- Science-fictionemes: the meta-local crossroads; the ecumenopolis; terraformed Mars; Spaceship Earth; the globalization chromosome; mutant physiologies that literally embody the transnational body politic

CHAPTER 2: "CYBERSPACE IN THE 1990S." Writers and thinkers in the 1990s who tried to describe cyberspace were faced with a number of problems. What does it mean to describe a virtual "space" whose existence is a nonvirtual fact? How is it possible to represent something whose chronological status cannot be fixed? Coined in 1981 by William Gibson, "cyberspace" originally referred to a mindscape generated by futuristic machines. Gibson used this imaginary mindscape as the setting for his Cyberspace Series: *Neuromancer* (1984), *Count Zero* (1986), and *Mona Lisa Overdrive* (1988). The novels quickly achieved cult-classic status, and Gibson's coinage became a buzzword among computer enthusiasts who found it a useful way of thinking about new tools (e.g., graphics-based browsers) that were revolutionizing telecommunications. By the mid-1990s, "cyberspace" had become synonymous with "Internet" and "World Wide Web." Because of this synonymy, and because of the abruptness with which the "Cyberspace Revolution" followed the publication of the Cyberspace Series, the Internet was widely perceived as the materialization of Gibson's prophetic vision. Whatever "cyberspace" referred to in the 1990s was not only a present-day technology that retained its earlier evocation of something futuristic and unreal, but also an unreal futurescape whose name was suddenly beginning to refer to part of the present-day world. Fittingly, it was Gibson who solved the problem of how to represent this elusive referent. In his Bridge Trilogy (1993–1999) cyberspace becomes available for representation through the science-fictional structure alluded to by the trilogy's title: a postapocalyptic San Francisco Bay Bridge. No longer operative as a mode of transport, the bridge now serves as a shantytown-like dwelling for visionaries and outcasts. Businesses on the bridge are unlicensed, laws are unspoken, pathways are densely mazelike, and homes are made of salvaged junk. By concretizing and consolidating a range of metaphors that had come to be associated with cyberspace in the 1990s (e.g., "cyberspace is a labyrinth," "cyberspace is a commune"), Gibson's bridge presents cyberspace as a physical entity whose features are readily intelligible to our bodies.

- Cognitively estranging referent: cyberspace in the 1990s
- Science-fictioneme: the bridge in Gibson's Bridge Trilogy

CHAPTER 3: "WAR TRAUMA." By definition, a traumatic event cannot be experienced while it is happening. Instead it is relived in delayed, repetitive form— through nightmares, hallucinations, flashbacks. Trauma, then, cannot be located in time. Yet trauma can be located in science fiction. This chapter explores the relationship between trauma and SF in four science-fictional testimonies to war trauma: Olaf Stapledon's *Last and First Men: A Story of the Near and Far Future* (1930), Kurt Vonnegut's *Slaughterhouse-Five* (1969), Joe Haldeman's *The Forever War* (1974), and Tim O'Brien's *The Things They Carried* (1990). Initially these texts may seem more dissimilar than alike: *Last and First Men*, for example, is seldom (if ever) considered a war novel, and *The Things They Carried* is seldom (if ever) considered science fiction. Yet to bring the four narratives into one another's vicinity is to discover that the variations among them are actually illustrations of the transcendent flexibility and expansiveness of science fiction as a representational form. In a multitude of ways and to varying extents, all four accounts of war trauma are remarkably self-reflexive, calling attention to the limits and possibilities of representation, raising questions about the capacity of language to accommodate extreme autobiographical realities, and probing the relationship between what is literally true and what is figuratively true. Dissociation finds mimetic counterparts in science-fictional metafiction and intertextuality. The impact of wounding finds itself recounted not as the straightforward memory of a past event but as the endlessly deferred possibility of a normal future. The unassimilated nature of trauma finds itself reflected in a narrative form that by nature resists assimilation. Shell shock finds testimonial expression in lyric voices—science-fictional voices—that speak from outside of ordinary temporality.

- Cognitively estranging referent: war trauma
- Science-fictionemes: dissociative cloning; involuntary time travel; time dilation; alien physiologies; alien telepathy

CHAPTER 4: "POSTMEMORY HAN." As Marianne Hirsch notes in her book *Family Frames* (1997), children of Holocaust survivors often "remember" a tragedy they did not experience firsthand. Hirsch uses the term "postmemory" to designate this form of intergenerational remembrance whereby the experience remembered is at once virtual and real, secondhand and familiar, long ago and present. In this chapter I investigate the ways in which SF has enabled Korean American writers to account for the paradoxes of postmemory. In particular, I examine SF representations of "postmemory han," by which I mean the transmission of *han* from Korean immigrants to their Korean American children. "Han," a word with no equivalent in English, refers to a Korean form of grief. According to Ishle Yi Park, "All Koreans feel it" because "our country has always had to shut up and listen to bigger countries" and "because of the war that split brother from sister and left everyone's family missing or dead." In *Dictee* (1982), Theresa Hak Kyung Cha invokes postmemory han by figuring herself as a bionic telepath who recalls distant events (e.g., her mother's near-death experience while exiled in Manchuria) with photographic exactness. And in *Notes from the Divided Country* (2003), Suji Kwock Kim renders postmemory han available for representation by describing it as a genetic condition. Made of "chromosomes" and "cells of history," her parents' han-filled memories permeated her body while she was in her mother's womb. Thus, in Kim's SF account of postmemory han, the Japanese occupation and Korean War—neither of which she experienced firsthand—have become part of her DNA.

- Cognitively estranging referent: postmemory han
- Science-fictionemes: the genetic transference of han-filled memories from Korean parent to unborn Korean American child; simultaneity of past and present within the Korean American psyche; the supernormal Korean American telepath

CHAPTER 5: "ROBOT RIGHTS." Suppose we lived in a world where humans coexisted with sentient robots. By "sentient robots," I mean human-made objects possessing human attributes such as selfhood and the capacity to love. What kinds of moral claims might such a creature have on us? Should a sentient robot be entitled, for example, to freedom of thought? While the ethical significance of such questions is already palpable—the American Society for the Prevention of Cruelty to Robots has been "upholding robot rights since 1999"—the moral claims of robots remain difficult to recognize. For one thing, artificial sentience is still a thing of the future. More important, however, the idea of a sentient robot is quintessentially "uncanny." How can one represent the moral claims of something whose status as a living entity may be impossible to determine? To explore what it means to ask such a question is the purpose of this chapter. Guided by the writings of Elaine Scarry and Masahiro Mori, I inspect humanoid artifacts in Shelley's *Frankenstein* (1818), Dick's *Do Androids Dream of Electric Sheep?* (1968), and the films *Blade Runner* (1982) and *A.I.* (2000). These are works in which images of robot uncanniness are meaningfully juxtaposed with situations where robots become identifiable as humans worthy of empathy—for example, an android soliloquizing about the nature of reality; a mechanical child pleading for its life. During such lyric moments, the uncanniness of robots is countervailed and the moral claims of robots become available for representation.

- Cognitively estranging referent: robot rights
- Science-fictionemes: lyric structures of voice where personification and apostrophe behave as forces that literally bestow humanity on nonhuman entities

What Science Fiction Is: Lyric Mimesis

By now it should be clear that *Do Metaphors Dream of Literal Sleep?* operates on a new definition of science fiction. Here is an informal version of the definition:

> Science fiction is a representational technology powered by a combination of lyric and narrative forces that enable SF to generate mimetic accounts of cognitively estranging referents.

Here is a more formal definition:

> Science fiction *(definiendum)* is a mode *(genus)* whose combined attributes— lyric/figurative and narrative/literal—together empower SF to render cognitively estranging referents available for representation *(differentiae specificae)*.

Three main factors are likely to make this definition "new" to most readers. The first factor is the definition's assignment to the *definiendum* a quality seldom thought of in conjunction with (or even in proximity to) science fiction: lyricism. Accordingly, most of this chapter has been charged with the task of demonstrating the ways in which lyricism inheres in science fiction. The second factor is the definition's assignment to the *definiendum* a quality usually thought of as antithetical to SF: the capacity for mimetic representation. Accordingly, each of the next five chapters of this book will demonstrate the ways in which a specific cognitively estranging referent becomes available for representation in works of science fiction. The third factor is the definition's classification of the *definiendum* as a "mode" rather than as a *"genre,"* which is how most people classify science fiction. (Some even classify SF as a "subgenre.") By "mode" I have in mind a category more expansive than "genre" and less determinable. Alastair Fowler captures the inexplicitness of "mode" in his insight that "modal terms never imply a complete external form" (107). Science fiction, being "modal," can assume a variety of "external forms"—electronica, concept art, prose fiction, film, architecture, etc.—while remaining recognizably science-fictional throughout.

Although *Do Metaphors Dream* operates on an unconventional definition of "science fiction," promoting a redefinition of the term is not my ultimate purpose here. The above formulations amount to a working definition rather than a conclusive argument. This working definition enables me to pursue the ultimate purpose of *Do Metaphors Dream:* to suggest a science-fictional theory of representation. As I proposed earlier, all representation is to some degree science-fictional because all reality is to some degree cognitively estranging. What most people call "realism," I said, is actually a low-intensity variety of SF, one that requires little energy to accomplish its representational work insofar as its referents (e.g., softballs) are readily susceptible to representation. Conversely, what most people call "science fiction" is actually a high-intensity variety of realism, one that requires exorbitant levels of energy to accomplish its representational work insofar as its referents (e.g., financial derivatives) challenge simple representation. In this book, "realism" means low-intensity mimetic representation, while "science fiction" means high-intensity mimetic representation. The continuum shared by realism and SF runs parallel to the continuum shared by all referents—from pebbles, dimes, and blueberries to cyberspace, black holes, and postmemory.

In addition to arguing that the difference between SF and realism corresponds to the difference in the degree to which their referents defy representation, I argued that the differences among various types of SF correspond to the various types of referents that require high-intensity representation. Surrealism, I said, is a type of SF mimesis whose cognitively estranging referent is the phenomenon of dreaming; utopianism is a type of SF mimesis whose cognitively estranging referent is the ideal polity; gothic is a type of SF mimesis whose cognitively estranging referent is the repressed-but-irrepressible unconscious; and so on. What unites these types of SF—what differentiates them from realism proper—is their ability to produce mimetic accounts of referents unavailable to straightforward representation.

Skeptical readers might wonder (understandably) why I use "science fiction" as an apparent synecdoche for the sum of so-called nonmimetic genres. Why do I posit science fiction (arguably a subgenre) as a mode encompassing fantasy, gothic, surrealism, etc.? Would it not be more accurate for me to reformulate my argument using the word "nonmimetic" instead of "science fiction"? Several reasons compel me to use "science fiction" to designate such a broad range of representational strategies. Replacing "science fiction" with "nonmimetic" would be potentially misleading insofar as my argument is precisely that "non-mimetic" texts are actually mimetic. Furthermore, there are distinct advantages to using SF as a means of framing and characterizing a theory of mimesis. To return to a claim made in the opening pages of this book: science fiction offers an uncannily opportune and prolific resource for generating brave new worldviews on an ancient topic. The discourses that already surround and constitute science fiction—the discourses that make science fiction what we perceive it to be—encompass a prodigious wealth of aesthetic and philosophical materials from which to construct a framework for thinking about mimesis. As the foregoing pages make obvious, two materials that I have found especially suitable for constructing a science-fictional theory of representation are the Suvinian vocabulary of "cognitive estrangement" and the tantalizingly deceptive absence of SF poems (i.e., the absent omnipresence of lyric in narrative SF). Less obviously, I have sought to enhance my argument by tapping the potent aura of iconic SF characters and texts (e.g., Jekyll/Hyde; *2001*) as well as the mental associations that attend the repertory of SF motifs (e.g., telepathy, aliens). But the material most vital to my project may be the phrase "science fiction" itself. It cannot be an accident that the phrase's original incarnation as "scientific fiction"—Hugo Gernsback introduced this coinage in the 1920s—rapidly mutated into "science fiction," which soon "prevailed over the original coinage" (Moskowitz, "How Science Fiction Got Its Name," 1127).[17] As noted earlier, "science fiction," unlike the modified noun "scientific fiction," is charged with lyric voltage generated by the shock of catachresis: the noun "science" has denotations and connotations that clash energetically with the denotations and connotations of the noun "fiction." At the same time, the etymological resonances of "science fiction" suggest that the voltage generated by the catachrestic joining of "science" and "fiction" is itself a generative force. "Science" comes from the Latin verb "sciere," to know. "Fiction" comes from the Latin verb "fingere," to make by shaping. Science fiction, in other words, equals the making of knowledge. This equation calls attention to the crucial epistemological work that science fiction performs. To make something available for representation is to make it knowable.

What Science Fiction Is *Not:* Allegory

If all representation is to some degree science-fictional, then what is *not* science fiction?

My answer: Allegory is not science fiction.

This claim may seem perverse. As Joanna Russ has noted, one of the most common responses to "What is science fiction?" is "Allegory" ("Speculations," 17). Certainly allegory and science fiction share salient attributes. Both are modes at once lyric and narrative, modes in which figurative structures are methodically literalized as large-scale features of narrative worlds. In fact, many of the ways in which scholars have characterized allegory can be used to characterize science fiction as well. In *Allegory: The Theory of a Symbolic Mode*, Angus Fletcher describes allegory as a "protean device" that embraces "so many different kinds of literature" that "no narrowly exclusive stipulated definition will be useful, however desirable it might seem, while formal precision may at present even be misleading to the student of the subject" (1). This description can be applied directly to science fiction without losing any of its veracity. To continue applying Fletcher's characterization of allegory to my own characterization of SF: science fiction encompasses an "extraordinary variety of literary kinds" (3). It is "a many-sided phenomenon" whose "overall purposes are capable of many minor variations" (23). Just as "there are degrees of allegory" (312), there are degrees of SF. Just as "we must be ready to discern in almost any work at least a small degree of allegory" (8), we must be ready to discern in almost any work at least a small degree of SF.

Such correlations, however, do not make allegory and science fiction identical. Instead they indicate that allegory and SF are commensurate in size, scope, and relevance. Allegory and SF may belong to the same *genus*—both are "modes"—but they do not share the same *differentiae specificae*. The defining qualities of allegory remain importantly distinct from the defining qualities of science fiction. Allegory is a mode whereby a text invites being construed "as if there were an 'other' sense to which it referred" (*New Princeton Encyclopedia*, 31). In particular, allegory involves what Gordon Teskey has identified as "an incoherent narrative" that "elicits continual interpretation as its primary aesthetic effect, giving us the feeling that we are moving at once inward and upward toward the transcendental 'other'" (4–5). As with intransitive verbs (e.g., "to blossom," "to evanesce," "to spiral"), allegory takes no direct object. A narrative in the allegorical mode need not be *about* something. The purpose of allegory is not to refer to a specific object but to incite the reader's mind to exegesis. Meanwhile, the purpose of science fiction is not to instigate exegetical activity in the reader's mind but to represent a cognitively estranging referent. Just as a transitive verb requires an object to complete its meaning ("to represent ___," "to address ___"), science fiction requires an object—or more precisely a referent—to complete its function.

Yet allegory and SF are not mutually exclusive. A text can qualify as both simultaneously. Consider the following two ways of approaching a grape. It is one thing to say: "This grape elicits continuous sense impressions in me: yellow-greenish hues; flavors sweet and slightly acidic. . . ." It is another thing to say: "This grape performs a certain function in my body, making available to the tissues of my body specific nutrients—vitamins, sugars, fiber. . . ." The analogy is imperfect, but the difference between the two approaches delineated above is not unlike the difference between allegory and science fiction. Both approaches to the grape, while dissimilar, can coexist without splitting the grape in half.

Let me discuss a literary case that serves more properly than the grape to illustrate the differences between allegory and science fiction. The case is a well-known Renaissance allegory: Alma's "House of Temperance" in book 2, canto IX of Spenser's epic poem *The Faerie Queene*. Alma, whose name means "soul," is a young woman, "full of grace and goodly modestee" (stanza 18), who resides in a diligently maintained and vigilantly guarded home that Spenser describes in detail over the course of numerous pages. Among the household members are a "Steward" named "Diet" who is "in demeanure sober, and in counsell sage" (27); an industrious "kitchin Clerke" named "Digestion" (31); and several unnamed workers who efficiently dispose of household waste by discarding it through "secret wayes" that lead discreetly "to the back-gate" (32). The air inside the house is kept temperate by a "huge great paire of bellowes, which did styre / Continually, and cooling breath inspyre" (30). Atop the house is a "stately Turret" (44) where "Two goodly Beacons" are "set in watches stead" (46). Seated "in siluer sockets bright," these beacons are composed "most subtilly" of "liuing fire" and "Couer'd with lids deuiz'd of substance sly, / That readily they shut and open might" (46). Interestingly, the walls of the architectural structure are "Not built of bricke, ne yet of stone and lime, / But of thing like to that Aegyptian slime" (21). Slime, then, is the primary building material that constitutes this building. Alma's house is made of actively ambiguous goo—a substance both living and inert, biological (mucus) and geological (mud). Since "no earthly thing is sure," the house of Alma eventually "must turne to earth" again (21). For the time being, however, the ooze is molded to the unthinkably intricate "workemanship" that distinguishes the overall structure of Alma's house:

> The frame thereof seemd partly circulare,
> And part triangulare, o worke divine;
> Those two the first and last proportions are,

The one imperfect, mortal, feminine;
Th' other immortall, perfect, masculine,
And twixt them both a quadrate was the base,
Proportioned equally by seven and nine;
Nine was the circle set in heavens place,
All which compacted made a goodly Diyapase. (Bk. 2, canto
    IX, stanza 22)

Such is the divine workmanship of Alma's house of temperance as delineated in a stanza that Thomas Roche has annotated as "the most obviously complicated of Spenser's stanzas" (1126).

As allegory, Alma's house arouses our curiosity. It kindles our desire to seek latent significances. It impels us to ask questions that might move us toward that elusive "something else" that we sense in Spenser's plan. What is the meaning of this strange residence? Why is it so heavily fortified? How can we decipher characters with names such as "Digestion" and "Diet"? Why is there so much secrecy surrounding the back-gate through which household waste is "privily" discarded? Are the two bellows that "inspyre" breath supposed to remind us of lungs and respiration? And the two watchful beacons set in bright sockets and covered with lids that shut and open—yes, those must be meant to remind us of eyes. Apparently, then, this architectural structure is designed to remind the reader of a human body. But whose body is it? Or what kind of body? Because the house is portrayed as rigorously maintained by its conscientious inhabitants, we may infer that the body evoked by Alma's house is a temperate one (as "House of Temperance" indeed suggests). He/she—the gender is ambiguous—obviously takes care of this body, is mindful of what enters and exits it, and is extremely protective of its borders. For what purpose is the body maintained so carefully? The unusual composition of Alma's house offers some clues. A structure made of something as slippery as slime must require rigorous maintenance to forestall dissolution. Moreover, an architectural design so transcendently charged with obscure symbolism that it hovers on the brink of unintelligibility[18] can have been created only by an entity whose handiwork demands to be treated with reverent devotion. Particularly intriguing here is the juxtaposition of obscure slime with obscure numerology—the juxtaposition, in other words, of ever obscurer levels of materiality (brute flesh constantly living and dying) with ever obscurer levels of abstraction (form that idealizes the body as more than merely flesh). The juxtaposition creates an effect at once stereoscopic and kaleidoscopic—stereoscopic because it synthesizes a three-dimensional illusion from two constituent images and kaleidoscopic because each image is forever shifting. Alma's house is an ever-evolving constellation of allegory effects. From one angle it evokes the body of a young woman. From another angle it evokes a slimy corpse. From yet another angle it evokes an architectural structure. It might be an unfinished sculpture of the boundary between outline and texture, the metaphysical boundary where the shapeliness of form simultaneously recedes into yet resurfaces from the shapelessness of matter. It might be a statue on the verge of coming to life. Whatever it is, it is always in the midst of transformation. It is a question of perspective—slowly but continuously mutating. It exists on the brink of indecipherability, just as it exists on the brink of the anthropomorphic. Reading Spenser's House of Alma as allegory is not unlike watching Optimus Prime (from the Transformers cosmos) in the midst of morphing intricately from truck to robot.

If the house of Alma in allegorical mode is an ongoing process of interpretive possibilities, the house of Alma in science-fiction mode is a powerful mimetic representation of a cognitively estranging referent, namely, the divinely awe-inspiring and exquisite workmanship of the human body. Spenser accomplishes this representational task by literalizing the metaphor of human body as house. There are various ways of figuring the human body: for example, the body as costume, the body as temple, the body as prison, the body as geography, the body as automobile. In the case of Spenser's temperate body, the metaphor of a house is appropriate because it allows Spenser to develop a narrative situation in which a house is maintained in an orderly fashion. Alma's residence is not just a representation of the human body; it is more specifically a representation of a human body that is healthy and well maintained. Accordingly, the metaphor literalized through Alma's house is not just the human body as a house but more specifically the healthy and temperate human body as a house whose slimy material composition entails vigilant maintenance and whose transcendent design entails worshipful devotion.

I have been using a sixteenth-century text to illustrate my point, but equally relevant illustrations of the difference between allegory and science fiction can be found in contemporary texts. Take, for example, the TV show *Lost* (2004–2010). As with *The Faerie Queene* and so many other texts, *Lost* qualifies as both science fiction and allegory, but what makes the show allegorical is not what makes it science-fictional. What makes *Lost* allegorical is the ongoing process of interpretation that the show elicits as its primary aesthetic effect: the series has generated a sizable and dedicated audience whose members use on-line forums to interpret, decode, and overanalyze every possible detail about the mysterious island. What makes *Lost* science-fictional is its power to make a cognitively estranging referent (the afterlife of 9/11 in America) available for representation.

Yet as I said earlier, allegory and science fiction, while distinct, are not mutually exclusive. Indeed, the two modes are intimately interrelated. Allegory plays a vital role in assisting in science-fiction mimesis: the aesthetic pleasure that a reader derives from the experience of "continuous interpretation" facilitates his or her recognition of whatever elusive referent is being made available for representation in a science-fiction text. Meanwhile, the alluring presence of a cognitively estranging yet ultimately knowable referent at the end of the interpretive process is what gives this process its final meaning and importance. Science fiction and allegory, then, have a reciprocal relationship. They are each other's significant other half. Each mode is the other mode's reciprocal. Each completes the other. Just as $1/x$ and x need to be multiplied by each other to equal one, allegory and science fiction need to be multiplied together to achieve the product of a total unity.

The Introduction Ends on a Historical Note

The science-fictional theory of representation offered in these pages may seem ahistorical. Insofar as elusive referents have always been around and are unlikely to disappear anytime soon, science fiction has always existed and will always continue to exist. That the term "science fiction" emerged in the 1900s need not prevent us from relating it to texts predating the twentieth century. To apply "science fiction" to, say, Shelley's *Frankenstein* is no more anachronistic than applying the word "literature" to the *Iliad, Macbeth,* and other texts predating the nineteenth century (when this sense of the word "literature" emerged).

Yet *Do Metaphors Dream* does have a kind of historical consciousness (or a historical unconscious). Most of the texts discussed in this book are from the twentieth and twenty-first centuries. "Mundane" reality has never been an uncomplicated matter, but the case could be made that everyday reality for people all over the world has grown less and less concretely accessible over the past several centuries and will continue to evolve in that direction for decades (if not centuries) to come. In other words, cognitively estranging referents are growing more and more prevalent. At the same time, the referents that constitute our everyday reality are growing progressively estranging. Financial derivatives are more cognitively estranging than pennies. Global climate change is more cognitively estranging than yesterday's local weather. Multinational conglomerates are more cognitively estranging than independent retail shops. Korean American identity is more cognitively estranging than Korean identity. Science fiction, then, is an increasingly appropriate and convenient language for handling questions about so-called mundane reality. The five referents discussed in the next five chapters of this book—the globalized world, cyberspace in the 1990s, war trauma, postmemory han, and robot rights—exemplify this trend whereby the referents that constitute everyday reality grow more elusive.

In the end (and as the epilogue will elaborate), *Do Metaphors Dream of Literal Sleep?* is a fragment of a vastly larger hypothetical book containing an infinite number of chapters corresponding to the infinite sum of referents that make up reality.

Do Metaphors Dream of Literal Sleep?

android: a human-made object that has the form, likeness, or nature of—but is not identical to—a human subject

metaphor: a figure of speech in which a phrase is transferred to an object that has the form, likeness, or nature of—but is not identical to—that to which the phrase is literally applicable[1]

To meditate on the title of Philip K. Dick's 1968 novel *Do Androids Dream of Electric Sheep?* is inevitably to find oneself probing its interrogative form. How should the title be answered? What style of question is being posed? If, for example, the question is hypothetical, then the grammatical mood should be modulated and the question rephrased: "Would androids, were they to exist in real life, dream of electric sheep?" Yet the mood of the title is *realis,* almost as though the capacity of androids to dream were a matter of knowable fact both inside and outside the novel's narrative reality. If the question is closed-ended and the answer is either "Yes" or "No," then the truth of the result cannot be verified on the evidence provided in the novel, whose pages never fully disclose whether Dick's android characters are capable of dreaming at all. If the title is a rhetorical question to which no instructive answer can be expected, then the question was designed to emphasize a specific point, the absence of which here suggests that the question must somehow be more (or less) than purely rhetorical. If the question is nonsensical, then at least the nonsense is plangently wistful in a manner reminiscent of "Greensleeves," whose archaic melody—as the science fiction writer Roger Zelazny once noted—eerily translates the title of Dick's novel into the first line of a futuristic hymn.[2] (Perhaps it is no coincidence that the first sentence of "What Child Is This," a nineteenth-century hymn set to "Greensleeves," is likewise interrogative in form: "What child is this who, laid to rest/On Mary's lap, is sleeping?") As for the remaining lines of the futuristic hymn, either they have yet to be written or else the opening is all that survives of a relic left incomplete by its mysterious transmission to us from the future.

Do androids dream of electric sheep? The question is haunted by manifold resonances, endlessly oblique, dissonant and harmonic by turns. Let us approach it as a reverberant maze whose invisible exit must be found by echolocation, a riddle whose key is concealed or revealed in the questioning that those six words perpetually elicit. Which sense, for instance, of the verb "dream" is intended? In the lone scene where the title is half-echoed, Deckard (the novel's human protagonist) wonders idly to himself if androids have "aspirations for something better. Do androids dream?" (184). A different sense of "dream," however, is much more vividly felt throughout the narrative, which opens with Deckard waking up and closes with Deckard falling asleep. If androids do sleep, is their unconsciousness a figure of speech? Whether they dream consciously or unconsciously, awake or while sleeping, why should androids dream of sheep that are mechanical instead of alive? Must an artificial person dream only of artificial things? It is Deckard who owns an electric sheep, a figure that possesses the form, likeness, and nature of—but is not identical to—a real sheep that he tended before it died of tetanus. Nowhere does the narrative mention the appearance of this sheep-like figure in the dreams of any character, android or otherwise. Do those who are "real" never dream of those that are "virtual"? Toward the end of the novel, Deckard hallucinates that he is turning into an artificial figure, a simulacrum of a human. Should his hallucination come to life, would he dream of what originally he had been? Will virtual humans dream of what eventually they might become, as humanlike figures on a Grecian urn might dream of inhabiting truer realms of truth? A figurative human capable of dreaming the limits to her unconsciousness must also be able to dream of transcending those limits and awaking to her own humanization. What if lyric figures could dream of their own literalization? What if metaphors dreamt of literal sleep—and thus of literal awakening?

This book is an exploration of the dream life of metaphors and other lyric figures, including robots. The questions raised in the preceding paragraphs—their timbres, echoes, tones—are meant to accompany the exploration like ambient music faintly heard. The universe in which the exploration takes place is composed not of stars, black holes, and interstellar matter, but of rhetorical novas, constellations of meaning, and conceptual event horizons. It is a paradoxical universe fraught with paradoxical phenomena such as literalized tropes and nostalgia for the future. It is a narrative universe where poetry is so nearly omnipotent that it need not take the physical shape of verse to make its absent omnipresence potently felt. It is a mind-bending universe where the literal activities of the figurative happen on a continuum with the figurative activities of the literal. Finally, it is a science-fictional universe where all aspects of reality (even extremely obscure referents) can ultimately become available for representation. In this universe, "dimensions" are more often narrative than physical or geometric. "Force" and "energy" are more often lyrical than gravitational or electromagnetic. A riddle such as "Do androids dream of electric sheep?" may find itself rhyming with an answering riddle such as "Do metaphors dream of literal sleep?" Powered by the literalization of lyric personification into narrative event, a humanoid robot may wake up fully sentient and human (only to decide, preferring reverie, to fall asleep again).

1

The Globalized World

The realm of the local is readily susceptible to straightforward representation. Only a single narrator is necessary for a given local reality to be described with the authority of unmediated experience. For instance, I might easily describe my local situation right now with the following simple narrative:

> I am sitting on a bench in a park in Flushing, NY (ZIP code: 11354). It is 3:06 PM on August 23, 2009. The air is warm. The afternoon sky is mostly cloudy.

What makes this situation so easily renderable is its proportionality to the human body. The local-as-it-is-subjectively-perceived-through-my-sensorium is consistent with the local-as-it-objectively-exists. My subjective perception of the air's warmth, for example, is consistent with the objective fact that the temperature of the air is 83 degrees Fahrenheit. Such uniformity is characteristic of local temporality as well: day here is identical to day; night is identical to night. When I am awake, most other humans in my local reality are likewise awake; when I am asleep, they too are sleeping. Together our bodies are synchronized to a single order of temporality whereby time moves in a unidirectional arc from morning to afternoon, from afternoon to evening, and so on.

Unlike the realm of the local, the realm of the global resists simple narration. If I were to give a firsthand experiential account of the globalized world right now in all of its complexity, I would need a body capable of simultaneously experiencing a huge range of localities—not only physical localities such as inner-city Rome, but also virtual localities such as http://ubuntuforums.org.

I would need a bodily clock synchronized to dozens of time zones, from Alaska Standard Time to the ghostly time zone of jet lag itself. I would need a brain versed in thousands of living languages. In short, I would need a body radically different from the human body as we know it today.

Although I have just classified Internet forums as localities and jet lag as a local time zone, such classifications are misleading. An international online forum is as much a translocal space as it is a local one: paradoxically, it is a local whole made up of global parts. The paradox obtains because the relationship of local to global is not (as one might initially assume) a simple opposition between part and whole. Consider the oxymorons that thinkers so often invoke in characterizing globalization. According to Fredric Jameson, for example, the globalized world is an "untotalizable totality" ("Preface" to *The Cultures of Globalization*, xii). According to the sociologist Roland Robertson, globalization is "the particularization of the universal and the universalization of the particular" (177–178). And according to the geographer John Rennie Short, globalization renders disparate local realities "closer apart" and "further together" (9). These definitions, strikingly reminiscent as they are of Zen *koans* (the riddles used in Zen Buddhism to assist in spiritual meditation), reflect the elusive logic that characterizes the relationship of global whole to local part. Whether the "parts" in question are tribes, nations, subcultures, monarchs, or local ecosystems, the globalized world cannot be conceptualized as a coherent whole composed of stable local parts.

The reason why the globalized world defies the logic of part and whole is that its literal dimensions operate independently of its figurative dimensions. Literally the globalized world is a concrete object: it has definite physical features (e.g., an oblate spheroid shape) and objectively measurable dimensions (e.g., a radius of approximately 6,378 kilometers). Figuratively, however, the globalized world is not a spherical object. It is an ever-mutating web wherein localities separated by geographic distance may suddenly find themselves rendered contiguous by the cable modem. Such technologies create a rift between the literal and figurative dimensions of the globalized world—a rift that we perceive through its hallucinatory epiphenomena: jet lag, rootlessness, culture shock, the illusion of sitting next to the person on the other end of a long-distance phone call, the nebulous sense of being implicated in a vast network of life-stories the intricacies of which defy straightforward apprehension. Common to all of these experiences is a certain phantasmagorical texture that realism cannot adequately represent.

To characterize globalization as an elusive referent, however, is not to characterize globalization as altogether insusceptible to representation. As I hope to show, science fiction is uniquely conducive to thinking and writing about globalization. In texts ranging from Octavia Butler's Xenogenesis Trilogy (1987, 1988, 1989) to Richard Powers's novel *Plowing the Dark* (2000), science fiction renders the global referent intelligible on a local scale while leaving the global nature of the referent intact. Moments ago I suggested that the cognitively estranging nature of the globalized world is generated by a rift between its literal and figurative dimensions. Science fiction transcends this rift. Indeed, science fiction can integrate the literal and figurative dimensions of the globalized world by literalizing figures of speech closely associated with globalization. Spaceship Earth; the global village; "global sapiens"; time-space compression: such figures of speech have the potential to serve as explanatory devices. Science fiction activates the power of such figures by literalizing and substantiating them into narrative situations: teleportation, for example, is a science-fictional narrative situation that literalizes the metaphorical "collapse of distance" often attributed to globalization. Through such literalizations, "closer apart," "further together," and other global paradoxes acquire proportions that the muscles, nerves, and sinews of our bodies can recognize kinesthetically. In analyzing some of these literalizations, I hope to demonstrate the capacity of science fiction to render our globalized world available for representation.[1] Moreover, I hope to show how these literalizations bring to life the complex nuances of ambivalence latent in figures of speech associated with the globalized world.

Globalization and Science Fiction:
A Mutual Attraction

Science-fiction writers and artists have historically been fascinated by the idea of globalization. As Gary Westfahl has noted, works of SF have long had "an international aura, routinely positing the future emergence of a world government" (2). Istvan Csicsery-Ronay Jr. offers a similar insight in "Dis-Imagined Communities: Science Fiction and the Future of Nations": the concept of nationality, Csicsery-Ronay points out, "is so rarely explored in sf's thought experiments that one might conclude that it has been rejected as something that cannot exist in any future" (218). Indeed, science-fiction writers were among the earliest theorists and proponents of a globalized future Earth transcending nationality. Olaf Stapledon, for example, was a passionate advocate for the League of Nations, voicing his support for the League in the preface to his 1931 novel *Last and First Men:* "There is today a very earnest movement for peace and international unity; and surely with good fortune and intelligent management it may triumph. . . . May the League of Nations, or some more strictly cosmopolitan authority, win through before it is too late!" (10–11). H. G. Wells was similarly enthusiastic about the notion of world governance. In a 1919 essay titled "The Idea of a League of Nations," he argues for an international institution promoting global peace and "unification of human affairs."[2] The language of science fiction has a noticeable presence throughout the essay. At one point Wells describes globalization in futuristic terms as a worldwide awakening "out of a dream of intensified nationality" and into "a new system of realities." And while discussing the relationship of technology to globalization, he invokes a classic text by iconic science-fiction author Jules Verne: "Instead of regarding *Around the World in Eighty Days* as an amazing feat of hurry, we can now regard a flight about the globe in fifteen or sixteen days as a reasonable and moderate performance." Years later, in the wake of the breakdown of the League of Nations, Wells would describe globalization as an elusive "force for world unity" that the League had failed to represent. Yet he remained hopeful: "This force is still seeking effective application," he wrote, characterizing "the idea of a League of Nations" as a strangely animate energy "seeking" a concrete representational medium *(A Short History of the World,* 295).[3] In a 1937 essay titled "World Brain," Wells envisioned this complex global "force" achieving realization through a planetary organ of human knowledge made from tissues of animated microfilm. Such an organ, he prophesied, would "pull the mind of the world together" into a "new all-human cerebrum" by way of "a world synthesis of bibliography and documentation with the indexed archives of the world." With "the concentration of a craniate animal" and "the diffused vitality of an amoeba," the planetary brain would allow information to "be reproduced exactly and fully" all over the globe—"in Peru, China, Iceland, Central Africa," and so on. This world brain, Wells believed, would succeed where the League of Nations failed: By "dissolving human conflict into unity" through the unification of human knowledge, it would offer a "way to world peace."

Not only have science-fiction writers such as Wells been drawn to the topic of globalization, but the converse is true as well: those who write and think about globalization have long been drawn to the language of science fiction. In theorizing what it means to live in a globalized world, these writers (with varying degrees of self-consciousness) have often found themselves using science-fictional images, metaphors, and allusions, and they have done so with a regularity suggesting that anyone who tries to write about globalization will almost inevitably turn to the language of science fiction. The economist Kenneth Boulding, among many others, has characterized the globalized world as a "Spaceship Earth."[4] Fredric Jameson has characterized our postmodern globalized world as a "hyperspace"—a "mutation in space"—comprising a "multidimensional set of radically discontinuous realities" (*Postmodernism*, 44, 413). The political theorist Paul Virilio has likened the globalized world to a flash of luminous energy: "Globalisation," he declares, "is the speed of light. . . . And it is nothing else!" Jutta Weldes, a scholar of international relations, has argued for the relevance of 1950s American science fiction to contemporary debates over globalization.[5] And as the sociologist John Gulick (2007) has observed, globalization is often imagined as a paranormal phenomenon, "a supernatural force beyond human control."

The Planetary Soul: East and West in Stereoscope

Even as far back as the nineteenth century, we find writers approaching the topic of globalization through the language of science fiction. Consider the writings of Percival Lowell (1855–1916), an American astronomer whose fascination with outer space was equaled by his fascination with Japan and Korea.[6] Lowell's astronomical imagination shaped the way he thought about the relationship between East and West. In his 1888 book *The Soul of the Far East*, a meditation on his travels through East Asia, Lowell imagines global subjectivity as a planetary apparition generated by an ocular machine. The importance of the Asian perspective, he proposes, lies in "the possibility of using it stereoptically":

> For his mind-photograph of the world can be placed side by side with ours, and the two pictures combined will yield results beyond what either alone could possibly have afforded. Thus harmonized, they will help us to realize humanity. Indeed it is only by such a combination of two different aspects that we ever perceive substance and distinguish reality from illusion. What our two eyes make possible for material objects, the earth's two hemispheres may enable us to do for mental traits. (3)

The stereoscope, invented in the 1830s, is an optical instrument containing two eyepieces that impart a spectral three-dimensional effect to a pair of photographs of the same scene taken from different angles. In Lowell's analogy, the soul of the Far East and the soul of the Far West constitute two separate "mind-photographs" of the same world. When juxtaposed and viewed as if through the eyepieces of a stereoscope, these "mind-photographs" together generate a polydimensional specter of planetary consciousness transcending its local parts. The planetary soul, then, is a prosthetic soul, a stereoscopic construct, a technology-generated synthesis of the Soul of the Far East and the Soul of the Far West.

The science-fictional effect of Lowell's account of planetary subjectivity is heightened by the way in which he accounts for the differences between the Eastern "mind-photograph" and the Western "mind-photograph." In the passage below, he whimsically suggests that such differences result from the physical shape of our world.

> The boyish belief that on the other side of our globe all things are of necessity upside down is startlingly brought back to the man when he first sets foot at Yokohama. If his initial glance does not, to be sure, disclose the natives in the every-day feat of standing calmly on their heads, an attitude which his youthful imagination conceived to be a necessary consequence of their geographical position, it does at least reveal them looking at the world as if from the standpoint of that eccentric posture. For they seem to him to see everything topsy-turvy. Whether it be that their antipodal situation has affected their brains, or whether it is the mind of the observer himself that has hitherto been wrong in undertaking to rectify the inverted pictures presented by his retina, the result, at all events, is undeniable. The world stands reversed, and, taking for granted his own uprightness, the stranger unhesitatingly imputes to them an obliquity of vision, a state of mind outwardly typified by the cat-like obliqueness of their eyes.
>
> If the inversion be not precisely of the kind he expected, it is none the less striking, and impressibly more real. If personal experience has definitely convinced him that the inhabitants of that under side of our planet do not adhere to it head downwards, like flies on a ceiling,—his early a priori deduction,—they still appear quite as antipodal, mentally considered. Intellectually, at least, their attitude sets gravity at defiance. For to the mind's eye their world is one huge, comical antithesis of our own. What we regard intuitively in one way from our standpoint, they as intuitively observe in a diametrically opposite manner from theirs. To speak backwards, write backwards, read backwards, is but the a b c of their contrari-

ety. The inversion extends deeper than mere modes of expression, down into the very matter of thought. Ideas of ours which we deemed innate find in them no home, while methods which strike us as preposterously unnatural appear to be their birthright. From the standing of a wet umbrella on its handle instead of its head to dry to the striking of a match away in place of toward one, there seems to be no action of our daily lives, however trivial, but finds with them its appropriate reaction—equal but opposite. (1–2)

According to this scenario, the diametric opposition between Eastern and Western mentalities is a "necessary consequence" of the spherical shape of the planet.[7] "On the other side of our globe," Lowell remarks, "all things are of necessity upside down": a person standing at any given point on the surface of the globe is simultaneously right-side up (from that person's perspective) and "topsy-turvy" (from the perspective of someone standing on the opposite side of the planet). This geographic fact, Lowell suggests, has influenced the development of Eastern and Western physiologies, shaping the "brain," our "retinas," and even the contours of our eyes. In turn, such physiological differences have shaped the differences between Western and Eastern attitudes and cultural practices. To the Westerner, the Easterner seems "to speak backwards, write backwards, read backwards"—and vice versa. Indeed, "the inversion extends deeper than mere modes of expression, down into the very matter of thought." To be sure, this explanation is much more fanciful than logical, and Lowell himself is obviously aware of the fanciful nature of his explanation. He signals the subjunctivity of his logic through the heavy use of words like "if," "whether," "seems," and "appears." And he openly acknowledges that any literal understanding of cultural disorientation as the result of physical disorientation is merely a "boyish belief" generated by "youthful imagination." Repeatedly calling attention to the fact that it is not meant to be interpreted on a literal level, this passage falls short of science fiction. Still, it is worth noting that Lowell approaches the topic of global subjectivity through a framework evocative of astronomical romance, explaining cultural disorientation in terms of a physical disorientation based on the shape of our planet.[8]

The Planetary Soul of an "Oriental Yankee"

Like Lowell, Korean American writer Younghill Kang describes global subjectivity through a framework evocative of astronomical romance. In his 1937 autobiographical novel *East Goes West: The Making of an Oriental Yankee,* the narrator—a native Korean who has just set foot in America for the first time—opens the narrative by invoking cosmic temporality. In particular, he describes the consciousness of his long-dead Korean ancestors gazing out of his own eyes at the sight of 1920s New York City, where he is a newly arrived immigrant.

> I seem to have traversed much time, more than most men, although I am still in the early thirties. To the old-fashioned Oriental, life goes back, step by step, to many forefathers, in unbroken chain, and onward into descendants which are somehow he, not in any abstract coldly philosophical sense, but as the solemn vehicle of his Ghost and his God, his most material ghost which eats with them. My own life in actual books still extant in my Korean village was traced far back in this way to ancestors with the bodies of men and heads of cows. This lifetime, threaded to theirs over the mellow-gold distances of time, can it be the same which now sees New York City?—And I ask myself, did I fall from a different star? (4)

Kang frames the feeling of cultural and geographic dislocation as a break in the fabric of temporality: observing that he seems to "have traversed much time," the narrator wonders what has happened to the link that "threaded" his life to those of his ancestors in Korea. Perhaps, he speculates, the thread was just an illusion and he is actually a homeless alien from "a different star." He continues to use the language of cosmology and astronomy in the novel's opening pages, describing the otherworldliness of the Western hemisphere as though it belonged not to Earth but to some other astronomical object floating in space:

> Up to a short while ago, the other side of this earth was like the turned face of the moon to people of the West. . . . It was my destiny to see the disjointing of a world. Upon my planet in lost time . . . I entered a new life like one born again. Here I wandered on soil as strange as Mars, seeking roots, roots for an exile's soul. (4–5)

Together, these passages articulate the disorienting experience of seeing America for the first time while simultaneously feeling one's life connected to the lives of ancestors who never left the other side of the planet. And even though Lowell's experience is that of a Westerner in the East and Kang's experience is that of an Easterner in the West, both identify the global experience of cultural and geographic dislocation with an extraterrestrial mindset evocative of science fiction.

The Global Soul: An Out-of-Body Problem

The appeal of science fiction to the global writer is perhaps nowhere more evident than in *The Global Soul: Jet Lag, Shopping Malls, and the Search for Home,* a collection of essays published in 2000 by the travel writer Pico Iyer. Born in Oxford to Indian parents, and raised in California and England, Iyer has lived in Japan and spent much (if not most) of his time traveling throughout the world. Drawing from his own personal experiences as well as from the experiences of many of his friends, colleagues, and acquaintances, Iyer posits the emergence of "a new kind of being" that he calls "the Global Soul." The Global Soul, he writes, is "a permanent alien" reminiscent of "a creature out of science fiction" (23, 100); in particular, it is a "creature" who has "grown up in many cultures all at once" and who therefore lives "in the cracks between them" (18). His repeated use of the word "creature" might evoke colorful images of some fantastical being. Yet Iyer himself supplies no solid images of this entity. Indeed, the Global Soul as it is characterized in Iyer's writing seems to lack a solid body. According to Iyer, Global Souls exist in an abstract state of "spaced-out dreaminess" (59). They inhabit "the metaphorical equivalent of international airspace" (19)—a "state of suspended animation, five miles above the sea," an "out-of-body state in which one's not quite there, but certainly not elsewhere," a state of "no-mind," "no-time," and "no-place" (59). They feel most at home in the "distant science-fiction land" of dreams (298).

To be sure, the Global Soul is hardly representative of everyone on the globe. Few people have the means, the opportunity, and/or the desire to travel as widely and as frequently as Iyer has traveled in his life. But Iyer's "Global Soul" is an extreme case of a type of subjectivity that has grown increasingly prevalent as air travel, computers, cell phones, television, and Internet access have become less expensive and more commonplace. Even while the Global Soul is not a monolithic entity—different individuals experience "Global Soulness" in different ways—there does seem to be a core set of experiences shared by individual global selves. An obvious example is the hallucinatory experience of jet lag.

Indeed, a striking feature that recurs across Iyer's account and other accounts of global subjectivity is the apparitional texture of the imagery. The problem with global subjectivity, such imagery suggests, is that it lacks a physical counterpart. Unlike the Local Soul, the Global Soul feels out of place in the human body. It needs a new kind of body, a new kind of sensorium, a new anatomical medium that will allow it to navigate through the unstable geographies of the globalized world. And unlike the Local Soul, the Global Soul feels not quite at home in the realm of the local. It seeks a new kind of at-homeness, a new architecture of habitation, a new type of environment capable of accommodating the pluralities and contradictions of global experience. In the absence of such physical counterparts, the Global Soul hovers on the brink of abstraction. To use Iyer's words, it remains "out-of-body," "not quite there, but certainly not elsewhere." In short, it remains a representational problem.

Science fiction, I propose, can solve this representational problem by providing physical counterparts for the global soul. In the remaining pages of this chapter, I will analyze some of the ways in which science fiction has imagined physical counterparts for global subjectivity. My analysis will have two parts. First, I will explore *science-fictional habitats* that allow global subjectivities to feel at home. Second, I will examine *science-fictional physiologies* that embody global subjectivities, giving them agency, mobility, and the ability to interact with the world at large.

Global Souls at Home in Science-Fictional Habitats

Each of the habitats that I am about to discuss is a literalization of what the geographer David Harvey (1990), among others, has described as "time-space compression." According to Harvey, one of the main effects of globalization has been to "revolutionize the objective qualities of space and time" so that "we are forced to alter, sometimes in quite radical ways, how we represent the world to ourselves" (240). In particular, globalization has brought about an unprecedented compaction in time and space: capitalism, Harvey explains, has caused a "speed-up in the pace of life, while so overcoming spatial barriers that the world sometimes seems to collapse inwards upon us" (240). To illustrate the concept of time-space compression, Harvey compares the average speed of the horse-drawn carriage (a mode of transportation common in the sixteenth century) with the average speed of the jet passenger aircraft. The average speed of the horse-drawn coach is 10 miles per hour. The average speed of a passenger aircraft is 600 miles per hour. If we use these numbers to calculate how much smaller our globe is now than it was 500 years ago, we arrive at the conclusion that the world is roughly 60 times smaller today than it was in 1500.

Of course, it is impossible to assign a precise number to the factor by which the world appears to have diminished in size. The jet passenger aircraft is just one of many modes of transportation used today, and these modes—from *human-transporting* subway trains to *data-transporting* broadband connections— vary widely in speed. Furthermore, it is only figuratively that our globe is smaller today than it was 500 years ago. In ordinary discourse, we use "time-space compression" as a figure of speech. And in using it as a figure of speech, we rarely stop to imagine what exactly it might mean for globalization to be compressing the dimensions of our planet. What does space-time compression look like? What does it feel like? What does it sound like? What are its shapes and textures? In the works of science fiction that I am about to discuss, such questions are brought to life in a variety of ways, specifically, through a variety of science-fictional habitats. I will explore four such habitats (in the reverse of the order in which they are listed here): Spaceship Earth, terraformed Mars, the ecumenopolis, and what I call the meta-local crossroads.

The Meta-Local Crossroads: Plowing the Dark, The Calcutta Chromosome, Tropic of Orange, Good Morning, Mr. Orwell, Bye Bye Kipling

By the meta-local crossroads, I mean a metaphysical location at which disparate localities momentarily intersect. The meta-local crossroads forms the crux of Richard Powers's 2000 novel *Plowing the Dark*. Set in the late 1980s and early 1990s, the novel contains two main storylines unfolding at the same time on opposite sides of the globe. For the most part, these two stories are unrelated. The protagonist of the first storyline is Adie Klarpol, an artist hired by a Seattle computer company to help design "the Cavern," a virtual reality chamber capable of reproducing famous paintings in multidimensional detail. Sheltered, naïve, and a pacifist by nature, Adie is horrified and disillusioned when she learns that the U.S. military has underwritten the Cavern for the purpose of creating highly sophisticated bombs and cruise missiles. The protagonist of the second storyline is Taimur Martin, an American schoolteacher who is abducted and held hostage for four years in Beirut. Starved, brutally tortured, imprisoned in a bare cell, and deprived of human contact, Taimur survives only by taking up residence in the virtual reality of his imagination.

Toward the end of the novel, the Cold War ends and the Gulf War breaks out, and it is against the backdrop of these global events that the two remote storylines inexplicably intersect. The intersection takes place in a virtual room that is neither the computer laboratory in Seattle nor Taimur's feverish imagination. The room transcends the dichotomy between the literal and the figurative: it is "more than allegory" yet "less than real"; it is "more than representation, but not yet stuff" (400). Space here behaves in non-three-dimensional ways: "The land's geometry is wrong" (401). Similarly, distinctions between pronouns such as "I" and "you" are immaterial. It is within this science-fictional room that Adie and Taimur, strangers who have never met and will likely never meet again, happen to come face to face for a fleeting moment that will haunt them both for the rest of their lives. The encounter is brief, speechless, and enigmatic. To Taimur, Adie is a celestial avatar fraught with despair, a grief-stricken "angel" terrified by the secrets she knows and desperate to redress the grievances of the world (414). To Adie, Taimur is an image of defenseless suffering, an innocent ghost trapped inside a dehumanizing machine, "an awed bitmap no artist could have animated" (399). Both Adie and Taimur identify each other as something less and more than completely human: an angel; a ghost. At the same time, these two strangers are united by a profoundly human longing for some kind of human connection powerful enough to transcend not only space and time but also the distances created by misunderstanding.

Many readers have found this moment of intersection baffling. The following quotation from a review on Amazon.com is representative of such bafflement:

> The two storylines come together in a way that to me, seems completely impossible and contrived. The end existed merely to bring an end to the book and to connect two completely disparate lives. . . . I felt cheated by the tenuous link forged between them. . . . They are not even remotely similar: an artist working on the age's greatest technological achievement and a captured Muslim-American. I certainly couldn't link the two together.

This reader misses the point of the inexplicability of the moment of convergence between the two storylines. What he describes as a "tenuous link" between "completely disparate" life-stories that "are not even remotely similar" is a fact of globalization. Such tenuous links are what make up the texture of global subjectivity. Suppose that while watching CNN you catch a live interview with a South Korean farmer protesting trade policies that directly benefit the U.S. rice supplier whose product formed part of the meal you ate last night. Neither you (sitting in an air-conditioned living room in a house in McLean, Virginia) nor the farmer (standing among thousands of other protestors in the streets of Seoul) is completely aware of the "tenuous link" that connects his life to yours and yours to his. But through your attention to his telepresent face, and through his awareness of the camera and of the viewers watching him from the other side of the lens, something like a moment of eye contact does take place even if you are not literally looking at each other. The crossroads in *Plowing the Dark*—the science-fictional juncture where Adie and Taimur are fleetingly brought face to face with one another—is a science-fictional representation of the media- and mind-generated site of time-space compression in which your consciousness and the consciousness of the South Korean farmer momentarily converge.

A similar meta-local crossroads forms the crux of Amitav Ghosh's 1995 novel *The Calcutta Chromosome*. Described by one of Ghosh's characters as "a technology for interpersonal transference" (107), the Calcutta chromosome brings people together by distributing first-person experience across diverse bodies throughout space and time. To pass through this crossroads, Ghosh tells us, is to become transposed. It is not only "to hear something said, and not to know who's saying it," but also to hear oneself speaking in someone else's voice in a foreign language (108). In terms of plot, the Calcutta chromosome is a junction in the narrative where multiple storylines (at least nine of them) intersect to create a densely intricate web. In terms of setting, this narrative junction is a supernatural border where various locations on the surface of the planet are somehow capable of existing side by side: at one point, for instance, a man inside his New York City apartment looks over his shoulder and sees "dark threatening clouds" approaching him from across the Maidan Park in Calcutta (310). As a meta-local crossroads, the Calcutta chromosome provides a science-fictional home for myriad aspects of global subjectivity: the jet-lag–induced hallucinatory sensation of inhabiting multiple localities at the same time; the disorientation that one might feel while following a simultaneous interpretation at an international conference; a vague awareness of being implicated in a vast network of life-stories the complexities of which defy straightforward comprehension.

A near-synonym for "Calcutta chromosome" is "Tropic of Orange," the name of a meta-local crossroads that occupies a central position in Karen Tei Yamashita's 1997 novel *Tropic of Orange*. Yamashita narrates a world in which the Tropic of Cancer—a globe-encompassing imaginary line traversing Mexico, Libya, Taiwan, and Bangladesh, among many other places—collides with Los Angeles, having been dragged northward by a navel orange that was plucked from a tree in Mazatlan and transported to California. As latitudinal lines become entangled on a traffic-jammed freeway in L.A., so do a number of seemingly unrelated but eventually crisscrossing storylines featuring a diversity of characters, including Bobby Ngu, a "Chinese from Singapore with a Vietnam name speaking like a Mexican living in Koreatown" (15); Arcangel, an ancient visionary performance artist who hails "from the very tip of the Tierra del Fuego" and whose voice is "a jumble of unknown dialects, guttural and whining, Latin mixed with every aboriginal, colonial, slave, or immigrant tongue" (47); Manzanar Murakami, "the first sansei born in captivity" during the internment of Japanese Americans in World War II, who quit his career as a surgeon to conduct L.A. freeway traffic from an over-pass as though the traffic were an orchestra (108); Buzzworm, an African American veteran of the Vietnam War who always wears at least two or three watches on each wrist and who listens to the radio—"rap, jazz, R&B, talk shows, classical, NPR, religious channels, Mexican, even the Korean channel"—twenty-four hours a day, seven days a week, on a Walkman plugged to one ear "like an inner voice" (29); a wrestler named SUPERNAFTA; and Gabriel Balboa, a Chicano journalist whose Japanese American girlfriend, a news-obsessed TV producer, encourages his growing addiction to the World Wide Web. The intersection of storylines and destabilization of geographic co-ordinates are accompanied by a deformation of space and time: as various characters observe, the landscape has become something capable of twisting, turning, stretching, and contracting. Like Ghosh's Calcutta chromosome, Yamashita's Tropic of Orange is a meta-local crossroads providing a science-fictional home for the mind-warping complexities of globalization.[9]

Meta-local crossroads need not be made of prose. Some of these cross-roads, like the satellite installations of Korean American video artist Nam June Paik, are constructed from the hi-tech media that are partially responsi-ble for globalization. On New Year's Day of 1984, Paik coordinated a video event titled *Good Morning, Mr. Orwell*. The extravaganza, hosted by George Plimpton, featured a multitude of celebrity artists, including Laurie Anderson, John Cage, Allen Ginsberg, and Peter Gabriel. Through satellite telecasts of simultaneous live international performances, *Good Morning, Mr. Orwell* linked WNET TV in New York with the Centre Pompidou in Paris, as well as broadcasters in South Korea and Germany. The intersection of these telecasts generated a real-time meta-local crossroads mimetic of global space-time compression. Paik continued to explore interactive global television communications in his 1986 piece *Bye Bye Kipling*, a live satellite installation linking Seoul, New York, and Tokyo. Significantly, the title of the piece alludes to a line from Rudyard Kipling's 1889 poem "The Ballad of East and West": "East is East, and West is West," Kipling writes, "and never the twain shall meet." In Paik's science-fictional artwork, the "twain"—East and West—literally do meet via satellite and video.

From Global Village to Ecumenopolis: Coruscant and Trantor

As I mentioned earlier, the meta-local crossroads is just one of many forms that the science-fictional literalization of space-time compression can take. The second form I want to discuss—the ecumenopolis—has its origins in the "global village," a trope that posits something of the magnitude of a planet compressed within a local unit. Marshall McLuhan famously introduced this phrase in the mid-twentieth century. We live in a "global village," McLuhan wrote in 1960. "Everything happens to everyone at the same time: everyone knows about, and therefore participates in, everything that is happening the minute it happens" (xi).[10] McLuhan was not the first to liken the globalized world to a local unit. In his essay on the League of Nations, Wells proposed a similar idea by invoking the "ennobled individual *whose city is the world.*" Indeed, "city" is more accurate than "village" as a figure for our globalized planet. As Iyer points out, "what we are entering is, in fact, much closer to a global city" than to a global village insofar as our world is marked by "all the problems of rootlessness and alienation and a violent, false denaturing that we associate with the word 'urban'" (28).

The idea of a global village (or global city) has become so widespread that by now it is a cliché: we rarely stop to visualize it as an image. Yet science fiction has the power to de-cliché this figure of speech. More specifically, the global city is literalized and thereby given new life through science-fictional visions of the *ecumenopolis*. This term (meaning "world city" in Greek) was coined in the 1960s by the Greek urban planner Constantinos Doxiadis. It refers to Doxiadis's prediction, extrapolated from current trends in urbanization and population growth, that expanding metropolitan areas will eventually fuse to create a single continuous megalopolis covering the entire planet. The most widely known science-fictional ecumenopolis in recent public memory is Coruscant, a city-planet in Star Wars mythology that provides much of the setting for episodes I *(The Phantom Menace)*, II *(Attack of the Clones)*, and III

(Revenge of the Sith). Coruscant is so heavily populated and so thoroughly ur-banized that virtually no natural topography remains: the entire surface of the planet is covered in an unbroken urban sprawl. Natural bodies of water have been drained and stored in cavernous subterranean reservoirs. Skyscrapers reach into the sky for miles. Newer buildings are densely layered over older buildings, forming an impossibly complex network of edifices aglow with artificial light-ing. When viewed from outer space, the texture of the planet coruscates.

Coruscant can be traced to an ecumenopolitan vision not quite as well known as that of George Lucas: the planetary cities in Isaac Asimov's Foun-dation Series (1951–1993). These novels (several of which actually precede Doxiadis's coinage) provide some of the most compelling illustrations of the ecumenopolis ever created. The stories are set among a vast array of planets, each of which, as Jutta Weldes has pointed out in "Globalisation Is Science Fiction," "is presented as a single entity, in fact a 'global village' of sorts" (661). Trantor, the center of the Galactic Empire, is not just a global village "of sorts." It is a full-blown and richly realized ecumenopolitan setting that vibrantly elaborates on the trope of the global city. Wrapped in 75 million square miles of metallic artifice, the planet is home to over 40 billion human beings (*Foun-dation*, 12).[11] Its population is spectacularly diverse, comprising almost a thou-sand different ethnic cultures (*Prelude to Foundation*, 470). Yet such differences are ultimately transcended by a single planetary identity. What distinguishes Trantor from other planets in the galaxy—what gives Trantor its unique fame—is the human-made roofing that encompasses the entire planet. Tran-torians literally live under one roof. Not only does this roof define their collec-tive identity as inhabitants of Trantor, but it also places all Trantorians inside a single climate-controlled situation. In the following passage, we get a vivid sense of what life is like inside the Trantorian ecumenopolis:

> The lustrous, indestructible, incorruptible metal that was the unbroken surface of the planet was the foundation of the huge, metal structures that mazed the planet. They were structures connected by causeways; laced by corridors; cubbyholed by offices; basemented by the huge retail centers that covered square miles; penthoused by the glittering amusement world that sparkled into life each night.
>
> One could walk around the world of Trantor and never leave that one conglomerate building. (*Foundation and Empire*, 85–86)

The effect of this narrative scenario is to generate a sense of planetary claus-trophobia mimetic of the effects of space-time compression. The surface of

Trantor—uniform in its dense metallic texture—is in essence one continuous edifice. Accordingly, there is no such thing here as vast outdoor space: A person could travel throughout the globe and remain indoors the entire time. The effect of planetary claustrophobia is enhanced in this passage by the use of anthimeria, a rhetorical device in which one part of speech is used as if it were another. Asimov conspicuously uses nouns as verbs: Trantor, he writes, is "mazed" with metal structures that are themselves "cubbyholed" by offices and "basemented" by retail centers. In using anthimeria, Asimov conjures up a world of increasing clutter where nouns are supplanting verbs, where the solidity of physical objects is supplanting the dynamic and ephemeral qualities of temporal action. Instead of unfolding through time—instead of taking place—actions take up space, replacing open air with dense materiality.

In addition to literalizing the metaphor of time-space compression, ecumenopolitan visions such as Trantor and Coruscant literalize synecdoche, a figure of speech in which a part is invoked as if it were a whole or a whole as if it were a part. I suggested earlier that the globalized world is difficult to imagine because it cannot be imagined as a coherent whole made up of stable parts. By positing the globe as a single city, Trantor literally invokes the global whole as a local part. Moreover, by invoking the global whole as a local part, Trantor forces us to consider the globe as if from outer space. In doing so, it posits the globalized world not as some unimaginably complex macrocosm made up of unstable parts but rather as a finite and readily imaginable part of a larger and more complex extraterrestrial totality. Here it is not the globe but the galaxy whose intricacy defies straightforward comprehension. Thus, the global horizon, itself contextualized by the broader horizon of outer space, no longer constitutes the ultimate frame of reference. Differences among human beings are supplanted by differences between humanity and extraterrestrial races. As a result, the global becomes acutely recognizable at a local level while remaining global in form.

Globalized Earth, Terraformed Mars

Trantor and Coruscant are just two of many science-fiction texts depicting the globalized world as a local part within a larger universe. Not all of these texts invoke the ecumenopolitan global city. In Kim Stanley Robinson's Mars Trilogy, published in the 1990s, Earth is framed as one of two planetary parts of a transplanetary whole. Set in the near future, and spanning multiple decades, the three novels tell the story of an international team of scientists, engineers, and politicians who leave Earth and settle on Mars with the intention of terraforming the extraterrestrial planet. "Terraforming," a word coined in the 1940s by science-fiction writer Will Stewart, denotes the hypothetical "process of transforming a planet into one sufficiently similar to the earth to support terrestrial life" (OED).[12] As I hope to show, Robinson uses the science fiction of terraforming to open up a narrative space in which globalization is made available for concrete representation.

That terraformed Mars is a representation of globalized Earth is observable on a superficial level. Much of Martian life is governed by the terrestrial politics of the United Nations. Moreover, the inhabitants of Mars come from all over Earth. They speak in a diversity of languages—for example, English, Arabic, French, Japanese—reminiscent of the diversity of languages spoken on their native planet. And the novels are narrated in a free indirect style that rotates through the memories and perspectives of characters of various nationalities, some of whom undergo nostalgic flashbacks to life in their home countries. Together, Robinson's characters form an ensemble no less conspicuously diverse in nationality than the panoply of flags outside the headquarters of the United Nations. As Fredric Jameson has noted of the Mars books: "It is a variety of Terran 'cultures' in the national and anthropological sense we are given to observe, from Arabs to Swiss to Japanese and South African (with Sufi interludes and Cretan overtones): indeed, few novels can have projected a global post-coloniality of such range and dimensions" (*Archaeologies of the Future*, 414).

But the representation of globalized Earth on Mars—the representation of Mars as a globalized Earth—is more complex than a superficial reproduction of the appearance of internationalism. Terraforming, I want to suggest, is a science-fictional representation of globalization. Central to both processes is the logic of simile, a figure of speech in which two things are compared explicitly. Many of the debates over globalization can be understood as a debate over precisely how explicit the comparability between the global and the local is or ought to be. Does—should—globalization homogenize the localities of our world? Or does globalization make the dissimilarities and inequalities among these localities more explicit? In the Mars books, the science-fictional scenario of terraforming brings such questions to life. The reader is constantly aware of the active dialectic of comparison that defines the relationship between the two planets. Parts of Mars, for instance, make up "a *kind* of Polynesia" (*Green Mars*, 341). And one colonist reflects that she has been "living in a huge analogy" on Mars, "understanding everything in terms of her past" on Earth (*Red Mars*, 141–142). Indeed, the central drama in the Mars Trilogy is the debate among colonists over how far to literalize the simile between Mars and Earth. Some are in favor of making the surface of Mars as much as possible like that of Earth. They want Mars to become a "green and blue" planet, with oceans and forests mimicking the terrestrial biosphere, and they want to establish a geopolitical world order similar to that of Earth. To these settlers, terraforming is not only desirable, it is inevitable. Just as Bill Clinton argued that "globalization is irreversible"—"we must embrace the inexorable logic of globalization," Clinton has said (quoted in Steger, 100)—pro-terraformers argue for the irreversibility, the inexorable logic, of terraforming: "It was not a question of whether but of when, and how much" (*Red Mars*, 169). Other settlers, known as the "Reds," want to keep Mars as non-Earth-like as possible. Extreme Reds who oppose terraforming altogether want to preserve Mars in its pristine original Martian state. Ann Clayborne, a leader of the Red Movement, at one point bitterly makes a prediction about the future of Mars: "We'll all go on and make the place safe. Roads, cities. New sky, new soil. Until it's all *some kind of Siberia or Northwest Territories*, and Mars will be gone and we'll be here, and we'll wonder why we feel so empty. Why when we look at the land we can never see anything but our own faces" (*Red Mars*, 158, emphasis added). For Ann and other Reds, the logic of simile at the center of terraforming is tantamount to the logic of imperialism—an attitude that resonates powerfully with the argument made by many today that globalization amounts to American imperialism.

At the same time that the process of terraforming represents the process of globalization, terraformed Mars is a concrete representation of globalized Earth. As I have been suggesting, the globalized world has two dimensions, literal (a spherical object with a radius of approximately 6,378 kilometers) and figurative (an ever-mutating web in which localities separated by geographic and cultural distance may suddenly find themselves rendered contiguous by technologies such as the cable modem). The globalized world, in other words, is not one Earth but two Earths: a literal Earth and its hallucinatory figurative "other." In my reading of the Mars Trilogy, Earth's hallucinatory "other" has been displaced from Earth itself and projected onto extraterrestrial Mars, where the psychic dramas of globalization are granted a concrete representational space though which to play themselves out. For example, the unearthly gravity on Mars literalizes the "floating dispassion" that Iyer (among others) associates with global subjectivity (258): "Her center of gravity was gone," Robinson writes of one Martian immigrant unaccustomed to Martian gravity: "Her weight had been shifted out to her skin, to the outside of her muscles rather than the inside" (*Red Mars,* 98). Furthermore, the unearthly size of Mars literalizes the metaphorical characterization of the globalized world as physically smaller than the world had been before globalization. On Mars, the sense of living on a shrunken planet is no mere subjective impression; it is a literal physical reality. "The horizon was closer than seemed right," one settler remarks (*Red Mars,* 98). Another settler realizes that his sense of living on a miniaturized planet is especially acute when the sun makes its daily disappearance below the western horizon: "It always seemed to him that sunset more than any other time of day made it clear that they stood on an alien planet; something in the slant and redness of the light was fundamentally wrong, upsetting expectations wired into the savannah brain over millions of years" (*Red Mars,* 13). More generally, to be on Mars is to experience distance and proximity as relative, unstable phenomena. Due to the effects—both immediate and long-term—of human terraforming, places on Mars are constantly shifting. Glaciers collapse. Bodies of water materialize where before there was desert. Even beneath the planet's surface, one might lose oneself in vast subterraneous mazes. Not only Martian space but Martian time is distorted. The Martian day is inherently longer than the terrestrial day. And due to special medical treatments, many humans on Mars live twice as long as they would in the pre-Mars days. As a result, units of time become compressed in relation to the life span of terrestrial human beings. What to us is a year would to them be (in effect) six months. Together, these narrative details convey the strangeness of living in a globalized world. Figuratively the globalized world is not the solid Earth as we know it but an otherworldly world, and in the Mars Trilogy this otherworldliness is made available for representation through the literal unearthliness of Mars—an unearthliness in which the Global Soul feels unsettlingly at home.

Spaceship Earth

As with Trantor, Coruscant, and terraformed Mars, Spaceship Earth—the last science-fictional habitat that I want to discuss—literalizes time-space compression by framing the globalized world as part of a much vaster whole.

To posit Earth as a spaceship is to imagine Earth as something that we think of as smaller in size than a planet; it is to depict Earth as an extremely confined space. Indeed, the phrase has often been used to illustrate the finiteness of our planet's resources. Economist Kenneth Boulding, for example, writes in his essay "The Economics of the Coming Spaceship Earth" (1966) that Earth has become "a single spaceship, without unlimited reservoirs of anything, either for extraction or for pollution, and in which, therefore, man must find his place in a cyclical ecological system which is capable of continuous reproduction of material form even though it cannot escape having inputs of energy." Like Trantor, Spaceship Earth elicits claustrophobia. But Trantor at least has an atmosphere and thus an outdoors, even if most Trantorians elect to stay beneath the planetary roof. Within a spaceship in outer space, there is no such thing as the possibility of open outdoors air.

Literalizations of Spaceship Earth abound in science fiction. Starship crews often function as microcosmic representations of the global community. And spacecrafts often provide the venue through which science-fictional scenarios richly evocative of contemporary global politics play themselves out. In the 2003–2009 television series *Battlestar Galactica*, for instance, the warship *Galactica* (the spacecraft after which the show is named) houses and shelters what is left of humanity after genocidal robots have destroyed much of human civilization. Members of the human race on *Galactica* struggle with many of the same kinds of issues that trouble those of us who inhabit a globalizing planet. The parallels between the spaceship *Galactica* and our own "Spaceship Earth" were made explicit on the evening of March 17, 2009, when the United Nations and the SCI FI Channel (rebranded "Syfy" in July 2009) cohosted a panel discussion devoted to exploring "themes that are of importance to both the United Nations and the critically acclaimed television show: human rights; terrorism; children and armed conflict; and reconciliation and dialogue among civilizations and faiths" (U.N. Press Release, Note No. 6192; March 16, 2009). Spacecrafts similar to *Galactica* can be found in the Star Trek mythology, where vehicles such as the U.S.S. *Enterprise* ("U.S.S." stands for "United Star Ship") literalize the metaphor of Spaceship Earth and thereby activate that metaphor's power to render the globalized world available for representation.

Another literalization of Spaceship Earth, one that is less obvious but ultimately more spectacular, comes from Octavia Butler's Xenogenesis Trilogy. These novels—*Dawn, Adulthood Rites,* and *Imago*—are set in the centuries following a nuclear war in which humankind has virtually annihilated itself. Earth is now inhabited by human survivors (few in number but diverse in nationality) and by benevolent extraterrestrial creatures known as the Oankali. In the wake of the apocalypse, Oankali have planted sentient village-organisms all over the planet. Part animal and part vegetation, each village entity originates as a tiny seed formed inside the reproductive organs of an Oankali. After extracting the seed from its own body, the Oankali buries the embryonic village in a carefully chosen plot of land. The flesh that emerges from the seed quickly blossoms and ramifies, growing over time into a compound of buildings whose walls, ceilings, furniture, and gardens constitute a living continuum. These living villages serve as habitats for humans, Oankali aliens, and their hybrid offspring. Together, each village and its transracial inhabitants make up a microcosmic ecosystem unmistakably evocative of the globalized world. At the same time, these habitats are temporary. Every village, we learn, is actually an immature organic spaceship. The village-organisms are gradually transforming Earth into a cluster of sentient organic vehicles that will in due course stop orbiting the sun and seek other life-forms in the universe. In this extraordinary science-fiction framework, the metaphors of Spaceship Earth and the global village are literalized and incorporated into a single narrative scenario.

In some works of SF, the spaceship serves not as a figure for the globalized world but as a figure for globalization itself. The extraterrestrial vehicles function as agents of globalization; in particular, they globalize Earth by forcing humans to unite, by forcing humans to see themselves as a single species, in the presence of alien others.[13] Susan Sontag has written on the connection between internationalism and the "aliens invade Earth" genre of SF film. Such movies, she notes in her 1965 essay "The Imagination of Disaster," almost always include a narrative stage in the course of which internationalism emerges as an explicit theme: "All international tensions are suspended in view of the planetary emergency"; the viewer is treated to "a rapid montage of news broadcasts in various languages"; a meeting of the United Nations takes place; and a "scientist generally takes sententious note of the fact that it took the planetary invasion to make the warring nations of the earth come to their senses and suspend their own conflicts" (210, 219). For example, in the 1951 film *The Day the Earth Stood Still* (a film that Sontag does not discuss), an alien visits Earth and is met with hostility by a human world more or less united by its fear of the extraterrestrial visitor—despite the fact that the alien is a pacifist whose purpose in visiting Earth is (ironically) to request a meeting with U.N. officials to advocate an end to hostilities among human nations.

A more recent illustration of Sontag's argument can be found in Steven Spielberg's 1977 film *Close Encounters of the Third Kind*. As a film that does not thematize war or invasion, *Close Encounters* does not exactly fit Sontag's description. Yet *Close Encounters* does bear meaningful similarities to the films Sontag describes. It establishes a difference between humanity and an alien "other" in order to render differences among human beings obsolete. Moreover, in establishing the difference between "human" and "alien," *Close Encounters* employs devices that can be thought of as variations on the devices employed in the films that Sontag discusses. One of the main characters of *Close Encounters* is a U.N. scientist investigating reports of UFO visits that initially seem to be isolated incidents. Because the sightings have happened all over the world, the scientist's travels take him and his team (and, by extension, the viewer) to a variety of international locations, including the Sonora Desert in Mexico; Indianapolis, Indiana; Dharamsala, Northern India; the Gobi Desert in Mongolia; and Moorcroft, Wyoming. As one might expect of a film set all over the world, characters speak in a diversity of languages—for example, English, French, Spanish—and translators are often needed for one character to understand another. Reinforcing the international scope of the film are various cartographic images, including a spherical model of the globe detached from its stand and rolling around on the floor of the Goldstone Observatory in California's Mojave Desert.

But the differences among various human localities are ultimately superseded by a meta-local consciousness of humanity as one part in a universal whole. The scientists realize that the ostensibly unconnected local sightings are actually part of a single planetary phenomenon: a visitation of Earth by otherworldly aliens who communicate through nonverbal music. Language differences are thus transcended by the melodic language from outer space. From the worshipers in Dharamsala to the three-year-old boy from Indiana, all humans understand the five-note motif emanating from the skies. The visual counterpart to this auditory image is the spectacular alien spaceship with which the team of international scientists conducts a musical dialogue during the climax of the film. Its design inspired by a giant oil refinery that Spielberg saw in India, the spaceship in *Close Encounters* is a vast, complex, radiant city in the sky. Basking in its presence, strangers are brought together into a shared wonderment. If globalization can be likened to a supernatural force that is palpable only through its effects—specifically, its effect of bringing humans closer together—then the spaceship in *Close Encounters* concretizes this impersonal and larger-than-life force. By uniting humans in a shared state of wonder in the presence of alien beings, the spaceship renders humanity acutely recognizable as a single biological species.

The utopian appeal of alien visitation as a vehicle for unifying humans across the globe is luridly thematized in *Watchmen* (1986–1987), a graphic novel by Moore and Gibbons set in an alternate 1980s America. Nixon here is still president; the United States has won Vietnam, due to the superhuman intervention of Dr. Manhattan; and a cold war between the United States and the Soviet Union is on the verge of exploding into nuclear holocaust. Adrian Veidt, a genius magnate who formerly battled crime as a costumed vigilante under the alias "Ozymandias," finds the idea of alien-visitation-as-a-vehicle-for-unifying-humanity so compelling that he turns it into a reality. Working in stealth over many years, and employing bleeding-edge technologies in the sciences (genetic engineering, quantum physics) and arts (avant-garde music, surrealist painting), Veidt painstakingly masterminds a simulated alien invasion with the purpose of rescuing humankind from imminent global apocalypse. Veidt and his creative team synthesize a sophisticated high-tech artifact that convincingly resembles an otherworldly monster. Tentacular, prodigious in size, hideously misshapen, the "alien" is programmed to materialize via teleportation in New York City, where its instantaneous death on arrival will trigger a psychic shockwave killing millions of people in the vicinity. This massacre, Veidt predicts, will motivate nations of the globe to abandon international hostilities and unite against a perceived extraterrestrial foe.

The strategy works. As Peter Paik remarks in *From Utopia to Apocalypse: Science Fiction and the Politics of Catastrophe,* "The shock of the ensuing carnage and mass death in Manhattan has its intended effect, as the superpowers draw back from [the] precipice of mutual annihilation with pledges of peace and mutual assistance in the face of this unforeseen and unprecedented threat to the human species" (26–27). But do the ends justify the means? The answer provided in *Watchmen,* Paik reveals, is graphic speechlessness. Examining the panels that depict the immediate aftermath of the catastrophe, Paik observes: "What might be most unsettling about this portrayal of mass death is the haunting atmosphere of absence and muteness it creates. There is not a single word or thought bubble in the large one-panel pages; the reader is confronted by a landscape filled by the objects of human production that have become voided of any living human presence, as inert and detached as the evidence at the scene of a crime" (51). Such speechlessness is discordantly amplified by its garish juxtaposition with the utopian vision behind the spectacle of carnage:

> And yet we are invited to read this extended scene of death and destruction as the signifiers for the near-miraculous founding of a new and peaceful order, a new golden age of international cooperation and solidarity, and regard the three million victims as a necessary and unavoidable sacrifice, the price to be paid for rescuing humanity from extinction. Indeed, the costumed heroes who track Ozymandias to his Antarctic lair find themselves trapped by a supremely fiendish version of the pallid dilemmas one finds in undergraduate ethics textbooks: Is it ever right to lie? Should one commit murder if that person's death will result in a cure for lethal diseases? Would you allow an act of injustice to go unpunished if the lives of billions depended on it? As might be expected, Ozymandias's former comrades are brought around without much difficulty into consenting to keep secret the truth behind the slaughter in New York. As Dr. Manhattan, who has teleported back to earth, concludes, "exposing this plot, we destroy any chance of peace, dooming earth to worse destruction," while the Silk Spectre, after being the first along with her former lover to witness the horrors in the city, rationalizes, "all we did was fail to stop him saving earth" (XII: 20). The only one among them who does not accede to Ozymandias's proposition is Rorschach ("Not in the face of Armageddon. Never compromise"), who is shortly afterwards incinerated in the Antarctic snows by Dr. Manhattan before he can set out on the long voyage back to the US to expose the truth and punish the crime. (51–52)

The "fiendish" moral dilemmas confronted by the superheroes in *Watchmen* and the dissonant silence emanating from the graphic spectacle of apocalyptic massacre are both mimetic of a violent ambivalence toward globalization. This conflictedness is as much a part of the cognitively estranging phenomenon of globalization as it is a reaction to globalization as a cognitively estranging phenomenon. We will see a similar science-fictional representation of such cognitively estranging ambivalence near the end of this chapter in a discussion of Olaf Stapledon's modernist novella *Odd John*.

Global Souls, Science-Fictional Bodies

To make humanity recognizable as a single species is to call attention to the fact that human beings are physical organisms, and it is on this note that I would like to turn to the second way in which science fiction provides images of physical counterparts that correspond to the global soul. The first way, as I have been discussing, is through science-fictional habitats that allow global subjectivities to feel at home. The second way is through science-fictional physiologies that allow global subjectivities to feel embodied, incorporated, and empowered to act upon the world.

Mutagenic Globalization

Let us revisit Iyer's formulation of the Global Soul as "a new kind of being." Iyer is not alone in identifying global subjectivity metaphorically as a new type of humanity. The mythology of a new global human species is pervasive in our culture, manifesting itself even in texts and contexts that are not obviously science-fictional. Consider, for example, the concept of "Davos Man." This term, coined in the 1990s by political scientist Samuel Huntington, designates the administrators, business leaders, and politicians who form our global ruling elite. "Davos" alludes to the World Economic Forum meeting that takes place annually in Davos, Switzerland. Reminiscent of "Neanderthal Man" *(Homo neanderthalensis)*, "Rhodesia Man" *(Homo rhodesiensis)*, and Wise Man *(Homo sapiens)*, the phrase "Davos Man" suggests that globalization is bringing about the evolution of a new human species or subspecies. A much more explicit manifestation of the idea of a new global human species can be found in the writings of Robert Muller, former assistant secretary general to the United Nations and chancellor emeritus of the United Nations. "The human species is becoming a global body," he remarks in a 1995 speech titled "Planning for the Next Millennium": "We have now a nervous system that encompasses the whole world. . . . We have become a totally different species. Our legs are extended, our hands are extended, we're a global human species on this planet. . . . We are all cells of one new global species."

Of course, Huntington and Muller are being metaphorical in their use of the rhetoric of a new globalized human species. As Fredric Jameson has remarked: we have yet to fulfill the imperative presented to us by the postmodern architecture of the globalized world—the imperative to "grow new organs, to expand our sensorium and our body to some new, yet unimaginable, perhaps ultimately impossible, dimensions" matching the hyperspace of contemporary global reality (*Postmodernism*, 39). Still, the existence of this metaphor is meaningful in itself. The idea of a new global human species is a tool that we use to make sense of our globalized world. And science fiction, by literalizing and embodying the metaphor, can make this explanatory tool infinitely more effective. In the texts that I am about to discuss, globalization is a mutagen transforming humanity as a species, changing the structure of our DNA and altering the genetic makeup of our cells. As I hope to show, this science-fictional narrative of genetic mutation offers a powerful way of describing and thinking about globalization. It bestows an anthropomorphic shape (however mutant this shape may be) on the global referent, rendering it imaginable as a person with whom one might relate, identify, come face to face, have a conversation, agree or disagree. It frames the drama of global identity as an exciting and often unpredictable dialectic between "descent" (relations of blood) and "consent" (relations of law and choice)—terms that Werner Sollors has shown to be extremely helpful in exploring "the whole maze of American ethnicity and culture," terms that will help us to explore the maze of globalized identity and culture as well (*Beyond Ethnicity*, 6). Finally, the science-fiction narrative of genetic mutation provides the Global Soul with sensuous physiologies capable of supporting the pluralities, contradictions, and dislocations that characterize life in a globalized world. From bodies immune to jet lag to bodies capable of occupying multiple locations simultaneously, these science-fictional physiologies make the condition of global subjectivity available for narrative experience.

The Globalization Chromosome

The literalized trope of genetic mutation is central to *The Calcutta Chromosome*. As discussed above, Ghosh's novel literalizes the metaphor of time-space compression through a "meta-local crossroads" whereby Manhattan and Calcutta (among other global locations) momentarily converge. But *The Calcutta Chromosome* also frames globalization as a phenomenon capable of altering human biology. The chromosome invoked in the novel's title operates on planes both figurative and literal. In dialogues between characters, it is referred to as a figure of speech. "If it is really a chromosome, it's only so by extension, so to speak—by analogy," one character says (250). But through the events experienced by these same characters, the Calcutta chromosome manifests itself as much more than a figurative expression. It affects both mind and flesh, expressing itself through symptoms such as fever and delirium. It transmits hereditary information from one human body to another on a cellular level, even when these bodies are not blood-related. Highly contagious, it easily erodes the boundaries that separate individual subjectivities, often gathering distantly related characters into a shared predicament. In short, the Calcutta chromosome is a "descent relation" capable of extending both temporally (from one generation to the next) and laterally in space (between, say, strangers in a taxicab who have just met for the first time).

What Ghosh calls "the Calcutta chromosome," Greg Bear calls "SHEVA": "Scattered Human Endogenous retroVirus Activation." In Bear's novels *Darwin's Radio* (1999) and *Darwin's Children* (2003), an ancient retrovirus, dormant in the human genome since prehistoric times, mysteriously becomes active in the twentieth century. Like the Calcutta chromosome, SHEVA turns out to be a descent relation that extends both laterally in space—SHEVA generates infectious particles that can move from cell to cell in horizontal transmission (*Darwin's Children*, 30)—and vertically/temporally from parent to offspring. The activated retrovirus causes alarmingly unusual miscarriages and abnormal pregnancies all over the world:

> SHEVA had turned out to be much more than a disease. Shed only by males in committed relationships, the activated retrovirus served as a genetic messenger, ferrying *complicated instructions for a new kind of birth*. SHEVA infected recently fertilized human eggs—in a sense, hijacked them. The Herod's miscarriages were first-stage embryos, called "interim daughters," not much more than specialized ovaries devoted to producing a new set of precisely mutated zygotes.
>
> Without additional sexual activity, the second-stage zygotes implanted and covered themselves with a thin, protective membrane. They survived the abortion of the first embryo and started a new pregnancy.
>
> To some, this had looked like a kind of virgin birth.
>
> Most of the second-stage embryos had gone to term. Worldwide, in two waves separated by four years, three million new children had been born. More than two and a half million of the infants had survived. There was still controversy over exactly who and what they were—a diseased mutation, a subspecies, or a completely new species.
>
> Most simply called them virus children. (*Darwin's Children*, 8, emphasis added)

Different cultures, the reader learns, react to the "virus children" in different ways. So-called traditional cultures such as "Muslims, Hindus, Buddhists" are "more accepting of the new children" (*Darwin's Children,* 387). The response in the United States, meanwhile, is less than fully accepting. Many people react (especially initially) with a mix of phobia, curiosity, disgust, mystification, and animosity. In a particularly charged scene unmistakably evocative of antiglobalization rallies that have taken place in recent decades, hundreds of protesters loudly denounce the "virus children" as "Virus Abominations genetically engineered by corporate mad scientists" (*Darwin's Children,* 92). One activist holds a sign that reads: "HEY HEY USA / DON'T FUCK WITH NATURE'S DNA!" (93). When interviewed by reporters, the protesters insist that the "virus children" are "artificial monsters designed to help corporations take over the world." Moreover, the protesters dehumanize the children with epithets such as "Lab Brats," "Monsanto's Future Toadies," and "GM Kids" (92). This last epithet is a telling pun, suggestive as it is of both "Genetically Modified Kids" and "General Motors Kids." To protest the existence of "GM Kids," this scene implies, is to protest the emergence and spread of multinational corporations and other global bodies.

The narrator never offers a detailed explanation of why the viral genes have suddenly become active in the twentieth century. However, one of the protagonists, a molecular biologist, does offer an intriguing conjecture: "When a problem in the environment is intractable," she muses, "long-term social stress in humans, for example . . . there's a major shift. Endogenous retroviruses express, carry a signal, coordinate the activation of specific elements in the genetic memory storage. Voila" (*Darwin's Children,* 243–244). Later in the same novel she reiterates her hypothesis: "Our genome is now responding to social change and the stress it causes" (341). The salient idea repeated in both passages is "social stress." While this phrase could be parsed in various ways, its narrative proximity to details such as the "anti-GM" protest indicates that "social stress" means globalization. The social stress of globalization is what has activated the retrovirus and resulted in SHEVA.

Xenogenesis: Children of Globalization

The link between SHEVA and globalization is borne out by the traits that distinguish SHEVA's end-product. SHEVA results in a new human subspeciation, *Homo sapiens novus,* whose members are manifestly born to thrive in a globalized world. These "novel" humans are strikingly different from their predecessors. As newborns, they are extraordinarily precocious: they can already focus, smile, recognize faces and voices, and even speak in brief sentences. Indeed, the SHEVA children possess an exquisitely multisensory talent for communication. Their faces are alive with vibrant melanophores—luminous melanin-containing pigment cells—that sparkle in various configurations on their faces, perpetually constellating and reconstellating into expressive dermal patterns. As they grow older, the SHEVA children learn that they can also communicate through "fever-scenting," a form of olfactory rhetoric. An intense fever-scenting conversation might smell "like an explosion in a cocoa factory, mixed with shocking and eye-stinging hints of musk and civet" (*Darwin's Children*, 466).

Vocally, too, Shevites are remarkably agile. Fluent in complex musical warbling and whistling, they can utter two streams of words simultaneously while readily comprehending other double-voiced stream of words. The split between overspeech and underspeech within such double-voiced utterances is typographically rendered on the page by a slash reminiscent of poetic line breaks. At one point, for example, a Shevite named Stella suddenly breaks into double-voiced utterance while talking to her non-Shevite father:

> "We need to be together/We're healthier together
> Everyone cares for the others/Everyone is happy with the others
> The sadness comes from not knowing/The sadness comes from being apart."
> (*Darwin's Children*, 270–271)

As a non-Shevite, Stella's father has trouble grasping his daughter's words: "The absolute clarity of the two streams astonished him. If he caught them immediately and analyzed, he could string them together into a serial statement, but over more than a few seconds of conversation, it was obvious he would get confused" (*Darwin's Children*, 271). Although this lack of facility in double-voiced language among non-Shevites problematizes dialogue between Shevites and non-Shevites, it also allows Shevite children to communicate secretly with one another during their many years of imprisonment—against their will and for no reason other than anti-Shevite phobia—in detention camps where they are treated inhumanely by their guardians. In one scene, for instance, Stella awakes to a surreptitious over-under songfest rich in information:

> The over was loud and almost tuneless; the under was subtle . . . it carried a lot of early-morning gossip . . . harshly sweet and sky-shaking laments, pushing sounds around both sides of their ridged tongues, circulating

breath through nose and throat simultaneously. The two streams of song began to play counterpoint, weaving in and out in a way designed to prevent any eavesdropping by the counselors. (*Darwin's Children*, 250)

Unlike their non-Shevite supervisors, whose attempts at "eavesdropping" are frustrated by the over-under songfests, the children of SHEVA are incapable of understanding the notion of coercion. They are incapable of rape (*Darwin's Children*, 404). They are also incapable of competition: "It hurts to make others fail" (*Darwin's Children*, 213). Instead of being prone to abusive behavior or fighting, Shevites have an innate gift for cooperation and consensus. They naturally form into consensual social units that they call "demes" (etymologically related to "democracy"). Each deme contains twenty to thirty individuals. "The deme is like a big family," Stella explains to her father: "We help each other. We talk and solve problems and stop arguments. We're so smart when we're in a deme. We feel right together" (*Darwin's Children*, 270). Unlike the heteronormative nuclear family, the deme is inherently decentralized and nebulous. Demes can "cloud" (a verb that non-Shevite characters have difficulty comprehending) just as individuals or clusters of individuals can "cloud" within and across demes. "When we cloud," Stella tells her father, "we're even more like brothers and sisters. Some of us become mama and papa, too, and we can lead cloud, but mama and papa never make us do what we don't want to do. We decide together" (*Darwin's Children*, 271). As Stella's use of the words "mama" and "papa" here suggests, Shevites regard "father" and "mother" not as essentialized identities but as roles that members of the deme take turns occupying temporarily. Along similar lines, Shevites do not regard romantic partnership and sexual partnership as necessarily coextensive: "Deme partners usually did not mate, though they could fall in love," and "infatuations seldom had anything to do with sex" (*Darwin's Children*, 466). Instead of longing for a significant other, each Shevite desires incorporation into a community of approximately twenty members who cohabitate within a single residence. The architectural features of the homes that the Shevites eventually build for themselves—for example, "bathrooms and toilet facilities without walls"; "narrow 'scent shafts' connecting adjacent homes" (*Darwin's Children*, 465)—maximize comfort insofar as Shevites feel "uncomfortable when deprived of company for more than a few hours" (*Darwin's Children*, 465). Addicted to multimedia information, profoundly dependent on live connections, at home in social-networking sites, Bear's Shevites science-fictionally personify many of the ways in which globalization has been affecting humanity in the late-twentieth- and early-twenty-first centuries. At the same time, Bear's Shevites personify the ways in which globalization is asking—even requiring—humanity to change if we are to avoid destroying ourselves and our planet. Generous, democratic, peaceful, and devoted to consensus decision making, Shevites would be exemplary citizens in a globalized world.

Shevites would likely get along quite well with the Xenogenetic offspring that Octavia Butler creates in her Xenogenesis Trilogy. As I mentioned earlier, *Dawn, Adulthood Rites, and Imago* are set during the centuries following a nuclear war in which humankind has nearly annihilated itself. Earth is now inhabited not only by surviving humans (few in number, significantly diverse in nationality) but also by the extraterrestrial Oankali and by their hybrid alien-human progeny. Known as "constructs," these hybrid children are literal incarnations of global subjectivity. The borders of their bodies are as active and porous as are the borders of our globalized world. Constantly shapeshifting in response to their physical and social environments, constructs are at risk of dissolving into amorphous matter in the absence of other people. The textures of their flesh—supple, alive to contingencies—play a vital part in Butler's representation of global subjectivity. In particular, such textures bring to life the transnational experience of identifying with (or without, or across, or despite, or notwithstanding) plural ethnicities and homelands.

Like the physical bodies of Oankali-human constructs, the structure of the Xenogenetic family unit brings to life the complexities of global subjectivity. Each "construct" has five parents: a human father, a human mother, an Oankali mother, an Oankali father, and finally what is known as an Oankali ooloi. Neither male nor female, the ooloi functions as the central medium of reproduction. It genetically engineers each child through a specialized bodily organ that the ooloi alone possess. Using hereditary material that it has extracted from the bodies of its four partners, the ooloi deliberately synthesizes an offspring that will differ radically from all five of its parents. Each offspring, in other words, is a mutant—an alien among differently alien kin—by definition and by design. The result is a familial configuration shaped, paradoxically, by a shared experience of mutual alienation. At the same time, family members are inextricably linked together by a biochemical interdependency so fierce that their bodies crave one another's proximity. What the Xenogenetic family configuration makes so richly available for representation is the sense of being at once deeply implicated in an interdependent globe and intimately familiar with the unfamiliarity of intimacy itself in a world where globalization brings people "closer apart." Indeed, Butler's description of the Xenogenetic family configuration is strikingly similar to Iyer's figurative account of global subjectivity: "The only home that any Global Soul can find these days," he writes, is "in the midst of the alien" (269); and "the very notion of home is foreign to me, as the state of foreignness is the closest thing I know to home" (24).

No discussion of globalization and mutancy would be complete without at least brief mention of the X-Men. (*Darwin's Children* includes a scene in which a non-Shevite detention guard gives Stella *X-Men* comics to read: "You'll like these," the non-Shevite presumes [266]. Ironically—or perhaps not—Stella finds the X-Men uninteresting.) Originating in the 1960s, the X-Men franchise (movies, comic books, television shows) has over the decades grown an enormous cast of superhuman mutants. With homelands from all over Earth—including Algeria, Greece, Kenya, Japan, Israel, Russia, Brazil, Afghanistan, Samoa, Ireland, Venezuela, Thailand, Australia, Mexico, Egypt, Poland, Morocco, Canada, Italy, Vietnam, Austria, Malaysia, Scotland, and India—today's X-Men constitute an astonishingly diverse transnational community. Mutants of similarly variegated backgrounds are featured in *Heroes*, a television show that debuted in 2006 and whose premise was surely inspired by the X-Men. The series follows the lives of individuals from all over the globe who discover that they possess superhuman abilities. "Heroes" and "X-Men" may come from different franchises, but they are clearly descended from the same species: globalized humanity.

While the global nature of these mutant humans is embodied in the diversity of their homelands, it is even more powerfully embodied in their superhuman capacities. Telepathy, flight, the ability to pass through solid objects: such powers correspond to the ways in which globalization has transformed our experience of space and time. In one episode of *Heroes*, for example, a mutant uses his superpowers to teleport himself instantaneously from Tokyo to Manhattan. His teleportation is a science-fictional concretization of the figurative collapse of distance brought about today by "tele-" technologies such as the telephone and television. Through such narratives of mutancy, Global Souls find themselves granted new forms of corporeal agency. No longer confined to the Local Body, the Global Soul can readily imagine navigating through and sensuously participating in the phantasmagorical topographies of the globalized world.

Modernist X-Men

Globalization is often thought of as a phenomenon that originated in the latter half of the twentieth century. Yet the origins of the globalized world as an
object of cognition can be located in the nineteenth century (if not even before then). As Stephen Kern points out in *The Culture of Time and Space: 1880–
1918*, the notion of global time-space compression was being discussed as
early as the 1890s: "Already in 1891 the editor of *Revue scientifique* wrote that
'to say that there are no longer distances is to utter a very banal truth'" (229).
At the beginning of this chapter I examined several accounts of globalization
from the late nineteenth and early twentieth centuries (Wells, Lowell, Kang,
etc.) before devoting the main body of the chapter to more recent texts. Now
I conclude the chapter by returning to the era of modernism.

Shevites, X-Men, and Oankali-human constructs have modernist precur-
sors in the science fiction of Olaf Stapledon (1886–1950). In particular, they
have progenitors in Stapledon's novel *Odd John* (1935), a science-fictional biography of a genetically mutated human. Narrated by a (nonmutant human)
family friend, *Odd John* begins with John's birth and ends with his eventual
suicide in 1933 at the age of twenty-three. In the storyline that bridges these
two events, John uses telepathy to track down others of his kind, eventually
locating fellow mutants in Russia, Britain, Abyssinia (Ethiopia), Sweden,
China, Turkey, the United States, India, Finland, and Tibet. To communicate among themselves, these mutants use a nonverbal form of mind-reading
that transcends language differences. Unified by the superhuman capacities
that distinguish them from the rest of humankind, the mutants found a com-
monwealth on an island in the South Pacific, where they identify themselves
as a new human species. (A remarkably similar scenario can be found in the
X-Men universe: the fictional island of Genosha, which first appeared in 1988
in *Uncanny X-Men* #235, serves for a time as the site of a mutant nation.)[14]

I interpret Stapledon's island nation of international mutants as a science-
fictional representation of the globalized world. Not only does the mutant
nation consist of individuals from all over the globe, but each individual mutant embodies global diversity. In ordinary speech, we often characterize the
globalized world as a transnational body politic. But rarely do we stop to
imagine this figure of speech as a tangible reality. In the following description
of Odd John, we find the figure of a global body politic literalized and incarnated as a mutant human creature—a living personification of the globalized

world—whose diverse body parts embody various nations from all over the planet:

> To those who had come to know him he seemed a creature of ever-novel beauty. But strangers were often revolted by his uncouth proportions. They called him spiderish. His body, they complained, was so insignificant, his legs and arms so long and lithe, his head all eye and brow. . . . His skin, burnt by the Polynesian sun, was of a grey, almost a green, brown, warming to a ruddier tint in the cheeks. His hands were extremely large and sinewy. Somehow they seemed more mature than the rest of his body. "Spiderish" seemed appropriate in this connection also. His head was certainly large but not out of proportion to his long limbs. Evidently the unique development of his brain depended more on manifold convolutions than on sheer bulk. All the same his was a much larger head than it looked, for its visible bulk was scarcely at all occupied by the hair, which was but a close skull-cap, a mere superficies of negroid but almost white wool. His nose was small but broad, rather Mongolian perhaps. His lips, large but definite, were always active. They expressed a kind of running commentary on his thoughts and feelings. Yet many a time I have seen those lips harden into granitic stubbornness. John's eyes were indeed, according to ordinary standards, much too big for his face, which acquired thus a strangely cat-like or falcon-like expression. This was emphasized by the low and level eyebrows, but often completely abolished by a thoroughly boyish and even mischievous smile. The whites of John's eyes were almost invisible. The pupils were immense. The oddly green irises were as a rule mere filaments. But in tropical sunshine the pupils narrowed to mere pinpricks. Altogether, his eyes were the most obviously "queer" part of him. (6–7)

To understand the representational work that John's body is performing here, we need to consider the lyric device of the blazon. The blazon is a poetic catalogue of various parts of a desirable human body, often using hyperbole to magnify this body's desirability. The following lines from Edmund Spenser's *Amoretti* (Sonnet 64) are illustrative of this poetic form:

> Her lips did smell lyke vnto Gillyflowers,
> her ruddy cheekes lyke vnto Roses red:
> her snowy browes lyke budded Bellamoures,
> her louely eyes lyke Pincks but newly spred,
> Her goodly bosome lyke a Strawberry bed,
> her neck lyke to a bounch of Cullambynes . . .

Notice how closely the syntax of Stapledon's description of Odd John parallels the syntax of the blazon in Spenser's poem. The description of John could

easily be transposed into a blazon with each line of verse corresponding to a
body part:

> His legs and arms were long and lithe,
> His head all eye and brow,
> His skin, burnt by the Polynesian sun, a grey-green brown,
> His hands extremely large, sinewy, like spiders,
> His head too big for his long limbs,
> His hair a close skull-cap of negroid white wool,
> His nose small but broad, rather Mongolian perhaps,
> His lips, large, definite, active,
> His eyebrows low and level,
> His eyes too big for his face,
> The whites of his eyes invisible,
> The pupils of his eyes immense,
> The oddly green irises mere filaments.

As a rhetorical form, the blazon is designed to elicit desire in the reader by
describing the subject's body lingeringly and in exaggerated detail. As the
subject of a blazon, Odd John does elicit a kind of desire in us—the desire to
understand the complexity of his foreignness. At the same time, John's other-
ness estranges us. Such estrangement is indissociable from our awareness that
Odd John is not just a blazon but a *literalized* blazon. The hyperboles of his
body are more than figurative. When the narrator says that John's eyes are
"much too big for his face," he is not exaggerating. Moreover, instead of constituting a seamless and organic whole, the parts of John's body literally stand
out as individual units. In Spenser's blazon, it is only figuratively that "lips"
and "cheeks" and "eyes" are visible as discrete segments. If you were actually
to look at the woman, you would see an aesthetically pleasing and seamless
organic unity. If you were to look at John's body, you would see not a seamless
organic whole but a patchwork of heterogeneous body parts from all over the
globe. The "oddness" of Odd John's physique emerges in and through the explicit separateness of its parts.

The weirdly synthetic nature of John's desirability is enhanced by other
contradictions. Although he is "uncouth," he also possesses "a curiously finished grace" (7). And although there is something "patriarchal" about him, he
is "far more like a boy than a man" (7). Boyish yet fatherly, young yet old, Odd
John possesses a non-Euclidean beauty suggesting that his body somehow
transcends the space-time continuum that the rest of us inhabit. Indeed, he

transcends the linear temporal continuum of natural biological reproduction. The multiracial characteristics that he embodies ("Mongolian" nose, the specifications of his racially typed hair and skin color) are genetically unaccountable: both of his biological parents, the narrator tells us, are of European ancestry. John's cohorts are equally strange composites whose "mongrel" features cannot be biologically explained. Meanwhile, the mutants themselves "reproduce" by way of an island laboratory—a collective reproductive matrix—in which embryological experiments signify the genesis of a new transnational humanity. What is most interesting about the mutants' attitude toward family is its conflation of "descent" with "consent." Ostensibly of heterogeneous descent, the mutants reach a consensus in which they identify themselves as descendents who share a single genealogical origin that exists in the future rather than in the past. Their "homeland" is not the place where they were born. It is the Pacific island transnation that they construct together in the future tense, a mutant homeland occupying a nonlinear temporality not unlike the International Date Line where the beginning of tomorrow and the end of yesterday meet along a vertical line through the Pacific Ocean.

The islanders' actions are characterized by a moral ambiguity that reflects a profound ambivalence toward globalization. The genesis of the new human species is made possible in the first place by genocide. Only by supplanting the island's aboriginal community, we learn, were the colonists able to found their nation in the first place. "They were simple and attractive creatures," John says of the native islanders, "but, of course, we could not allow them to interfere with our plans. . . . So we decided to destroy them" (124). The narrator struggles to rationalize the genocide by contrasting it with what Europeans might have done: "They would probably have baptized the natives, given them prayer books and European clothes, rum and all the diseases of the White Man. They would also have enslaved them economically, and in time they would have crushed their spirits by confronting them at every turn with the White Man's trivial superiority" (124). Ultimately, however, the rationalization can only be (at best) a thought experiment, insofar as the superhuman motives behind the genocide are psychologically unavailable to John's human biographer. As characters whose inner experiences remain opaque to us, Odd John and his cohorts exist at the limits of human psychology. Consequently, the narrator accounts for the ethnocide by remarking: "Whether the end which they so ruthlessly pursued did in fact justify the means, I simply do not feel competent to decide. All my sympathies lie with the view that murder can never be justified. . . . But who am I that I should judge beings who in daily contact with me constantly proved themselves my superior not only in intelligence but in moral insight?" (125). The narrator's inability to judge the genocide, I would argue, represents an inability to form an unambiguous judgment about globalization.

The Pacific island once again becomes the site of genocide at the end of the book. This time, the people destroyed are the superhuman colonists themselves. After years of living in peaceful isolation from the rest of the world, the island nation, we learn, is discovered by a British warship. What follows is a surreal parody of international conflict. The "Six Powers"— which the narrator lists as Britain, Japan, Russia, France, Holland, and the United States[15]—make repeated attempts to conquer the island, only to find themselves psychologically vanquished by the telepathic weaponry (nightmares, panic, despair) that the supernormals use to defend themselves. While the psychical ordeal that these men undergo resembles the effect of war on the mind, the cause itself—war—does not physically "happen": the source of trauma has no stable location. Likewise, the moment of genocide itself complicates the structure of accountability. Faced with the prospect of submitting to the Six Powers, the islanders commit mass suicide. Critics have tended to read *Odd John* as a tragic political fable in which the heroic superhumans represent Stapledon's vision of an ill-fated transnational community. Such a reading maps the opposition between Odd John and the Pacific Powers onto a morally charged dichotomy between utopian hope and dystopian reality. But John himself is a morally problematic character, and the British officers are victims of torture inflicted by the mutants. Even today, over seventy years after the publication of *Odd John,* readers may find its pages reflecting their own conflictedness about the mutations that are globalizing the world as we know it (or the globalization that is mutating the world as we know it).

A Global "Eve"

Such ambivalence is further reflected in another Stapledon novel from the 1930s, *Last and First Men.* In most respects these two works are extremely different. *Odd John* is a brief "biography" spanning a quarter of a century. *Last and First Men,* by contrast, is a cosmic romance chronicling two billion years of human culture, at a pace so fast—the passages of time so massive, the account itself so relatively small—that panoramic summary forms the book's dominant unit of description. The opening chapters relate the rise and fall of the "First Men," to which we ourselves belong, while the concluding chapters give an account of the unearthly "Last Men" who inhabit the remote future. Together these chapters encompass a vast ethnographic fantasia chronicling the evolution of humanity. Thus, the narrative renders the "present moment" (namely, the 1930s) the increasingly distant prehistory of an ever-unfolding future.

For all the differences between these two novels, they do share a meaningful intertext: an island in the Pacific that serves as the site of the genesis of a new world order. Although this island appears only briefly in *Last and First Men*, the episode in which it appears is worth examining as a science-fictional account of globalization. The episode begins, we are told, in "the twenty-sixth year" of a global war between America and China. Two men from each geopolitical hemisphere meet secretly on the beach of a South Pacific island. The agenda of their meeting is to "re-arrange the planet"—"in place of the national governments, a World Finance Directorate was to be created" (51)— so that both men gain positions of power, the American as the president of the world and the Chinese as vice-president.[16] The meeting is interrupted when a mysterious young woman emerges from the ocean's depths and walks out of the water toward the "creators of the World State." Her sudden appearance from out of nowhere instantly polarizes the two men. Vitally and revealingly different, their reactions to her presence put into motion what will unfold as an asymmetrical flow of power among these three individuals and, eventually, throughout the world at large. What the American disguises as scorn—namely, desire—the Chinese voices by way of reverie:

> "Who are you? Of what race are you? My anthropological studies fail to place you. Your skin is fairer than is native here, though rich with sun. Your breasts are Grecian. Your lips are chiseled with a memory of Egypt. Your hair, night though it was, is drying with a most bewildering hint of gold. And your eyes. . . . Long, subtle as my countrywomen's, unfathomable as the mind of India, they yet reveal themselves to your new slave as not wholly black, but violet as the zenith before dawn. Indeed this exquisite unity of incompatibles conquers both my heart and my understanding." (52)

Like Odd John, this enigmatic "Daughter of Ocean" (as the Chinese speaker denominates her) embodies a literalized blazon whose components come from all over the globe. And as with John, the nature of the desire she evokes is complicated. The speaker addresses her body by listing part by part—bronze skin, Grecian breasts, Egyptian lips, black hair streaked with gold, violet eyes—only to find that such analysis makes him discover in her an "exquisite unity of incompatibles" that both eludes and "conquers" him. Her attractiveness, like that of Odd John, is weirdly synthetic, non-Euclidean, superhuman. It elicits in us a strange desire mimetic of our strange fascination with the emerging globalized world.

To complicate matters, the young woman (supposedly indigenous to the South Pacific island) startles us by answering the Chinese man's question in an unreal "old-time English accent" (53):

> "I am certainly a mongrel. You might call me, not daughter of Ocean, but daughter of Man; for wanderers of every race have scattered their seed on this island. My body, I know, betrays its diverse ancestry in a rather queer blend of characters. My mind is perhaps unusual too, for I have never left this island. And though it is actually less than a quarter of a century since I was born, a past century has perhaps had more meaning for me than the obscure events of today. A hermit taught me." (53)

By generalizing her ancestors and thereby voiding them of specific identity, the "Daughter of Man" casts herself as a figure who exists beyond the natural continuum of human reproduction. Of puzzling origin in every possible way—where did she come from? how was she born? who are her parents? what is her precise genetic make-up?—she signifies not only blank provenance but also a discontinuous genealogy. At once "primitive" and hypercultured, at once quaint and futuristic, she is a science-fictional representation of the mutational space between the end of the past and the beginning of the global world order.

Indeed, the "Daughter of Man" goes on to become a kind of Eve who begets Future Humankind by consenting to be the President of the World's lover.[17] We are told that the President's "scandalous" connection with the "woman who now styled herself the Daughter of Man" is "expected to enrage the virtuous" public. But the American President of the World rationalizes his bigamy with the following sophistry:

> By a stroke of genius the President saved both himself and the unity of the world. Far from denying the charge, he gloried in it. . . . Without this daring sacrifice of his private purity, he would never have been really fit to be President of the World; he would have remained simply an American. In this lady's veins flowed the blood of all races, and in her mind all cultures

mingled. His union with her, confirmed by many subsequent visits, had taught him to enter into the spirit of the East, and had given him a broad human sympathy such as his high office demanded. As a private individual, he insisted, he remained a monogamist with a wife in New York. . . . But as President of the World, it was incumbent upon him to espouse the World. And since nothing could be said to be real without a physical basis, this spiritual union had to be embodied and symbolized by his physical union with the Daughter of Man. . . . He had consummated his marriage with the World. . . . The lovely form of the Daughter of Man (decently clad) was transmitted by television to every receiver in the world. Her face, blended of Asia and the West, became a potent symbol of human unity. Every man on the planet became in imagination her lover. Every woman identified herself with this supreme woman. (57–58)

This scenario explicitly literalizes the metaphor of "espousing the world"—not just as a consensual and polygamous triangle among "American President of the World," "Wife in New York," and "Daughter of Man," but also as a consensual and technologically mediated marriage between "every man on the planet" and the televised image of the Daughter of Man. While the passage implies that the situation is unnatural, it also represents this scenario as a confusingly attractive prospect. Such confusion, as with our confusion toward Odd John, reflects a profound ambivalence about globalization—an ambivalence that is symptomatic of the cognitively estranging nature of the globalized world.

Earth after Globalization?

Some might take issue with my largely ahistorical characterization of the cognitively estranging nature of the globalized world. To be sure, the globalized world is cognitively estranging only inasmuch as the world has not yet been completely globalized. In other words, the closer the process of globalization is to completion, the less and less cognitively estranging the globalized world will become. Thus the concept of a globalized world, while cognitively estranging today, was of course more so before the word "globalization" entered common usage in the 1960s. And it is likely that the cognitively estranging nature of the globalized world will diminish over time. Through technological advances, we may eventually outgrow the limits of the individual human body. Jet lag may one day somehow become a distant thing of the past. The idea of inhabiting two or more places simultaneously may cease to be merely an idea; it may eventually become a reality.

But the twenty-first century is not yet in its teens. The technologies mentioned above are so far off that—for our purposes, at least—the cognitively estranging nature of the globalized world might as well be ahistorical. The globalized worldview, for now, remains more abstract than concrete, more elusive than intuitive. As scholars such as Gayatri Chakravorty Spivak, Paul Gilroy, and Wai Chee Dimock have noted, to use the "planet" as a frame of reference for studying literature and culture today is to invoke a framework not yet fully in existence. In her introduction to *Shades of the Planet: American Literature as World Literature*, Dimock paraphrases arguments made by Spivak in *Death of a Discipline* (2003) and by Gilroy in *After Empire* (2004) about the intriguing half-reality of a global framework whose complete realization is yet to come:

> "Planetarity" is a term worth exploring precisely because it is an unknown quantum, barely intimated, not yet adequate to the meaning we would like it to bear, and stirring for just that reason. It stands as a horizon impossible to define, and hospitable in that impossibility. . . . The concept can be helpful only in the optative mood, as a generative principle fueled by its less than actualized status. For its heuristic value lies in its not having come into being: it is a habitat still waiting for its inhabitants, waiting for a humanity that has yet to be born. (5)

The time when the globalized world becomes readily susceptible to straightforward comprehension is still in the remote future. In the meantime, we can rely on science fiction to describe and make sense of the globalized world.[18]

2

Cyberspace in the 1990s

As we saw in the preceding chapter, the globalized world has two dimensions, literal and figurative. The subject of this chapter has much in common with the "ever-mutating web" that makes up the figurative half of the globalized world. However, enough differences exist between the two entities to justify an analysis of cyberspace on its own terms as a cognitively estranging referent independent of the globalized world. What does it mean to create a mimetic account of cyberspace? To ask this question is in fact to ask three separate questions, for there are three separate components to the difficulty of making cyberspace available for representation.

First, what does it mean to represent something whose existence is both virtual and nonhypothetical? According to a 1997 entry in the *Oxford English Dictionary*, cyberspace is "space perceived as such by an observer but generated by a computer system and *having no real existence*" (emphasis mine). By its very definition, then, cyberspace—the illusion of space that we experience when we stare into a computer screen, sign in to a network of computers, and interact with the ever-changing collection of data that these networked computers share—is a figure of speech. Just as a chatroom is not actually a room, cyberspace is not actually a space. Yet this illusory "space" does, paradoxically, exist. As one writer has observed, the "place" of cyberspace is "as real as the work and play conducted 'in' it" (Nunes, 61). Although cyberspace is of the nature of figuration, its existence is a literal fact.

Second, what does it mean to represent something whose structure defies not only the linearity of the sentence but also the planarity of the canvas and

the three-dimensionality of sculpture? Cyberspace may be perceived as a spatial phenomenon, but the "space" constituted by this illusion is non-Euclidean.
In cyberspace, the concept of distance is incoherent. There is no such thing as
a "center" relative to which every other point has a fixed location. Like the
God of Saint Augustine's imagination, cyberspace can be described as a
"mystical circle whose center is everywhere and circumference nowhere: every
user regards his home site as the heart of the system, and there is no limit on
how far the system can reach" (Ryan, "Cyberspace, Virtuality, and the Text,"
86).[1] Accordingly, the orientation of items in cyberspace—for example, the
relationship between two websites—cannot be described using terms such as
"inside," "outside," "above," or "below." Instead of obeying the laws of Euclid-
ean geometry, cyberspace obeys the laws of hypertextual technology. Hypertext, a computer-based system for retrieving information, is organized so that
related "lexias"[2] or fragments of data are interconnected in a nonlinear manner through what are known as "hyperlinks." The shape of hypertext is never
stable: lexias are frequently updated, links can easily be added or removed,
and the pattern of lexias—each of which contains at least several different
hyperlinks—shifts according to which links individual readers decide to click
(or not to click). Moreover, the very shape of the hyperlink is inherently unstable: although it creates continuity between lexias, the link is itself of the
nature of discontinuity. Neither preposition nor conjunction, the link is a
gaplike structure that simultaneously disjoins and conjoins, as much a unit
of curiosity and anticipation (click: question?) as it is a unit of epistemological gratification (download: answer). To be "inside" the "space" of cyberspace is therefore to experience information as an actively complicated web
whose complexity behaves in ways that are neither zero- nor one- nor two-
nor three-dimensional.

Third, what does it mean to represent something whose chronological status during the 1990s could not be defined? Coined in 1981 by science-fiction
writer William Gibson, the word "cyberspace"[3] originally referred to an intersubjective mindscape generated by futuristic machines. Gibson used this
imaginary universe as the primary setting for his Cyberspace Series:[4] the short
story "Burning Chrome" (1981) and the novels *Neuromancer* (1984), *Count
Zero* (1986), and *Mona Lisa Overdrive* (1988). These novels—*Neuromancer* in
particular—quickly achieved cult-classic status, and Gibson's coinage became
a buzzword among computer enthusiasts who found it a useful way of thinking
about the emerging technology of virtual reality (Ryan, "Cyberspace, Virtual-

ity, and the Text," 78). More importantly, however, the media began using the term "cyberspace" in reference to new tools (for instance, graphics-based Web browsers) that were revolutionizing data processing and telecommunications. By the mid-nineties, "cyberspace" had become a popular synonym for "the Internet," "the Net," and "the World Wide Web." Because of this synonymy, and because of the abruptness with which the "Cyberspace Revolution" followed the publication of the Cyberspace Series,[5] the Internet was widely perceived to be the materialization of Gibson's prophetic vision.[6] A 1995 piece in *Time Magazine*, for example, conflates Gibsonian cyberspace with cyberspace-as-Internet: "Hardly a day goes by without some newspaper article, some political speech, some corporate press release invoking Gibson's imaginary world" (Elmer-DeWitt). Similarly, a 1995 article in the *New York Times* finds irony in the fact that the man who coined the word "cyberspace" is unfamiliar with the online world: "Until late last week, Mr. Gibson had never logged onto a computer network to witness first-hand the cyberspace realms that he so evocatively described" (Lewis, "Present at the Creation, Startled at the Reality"). A 1997 Amazon.com review of *Neuromancer* goes so far as to credit Gibson as the creator of the Internet: "The last thirteen years have delivered some technologies that are much closer to those Gibson 'invented'" (emphasis in the original).[7] As these comments reveal, whatever "cyberspace" referred to in the 1990s was simultaneously past, present, and future tense. It was an unreal futurescape whose name was suddenly beginning to refer to part of the present-day world. At the same time, it was a present-day technology that retained its earlier evocation of something futuristic and unreal.

Indeed, cyberspace has never been more cognitively estranging than it was during its transformation in the 1990s from futuristic vision to unfamiliar new reality. While the first and second components to the challenge of describing cyberspace may still challenge us today, they will never daunt us the way they daunted writers and thinkers in the 1990s. This chapter will therefore focus on *cyberspace in the 1990s* as a cognitively estranging referent. Accordingly, most of the texts that I discuss were written in the 1990s.

Gibson never anticipated that his coinage would become so influential, and he has made a habit of disavowing (or pretending to disavow) his so-called invention. "I don't even have a modem or e-mail," he claimed in a 1994 interview; "my computer is outdated by any standards of criteria" (interview with Salza). In his 1991 essay "Academy Leader," he calls attention to the ambiguity that has come to characterize his status as the "author" of cyberspace in the aftermath of the Cyberspace Revolution. "Assembled word cyberspace. . . . Now other words accrete in the interstices," he writes elliptically, omitting the nominative "I" and thereby enacting on a syntactic level how cyberspace has outgrown its original identity as the creation of an individual mind (27).[8] Yet Gibson's disavowal of cyberspace belies his intense fascination with the phenomenon to which his coinage has come to refer. In a 1996 essay titled "The Net Is a Waste of Time," he struggles to find the right language to characterize the elusiveness of his subject. Cyberspace, he muses, is "half-formed," "growing," "clumsy," "larval," and "curiously innocent." It is as blank and amorphous as the feeling of "staring into space." It "is not what it was six months ago," and six months from today "it will be something else again." In another essay from the nineties, Gibson discusses the ungraspable nature of cyberspace in terms of his addiction to eBay. Online auctions appeal to him, he writes, because they allow him "to import a unique object, physically, out of cyberspace"; that is, they allow him "to turn the not-so-clear scan on my screen into a physical object on my desk" ("My Obsession"). His addiction to eBay—his longing to transform the "not-so-clear scan" into "a physical object"—is a manifestation of a deeper longing that many Internet users share: the desire to transform the elusiveness of cyberspace into the describable concreteness of a solid object.

While Gibson's preoccupation with the difficulty of representing cyberspace is evident in his nonfiction, it might seem to be missing from the *fiction* that he wrote in the wake of the Cyberspace Revolution. In his Bridge Trilogy— *Virtual Light* (1993), *Idoru* (1996), and *All Tomorrow's Parties* (1999)—most of the action takes place in the physical world, and the word "cyberspace" itself is conspicuously absent. (This absence is deliberate. "How can I create a fictional continuum in which people use a word that originated in a William Gibson story?" he once asked in a 1996 interview [quoted in Wallis].) Yet cyberspace is precisely what the Bridge Trilogy is all about. More specifically, these novels solve the problem of how to create a mimetic account of cyberspace, and they do so by drawing on the representational strategies of science fiction. Science fiction, I have been arguing, is a mode in which lyric figures are literalized as the features of a narrative world: apostrophe, for example, is often literalized as telepathy, and personification is often literalized as the animation of an inanimate robot. As a mode in which figures of speech operate on a literal level without losing their figurative power, science fiction can represent phenomena that are themselves neither purely literal nor purely figurative. In the Bridge Trilogy, cyberspace becomes available for representation through the science-fictional entity alluded to by the trilogy's title: a postapocalyptic San Francisco Bay Bridge set in the early twenty-first century. No longer operative as a mode of transportation—it was damaged beyond repair by a mythical earthquake—the bridge now serves as a shantytown-like dwelling for visionaries, outcasts, and refugees. Laws here are unspoken, businesses are unlicensed, pathways are densely mazelike, and homes are made of salvaged junk. By literalizing a wide array of figures of speech that have been associated with cyberspace—for example, "cyberspace is a labyrinth," "cyberspace is a junkyard"—Gibson's bridge constitutes a framework through which cyberspace becomes something that we recognize kinesthetically, something that makes immediate sense to our bodies. Moreover, by literalizing the eternal "now" of lyric time, Gibson's bridge constitutes a nonlinear space in which past and present and future coexist. In these ways, Gibson's science-fictional bridge is able to accommodate those qualities of cyberspace that make it so cognitively estranging: its paradoxical status as both literal and figurative, its intricately nonlinear structure, and its ambiguous place on the temporal continuum.[9]

Approaching Cyberspace

The idea of cyberspace occurred to Gibson in the late 1970s and early 1980s. Watching teenagers play video games in an arcade in downtown Vancouver, he was struck by "the physical intensity of their postures," "how *rapt* these kids were," the way they "clearly *believed* in the space the games projected" (quoted in Turkle, 265, emphasis in the original). What fascinated him was their "intuitive faith that there's some kind of actual space behind the screen"—a faith, he noted, that the video game players share with "everyone who works with computers" (quoted in Turkle, 265). In the Cyberspace Series, Gibson depicts this "intuitive faith" as a technological device. His characters use "cyberspace decks" to connect their brains to a "graphic representation of data abstracted from the banks of every computer in the human system" (*Neuromancer*, 51). The disembodied consciousness of the jacked-in operator is projected into a worldwide "consensual hallucination" (*Neuromancer*, 5, 51) that can be navigated as though it were a physical environment.

Much of what makes Gibson's futuristic vision so powerful—indeed, much of what would make it so influential during the nineties—is its active indeterminacy. At times cyberspace is as starkly simple as "an abstract representation of the relationships between data systems" ("Burning Chrome," 169). At other times cyberspace is marked by "cluttered vastness" (*Mona Lisa Overdrive*, 49) and "unthinkable complexity" (*Neuromancer*, 51). At times cyberspace is a state of imprisonment: One character likens it to "an infinite cage" (*Mona Lisa Overdrive*, 49). At other times cyberspace is a state of freedom: it possesses "unlimited subjective dimension" (*Neuromancer*, 63), and to inhabit it is to experience "bodiless exultation" (*Neuromancer*, 6). At times cyberspace is portrayed in highly rational terms—"bright lattices of logic" (*Neuromancer*, 5), "a 3D chessboard, infinite and perfectly transparent" ("Burning Chrome," 168). At other times cyberspace is portrayed as a world dominated by irrational forces: in *Count Zero* and *Mona Lisa Overdrive*, cyberspace is haunted by ghosts and voodoo gods. At times cyberspace is a world of sensory deprivation—a "monochrome nonspace" ("Burning Chrome," 170), a "colorless void" (*Neuromancer*, 5). At other times cyberspace is a world of sensory hyperstimulation—a world filled with "shifting rainbow strata" (*Neuromancer*, 180), "silver phosphenes" (*Neuromancer*, 52), "walls of emerald green, milky jade" (*Neuromancer*, 256), "bright primaries, impossibly bright in that transparent void, linked by countless horizontals in nursery blues and pinks" ("Burning Chrome," 178), and "data so dense you suffered sensory overload" (*Count Zero*, 39).

Not only does Gibson endow cyberspace with contradictory qualities, he also uses a broad range of metaphors and discourses to describe this virtual realm. Among these many discourses are *astronomy* (cyberspace consists of "constellations of data" [*Neuromancer*, 51]; it is a space "where the only stars are dense concentrations of information, and high above it all burn corporate galaxies" ["Burning Chrome," 170]), *architecture* (cyberspace has "walls" and "windows" [*Neuromancer*, 5]; parts of it assume the shape of the "gleaming spires of a dozen identical towers" [*Neuromancer*, 257]), *urban space* (cyberspace is an "endless neon cityscape" [*Neuromancer*, 256]; it looks "like city lights, receding" [*Neuromancer*, 51]), *neurology* (cyberspace is "mankind's extended electronic nervous system" ["Burning Chrome," 169], an "infinite neuroelectronic void" [*Neuromancer*, 115] with "extended crystal nerves" [*Neuromancer*, 258]), *mathematics* (cyberspace contains "bright geometries" ["Burning Chrome," 169], rectangles and cylinders dancing along the "planes of a three-dimensional grid" [*Count Zero*, 82]), *nationalism* (to one hacker, cyberspace is "his distanceless home, his country" [*Neuromancer*, 52], *decorative art* (cyberspace "folds itself around me like an origami trick" ["Burning Chrome," 188]; it evokes a "neon prayer rug on the screen" ["Burning Chrome," 181]), and *transportation* (in cyberspace, "core data tower around us like vertical freight trains" ["Burning Chrome," 178]).

If Gibson's vision of cyberspace is difficult to define, then the term that he invented to refer to this vision is even less definite. In *Control and Freedom*, Wendy Chun illuminates the obscurity peculiar to the word "cyberspace" by comparing it with words that denote other modes of communication:

> *Cyberspace* is an odd name for a communications medium. Unlike *newspaper* (news + paper) or *film*, it does not comprise its content or its physical materials. Unlike *movies*, derived from "moving pictures," it does not explain its form; unlike *cinema* (short for cinematograph: Greek *kinhma*, *kinhmato* [motion] + graph [written]), it does not highlight its physical machinery. Further, unlike *television* (tele + vision; vision from afar), cyberspace does not explain the type of vision it enables, and unlike *radio*, it does not reference its means of transmission (radiation). Although all these names—newspaper, film, movies, cinema, television, and radio—erase sites of production, cyberspace erases all reference to content, apparatus, process, or form, offering instead a metaphor and a mirage, for cyberspace is not spatial. (39)

The relationship between "cyberspace" and cyberspace, Chun's analysis shows, is strikingly illogical. Gibson himself has acknowledged that he had no specific referent in mind when he coined the term "cyberspace." As he revealed in a 1996 interview, the term was designed to be open and ambiguous: "What I wanted was an exciting buzzword somewhat devoid of meaning" (quoted in Wallis). Begotten spontaneously through what Gibson has elsewhere described as a "neologic spasm," "cyberspace" entered the world in the form of a "slick and hollow" signifier that whimsically "preceded any concept whatever" ("Academy Leader," 27). Brand-new, it existed in a state of "awaiting received meaning" (27). It evoked. It did not yet denote.

The vagueness of Gibson's coinage helps to explain why "cyberspace" prevailed as a catchphrase in the nineties. Unlike less popular synonyms such as "the Information Superhighway" and "the Electronic Frontier," the word "cyberspace"—like Gibsonian cyberspace more generally—was as indeterminate, as charged with potential, as open to various uses and interpretations, as was the emerging Internet technology to which "cyberspace" would come to refer. What gave "cyberspace" its peculiarly evocative power was the prefix. "Cyber" famously comes from "cybernetics," a term first used by the American mathematician Norbert Wiener in the 1940s to designate the study of communication and control in machines and living organisms. Mystifying and incantatory, this prefix alone became a buzzword in the nineties. Often unmindful of its etymological origins in the Greek verb for "to steer," writers and advertisers invoked "cyber" to generate widely ranging (and frequently nonsensical) neologisms such as "cybercafe," "cyberporn," "cyberhymnal," "cyberzoo," "cyberculture," "cybernation," "cyberliberty," "cyberkid," "cyberpolitics," and "cybershine." In 1995, *Time* magazine called "cyber" the "prefix of the day," noting that "a Nexis search of newspapers, magazines and television transcripts turned up 1,205 mentions of cyber in the month of January, up from 464 the previous January and 167 in January 1993" (Elmer-DeWitt). A year later, the *New York Times* reported that "cyber" had become a cliché: "Much to the chagrin of Internet aficionados, the ubiquitous prefix has replicated faster than a powerful computer virus" (Wallis). Gibson himself commented that the overuse of "cyber" had vitiated its meaning. "I knew 'cyber' was getting out of control at least a decade ago," he said in 1996. "I was in Tokyo and passed a department store window full of boring-looking madras-plaid sports jackets. Behind the sports jackets was a huge sign that read CYBERSUMMER! If those jackets can be cybersummer, then cyber can mean anything" (quoted in Wallis).

If "cyber" could "mean anything," then what could "cyberspace" mean? The difficulty of addressing this question is evidenced by the ways in which writers have attempted to frame their answers. Some writers, for example, have tried to identify what cyberspace is by identifying what cyberspace is *not*. "It isn't a thing, it isn't an entity, it isn't an organization," James Gleick remarks in a 1994 newspaper article: "No one owns it; no one runs it" ("The Information Future: Out of Control"). Likewise, Marie-Laure Ryan uses the language of negation in a 1999 essay: cyberspace is "neither a palpable thing, nor a scientific or philosophical concept, nor even a technology" ("Cyberspace, Virtuality, and the Text," 79). Meanwhile, those who have tried to describe what cyberspace "is" have been unable to do so in literal terms. How is it possible, after all, to give a literal account of something that is of the nature of figuration? One of the most striking things about writings on cyberspace is the lush proliferation of metaphors and similes. What follows is a partial list of these figures of speech (some of which overlap with one another and many of which overlap with those that Gibson uses in his Cyberspace Series): *transportation* (cyberspace is "an instrumented bridge" congested with "the global traffic of knowledge" [Benedikt, "Introduction," 2], a "Superhighway" with "tolls and bridges, on-ramps (sort of) and potholes (unquestionably)" [Gleick]), *ecology* (cyberspace "grows on its own like an ecosystem" [George Johnson] that "grows not by design but by accretion" [Gleick]; it is an "endless wilderness" [Johnson] inhabited by a "new kind of organism" [Turkle]—"a protoplasmic organism, or colony of organisms" [Gleick]), *architecture* (cyberspace has "corridors" [Benedikt, "Introduction," 2], "leaky pipes and exposed wires" [Erik Davis, 312], and "edifices" [Benedikt, "Introduction," 18]; it is an "architecture nested within architecture" wherein "cities can exist within chambers as chambers may exist within cities" [Novak, 249] and a "maze" of "hidden byways snakes around with no apparent center" [Heim, 77]), *urban space* (cyberspace is a "city" [Benedikt, "Introduction," 2], a "megalopolis" [Heim, 77]), *archival research* (cyberspace is a repository of "vast databases that constitute the culture's deposited wealth" from which "every document is available, every recording is playable, and every picture is viewable" [Benedikt, "Introduction," 2]), *neurology* (cyberspace is a "great terrestrial brain" [George Johnson], a "collectivization of the human sensorium" [Tomas, 36], a neural organ "growing up out of the connections that an infant makes, sights to sounds" [quoted in Turkle, 45]), *meteorology* (cyberspace is a "soft hail of electrons" [Benedikt, "Introduction," 3] or perhaps a sky filled with "thunderstorms of congestion" [George Johnson]), *business* (cyberspace is "a shopping mall" [Elmer-DeWitt], a "junkyard" where salvage is resold [Gleick], "a giant and unbounded world of virtual real estate" [Dyson] spangled with the "visual pageantry" of "flashing billboards" [Murray, 112], "a place of circulation, trading, speculation, and relentless activity—the dynamics of capitalism turned into a spectacle" [Ryan, "Cyberspace, Virtuality, and the Text," 83]), *cosmology* (cyberspace is "a new universe, a parallel universe" [Benedikt, "Introduction," 1]), *sociopolitics* (cyberspace is "a commune with 4.8 million fiercely independent members" [Elmer-DeWitt], "a town that leaves its streets unmarked on the principle that people who don't already know don't belong" [Gleick]), *the sport of surfboarding* (cyberspace is like "surfing on top of a wave" [Ryan, "Cyberspace, Virtuality, and the Text," 84] or like "a great ocean on which you surf from site to site" [Johnson]), *housing* (cyberspace is "a home" [Benedikt, "Introduction," 2], a "habitat for the imagination" [Novak, 225], a "cozy habitat" [Ryan, 84]), *geopolitics* (cyberspace is a "country nowhere to be found on the map" [Ryan, "Cyberspace, Virtuality, and the Text," 86]), *metaphysics* (cyberspace is "a metaphysical laboratory, a tool for examining our very sense of reality" [Heim, 59]; cyberspace "sidesteps Einsteinian space-time, giving birth to a kind of digital metaphysics—or, perhaps more properly, 'netaphysics'" [Erik Davis, 392]), *pageantry* (cyberspace is "a full-scale Mardi Gras parade" [Bruce Sterling, quoted in Elmer-DeWitt]), and *mysticism* (cyberspace inspires "religious fervor" [Elmer-DeWitt]; it is a "fantastic world" [Lewis, "Put On Your Data Glove"], "a Borgesian library" [Benedikt, "Introduction" 2], an "alchemical beaker" [Erik Davis, 392], "a landscape of rational magic, of mystical reason" [Novak, 226], "another venue for consciousness itself" [Benedikt, "Introduction," 124]; cyberspace is "Oz—it is, we get there, but it has no location" [Stenger, 53]).

Sometimes the metaphors are mixed. One figurative expression, for instance, combines physics with mystical philosophy: cyberspace is "a wavelength of well-being where we would encounter the second half of ourselves" (Stenger, 50). Another figurative expression combines physics with transportation: cyberspace is "a dynamic environment, a slick surface, a force to catch in order to be transported elsewhere" (Ryan, "Cyberspace, Virtuality, and the Text," 84). A third figurative expression combines the discourses of war, peace, mysticism, and cosmology: cyberspace is "the new bomb, a pacific blaze that will project the imprint of our disembodied selves on the walls of eternity" (Stenger, 51). A fourth figurative expression combines topography, botany, geophysics, and visual spectacle: cyberspace is a collection of "sights, sounds, presences never seen on the surface of the earth blossoming in a vast electronic night" [Benedikt, "Introduction," 1]. A fifth figurative expression combines topography, linguistics, animal reproduction, and philosophy: cyberspace is "a frontier awaiting exploration, promising discovery, threatening humanistic values, hatching new genres of discourse, altering our relation to the written word, questioning our sense of self and of embodiment" (Ryan, "Introduction," 1). A sixth figurative expression combines topography, psychology, anatomy, musical performance, and business: cyberspace is a "territory swarming with data and lies, with mind stuff and memories of nature, with a million voices and two million eyes in a silent, invisible concert of enquiry, deal-making, dream sharing, and simple beholding" (Benedikt, "Introduction," 2). Some researchers, moreover, have created cartographic diagrams of cyberspace that inspire their own metaphors and similes. One journalist, writing in 1999, likens the cyberspace maps to "pointillist paintings," "doodles from a brainstorming session," and "promiscuously propagating sea ferns, with countless feathery vines" (O'Connell).

Complicating this list of metaphors and similes are the figures of speech that scholars have used to describe cyberspace's hypertextual structure. Several of these figures—"link," "web" "network"—are so common that they have become part of our global vernacular. Other figures, while less common, are still influential. One such figure is the metaphor of the visual collage. George P. Landow explicitly uses this metaphor when he notes that "all hypertext webs, no matter how simple, how limited, inevitably take the form of textual collage, for they inevitably work by juxtaposing different texts" (*Hypertext 2.0*, 171). Similarly, Marie-Laure Ryan remarks that hypertext can be thought of on the analogy of "bricolage," whereby "autonomous fragments, the verbal equivalent of objets trouvés," are pasted together into a "patchwork" whose "shape and meaning(s) emerge through the linking process" (Ryan, *Narrative as Virtual Reality*, 7). Related to the metaphor of the visual collage is that of the kaleidoscope. According to Landow, hypertext "provides an infinitely recenterable system whose provisional point of focus depends upon the reader"—just as a kaleidoscope provides an infinitely recenterable pattern of colors whose provisional point of focus depends on how the viewer rotates the optical tube (*Hypertext 2.0*, 36). Ryan, too, invokes this metaphor, characterizing hypertext as "a collection of fragments that can be combined into ever-changing configurations through the random choices of the reader" (*Narrative as Virtual Reality*, 219). And Michael Joyce invokes the metaphor of the kaleidoscope when he describes hypertext as a "visual form" of "constant reconfiguration" in which "a complex network of signs . . . presents texts and images in an order that the artist has shaped but which the viewer chooses and reshapes" (206). Yet another figure for hypertext is the metaphor of the funhouse. According to Landow, hypertext is an architectural structure whose "multiple entryways and exits" can disorient the visitor (*Hypertext 2.0*, 40). Along similar lines, Ryan describes hypertext as a funhouse in which moving from one joltingly surreal room to the next can feel like being "teletransported to more or less random destinations" (*Narrative as Virtual Reality*, 73–74). Because the reader of hypertext rarely stays in a single place "long enough to let an atmosphere sink in" (*Narrative as Virtual Reality*, 262), the layout of the metaphorical funhouse is unmemorizable: one is unable to "familiarize oneself" with a single aspect of a hypertext. Furthermore, there is no such thing here as a transparent window that looks out onto the outside world. In the funhouse of hypertext, "windows" behave like illusive screens that distort perception by breaking down sensory experience into its discrete components: "One window may offer text, another sound, a third pictures or film" (*Narrative as Virtual Reality*, 215).

Gibson himself contributed to the profusion of figures of speech for cyberspace-as-Internet in the 1990s. One of his figures for the Internet is the urban metaphor: the web, he writes in a 1996 essay, "is happening the way cities happened. It is a city" ("The Net Is a Waste of Time"). A second Gibsonian figure for cyberspace-as-Internet is the metaphor of the bazaar. In a 1999 essay, he likens the World Wide Web to a "flea market or garage sale" ("My Obsession"), and in another essay he characterizes the activity of web-surfing in terms of "rummaging in the forefront of the collective global mind" ("The Net Is a Waste of Time"). The most significant Gibsonian figure of speech for cyberspace-as-Internet is the Hak Nam communal website that he describes in segments of *Idoru* and *All Tomorrow's Parties*. Although Gibson never uses the word "cyberspace" in the Bridge Trilogy, he does mention the Internet as part of his characters' world, and the only time he describes the "Net" in detail is when he is describing Hak Nam. The website therefore functions as a synecdoche for cyberspace: it is a cyberspatial part representative of the cyberspatial whole. Not only is Gibson's Hak Nam a synecdochical figure, but it is an elaboration of the urban metaphor. The website was named (both by Gibson and by the fictional hackers who founded the website) after a real-life place known variously as Hak Nam, City of Darkness, and Kowloon Walled City. Built as an outpost in the nineteenth century, the Walled City became the site of a Chinese enclave in the middle of British Hong Kong. Because the police had no jurisdiction over this district, the Walled City attracted squatters, drug addicts, and criminals. During the second half of the twentieth century, its inhabitants gradually transformed what used to be a fortress into a mazelike and densely populated ghetto-space. (The Walled City no longer exists; in 1993, it was torn down and replaced by a city park.) The communal website in *Idoru* and *All Tomorrow's Parties* is modeled on the urban labyrinth of Hak Nam. Here there are "no laws," "only agreements" (*Idoru*, 225). Here, moreover, are "jumbled shapes and textures" (*Idoru*, 225), "thousands of small windows," "countless unplanned strata," and an "accreted patchwork of shallow random balconies" where "nothing" is "even or regular" (*Idoru*, 195). Like the intricacy of the real-life Hak Nam, the intricacy of the virtual Hak Nam has a kind of organic quality. Gibson's descriptions of the website evoke images of insects, plant life, and mammalian hair. Surrounding the city, for example, is "a black fur of twisted pipe, antennas sagging under vine growth of cable" (*Idoru*, 195). To enter the city is to experience a kind of "squirming density" (*Idoru*, 195). To be inside the city is to inhabit a place that exists both in a state of aggressive vegetation (it is constantly "growing" and "being grown" [*Idoru*, 305]) and in a state of decomposition ("the Walled City luxuriates in apparent frank decay, in texture maps that constantly unravel, revealing of other textures, equally moth-eaten" [*All Tomorrow's Parties*, 193]). Together, the synecdoche of the Hak Nam website and the metaphor of the real-life Walled City depict cyberspace-as-Internet as an ecosystem where city-dwellers coexist in natural harmony with a jungle-like urban environment textured by organic disarray.

If the necessity of using figures of speech to describe cyberspace demonstrates that cyberspace eludes purely literal description, then the astonishing heterogeneity of these figures of speech demonstrates that cyberspace eludes purely figurative description as well. As one journalist observed in 1999, "it is hard to find the right metaphor for something so strange," and "the metaphors inevitably clash" (Johnson). Cyberspace, in other words, is so massive, so intricate, and so charged with contradictions that it cannot be compared directly to any one thing. To come up with a metaphor for cyberspace is only to bring attention to the poverty of that one metaphor and the wealth of alternative and equally valid metaphors. Perhaps this is why some commentators, such as Marcos Novak, have found it pointless to try to find the "right" metaphor for something so strange, instead creating metaphors that are willfully opaque: "Cyberspace is poetry inhabited," Novak writes cryptically, "and to navigate through it is to become a leaf on the wind of a dream" (229).

Other commentators, however, have responded to the language-defying nature of cyberspace not by creating metaphors for cyberspace's ineffability but rather by approaching this ineffability as a technical obstacle that will eventually be surmounted. One such commentator, a consultant for American Express, remarked in 1990 that "the hardware is available, the software is available, but the metaphor isn't" (Aiden McManus, quoted in Lewis, "Put On Your Data Glove"). Implicit in this remark is the idea that our lyric technologies—technologies of figuration such as metaphor and simile—are not yet now but will someday be equipped to represent "something so strange" as cyberspace. To take this idea one step further: what we need to represent cyberspace is a technology capable of describing something whose existence is both virtual and nonhypothetical, something whose structure defies not only the linearity of the sentence but also the planarity of the canvas and the three-

dimensionality of sculpture, something whose place on the temporal continuum cannot be defined.

Grasping the Presence of Cyberspace

Science fiction made it possible for Gibson to develop a representational technology advanced and sophisticated enough to accommodate "something so
strange" as cyberspace. More specifically, science fiction made it possible for
Gibson to create the bridge that forms the primary setting of *Virtual Light*
and *All Tomorrow's Parties*. To understand the bridge's function as a representational medium, one must first understand the place of the bridge in the
narrative world of the Bridge Trilogy. As we learn through flashbacks, the
earthquake-damaged Bay Bridge was raided and colonized by homeless people at some point in the trilogy's prehistory.[10] ("They climbed the wire fences,
the barricades, in such numbers that the chain link twisted, fell. They had
climbed the towers, then, more than thirty falling to their deaths. But when
the dawn came, survivors clung there, news helicopters circling them in the
gray light like patient dragonflies" [*Virtual Light*, 103].) Over the years, these
vagrants have transformed what used to be a thoroughfare between Oakland
and San Francisco into an intricate architectural structure reminiscent of the
favelas of Brazil (*All Tomorrow's Parties*, 18). Vibrant, labyrinthine, and "startlingly organic," this superstructure has grown "piecemeal, to no set plan"
(*Virtual Light*, 69), eventually becoming a "formless mass of stuff" in which
"no two pieces" are identical (*Virtual Light*, 194). Pathways through this
shantytown-like structure are made up of a "random mosaic of impacted lit-
ter" (*All Tomorrow's Parties*, 19). Similarly, homes are built from a wide assort-
ment of "scavenged surfaces" (*Virtual Light*, 70) that include "polished brass"
(*Virtual Light*, 70), "turquoise Formica" (*Virtual Light*, 194), "corroded alumi-
num" (*All Tomorrow's Parties*, 81), "mirrors" (*Virtual Light*, 70), "fake brick"
(*Virtual Light*, 194), "white-painted plywood" (*Virtual Light*, 101), "broken
marble" (*Virtual Light*, 70), "corrugated plastic" (*Virtual Light*, 70), and "green-
and-copper slabs of desoldered component-board" (*Virtual Light*, 194). Those
who live on the bridge, moreover, are "as mixed a bunch as their building
materials" (*Virtual Light*, 194). Known as "the bridge people," they are made
up of "all ages, races, colors"—from "the Korean boy with the bad leg, rum-
bling his father's soup wagon along as though it should have brakes" (*All
Tomorrow's Parties*, 80), to the forty-eight-year-old Jamaican woman whose

eyes are "a green pale as drift glass, DNA-echo of some British soldier" (*All Tomorrow's Parties*, 95).

The functions performed by the bridge are themselves wildly miscellaneous. In addition to serving as a massive housing complex, the bridge serves as a busy marketplace where the businesses are (fittingly) as "mixed" as are their owners and the materials out of which the bridge is made: a hair salon, for example, sells oysters, and a tattoo parlor serves breakfast (*All Tomorrow's Parties*, 67). The bridge is also a human ecosystem, an ecological unit composed of a community of organisms (rats, feral cats, mutant fish, the bridge people themselves) and the hybrid natural-artificial environment in which they live (an "organic complex" [*All Tomorrow's Parties*, 80] of hydroponic gardens, nests of decaying garbage, sewage hoses reminiscent of neural "ganglia" [*Virtual Light*, 100]). Moreover, the bridge is an experimental society, an "autonomous zone" where the law does not apply, a place where modern civilization goes to dream (*All Tomorrow's Parties*, 174). As the site of a kind of cultural subconscious, the bridge inspires irrational feelings, one of which is phobia: mystified outsiders allege that the bridge is populated by cannibals and anarchists who "just let [in] their own kind . . . like a cult" (*Virtual Light*, 165). Another irrational feeling is awe: the bridge is a spectacular work of art, a fabulous large-scale sculpture that attracts tourists from all over the globe. Often the awe and fear coincide, as when tourists and residents alike sense something eerily sentient about the physical structure of the bridge. At times, for instance, the bridge seems to sing to itself. "You can press your ear against it and hear the whole bridge sing," one bridge-dweller says (*Virtual Light*, 50), and a visitor from Japan identifies the voice of the bridge as a "strange music emerging from the bundled cables" (*Virtual Light*, 181). To those who behold it, moreover, the bridge often gives the feeling of being beheld in return: "The bridge seemed to look down at her, its eyes all torches and neon" (*Virtual Light*, 181). Indeed, the bridge is reminiscent of the artificial superintelligences that populate Gibsonian cyberspace. In *Virtual Light*, a philosopher likens the bridge to a computerized "mind" that has somehow attained an alien level of consciousness (71).

Its aura of artificial intelligence is not the only way in which the bridge resonates with Gibson's vision of cyberspace from the 1980s. The bridge intertextually incorporates numerous characteristics of the imaginary future-scape from Gibson's earlier work. For example, the vocabulary of altered consciousness that Gibson frequently uses in reference to the bridge—the entrance is a "gateway to dream and memory" (*All Tomorrow's Parties*, 19) and the bridge itself is "an accretion of dreams" (*Virtual Light*, 70)—resonates with Gibson's definition of cyberspace in *Neuromancer* as a "consensual hallucination." The geometric forms that can be found throughout the bridge's superstructure—a "cube of plywood" (*All Tomorrow's Parties*, 65), "rhomboids streaked with rust" (*All Tomorrow's Parties*, 17), an "oval segment" resembling "some mathematical formula barely breaking a topological surface in a computer representation" (*Virtual Light*, 226)—resonate with the complicated geometries of Gibsonian cyberspace. The supernatural qualities of the bridge—one character refers to it as a "fairyland" (*Virtual Light*, 70) and another ascribes a "fairy" quality to it (*All Tomorrow's Parties*, 18)—resonate with the voodoo ghosts from *Count Zero* and *Mona Lisa Overdrive*. The apocalyptic event that forever changed the nature of the bridge—after the mythical earthquake, the bridge would never again be the same—resonates with the apocalyptic "When It Changed," the mythical union of artificial intelligences, after which the world of cyberspace in Gibson's early fiction was never the same. The disorganized intricacy of the bridge—its superstructure, constructed "in the most random way possible," evokes "apparent disorder arranged in some deeper, some unthinkable fashion" (*All Tomorrow's Parties*, 120, 273)—resonates with the "unthinkable complexity" and "cluttered vastness" that characterize Gibsonian cyberspace. Finally, the overpowering effects of the bridge's immersive environment—to be inside the bridge is to be inundated with sensory information—resonate with Gibson's description of cyberspace as a place where the data is "so dense" that "you suffered sensory overload." So engulfing is the environment of the bridge that being inside it, according to one visitor, can feel like being submerged in an underwater realm (*All Tomorrow's Parties*, 185). Another visitor undergoes an experience akin to flat-lining while staring into the bridge's "cavern-mouth" entrance: "Steam was rising from the pots of soup-vendors, beneath a jagged arc of scavenged neon. . . . Rain-silvered plywood, broken marble from the walls of forgotten banks, corrugated plastic, polished brass, sequins, painted canvas, mirrors, chrome gone dull and peeling in the salt air. *So many things, too much for his reeling eye*" (*Virtual Light*, 70, emphasis added).

Not only does the bridge intertextually incorporate many of the features of Gibsonian cyberspace, but it also literalizes a multitude of key figures for cyberspace—figures both from Gibson's early fiction and from writings on cyberspace in the nineties. Cyberspace is a space. Cyberspace is a bridge.

Cyberspace is a city. Cyberspace is a junkyard. Cyberspace is a visual spectacle. Cyberspace is a commune. Cyberspace is an ecosystem. Cyberspace is a habitat. Cyberspace is a marketplace. Cyberspace is an architectural structure. Cyberspace is a venue for experimental consciousness. In the bridge, these and many other disparate figures of speech consolidate into the material features of a coherent and dynamic narrative world. The bridge is a space. The bridge is a bridge. The bridge is a city. The bridge is a junkyard. The bridge is a visual spectacle. The bridge is a commune. The bridge is an ecosystem. The bridge is a habitat. The bridge is a marketplace. The bridge is an architectural structure. The bridge is a venue for experimental consciousness.

By literalizing this intricate array of figures of speech, and thereby transcending the dichotomy between the literal and the figurative, Gibson's science-fictional bridge is able to describe an intricate referent that itself transcends the dichotomy between the figurative and the literal. As I suggested in the introduction to this book, science fiction is a heightened version of the verbal arts, which Elaine Scarry has identified as at once counterfactual (bringing into existence things not previously existing in the world) and counterfictional (displacing the faintness and two-dimensionality of imagining with the vivacity and solidity of the perceptible world). Not only is science fiction at once counterfactual and counterfictional, but it is also at once counterliteral and counterfigurative. Like the metaphor, science fiction is counterliteral: both the metaphor and science fiction bring into imagined existence things that do not exist in the world of literal facts. Hence, Gibson's science-fictional bridge brings into imagined existence cyberspace-as-bridge, cyberspace-as-junkyard, and other figures of speech for cyberspace. But science fiction is also counterfigurative, displacing the ordinary attributes of figurative language—its weightlessness, virtuality, as-if-ness, dependence on cognitive labor—with the vivacity, solidity, persistence, and givenness that characterize the perceptible world of literal facts. As a result of this literalization, cyberspace becomes something palpable, something we can recognize kinesthetically, something that makes immediate sense to our bodies. By working counterfiguratively, by literalizing figures of speech for cyberspace, Gibson's science-fictional bridge renders cyberspace available for representation.

The most prominent figure of speech literalized by the bridge is a compound metaphor that combines the metaphors of space, city, architecture, commune, lawless zone, subculture, habitat, and ecosystem, namely, the

Walled City as a metaphor for cyberspace. The two structures—Walled City and bridge—are strikingly similar. Almost all of the phrases that Gibson uses to describe Hak Nam can be used to describe the bridge as well: "jumbled shapes and textures," "thousands of small windows," "accreted patchwork," "no laws," "countless unplanned strata," "nothing about it even or regular," "vine growth of cable," "squirming density," "growing" and "being grown," "frank decay." In fact, Gibson explicitly identifies the Walled City as the inspiration for the bridge in the acknowledgments to *Idoru:*

> Sogho Ishii, the Japanese director, introduced me to Kowloon Walled City via the photographs of Ryuji Miyamoto. It was Ishii-san's idea that we should make a science fiction movie there. We never did, but the Walled City continued to haunt me, though I knew no more about it than I could gather from Miyamoto's stunning images, which eventually provided most of the texture for the Bridge in my novel *Virtual Light*. (*Idoru*, "Thanks")

As Gibson's comments here indicate (and as the novels themselves already suggest), the bridge and the Hak Nam website share the same texture—namely, the texture of the Walled City. But in the Hak Nam website, the city is merely figurative and this texture is merely virtual. The bridge literalizes and substantiates this texture. It is literally a densely populated urban space. It is literally a massive habitat. It is literally a labyrinthine architectural structure. It is literally a patchwork accretion of junk. It is literally a haven for outlaws and subcultures. By literalizing what in the Walled City website remains merely virtual, Gibson's bridge literalizes both the synecdochical relation of cyberspace to the Walled City website and the metaphorical relation of cyberspace to the real-life Walled City.

In addition to literalizing Hak Nam, the bridge literalizes an array of specific metaphors for cyberspace—some of which I have already mentioned in brief. As a marketplace, the bridge literalizes the metaphor of commerce. As a piece of freeway, the bridge literalizes the metaphor of transportation. As a site of visually spectacular parades and public rituals, the bridge literalizes the metaphor of pageantry. As an oracular medium whose cables frequently transmit "some message of vast, obscure moment" (*Virtual Light*, 226), the bridge literalizes the metaphor of mysticism. As a repository where remnants of culture (dolls, antique watches, the "wingless carcass of a 747" [*Virtual Light*, 71]) are collected and stored, the bridge literalizes the metaphor of the archive. And as a physical extension of the human sensorium—its manifold cables and fibers conduct information in the form of vibrations—the bridge literalizes the neurological metaphor.

Furthermore, Gibson's bridge evokes and literalizes key figures of speech associated with hypertext. Most obviously, the bridge literalizes the metaphor of the web. It is literally a complex, interconnected arrangement. Its nodal structures are "crazy little shanties" and "whole house-trailers" (*Virtual Light*, 193) that the bridge people have "lashed up" (*All Tomorrow's Parties*, 85) and "glued into the suspension with big globs of adhesive, like grasshoppers in a spider-web" (*Virtual Light*, 193). Interlinking these nodes are plastic tubing, aircraft cable, "webworks of two-by-four fir" (*All Tomorrow's Parties*, 108), and the original cables of the bridge (each of which, we are told, contains 17,464 strands of wire [*Virtual Light*, 50]). Through the "crazy tangle" of the bridge's porous openwork (*Virtual Light*, 195), the multilinear intricacy of hypertext becomes readily graspable.

The bridge also literalizes the metaphor of the visual collage. Literally a giant patchwork of found objects, the bridge incorporates old fragments into new contexts: "There was a different material anywhere you looked, almost none of it being used for what it had originally been intended for" (*Virtual Light*, 194). In recontextualizing fragments, the bridge often juxtaposes dissonant elements. A flight of steps is made up of "all different kinds of stairs patched in under there, plywood and welded steel" (*Virtual Light*, 193–194). The façade of a shop is an assemblage of "turquoise Formica, fake brick, fragments of broken tile worked in swirls and sunbursts and flowers" (*Virtual Light*, 194). A piece of furniture that has been "*collaged* from paint-flecked oak" is composed of different wooden surfaces "scavenged from the shells of older houses" (*All Tomorrow's Parties*, 80, emphasis added). Each of these instances of juxtaposition is a small-scale collage that contributes to the large-scale collage of the bridge as a whole. Through this vivid collage, the juxtapositions of hypertext—the ways in which the linking process can simultaneously conjoin and disjoin radically diverse images and texts—become readily graspable.

Similarly, the bridge literalizes the kaleidoscopic metaphor. It is literally an optical instrument: "the central pier," we are told, functions as "one of the world's largest pinhole cameras" by allowing "light shining in through a single tiny hole" to project "a huge image of the underside of the lower deck, the nearest tower, and the surrounding bay" (*Virtual Light*, 226). More important, the bridge is a space of perpetual reconfiguration and permutation. No version of the bridge is ever final. As one bridge-dweller observes, the bridge "grew a little, changed a little, every day" (*Virtual Light,* 150). Restaurants and shops have frequently "changed names on the bridge" and "changed size and shape too" (*All Tomorrow's Parties,* 67). Moreover, the point of focus of the bridge is always contingent on the random wanderings of the individual bridge-dweller or visitor. Each person experiences the bridge as a unique configuration of fragmentary images. The kaleidoscope of the bridge, in other words, is less a thing as it is and more a thing as it is subjectively perceived. Through the bridge's literally kaleidoscopic nature, the interactive complexity of hypertext becomes readily graspable.

Finally, the bridge literalizes the metaphor of the funhouse. The bridge disorients. Originally designed as a medium of in-between transit—transit between San Francisco and Oakland, which Gertrude Stein famously characterized as "no there there," as Gibson himself has characterized cyberspace[11]— the postapocalyptic bridge is now a point of destination. It is a bridge that cannot take you across. At once interstitial and terminal, it has no clear beginning or end, no clear entryway or exit, no clear boundary between inside and outside. To explore it is to lose oneself in an architectural space marked everywhere by discontinuity. As one tourist observes: the bridge is made up of "lots of narrow little stairways snaking up between stalls and shuttered microbars, and no pattern to it at all. He guessed they all led up into the same ratsnest, but there was no guarantee they'd all connect up" (*Virtual Light,* 195). This effect of spatial disorientation is enhanced by the many sources of hallucinatory sensory stimulation that are installed throughout the bridge. To be inside the bridge's environment is to experience the kinds of psychedelic imagery that one might find in a carnival: "halogen-shadows" (*Virtual Light,* 87), the garish light of "Christmas bulbs" and "recycled neon" (*Virtual Light,* 69), and "outsize leaf shadows" cast by "the unearthly light of a hydroponics operation" (*All Tomorrow's Parties,* 80). Through the funhouse of the bridge, the disorienting nature of cyberspace becomes readily graspable.

At the same time that the bridge *literalizes* metaphors for hypertext, the verbal form of the bridge—the prose that *literally* generates the bridge's representational technology—is *figuratively* hypertextual. In describing the bridge, Gibson often uses parataxis, a rhetorical device whereby multiple clauses or phrases are juxtaposed without conjunctions and/or without being subordinated to an "if/then" syntactic structure. As George Landow has pointed out, parataxis and hypertext are alike in that both are nonsequential: just as the order of lexias is not what determines the essential meaning of a hypertext, the order of items in a paratactic list is not what determines the essential meaning of the list. By using parataxis, then, Gibson describes the bridge in figuratively hypertextual prose that aspires to the nonhierarchical condition of hypertext. In the following sentence, for example, each item is a figurative lexia whose place in the list is irrelevant to the description's overall effect: "He passed stalls faced with turquoise Formica, fake brick, fragments of broken tile worked into swirls and sunbursts and flowers" (*Virtual Light*, 194). The effect of this description would remain unchanged if it were rewritten as follows: "He passed stalls faced with fake brick, turquoise Formica, swirls of tile worked into broken flowers and fragmentary sunbursts." Likewise, Gibson's description of the bridge as a patchwork of "rain-silvered plywood, broken marble from the walls of forgotten banks, corrugated plastic, polished brass, sequins, painted canvas, mirrors, chrome gone dull and peeling in the salt air" (*Virtual Light*, 70) would not be changed in meaning if it were rewritten as "mirrors, sequins, polished brass, painted canvas, chrome gone dull and peeling in the salt air, corrugated plastic, rain-silvered plywood, broken marble from the walls of forgotten banks." And Gibson's account of the contents of one bridge person's room—"small glass jars of spices, identical jars containing steel screws, an ancient Bakelite telephone reminding him of the origin of the verb 'to dial,' rolls of many different kinds and colors of adhesive tape, twists of heavy copper wire, pieces of what he took to be salt-water tackle, and, finally, a bundle of dusty candle-stubs secured with a rotting rubber band" (*Virtual Light*, 225)—would be unchanged if the "lexias" were reorganized: our impression of the room would remain the same regardless of the sequence in which the images are catalogued.

There is, however, one paratactic passage whose meaning would be altered by the rearrangement of items. But this is only because to rearrange the items listed in this passage would be to interfere with the passage's enactment of another principle of electronic textuality: "copy and paste." This term refers to a procedure that allows the computer user to "select" and "copy" a fragment of text from a source and "paste" this fragment of text onto a destination. The following description of the bridge from *Virtual Light* is a figurative copy-and-paste destination.

Its steel bones, its stranded tendons, were lost within an accretion of dreams: tattoo parlors, gaming arcades, dimly lit stalls stacked with decaying magazines, sellers of fireworks, of cut bait, betting shops, sushi bars, unlicensed pawnbrokers, herbalists, barbers, bars. Dreams of commerce,

their locations generally corresponding with the decks that had once carried vehicular traffic; while above them, rising to the very peaks of the cable
towers, lifted the intricately suspended barrio, with its unnumbered population and its zones of more private fantasy. (70)

The source from which this fragmentary verbal texture has been extracted is a
description of virtual reality from Gibson's 1991 essay "Academy Leader."
"The architecture of virtual reality," he writes in this earlier text, is

> imagined as an accretion of dreams: tattoo parlors, shooting galleries, pin-
> ball arcades, dimly lit stalls stacked with damp-stained years of men's
> magazines, chili joints, premises of unlicensed denturists, of fireworks and
> cut bait, betting shops, sushi bars, purveyors of sexual appliances, pawn-
> brokers, wonton counters, love hotels, hotdog stands, tortilla factories,
> Chinese greengrocers, liquor stores, herbalists, chiropractors, barbers, bars.
>   These are dreams of commerce. Above them rise intricate barrios, zones
> of more private fantasy. (28)

While the two passages are not exactly identical, they are close enough in
form and content to evoke the electronic textuality of "copy and paste." By
figuratively incorporating this cut-and-paste method, Gibson's prose description of the bridge aspires to the collage-like condition of hypertext. To put it
otherwise, Gibson's cut-and-paste collage-like prose aspires to the condition
of what Marie-Laure Ryan has identified as a form of writing in which text is
not "a unified work to be experienced in its totality" but rather "a mass substance," a "resource that can be scooped up by the screenful" ("Cyberspace,
Virtuality, and the Text," 99).

Beyond incorporating the collage-like nature of electronic cut-and-paste,
the intertext above is remarkable for its imagery of materiality. Like the passage from "Academy Leader," which depicts virtual reality in terms of palpable
objects such as "damp-stained years of men's magazines," the bridge as a whole
represents cyberspace in strikingly material terms. In contrast to cyberspace,
which is a notional environment populated by disembodied minds, the bridge
is a concrete environment populated by physical bodies. To some extent, the
materiality of Gibson's bridge is a consequence of the bridge's science-fictional
nature: the bridge is a literalization of metaphors, and to literalize a metaphor—to subject a metaphor to counterfigurative procedures—is to augment
the metaphor's sensuous vivacity, to incorporate the metaphor into the world of
material details. But there is another dimension to the bridge's materiality. The

bridge literalizes the "materialization"—the actualization—of cyberspace in real life. In doing so, the bridge helps us to grasp something whose place in time was unstable during the nineties—something that was in the middle of changing from imaginary futurescape to everyday actuality.

Nostalgia for Cyberspace

The literalization of cyberspace's "materialization" is not the only way in which Gibson's bridge helps us to grasp cyberspace's ambiguous location on the temporal continuum. The bridge also (and more importantly) literalizes lyric time. As I mentioned in the introduction, a study by George Wright has shown that the tense most characteristic of poetry is the simple present. Paradoxically, the simple present is almost never used in spoken English to indicate simple present-tense action. Unlike the present progressive, which situates the action in a palpable context of "now," the simple present tense is fraught with multiple temporal features: timelessness, duration, pastlikeness, futurity. In using this tense without specifying the time of action, poets locate their poetry in what Wright describes as "a realm outside our normal conscious time world" (565).

That Gibson's science-fictional bridge literalizes the lyric tense is evident in the following scene from *Virtual Light*. A tourist, lost inside the mazes of the bridge, suddenly undergoes an epiphany: he realizes that he is standing in the middle of a place where the obsolescence of the postmillennial occurred long ago:

> *We are come not only past the century's closing,* he thought, *the millennium's turning, but to the end of something else. Era? Paradigm? Everywhere, the signs of closure.*
> Modernity was ending.
> Here, on the bridge, it long since had. (105)

Unlike the nonbridge world, where time flows in a single direction from past to present to future, the bridge is a world in which the present has "long since" become a thing of the past. Here, that which is posthistoric and still to come has already taken on the attributes of the "ancient and eternal" (*All Tomorrow's Parties*, 273). To be inside the bridge is to find oneself occupying the same temporal universe occupied by the figures on Keats's Grecian urn—a universe that exists beyond the successiveness of ordinary levels of time.

Only a narrative universe that literalizes lyric time has the capacity to represent cyberspace, for cyberspace exemplifies what Philip Fisher has identified as the unstable temporal realities that characterize our world of competitive technological capitalism. The world in which we live, Fisher observes, is one in which

> the future and the possible, the promising idea and the articulated plan, have a complex reality long before they are real. Fictions that in stable systems are the marks of fraud and the work of charlatans are in unstable systems the sketch, or one possible sketch, of what will turn out to be the real just slightly later in one lifetime. Equally important is the fact that everything that is now fully real becomes potentially unreal because it is or might be threatened by some new scheme of things in which it would disappear or become merely decorative, as horses are today now that they are no longer primarily used for farm work. What does not exist, but might someday, takes on a half-real, half-unreal quality long before it exists. But all that now exists is equally half-real, half-unreal because it exists under the threat that it might soon become obsolete or be discarded. (*Still the New World*, 13)

Fisher's insights about technological change help to account for the intricacy of cyberspace's ever-evolving status as part of "reality." During the early 1980s, cyberspace already possessed "a complex reality" as a "possible sketch" of the future; that is, it had already taken on "a half-real, half-unreal quality" years before the technology actually materialized. During the late 1980s and early 1990s, Gibson's "promising idea" began to take on the qualities of fact, but it had not yet completely lost the aura of a futuristic fantasy. By the turn of the century, cyberspace had become what it is today: an everyday part of most people's lives and therefore a "fully real" phenomenon. Yet this phase of cyberspace, like every other phase of cyberspace, is only temporary. As Fisher points out, "all that now exists is equally half-real, half-unreal because it exists under the threat that it might soon become obsolete or be discarded." It is not too difficult to imagine a future world in which cyberspace, like the horse that is no longer used for farm work, has become an obsolete and "merely decorative" relic.

The lyric framework of the bridge retrospectively accommodates all the different versions of cyberspace: the futuristic sketch that Gibson drew in the early eighties; the exotic new technology that generated headlines in the late eighties and early nineties; the everyday household tool that we began to take for granted in the late nineties; and the antique relic that cyberspace will inevitably have become at some point in the not-too-distant future. The bridge forces us to reminisce about—to look back on—something that we still think of as actively "now." What results from this reminiscence is a strangely dislocating sense of nostalgia for cyberspace. If, as Fredric Jameson has suggested, science fiction makes us conscious of the present as the past of some unexpected future rather than as the future of a past,[12] then the bridge makes us feel nostalgic for the future of a past that used to be the past of some unexpected future. Through this future-perfect nostalgia, the intricacy of cyberspace's place in history becomes available for representation.

Nostalgia for cutting-edge technology is an emotion to which Gibson seems exquisitely susceptible.[13] "My first impulse, when presented with any spanking-new piece of computer hardware, is to imagine how it will look in 10 years' time, gathering dust under a card table in a thrift shop," he reveals in a 1999 essay. And in his afterword to the 1992 electronic edition of the Cyberspace novels, he confesses that it gives him great pleasure to "contemplate that process whereby every tech, however sharp this morning, is invariably supplanted by the new, the unthinkable, and to imagine these words, unread and finally inaccessible, gathering dust at the back of some drawer in some year far up the road." As a structure whose façade is decidedly low-tech—it has a "queer medieval energy," and during the day it resembles "the ruin of England's Brighton Pier, as though viewed through some cracked kaleidoscope of vernacular style" (*Virtual Light*, 69–70)—the bridge invites being construed as Gibson's vision of an obsolete cyberspace "gathering dust" in "some year far up the road." Indeed, the bridge radiates the aura of an antique object. As more than one reader has noted, Gibson's bridge evokes the nostalgic artwork of Joseph Cornell, a modernist sculptor who used glass-fronted boxes as the settings for careful arrangements of dried flowers, Victorian toys, fading newsprint, sepia-toned photographs, and other such relics.[14] Cornell is one of Gibson's favorite artists, and in some sense the bridge can be thought of as a Cornell-like shadow-box collage. Its architectural framework is the setting for evocative patterns that Gibson has carefully constructed from outdated buzzwords, allusions, metaphors, images, and other bits of cyberspace debris.

To focus on the low-tech façade of the bridge, however, is to overlook its actual high-tech capabilities. As I have tried to show, the prose-generated space of the bridge functions as a powerful and sophisticated representational technology. Gibson's science-fictional bridge has the storage, the memory, and the bandwidth to represent "something so strange" as cyberspace. To echo the words of the consultant for American Express: the hardware and software for cyberspace have been available for some time. With Gibson's bridge, the language for representing cyberspace becomes available too.

3

War Trauma

Yesterday preceded today. Today precedes tomorrow. Past events stay in the past. Consciousness is an embodied experience that occurs in the first-person "I."

Such axioms are taken for granted in the narrative of everyday reality. They are incompatible with the psychological reality of trauma. Traumatic events by definition elude immediate first-person embodied experience, and they tend not to stay within their native chronological and spatial contexts. As Cathy Caruth has remarked, trauma is "locatable not in the simple violent or original event in an individual's past, but rather in the way that its very unassimilated nature—the way it was precisely not known in the first instance—returns to haunt the survivor later on" (Caruth, *Unclaimed Experience*, 4). A traumatic event, in other words, is so overpowering that it cannot be experienced while it is happening. Instead it is reexperienced in delayed, repetitive form—through flashbacks, nightmares, intrusive hallucinations, bodiless memories of missing subjectivity.

As a phenomenon whereby "the most direct seeing of a violent event may occur as an absolute inability to know it" (Caruth, *Unclaimed Experience*, 91–92), trauma constitutes a paradox. How is it possible for the "most direct" knowledge of an event to occur as that event's "absolute" unknowability? The difficulty of resolving this paradox is evidenced in nonfiction accounts of trauma by a persistent recourse to figurative language: trauma is (figuratively) an "out-of-body" experience in which the victim (figuratively) "relives" the event that caused the psychic wound or the survivor inhabits a reality that is (figuratively) "otherworldly." Even in matter-of-fact accounts, trauma is characterized in figurative terms. Such counterliteral expression often takes the form of similes in which the explicitness of the figuration is indicated (almost imperceptibly) by subtle phrases such as "as if" or "as though." For example, according to the diagnostic criteria for post-traumatic stress disorder (PTSD) outlined in 2000 by the American Psychiatric Association in the fourth edition of the *Diagnostic and Statistical Manual of Mental Disorders (DSM-IV-TR)*, symptoms of PTSD include "feeling as if the traumatic event were recurring." Likewise, according to *The Body Remembers: The Psychophysiology of Trauma and Trauma Treatment* (2000) by Babette Rothschild, someone undergoing a traumatic incident may "feel as if he had become disembodied," and a traumatic flashback "may feel as though it is happening now" (65, 130). Other nonfiction accounts of trauma make more vivid use of figurative language. In *Traumatic Realism: The Demands of Holocaust Representation* (2000), Michael Rothberg situates the unthinkable imperative of documenting the trauma of genocide (can a reality-shattering event such as the Holocaust possibly share representational space with the familiar reality of everyday existence?) within a conspicuously metaphorical location: "Trauma resides not in the extreme event itself but in the barbed wire that holds together and separates life and death, the inside and the outside, the familiar and the radically foreign" (136). In *Writing History, Writing Trauma* (2001), the historian Dominick LaCapra applies various metaphors—for example, the metaphorical "implosion" of verb tenses—to characterize psychological trauma: "The past returns and the future is blocked or fatalistically caught up in a melancholic feedback loop. In acting out, tenses implode, and it is as if one were back there in the past reliving the traumatic scene" (21).

One of the most dramatic instances of figurative language in nonfiction accounts of trauma can be found in Roger Luckhurst's 1998 essay "The Science-Fictionalization of Trauma." Noting the increasing frequency with which survivors of abuse in contemporary America have turned to the alien abduction narrative as a way of explaining psychological trauma, Luckhurst employs the trope of apostrophe to invoke and bring to life the archetypical trauma-victim-as-abductee:

> You suffer aversions, phobias (to specific places, sleeping at night, sex, medical doctors, dentists, perhaps children), and you have a profound dread, built around an absence, a gap, that you feel is structural to your life. This gap can range from the vague to a specific moment: a disturbed night, the

oppressive residues of a nightmare, perhaps coupled with the distress of nosebleeds or puzzling marks on the body; a sense of confused temporality which constitutes a determinable gap of "missing time." Your phobias may become increasingly unmanageable, forcing you to seek help, or else (more commonly) flashes of content begin to return to fill in the absence. . . . This is what you will remember: you wake at night/your car fails on a lonely road, and you become aware of small figures surrounding you. They are small, gray, and not human. Your partner/passenger is immobile, somehow "switched off." You are injected or pierced by a beam of light. Either you feel yourself floating off the bed/out of the car, or, without transition, you reawake to find yourself naked and paralyzed on a table in an unfamiliar room. The figures gather around you, and proceed to examine you. . . . You survive this, only to experience the intense gaze of one, perhaps differentiated being, who seems to penetrate your mind, implanting messages, most often of the kind: "You will not remember." (30–31)

In this eerie, incantatory, and oddly lyrical second-person invocation of the trauma-victim-as-abductee, an intriguing conundrum emerges. Why exactly does the victim, when confronted with a mysterious gap in memory, fill that gap with spectral images of extraterrestrial captors? Why, in other words, do victims find the science-fictional scenario of alien abduction so compelling as an etiological framework for understanding traumatic experience? Luckhurst's answer to such questions is a historicized one. He argues that the emergence of the trauma-victim-as-abductee is a recent development in American culture. According to Luckhurst, the factors behind this development include growing fears surrounding the pervasiveness of technology in our lives, the rise of New Age countercultures that challenge the authority of scientific discourse, and the emergence of abuse as "the determining 'secret' of contemporary subjectivity" (32). Together, such historical determinants have contributed to what Luckhurst identifies as the "science-fictionalization of trauma" in the late twentieth century.

My own answer to the questions posed above is not historical. The reason why so many trauma victims fill the gap in memory with science-fictional images is that trauma is always already science-fictionalized. Moments ago I cited several instances of the way in which nonfiction texts, in attempting to accommodate representations of trauma, have persistently sought the resources of figurative language. It is even more strikingly and importantly the case that "realistic" texts (whether fiction or nonfiction), in attempting to accommodate representations of trauma, have persistently sought the resources of science fiction. (Where realist accounts of trauma do not seek the resources of science fiction, they often instead call attention to the deficiencies of realism as a representational resource: hence the painful eloquence of mutism, for example, in Pat Barker's 1991 historical novel *Regeneration*, based on the experiences of British soldiers being treated for shell shock during the Great War.) Science-fiction icons, scenarios, and motifs offer a strangely accurate lexicon for articulating the most elusive aspects of psychological trauma. The psychiatrist and trauma expert Judith Lewis Herman identifies one such motif when she remarks that trauma "gives rise to complicated, sometimes uncanny alterations of consciousness, which George Orwell, one of the committed truth-tellers of our century, called 'doublethink,' and which mental health professionals, searching for a calm, precise language, call 'dissociation'" (*Trauma and Recovery*, 1). While Herman posits a correspondence between traumatic dissociation and the SF scenario of Orwellian "doublethink," the literary and cultural theorist Kirby Farrell posits a correspondence between dissociative fugue states and the SF scenario of time travel: both, Farrell observes, involve wandering "out of the conventional mind," "beyond creaturely limits," and "into the oblivion of time" (*Post-Traumatic Culture*, 106).

The appeal of time travel, alien abduction, and other SF motifs as strategies for narrating traumatic experience lies in their capacity to substantiate metaphors for psychological trauma. In science fiction, figurative expressions surrounding trauma are granted literal veracity: trauma is literally an out-of-body experience; the traumatic event is literally relived in time; the reality inhabited by the survivor of trauma is literally unearthly. Axioms taken for granted in everyday reality—axioms inconsistent with the psychological reality of trauma—cannot be taken for granted in science fiction. Tomorrow may precede yesterday. Consciousness may transcend the embodied "I." Past events may refuse to stay in the past. Trauma's otherworldly temporality, which in the world of realism must be characterized as occurring subjectively inside one person's mind, can become externalized and validated in science fiction as objective fact. By allowing trauma a concrete, logical, nonparadoxical part in the fabric of existence, science fiction operates as a powerful testimonial framework in which trauma can become available for representation.

In this chapter, I explore four science-fictional testimonies to war trauma: Olaf Stapledon's *Last and First Men: A Story of the Near and Far Future* (1930), Kurt Vonnegut's *Slaughterhouse-Five* (1969), Joe Haldeman's *The Forever War*

(1974), and Tim O'Brien's *The Things They Carried* (1990). While these texts are linked by a number of self-evident commonalities—all four are twentieth-century prose narratives that revolve around catastrophic events—they will appear more dissimilar than alike to most readers. *Last and First Men* is outwardly perceptible and generally perceived as a sweeping cosmological romance, a starry fantasia with little basis in worldly reality. *Slaughterhouse-Five* overtly frames itself as a semiautobiographical science-fiction tale based on Vonnegut's own experiences as an American POW who survived the 1945 firebombing of Dresden in World War II. *The Forever War* is a work of futuristic military science fiction that, while not manifestly autobiographic, has come to be associated intimately with Haldeman's personal experiences as a combat engineer in Vietnam. *The Things They Carried*, widely considered an autobiographical collection of short fiction about O'Brien's struggle as a veteran to come to terms with his painful memories of the Vietnam War, is rarely (if ever) approached as science fiction.

Yet to bring the four narratives into one another's vicinity—to juxtapose them within a single conceptual zone—is to discover that the variations among them are actually illustrations of the transcendent flexibility and expansiveness of science fiction as a representational form. In a multitude of ways and to varying extents, all four accounts of war trauma are remarkably self-reflexive, calling attention to the limits and possibilities of representation, raising questions about the capacity of language to accommodate extreme autobiographical realities, and probing the relationship between what is literally true and what is figuratively true. Dissociation finds mimetic counterparts in science-fictional metafiction and intertextuality. The impact of wounding finds itself recounted not as the straightforward memory of a past event but as the endlessly deferred possibility of a normal future. The unassimilated nature of trauma finds itself reflected in a narrative form that by nature resists assimilation. Shell shock finds testimonial expression in lyric voices—science-fictional voices—that speak from outside of ordinary temporality.

Perhaps it is inevitable, given the nature of our subject matter, that "War Trauma" should divagate from linear chronology. The body of this chapter will begin with a topically organized discussion of the three most recent texts (Vonnegut, Haldeman, O'Brien). It will conclude with a close analysis of the text that among the four is chronologically earliest. Although the SF elements of Stapledon's narrative are plain, *Last and First Men* is, of the four main cases under consideration, the case whose relevance to war trauma is least apparent. By examining this ostensibly out-of-place specimen in the wake of a discussion of examples that more obviously exemplify the correlations between SF and trauma, I hope to show that *Last and First Men* is actually a text in which these correlations are most vividly exemplified.

From Autobiographical Paratext to SF Metafiction

Slaughterhouse-Five is practically a textbook case of a science-fictional representation of war trauma. In particular, it is a text in which war trauma, autobiography, paratext, metafiction, and science fiction—elements all co-present, albeit in different ways and to varying degrees, in the other three cases—are presented as explicitly interrelated. To open with *Slaughterhouse-Five* will therefore establish a helpful context in which to understand the science-fictional testimonies to trauma in other cases of war literature.

Slaughterhouse-Five is a meta-science-fictional novel. It self-consciously calls attention to the relationship of science fiction to trauma and the corresponding relationship of science fiction to autobiography. Vonnegut calls attention to his subject matter even before the narrative has begun. In the title page, directly below the author's name, are the following lines:

> A FOURTH-GENERATION GERMAN-AMERICAN
> NOW LIVING IN EASY CIRCUMSTANCES
> ON CAPE COD
> [AND SMOKING TOO MUCH],
> WHO, AS AN AMERICAN INFANTRY SCOUT
> HORS DE COMBAT,
> AS A PRISONER OF WAR,
> WITNESSED THE FIRE-BOMBING
> OF DRESDEN, GERMANY,
> "THE FLORENCE OF THE ELBE,"
> A LONG TIME AGO,
> AND SURVIVED TO TELL THE TALE.

> THIS IS A NOVEL
> SOMEWHAT IN THE TELEGRAPHIC SCHIZOPHRENIC
> MANNER OF TALES

OF THE PLANET TRALFAMADORE,
WHERE THE FLYING SAUCERS
COME FROM.
PEACE.

Paradoxically, these lines call attention to the connection between science fiction and autobiography by framing this connection asyndetically as a disconnection. The first twelve lines refer to the novelist's wartime experience. The subsequent six lines refer to the science-fictional content of the novel. How exactly the two parts are connected is left unexplained: they are simply juxtaposed in a paratactic manner without any explicit conjunction or transition. (I inserted the horizontal slash to make the absence of an explanatory transition/conjunction emphatically visible.) The abruptness of the juxtaposition—the conspicuous absence of a logical connection—generates a question in the reader's mind: What is the link between the author's traumatic experience and the science-fictional mode in which the novel is written?

The answer emerges in the preface to the book. *Slaughterhouse-Five* opens with an autobiographical paratext in which Vonnegut describes his personal struggle with the challenge of representing traumatic experience. A paratext, as Gerard Genette has explained, is a framing device that presents a text as a book to its readers. Examples include titles, epigraphs, prefaces, and dust jackets. In *Slaughterhouse-Five,* the function of the paratext (in the form of title page and preface) is to institute a conspicuous boundary between the world outside the text and the world inside the text. By instituting this boundary, the paratext calls attention to the inability of ordinary language to represent trauma and the ability of science fiction to represent trauma. It is only when the paratext ends and the science fiction begins that Vonnegut is able to narrate the story of trauma. In other words, it is only when Vonnegut leaves behind the ordinary realistic language of straightforward first-person autobiography (the discursive reality outside the text) and enters the lyric otherworldly realm of science fiction (the discursive reality inside the text) that he is able to bring his traumatic experience to representation. Without the paratext, the book would not be meta-science-fictional; it would not set up and thereby call attention to the contrast between the two discursive worlds.

That the difficulty of representing trauma haunts the discursive reality outside the text is made clear at the very beginning of the preface:

When I got home from the Second World War twenty-three years ago, I thought it would be easy for me to write about the destruction of Dresden, since all I would have to do would be to report what I had seen. . . . But not many words about Dresden came from my mind then—not enough of them to make a book, anyway. And not many words come now, either. (2)

Vonnegut's wish to perform the straightforward act of recording his wartime experience—"All I would have to do would be to report what I had seen"— is defied by the nonstraightforward structure of the experience itself. As Vonnegut has put it elsewhere, in an interview:

There was a complete blank where the bombing of Dresden took place, because I don't remember. And I looked up several of my war buddies and they didn't remember, either. They didn't want to talk about it. There was a complete forgetting of what it was like. There were all kinds of information surrounding the event, but as far as my memory bank was concerned, the center had been pulled right out of the story. (W. Allen, 94)

Ordinary language cannot fill the "complete blank" where there ought to be memories of the bombing of Dresden. Speech cannot fill the place in Vonnegut's mind where "the center had been pulled right out of the story." Even the simplest visual imagery cannot adequately fill this void. At one point in the preface to *Slaughterhouse-Five*, Vonnegut relates his attempt to draw a picture of his experience in Dresden:

I had outlined the Dresden story many times. The best outline I ever made, or anyway the prettiest one, was on the back of a roll of wallpaper.
    I used my daughter's crayons, a different color for each main character. One end of the wallpaper was the beginning of the story, and the other end was the end, and then there was all that middle part, which was the middle. And the blue line met the red line and then the yellow line, and the yellow line stopped because the character represented by the yellow line was dead. And so on. The destruction of Dresden was represented by a vertical band of orange cross-hatching, and all the lines that were still alive passed through it, came out the other side. (5)

Instead of creating a visual illustration of his experience, Vonnegut illustrates the difficulty of bringing this experience to representation. Opaque and diagrammatic, the picture is virtually empty of details. The deployment of various colors ("a different color for each main character") might suggest that some kind of code is at work here, but the code (insofar as one exists) is indecipherable: Vonnegut's explanation of the diagram is itself virtually empty of details.

What the crayoned picture renders so visible is the "complete blank where the bombing of Dresden took place." It is this "blank"—what Caruth describes as "a gap that carries the force of the event and does so precisely at the expense of simple knowledge" ("Trauma and Experience," 7)—that makes it impossible for Vonnegut to produce a straightforward account of his experience.

Other-Than-First-Person Automata: Billy Pilgrim, Tim O'Brien

While the representational crisis of trauma haunts the preface to *Slaughterhouse-Five*, the crisis subsides once we have entered the discursive world inside the novel. The crisis is resolved, more specifically, through the science-fictional figure of Billy Pilgrim. In some ways, Billy is a double for Vonnegut himself. Both Pilgrim and Vonnegut served in the U.S. Army during World War II while in their early twenties. Both were captured by Germans during the Battle of the Bulge in 1944. As American prisoners of war, both witnessed the fire bombing of Dresden, Germany, by Allied Forces in February of 1945—an event that would haunt both Pilgrim and Vonnegut for the rest of their lives. But Billy is not identical to Vonnegut. This is made clear in two places in the novel where the author appears—fleetingly—as a personage separate from Billy. One of these appearances occurs in a scene where Pilgrim is being sorted along with other prisoners of war captured by the Germans. "I was there," Vonnegut suddenly interjects before bringing the scene to an abrupt close (67). A second appearance occurs at the end of a scene in which the prisoners of war arrive in Dresden.

> The skyline was intricate and voluptuous and absurd. It looked like a Sunday school picture of Heaven to Billy Pilgrim.
> Somebody behind him in the boxcar said, "Oz." That was I. That was me. The only other city I'd ever seen was Indianapolis, Indiana. (148)

In both of the passages cited above, the intrusion of the author's presence occurs at the end of a scene: having suddenly materialized out of nowhere, Vonnegut quickly disappears back into that same mysterious void. The ellipsis that follows each appearance—the ellipsis that temporarily suspends the narrative—marks the author's inability to elaborate on his participation in the war. These are the most direct references to his own experience that Vonnegut can allow himself to make in the novel: brief, stark, scarce sentences such as

"I was there." Vonnegut's powerlessness to narrate the story directly in the first-person "I" is apparent not only from the extreme brevity of his appearances but also from the syntactic alignment of "I" with "somebody" (indicating an unspecified or unknown person) and "that" (indicating an entity less immediate than "this"). Even when using the word "I," Vonnegut is not truly occupying the immediate nominative first-person pronoun. Vonnegut himself—Vonnegut-as-Vonnegut—cannot tell the story through a simple first-person "I"; he can barely even make the simple assertion that he was there.

Billy, then, is not commensurable with Vonnegut, and this is precisely why Vonnegut is able to tell the story of Dresden through him. More object than subject, Billy Pilgrim constitutes an other-than-first-person medium through which Vonnegut can tell the story of trauma at a remove. As such, the character of Billy has an army of analogues in a range of war literature. Some of the most striking analogues can be found in poetry written by soldiers who fought in World War I. One example is the addressee in Edgell Rickword's poem "The Soldier Addresses his Body." "I shall be mad if you get smashed about," Rickword writes, referring to his body not as a medium of first-person experience but as a separate second-person "you" (138). Another example can be found in Edmund Blunden's poem "Come On, My Lucky Lads":

> In what subnatural strange awaking
> Is this body, which seems mine?
> These feet towards that blood-burst making,
> These ears which thunder, these hands which twine
>
> On grotesque iron? (104)

Instead of using "mine" in reference to his body, Blunden uses this first-person possessive to evoke what his body *"seems"* to be. Moreover, instead of characterizing his body as an integral first-person whole, he characterizes his body as a collection of non-first-person parts: "these feet" (not "my feet"), "these ears" (not "my ears"), "these hands" (not "my hands"). A similarly alienated attitude toward the body can be found in Wilfred Owen's poem "The Show." At the end of the poem, Death (personified) reveals to Owen the spectacle of his own decapitated corpse:

> He [Death], picking a manner of worm, which half had hid
> Its bruises in the earth, but crawled no further,
> Showed me its feet, the feet of many men,
> And the fresh-severed head of it, my head. (199)

In each of these poems, the lyric speaker's body is framed as something other than first-person. Whether identified with the pronoun "you," "these," or "it," somehow the body is disconnected from the lyric speaker. And it is only through this other-than-first-person body that the speaker is able to narrate the effects of wartime trauma. Instead of saying, "I shall be mad if I get smashed about," or "I half had hid my bruises in the earth," the lyric speaker presents his body as something separate from himself. As with Billy Pilgrim, this other-than-first-person "something" registers the catastrophic impact of war on behalf of the first-person "I."

There is a subtle distinction, however, between the bodies described in the poems cited above and the character of Billy Pilgrim. In the poems, the displacement in the poems is figured largely in a manner of speaking. In "The Show," for example, the speaker's body is "a manner of worm." Hence the reader is discouraged, even if subliminally, from construing the displacement as anything other than a powerful lyric figure of speech. In *Slaughterhouse-Five*, the displacement is thoroughly and systemically literalized. The objectified body has fully become its own literary character. The empty vortex in Vonnegut's mind where the center had been pulled right out of the story—the void that bore the force of the event precisely at the expense of plain knowledge—is also the science-fictional matrix from which the shell-shocked "I" has been cloned into an other-than-"I" automaton named Billy Pilgrim.

The same phenomenon can be observed in what might initially seem an unlikely site of science-fictional cloning: Tim O'Brien's *The Things They Carried*. The twenty-two stories are unified not only by a common subject matter (Vietnam) but also by a common set of characters, including Tim O'Brien, who narrates the book. Like *Slaughterhouse-Five*, *The Things They Carried* includes metafictional passages in which the author makes self-consciously autobiographical gestures calling attention to the difficulty of representing trauma. "I was afraid to speak directly, afraid to remember," O'Brien confesses when recounting a past attempt to write about one of his traumatic experiences in Vietnam, "and in the end the piece had been ruined by a failure to tell the full and exact truth" (159). Yet in *Slaughterhouse-Five* the metafictional account of the author's struggle to recount the war is largely confined to the autobiographical realm of the paratextual preface. By departing the metafictional paratext and entering the otherworldly science-fictional realm inside the text itself, Vonnegut leaves behind self-conscious references to his own struggles with writing about the war. In *The Things They Carried*, the metafictional account of the author's struggle to recount the war is explicitly present in the text itself. The line cited above ("I was afraid to speak directly . . .") comes from a story located well within the body of the book, far from paratextual front or back matter. Moreover, the line is not an isolated occurrence. O'Brien makes similarly self-conscious metafictional references to the difficulty of representing trauma in numerous places across the stories.

In what sense, then, can *The Things They Carried* be characterized as a science-fiction account of war trauma comparable to *Slaughterhouse-Five?* Certainly there is something science-fictional about the stories' setting in a landscape where "crickets talk in code," "night takes on a weird electronic tingle," and U.S. soldiers are haunted by "forces that did not obey the laws of twentieth-century science" (205, 202). Such hallucinatory details vividly convey the hallucinatory texture of traumatic experience. But what is even more crucially science-fictional than this surreal atmosphere is O'Brien's portrayal of dissociative self-cloning in "The Man I Killed." Physically situated almost exactly at the center of the collection, "The Man I Killed" represents the void in O'Brien's mind where the center has been pulled right out of the story. As in Vonnegut's case, this empty vortex is also the matrix from which the shell-shocked "I" finds itself cloned into an other-than-"I" automaton. Throughout the seven-page-long piece, O'Brien does not narrate himself speaking aloud. Even in his capacity as the story's narrator, O'Brien is scarcely present. He uses the pronoun "I" in reference to himself fewer than a handful of times. Each time the "I" appears in connection to O'Brien, it is part of the same refrain: "the man I killed." The man alluded to in this refrain (and in the story's title) is a young Vietnamese soldier whom O'Brien has moments ago inadvertently hit with a grenade. As the story opens, O'Brien stares at the dead man's body in a state of shock, cataloging and compiling the physical features of the corpse into a morbid blazon:

> His jaw was in his throat, his upper lip and teeth were gone, his one eye was shut, his other eye was a star-shaped hole, his eyebrows were thin and arched like a woman's, his nose was undamaged, there was a slight tear at the lobe of one ear, his clean black hair was swept upward into a cowlick at the rear of the skull, his forehead was lightly freckled, his fingernails were clean, the skin at his left cheek was peeled back in three ragged strips, his right cheek was smooth and hairless, there was a butterfly on his chin, his neck was open to the spinal cord and the blood there was thick and shiny and it was this wound that had killed him. (124)

In a reverie induced by his own mute recitation of the dead man's body parts, O'Brien imagines the life the man lived before he died:

> He had been born, maybe, in 1946 in the village of My Khe near the central coastline of Quang Ngai Province, where his parents farmed, and where his family had lived for several centuries, and where, during the time of the French, his father and two uncles and many neighbors had joined in the struggle for independence. He was not a Communist. He was a citizen and a soldier. . . . He was not a fighter. His health was poor, his body small and frail. He liked books. He wanted someday to be a teacher of mathematics. At night, lying on his mat, he could not picture himself doing the brave things his father had done, or his uncles, or the heroes of the stories. He hoped in his heart that he would never be tested. He hoped the Americans would go away. Soon, he hoped. He kept hoping and hoping, always, even when he was asleep. (125)

Throughout the story, as O'Brien stares at the dead man's body and reconstructs the dead man's life, O'Brien's fellow soldier and friend Kiowa tries to console O'Brien. The narrator's trancelike descriptions of the man's dead body and life before he died are punctuated by Kiowa's repeated—and repeatedly unsuccessful—attempts to engage O'Brien in dialogue: "Come on, stop staring" (126); "You want to trade places with him?" (126); "Tim, it's a war. The guy wasn't Heidi—he had a weapon, right?" (126); "Listen to me" (127); "Stop staring" (128); "You okay?" (129); "The guy was dead the second he stepped on the trail. Understand me? We all had him zeroed" (129); "So listen, you best pull your shit together. Can't just sit here all day" (129); "Why not talk about it?" (130); "Come on, man, talk" (130). But O'Brien remains unresponsive. The dialogue between Kiowa and O'Brien in this story is not, in fact, a dialogue at all. Instead it is a kind of lyric apostrophe operating in reverse. The "I" of the narrator here is the object of address—rendered progressively absent and inanimate by his shock, his guilt, and by his own strange mute identification with the man he killed, with the corpse at which he cannot stop staring. That the "I" becomes increasingly absent and abstract over the story's course is confirmed by the line with which the story concludes: " 'Talk,' Kiowa said" (130). Even by the story's end, Kiowa's repeated appeals to O'Brien have failed to reanimate the second-person object of address (who is ordinarily the first-person narrator) into a human state of responsiveness and active subjectivity. In being apostrophized—in being addressed *as though* alive, present, and human—O'Brien-as-first-person-subject is automatically posited as an inanimate second-person object, despite the fact that O'Brien is literally human, present, and alive while being apostrophized. Meanwhile, Kiowa, by participating in this paradoxical structure of address, in some sense helps to midwife the other-than-"I" automaton that displaces the "I" and that mechanically registers the impact of catastrophe on behalf of the first-person human subject.

If "The Man I Killed" lays bare the matrix from which the shell-shocked "I" is cloned into and displaced by an other-than-"I" automaton, then the subsequent story "In the Field" is where the automaton appears most prominently as a literary character independent of O'Brien-the-first-person-narrator. Set in a monsoon-drenched sewage field where the soldiers have been bivouacking, "In the Field" begins at daybreak in the wake of a nighttime mortar fire attack on the platoon. The mortar fire, we learn, has killed Kiowa, and his body is now missing—submerged somewhere in the sewage field's appalling depths. As the soldiers wade through thigh-high muck searching for Kiowa's remains, First Lieutenant Jimmy Cross notices a stray member of the platoon standing "off by himself at the center of the field in knee-deep water, reaching down with both hands as if chasing some object just beneath the surface" (163). Significantly, the narrative identifies the young soldier as unidentifiable: "The boy's face was impossible to make out. The filth seemed to erase identities, transforming the men into identical copies of a single soldier" (163). To Cross, who vaguely remembers "the kid's face but not the name" (172), the young soldier seems almost an uncanny stranger of mysterious provenance. Cross tries to get the soldier's attention, but the soldier does not respond. Mechanically, single-mindedly, his movements "random and jerky" (172), the young soldier performs the same action over and over again—plunging his hands into the water, groping for some vanished belonging, a damaged machine eerily reduced to repeating a single function.

The anonymous soldier, however, is not merely an opaque object. In several places throughout the story, the reader is given extensive free indirect access to the enigmatic soldier's interiority. From these passages we learn that the soldier feels personally responsible for Kiowa's death and is engulfed in grief:

> He pictured Kiowa's face. They'd been close buddies, the tightest, and he remembered how last night they had huddled together under their ponchos, the rain cold and steady, the water rising to their knees, but how Kiowa had just laughed it off and said they should concentrate on better things. And so for a long while they'd talked about their families and

hometowns. At one point, the boy remembered, he'd been showing Kiowa a picture of his girlfriend. He remembered switching on his flashlight. A stupid thing to do, but he did it anyway, and he remembered Kiowa leaning in for a look at the picture—"Hey, she's cute," he'd said—and then the field exploded all around them.

Like murder, the boy thought. The flashlight made it happen. Dumb and dangerous. And as a result his friend Kiowa was dead.

That simple, he thought.

He wished there were some other way to look at it, but there wasn't. Very simple and very final. He remembered two mortar rounds hitting close by. Then a third, even closer, and off to his left he'd heard somebody scream. The voice was ragged and clotted up, but he knew instantly that it was Kiowa.

He remembered trying to crawl toward the screaming. No sense of direction, though, and the field seemed to suck him under, and everything was black and wet and swirling, and he couldn't get his bearings, and then another round hit nearby, and for a few moments all he could do was hold his breath and duck down beneath the water.

Later, when he came up again, there were no more screams. There was an arm and a wristwatch and part of a boot. There were bubbles where Kiowa's head should've been. (170–171)

"In the Field" never explicitly identifies or names the enigmatic young soldier. But we recognize him as the automaton whose birth Kiowa himself helped to midwife in "The Man I Killed." Our recognition of the soldier as O'Brien's proxy is strengthened by the conspicuous nonappearance of O'Brien-the-first-person-narrator-and-protagonist in "In the Field." Whether grammatically second person (as in "The Man I Killed") or grammatically third person (as in "In the Field," which in some sense could also be titled "The Man I Killed"), the other-than-first-person automaton has displaced O'Brien's "I." Like Billy Pilgrim, O'Brien's surrogate automaton is more object than subject. It mechanically registers the impact of catastrophe on behalf of the first-person self. In doing so, it allows the "I" to narrate trauma at a remove.

Yet the distinction between O'Brien-the-narrator and his other-than-first-person surrogate is less distinct than I have been making it out to be. Even O'Brien-the-first-person-narrator—even the "I" who speaks with such raw and intimate honesty throughout *The Things They Carried*—even he is a proxy. The cloning of surrogates for Tim O'Brien precedes the opening sentence of the first story. O'Brien-the-author is not identical to O'Brien-the-narrator.

As counterparts, of course, they share many attributes. Like his real-life namesake, the fictional Tim O'Brien grew up in Minnesota, graduated Phi Beta Kappa from Macalester College, reluctantly fought in Vietnam, survived the war, and attended graduate school at Harvard. Both versions of Tim O'Brien, furthermore, went on to become well-known authors of books titled *If I Die in a Combat Zone* and *Going After Cacciato*. And both versions of Tim O'Brien were in their early forties when *The Things They Carried* was being written. Such similarities between O'Brien the author and O'Brien the narrator, however, are offset by a number of important differences. For example, the fictional O'Brien has a young daughter named Kathleen, while the real-life O'Brien does not. Thus the paratextual title page and back cover of *The Things They Carried* identify the book as "fiction" rather than "memoir." At the same time, other paratextual details complicate the book's identity as fiction. Most notably, the front matter includes a statement that *The Things They Carried* is "lovingly dedicated" to Kiowa, Jimmy Cross, Rat Kiley, and several other soldiers who appear as literary characters within O'Brien's "fiction" about Vietnam. Their status as fictional characters is potentially contradicted by the memorial inscription of their names in the conventionally nonfictional space of the paratextual dedication. Were these men actual people? Did the real Tim O'Brien know them personally? To what extent is *The Things They Carried* fact-based autobiography? To what extent are the stories fictive?

Such questions are not new. Many readers and scholars (e.g., Catherine Calloway, Mark Heberle, Tobey Herzog, David Jarraway, Robin Silbergleid) have investigated the ways in which *The Things They Carried* resists, experiments with, and transcends the dichotomy between fiction and nonfiction. But the first person who investigated the difficulties of evaluating the "truth" of *The Things They Carried* is the man who wrote it, and the place where he investigated such difficulties was in the object of investigation itself. *The Things They Carried* may be partially fictional and partially autobiographical, but it is wholly metafictional.

The metafictional nature of *The Things They Carried* is transparent. As I mentioned earlier, the stories abound with passages in which O'Brien-the-author self-consciously reflects on what it means to write about war trauma. Some of these passages are aphoristic and almost didactic in their tendency toward generalization: "In any war story, but especially a true one, it's difficult to separate what happened from what seemed to happen" (71); "Stories are for eternity, when memory is erased, when there is nothing to remember except the story" (38). Other metafictional passages comment specifically on earlier parts of *The Things They Carried.* Often O'Brien uses this latter category of metafictional passages to confide to the reader that certain details in the book have been fabricated. In "Good Form," for instance, he reveals that he did not actually kill the man in "The Man I Killed":

> I want to tell you this: twenty years ago I watched a man die on a trail near the village of My Khe. I did not kill him. But I was present, you see, and my presence was guilt enough. I remember his face, which was not a pretty face, because his jaw was in his throat, and I remember feeling the burden of responsibility and grief. I blamed myself. And rightly so, because I was present.
>
> But listen. Even that story is made up.
>
> I want you to feel what I felt. I want you to know why story-truth is truer sometimes than happening-truth.
>
> Here is the happening-truth. I was once a soldier. There were many bodies, real bodies with real faces, but I was young then and I was afraid to look. And now, twenty years later, I'm left with faceless responsibility and faceless grief.
>
> Here is the story-truth. He was a slim, dead, almost dainty young man of about twenty. He lay in the center of a red clay trail near the village of My Khe. His jaw was in his throat. His one eye was shut, the other eye was a star-shaped hole. I killed him. (179–180)

There are multiple possible effects that such a metafictional revelation might have on the reader. One possible effect is a sense of having been deceived or betrayed by the author. Another effect may be a heightening of the illusion that the stories are meant to be nonfiction: Why else would the fictionalization of a detail be worth revealing? To me, the most interesting effect of this metafictional revelation is a science-fictional one. What O'Brien calls "happening-truth" in the paragraphs above is, in my reading, the cognitively estranging reality of war trauma. Happening-truth eludes direct representation. It is a psychological force-field so intent on abstraction that it inexorably leaves memories of faces effaced, bodies disembodied, and overwhelming grief bereft of any physical medium of expression. By the standards of happening-truth, a statement such as "This feeling of faceless guilt is as real as it would be if I had killed someone" can be true only as a figure of speech. But by the standards of what O'Brien calls "story-truth," the same statement can be true both literally and figuratively. Unlike happening-truth, story-truth fully accepts and validates the reality of catastrophic psychological states. Story-truth is the science-fictional medium that enables O'Brien to literalize and substantiate the figurative expression "The guilt feels as real as if I had killed someone." Story-truth is the science-fictional substance out of which O'Brien can sculpt a slim, dead, almost dainty young man of about twenty, whose jaw is in his throat, whose one eye is shut, whose other eye is a star-shaped hole. Story-truth is the science-fictional process through which O'Brien's "faceless grief" and "faceless responsibility" acquire a human face—a face that can be confronted, remembered, mourned.

As much as story-truth enables confrontation with the traumatic past, it paradoxically allows this face-to-face confrontation to happen indirectly. The paradox obtains because O'Brien-the-narrator is the one directly facing the grief on behalf of O'Brien-the-author, who can then, in turn, face that grief at a remove. Throughout *The Things They Carried*, metafiction and trauma and science fiction revolve around this paradox. Again and again O'Brien metafictionally thematizes the science-fictional process of dissociative self-cloning, often while concurrently formalizing the process at the level of the sentence. "When a booby trap explodes, you close your eyes and duck and float outside yourself," O'Brien relates; "When a guy dies, like Curt Lemon, you look away and then look back for a moment and then look away again. The pictures get jumbled; you tend to miss a lot" (71). Elsewhere, in a later piece: "By telling stories, you objectify your own experience. You separate it from yourself" (158). Both of these passages are narrated in the first person "I." Both of these passages are narrated in the second-person "you." There is no contradiction between the two grammatical persons. For in both passages the "I" (the "I" who would otherwise have to say "When the booby trap exploded, I closed my eyes and ducked and floated outside myself") is apostrophizing its own self. By being turned into an other-than-first-person object of address, the "I"—the "you"—donates life back to the "I." Thus the survivor is permitted to continue living.

Alien Veteran

Like O'Brien-the-narrator, and like Billy Pilgrim, William Mandella, the protagonist of Joe Haldeman's *The Forever War*, is to some extent a double for the author himself. Both Haldeman and Mandella—together their surnames are nearly a palindrome—were drafted into military service in seemingly interminable wars. The maiden name of Mandella's wife, "Marygay Potter," is virtually indistinguishable from the maiden name of the author's real-life wife: "Mary Gay Potter." In *Vietnam and Other American Fantasies* (2000), H. Bruce Franklin voices a perception shared by many readers when he identifies *The Forever War* as "a kind of autobiography" (165). Haldeman himself, in an autobiographical essay posted on his homepage, characterizes *The Forever War* as a "treatment of what I'd seen and learned in Vietnam."

Haldeman and Mandella, however, are clearly not identical. Even though Mandella is the first-person narrator of *The Forever War*, the distance between his "I" and Haldeman's "I" surpasses terrestrial measure. The war that Haldeman survived took place in Southeast Asia and spanned two decades (from the 1950s to the 1970s). The war that Mandella survives takes place in outer space, light-years away from Earth, and ends up spanning over a millennium (from the late twentieth century to the year 3143). The "enemies" in the war that Haldeman survived are human. The "enemies" in the war that Mandella survives are extraterrestrial life-forms scarcely humanoid in shape and utterly impossible to fathom psychologically. So drastic are the differences between Haldeman and Mandella that one might reasonably question the basis of *The Forever War* in terrestrial sublunary reality. In the novel, the Vietnam War is mentioned only briefly, in passing, at the beginning of the narrative, and it is mentioned as something that happened decades ago in the novel's prehistory (12, 14). What is the link between the author's traumatic experience and the science-fictional mode in which the novel is written?

The answer, as in *Slaughterhouse-Five*, can be found in the paratext, which in the 2009 edition of *The Forever War* refers to Vietnam no fewer than nine times within five pages. The profusion of such paratextual references at once reflects, reaffirms, and advertises the fact that *The Forever War* is preceded and framed by its reputation as a novel about Vietnam. A blurb by Iain Banks calls *The Forever War* "a great Vietnam war novel." A blurb by Junot Diaz calls *The Forever War* "perhaps the most important war novel written since Vietnam" and notes that Haldeman is "a veteran" of the war. A blurb by Thomas Disch remarks that *The Forever War* "is to the Vietnam War what *Catch-22* was to World War II, the definitive, bleakly comic satire." The foreword to the novel takes the form of an open letter to Haldeman from John Scalzi, who at one point remarks: "It's no secret, to you or me or most of the people peering over our shoulders here, that *The Forever War* comes out of the crucible of the Vietnam War, in which you served, and which, as I understand, marked you for its own, as it did with many who served in it" (xi–xii). Scalzi goes on to praise *The Forever War* as a successful attempt "to explain to people who hadn't been there the confusion and bureaucracy, the muddled aims and random horror" (xii).

Even if someone with no prior knowledge of the book were asked to guess the topic of *The Forever War* simply by glancing at the cover of the 2009 edition, he or she might very well offer Vietnam as a possible answer. In the cover illustration, by Tomislav Tikulin, a lone soldier is walking away from the viewer—he seems roughly twenty feet away from us—and into a dense tropical forest. Nothing about the image is blatantly or necessarily science-fictional. The military gear worn by the soldier could easily be construed as dating from the twentieth century; only on close inspection does the gear strike the viewer as potentially futuristic (and hardly futuristic at that). The texture of the dirt beneath the soldier's boots, the fronds and other leaves of the proliferating vegetation—all these details are recognizably terrestrial. Dominated by hues of green and brown and gray, the image as a whole evokes military camouflage and earthbound reality.

Tikulin's cover art is arguably truer to the science-fictional nature of the book than its more overtly science-fictional predecessors have been. The previous covers depict soldiers bedecked in exotically high-tech paraphernalia and/ or cosmic backdrops populated by spaceships and shimmering orbs. *The Forever War* does indeed take place for the most part in extraterrestrial settings: space-vessels, stargates, otherworldly planets. But the most radically science-fictional moments in the narrative occur when Mandella, having completed an intergalactic tour of duty, reenters terrestrial reality only to realize that this once-familiar terrestrial reality now seems to him unearthly and surreal. Since the battlegrounds of the "forever war" are located light-years away from Earth, soldiers must rely on "collapsar jumps" (sites in space-time eternally suspended in a state of gravitational implosion) for speed-of-light transport, the severe relativistic effects of which leave them chronologically stranded upon homecoming. Due to time dilation, soldiers who subjectively experience several years of being away from their native Earth may end up returning to what is, in effect, a futurescape where centuries have passed since their departure and in which they are now living anachronisms. Mandella, who through skill and sheer luck manages to survive the entire "forever war," returns "home" more than once to find himself an alien figure in an alien land. On his first homecoming, for instance, he is astonished to learn that overpopulation has compelled governments to promote "homolife" as "the one sure method of birth control" (118). With each leave of absence from terrestrial reality—with each return to terrestrial reality—the alienation grows more acute. Once homosexuality has become the norm among humans, Mandella, who is heterosexual, must accept the fact that his "fellow" humans consider him an aberration from humanity. Near the close of the narrative, over a millennium into the future, Mandella returns to an Earth where mammalian humans have been displaced by billions of clones of a single gender-neutral individual who embodies "the perfect pattern" of humanity (260). In a world where "human being" has been dramatically redefined, Mandella is by definition no longer human. His alienation now thoroughly literalized, Mandella's conversion from member of human society into veteran alien "other" is complete.

This is why the lone soldier portrayed in the cover art is turned away from us. We who are human cannot see his alien face. We who are alien cannot see his human face. He exists at a threshold of perception, of representation, of science fiction. He is Mandella returning to a terrestrial reality grown unreal. More important, he is Haldeman science-fictionally approaching the cognitively estranging reality of what happened in Vietnam—which is also to say the cognitively estranging reality of what happened to "home" during his absence. As Scalzi remarks in his letter to Haldeman, *The Forever War* illustrates the "alienation" undergone by veterans who "came back home to a nation and culture that they no longer quite fit into, because both had changed" (xii). Bruce Franklin similarly notes that *The Forever War* "extrapolates both kinds of extreme alienation experienced by U.S. veterans—first as alien invaders of a foreign land, then as aliens returning to what no longer seems their own society—into the experience of becoming both extraterrestrial invaders of alien planets and exiles in time and space from planet Earth" (165).

The figure of the alien veteran is not unique to Vietnam. Recall the lyric speaker in Wilfred Owen's poem "The Show," who envisions his body as a "manner of worm" lying on an unearthly landscape "cratered like the moon." The afterlife of shell shock is externalized here as the spectacle of a grossly alien-like body trapped on an otherworldly landscape observed from a disembodied viewpoint. In *Slaughterhouse-Five*, Billy Pilgrim literally becomes an alien spectacle in an extraterrestrial world when he is abducted by the Tralfamadorians in 1967. As organisms who perceive time four-dimensionally, Billy's captors view human beings not as two-legged creatures but "as great millipedes—'with babies' legs at one end and old people's legs at the other'" (87). On the planet Tralfamadore, where he is "displayed naked in a zoo"

(25), Billy is literally an alien manner of worm (or manner of millipede) trapped on a landscape that is literally unearthly.

The Science-Fictional Temporality of Trauma

In addition to reflecting the alienating and hallucinatory aspects of traumatic experience, the human millipede reflects the distorted temporality of trauma: it is through being viewed four-dimensionally that Pilgrim is turned into a grotesque millipede. Likewise, it is via the relativistic distortions of time dilation that Mandella is turned into a no-longer-human alien on his own home planet Earth in *The Forever War*. One of the most estranging aspects of trauma is its impact on the subjective experience of time, both during the moment of wounding and afterward. "I'm forty-three years old, and a writer now, and the war has been over for a long while," Tim-O'Brien-the-narrator relates in *The Things They Carried:*

> Much of it is hard to remember. I sit at this typewriter and stare through my words and watch Kiowa sinking into the deep muck of a shit field, or Curt Lemon hanging in pieces from a tree, and as I write about these things, the remembering is turned into a kind of rehappening. Kiowa yells at me. Curt Lemon steps from the shade into bright sunlight, his face brown and shining, and then he soars into a tree. The bad stuff never stops happening: it lives in its own dimension, replaying itself over and over. (32)

This "dimension" where trauma "lives," where the "bad stuff never stops happening," is itself a collapsar—a terrible portal through time-space where the past collapses into now, where remembering turns to rehappening, where tenses literally implode into the simple present ("Kiowa yells at me"; "Curt Lemon steps from the shade"). In his online autobiography, while recounting an explosion that left him gravely injured in Vietnam, Haldeman veers—as O'Brien does in the passage above—from the difficulty of remembering the traumatic event to the science-fictional temporality of trauma. In this instance, however, time dilates instead of collapsing.

> It's hard to remember, let alone describe, what that explosion felt like. In one instant I sustained a couple of hundred small puncture wounds, a couple of dozen serious bullet and shrapnel wounds, and one killer—a .51 caliber machine gun bullet to the thigh. . . . The passage of time got strange as I faded into shock, but I guess it was only a couple of minutes before the medic came back.

What the clock measures objectively as "only a couple of minutes" is subjectively undergone as a diffusive expansion of time. In *The Forever War* this relativistic slowing down of time's passage in the immediate wake of a catastrophic event is systematically literalized. The novel opens in 1997 on Earth and ends in the year 3143 on a planet in the vicinity of the Mizar star system. Section titles chronically remind the reader of the dilated time scale: "Sergeant Mandella: 2007–2024 A.D."; "Lieutenant Mandella: 2024–2389 A.D."; "Major Mandella: 2458–3143 A.D." By the end of the book, Mandella—the "oldest" surviving soldier in the war—has survived almost a full millennium of military service that he experiences subjectively as four years.

Although strictly speaking the narrative follows a linear chronology (e.g., there is no out-of-sequence time traveling), Mandella almost never perceives temporality as anything other than nonlinear. "I'd been in the army ten years, though it felt like less than two," Mandella muses at one point. "Time dilation, of course; even with the collapsar jumps, traveling from star to star eats up the calendar" (84). Elsewhere in the narrative, the soldiers find themselves in a situation in which their enemies are chronologically ahead and therefore more advanced: "Relativity traps us in the enemy's past; relativity brings them from our future" (105). The high-tech military training to which Mandella is subjected further disorganizes his sense of time. Immersed in a tank of oxygenated fluorocarbon, attached to dozens of electrodes, and hooked to an "accelerated life situation computer" (ALSC), he undergoes indoctrination and military education in a virtual environment. "In three weeks I killed several regiments of electronic ghosts. It seemed more like a year to me, but the ALSC does strange things to your sense of time" (182). Together such science-fictional details made vivid the ways in which trauma can permanently alter how it feels to anticipate the future, what it means to remember the past, and whether inhabiting the present seems possible at all. The temporality of trauma gives war the ghastly ability to survive peace. Trauma has the potential to render any war a "forever war."

Indeed, "The Forever War" could readily serve as an alternate title to *Slaughterhouse-Five*, whose other-than-first-person protagonist is at the mercy of forces that can at any moment abduct him from chronology and trap him inside that timeless dimension where the "bad stuff never stops happening." Billy Pilgrim is continually becoming "unstuck in time." This happens most prominently in December 1944, while he is a soldier in World War II. Lost behind new enemy lines, Billy suddenly finds himself displaced from the present moment:

> His attention began to swing grandly through the full arc of his life, pass-
> ing into death, which was violet light. There wasn't anybody else there, or
> any thing. There was just violet light—and a hum.
>   And then Billy swung into life again, going backwards until he was in
> pre-birth, which was red light and bubbling sounds. (43)

More than one reader has noted the connection between psychic trauma and Billy's time travel in *Slaughterhouse-Five*. Alberto Cacicedo has argued that "Billy Pilgrim is insane, precisely because his time traveling prevents him from coming face to face with the traumatic event around which his whole life has formed itself" (363). And Susanne Vees-Gulani has argued that Billy's time travel is "a metaphor for Billy's repeatedly re-experiencing the traumatic events he went through in the war, particularly as a POW during the Dresden bombings. Psychologically, Billy has never fully left World War II" (177). In my view, however, time travel is neither something that "prevents" Billy from "coming face to face with his trauma," nor is it quite a "metaphor for Billy's repeatedly re-experiencing the traumatic events he went through in the war." Rather, Billy's being "unstuck in time" is a figure of speech literalized as a narrative reality that enables Vonnegut to document his experience of trauma.

To understand how the literalization of trauma's atemporality as time travel makes trauma more readily susceptible to representation, we might think about some of the ways in which *Slaughterhouse-Five* differs narratologically from a realist novel. Consider, for example, the following passage:

> Billy Pilgrim has come unstuck in time.
>   Billy has gone to sleep a senile widower and awakened on his wedding
> day. He has walked through a door in 1955 and come out another one in
> 1941. He has gone back through that door to find himself in 1963. He has
> seen his birth and death many times, he says, and pays random visits to all
> the events in between. . . . Billy is spastic in time, has no control over where
> he is going next, and the trips aren't necessarily fun. (23)

To the reader accustomed to realist fiction, these sentences might initially seem to provide free indirect access to Billy's imagination. Free indirect discourse is a mode of third-person narration that presents a character's inner thoughts as if from his or her perspective. Construed in this light, the passage above would be paraphrased: "Billy dreamt that he had come unstuck in time.

He had gone to sleep a senile widower and awakened on his wedding day. He had walked through a door in 1955 and come out another one in 1941. . . ." But *Slaughterhouse-Five* is not a realist novel. Unlike the abductees described in Luckhurst's article, Billy literally inhabits a science-fictional universe. Accordingly, his traumatic flashbacks are more than purely notional. Instead of constituting a subjective interior fantasy, the time travel that he undergoes constitutes an objective externalized fact. In the science-fictional framework of *Slaughterhouse-Five*, that which is elusive about trauma—its notional status, its unsharability, the fact that it happens solipsistically inside one person's head—becomes externalized, objectified, and substantiated at the same time that trauma's extraordinary structure remains intact.

Like Billy's life, *Slaughterhouse-Five* does not follow a linear path. The plot is nonlinear, often changing abruptly from the future to the past to the present and so on. We frequently encounter abrupt changes in scene such as the following three-sentence passage, which begins on the night of Billy's abduction in 1967 and ends more than two decades earlier while Billy is a prisoner of war in Germany:

> The terrific acceleration of the saucer as it left Earth twisted Billy's slumbering body, distorted his face, dislodged him in time, sent him back to the war.
> When he regained consciousness, he wasn't on the flying saucer. He was in a boxcar crossing Germany again. (77)

Once again, a narratological consideration of *Slaughterhouse-Five* will help us to understand the book's representation of trauma. To the reader accustomed to the realist novel, the nonlinear nature of events in *Slaughterhouse-Five* might seem to be the result of narratorial intervention. In other words, it might seem as if the disarray of events is taking place not at the level of fabula (the chronological order of events as they *actually* occur in the time-space of the narrative universe) but at the level of syuzhet (the order of events as they are selected, arranged, and manipulated by the narrator). But *Slaughterhouse-Five* is a science-fiction novel. Accordingly, the disorder of events is happening simultaneously at the levels of fabula and syuzhet. The events themselves occur out of chronological order, and the narrator faithfully represents the events in the (dis)order in which they occur.

Vonnegut's commitment to representing the atemporality of trauma is reflected not just in the book's narrative structure but also in its prose style. Many sentences are short. Some sentences repeat themselves throughout the

book. "So it goes" is one such sentence. Often, too, sentences seem disconnected, randomly juxtaposed, or joined only by the most evasive logic: "Billy
sat up in bed. He had no idea what year it was or what planet he was on.
Whatever the planet's name was, it was cold. But it wasn't the cold that had
awakened Billy. It was animal magnetism" (136). When Vonnegut apologizes
in his preface for the "jumbled and jangled" form of his novel (19), he is really
apologizing for the "jumbled and jangled" nature of his subject matter. The
form of *Slaughterhouse-Five* is jumbled and jangled because it is mimetic of a
referent that is itself scrambled, discordant, confused.

The Great War

Unlike the narratives discussed so far, *Last and First Men* is not immediately
identifiable as a war memoir. Published in 1930, when Olaf Stapledon was 44,
the novel—his first—accounts for roughly two billion years of human history.[1]
The opening chapters relate the rise and fall of the "First Men," to which we
ourselves belong, while the concluding chapters describe the Neptunian "Last
Men" who inhabit the remote future. Together these chapters encompass a
panoramic fantasia in which the evolving human race undergoes a long succession of permutations. Each new species—there are eighteen in all—is less recognizably human than the ones preceding it. The narrator of this chronicle, we
are told at the outset, is "one of the Last Men" speaking retrospectively from the
end of time. By way of telepathy, he is using the "actual writer" (13)—Stapledon—
as a means of recounting to members of the "First Men" what for us constitutes
the future but what for him constitutes the receding past.

Described in this way, *Last and First Men* might seem to exemplify science
fiction at its most fantastic. Indeed, this is how *Last and First Men* has most
often been understood: as an "ontological epic prose poem" (Brian Aldiss,
quoted in Benford, x), as a cosmological romance where "items of humanity
may suffer and be swept away in the interest of cosmic wholes and billion year
cycles" (Lessing, "Afterword," 306). To read *Last and First Men* along these
lines is to posit a text whose referents are speculative or imaginary—a text
whose chapters become less and less referential as they become more and
more fantastical. But as I will try to show, *Last and First Men* is actually a text
whose chapters grow increasingly mimetic of a nonimaginary referent: the
trauma of World War I. *Last and First Men* can be understood as a war memoir no less autobiographical than *Slaughterhouse-Five*, *The Things They Carried*,

or *The Forever War.* As an ambulance driver for the Quakers Society of Friends during the Great War, Stapledon endured shell shock, witnessed bloody attacks, and often endangered his own life to rescue wounded soldiers.[2] Indeed, it was during the war that Stapledon began writing *Last and First Men* (Crossley, 139).

It may seem strange to assign the label "World War I memoir" to a narrative set almost entirely in the future, a narrative that contains virtually no explicit reference to World War I. But the absence of direct reference to the trauma of World War I is, in fact, mimetic of this trauma itself. Trauma cannot be referred to directly, and Stapledon tells the story of wartime trauma precisely as a story that cannot be told directly. Those few sentences that do make direct reference to the Great War are bloodless and devoid of imagery. Located at the beginning of the narrative, they take the form of brief synopsis.

> The European War, called at the time the War to End War, was the first and least destructive of those world conflicts which display so tragically the incompetence of the First Men to control their own nature. At the outset a tangle of motives, some honorable and some disreputable, ignited a conflict for which both antagonists were all too well prepared, though neither seriously intended it. . . . Out of the conflict of the tribes arose, at least for a while, a spirit loftier than tribalism. But this fervor lacked as yet clear guidance. (*Last and First Men*, 18–19)

"Stunning indifference," "comprehensive serenity": these are words that John Huntington has used to describe the narrative voice of the Neptunian Last Man, and one might be tempted to apply them to the passage above (260, 263). Yet the voice of the Last Man is less "indifferent" than detached from life, less "comprehensively serene" than disturbingly vacant and inert. It is a voice whose strange hollowness is echoed by the "complete blank" in Vonnegut's memory where there should be memories of the bombing of Dresden. It is a voice whose reticence about World War I is echoed by the stark brevity of sentences such as "I was there" and "That was I" in *Slaughterhouse-Five.*

The abstract quality of the narrator's voice is achieved in no small part by his recurrent use of phrases such as "generation by generation" (76, 96), "century by century" (97, 140), "age after age" (136), and "epoch by epoch" (140)—phrases reminiscent of the monotone "So it goes" that recurs throughout *Slaughterhouse-Five.* As these phrases suggest, *Last and First Men* is a narrative haunted by the specter of the iterative. Indeed, Stapledon narrates the trauma of World War I as a story that cannot be described in terms of a single event in time, a story in which the same thing keeps happening time and again. He refers to the impact of World War I by chronicling everything that happens in its wake, which turns out to be a two-billion-year-long variation on the war itself. Epoch after epoch, the human race dies eighteen times in a variety of ways: bacterial plague, meteorological catastrophe, the breakdown of the solar system. Each time humanity dies, the Great War reenacts itself in belated and hallucinatory form. Although it is the future—the "next" phase of humankind—that appears to be displacing reality, what is actually disrupting the historical continuum over and over is the reliving of a past disaster that never stops invading the present moment. *Last and First Men* is structured invisibly by the returning shock of an event that is too large, too sudden, to stay where it happened in the receding past. In exactly so far as the horror of the Great War is missing from the brief reference at the beginning of the book, this same horror registers its impact on every future iteration of humanity.

As a narrative haunted by recurrence, *Last and First Men* is as much a story of repeated survival as it is a story of repeated destruction. "For those who undergo trauma, it is not only the moment of the event, but of the passing out of it that is traumatic," Caruth has observed: "*Survival itself, in other words, can be a crisis*" ("Trauma and Experience: Introduction," 9, emphasis in the original). *Last and First Men* represents the afterlife of World War I as the endless alternation between a crisis of death and a reciprocal crisis of survival. The narrative's chronic beginnings and ends signify the ongoing struggle to secure a perception of reality that is repeatedly disrupted. Indeed, the experience of waking—the experience of survival—is what constitutes the reliving of the trauma. Just as the protagonist of Kafka's "Metamorphosis" wakes up one day to find himself replaced by the body of an enormous insect, Stapledon's reader wakes up chapter after chapter—species after species—only to find herself replaced by something else: a twelve-fingered creature, or a disembodied brain, or a fur-skinned giant, or a seven-hundred-year-old child. The replacements grow stranger and stranger over time, much as humanity on Earth grows less and less recognizable to the increasingly bewildered narrator of *The Forever War*. Moreover, as with the "manner of worm" in Owen's poem and the human millipede in *Slaughterhouse-Five*, Stapledon's monsters literalize the hallucinatory nature of traumatic experience in external form.

Yet these monsters have also *internalized* the shell shock of the Great War. Some of the futuristic humans are "sleep-walkers" who exist "always in a kind of rapt absent-mindedness," as if "they were ever trying to remember something important which escaped them" (139). Others are telepaths who have seen "past events through the mind of some past organism, no longer living" (181). Having "encountered regions of eternal agony" while traveling in the past, such telepaths, we are told, inevitably "fell into despair. At all times, in all pursuits, the presence of the tragic past haunted them, poisoning their lives, sapping their strength" (182–183). What Stapledon's sleepwalkers and telepaths dramatize is the ineluctable futurity of traumatic experience. As Caruth has remarked, the content of a traumatic flashback is "a history that literally has no place, neither in the past, in which it was not fully experienced, nor in the present, in which its precise images and enactments are not fully understood" ("Trauma and Experience: Introduction," 153). Displaced from past and present, the experience of trauma must instead take place as the endlessly deferred possibility of a normal tomorrow. Stapledon's telepaths are casualties of a future already disordered by the violence of a past that will never become obsolete.

The narrator himself is one of the telepaths infected by the distorted temporality of traumatic experience. As a member of the Last Men, he has the ability to enter into the minds of humans from the distant past and influence those past minds by using them to "suggest some very vague intuition which is then 'worked up' by the individual himself" or by using the past minds as "passive instruments for the conveyance of detailed ideas" (240). We are first alerted to the narrator's telepathic powers in one of the novel's paratexts, an "Introduction by One of the Last Men." Like the preface in *Slaughterhouse-Five*, Stapledon's "Introduction by One of the Last Men" serves the purpose of making trauma available to representation. But the paratexts differ in the mechanisms through which they serve this purpose. Vonnegut's preface highlights the boundary between the discursive worlds outside and inside the novel, thereby calling attention to the power of science fiction—and the inability of realism—to describe trauma. By contrast, Stapledon's "Introduction" incorporates the author himself into the science-fictional apparatus of *Last and First Men*, thereby heightening the mimetic correspondence between the book's narrative structure and the out-of-body structure of traumatic experience. "This book has two authors," we are told,

> one contemporary with its readers, the other an inhabitant of an age which they would call the distant future. . . . The actual writer thinks he is merely contriving a work of fiction. Though he seeks to tell a plausible story, he neither believes it himself, nor expects others to believe it. Yet the story is true. . . . A being whom you would call a future man has seized the docile

but scarcely adequate brain of your contemporary, and is trying to direct its familiar processes for an alien purpose. Thus a future epoch makes contact with your age. . . . You cannot believe it. . . . But no matter. Do not perplex yourselves about this truth, so difficult to you, so familiar to us of a later aeon. Do but entertain, merely as a fiction, the idea that the thought and will of individuals future to you may intrude, rarely and with difficulty, into the mental processes of some of your contemporaries. Pretend that you believe this, and that the following chronicle is an authentic message from the Last Men. Imagine the consequences of such a belief. (13)

Notice the complexity that this paratext attributes to the voice of trauma. "The actual writer thinks he is merely contriving a work of fiction," we are told. At the same time, the actual narrator—the futuristic Neptunian who is (in some sense) Stapledon's muse and hence the true "actual writer" of the book—knows that the fictionality of the story is itself a fiction: "Yet the story is true." Meanwhile, the reader is instructed to "pretend that you believe" that the novel "is an authentic message from the Last Men." To complicate matters further, the "Introduction by One of the Last Men" is preceded by yet another paratext in which Stapledon—"the actual writer"—explains why he has chosen to write in the genre of speculative fiction. Yet this preface is anything but explanatory. It teems with paradoxes, double negatives, self-qualifications, and contradictory statements:

> I have tried to invent a story which may seem a possible, or at least not wholly impossible, account of the future. . . . To romance of the future may seem to be indulgence in ungoverned speculation for the sake of the marvelous. Yet controlled imagination in this sphere can be a very valuable exercise for minds bewildered about the present and its potentialities. (9)

Active with equivocation, these lines divide the voice—the authority—of the first-person author. "Controlled" yet "bewildered," this voice becomes at once more studied and more histrionic:

> While gladly recognizing that in our time there are strong seeds of hope as well as of despair, I have imagined for aesthetic purposes that our race will destroy itself. There is today a very earnest movement for peace and international unity; and surely with good fortune and intelligent management it may triumph. Most earnestly we must hope that it will. But I have figured things out in this book in such a manner that this great movement fails. . . . May this not happen! May the League of Nations, or some more strictly cosmopolitan authority, win before it is too late! Yet let us find room in our

minds and in our hearts for the thought that the whole enterprise of our race may be after all but a minor and unsuccessful episode in a vaster drama, which also perhaps may be tragic. (9–11)

Does despair here impersonate a strangely forced counteroptimism, or is it the other way around? The mood of the exhortation is impossible to determine inasmuch as it leaves radically unclear which outcome—world peace or calamity—is more likely to follow the temporal brink at which the book situates us. Together, these paratexts obscure the lines not only between text and paratext but also between paratext and real-life context, between the plausible and the implausible, between the rational and the irrational, between the "actual" author and the "actual" narrator of the book. The obscurity generated by Stapledon's paratexts indicates the impact of World War I, an impact that has damaged the frame of reference that would normally differentiate reality from that which reality is not.

The narrative framework of *Last and First Men* cannot be adequately understood without a consideration of Stapledon's second work of fiction. Published in 1932, *Last Men in London* is the sequel to Stapledon's first novel. The two books share the same extraterrestrial narrator who addresses the "First Men" from two billion years into the future. At the end of *Last Men in London*, in an intricately metafictional paratext titled "Epilogue by the Terrestrial Author of this Book," Stapledon addresses the relationship between the two novels:

> Readers of my earlier book, *Last and First Men*, may remember that it closed with an epilogue which my Neptunian controller claimed to have transmitted to me from a date in Neptunian history many thousands of years after the communication of the body of the book. The present book was obviously originated at a Neptunian date shortly after the transmission of the main part of the earlier book, but very long before its epilogue. Now I have reason to believe that at some date long after the communication of that former epilogue itself, my controller attempted to give me an epilogue to the present volume, but that owing to the serious disintegration of the most delicate brain tracts of the Last Men, and the gradual break-up of their world society, the result has been extremely confused and fragmentary. (601)

The Neptunian's communication is identified here as a text whose "confused and fragmentary" nature has resulted from some future Neptunian catastrophe. But the Neptunian's "confused and fragmentary" communication is itself a representation of the confused and fragmentary text—or web of texts,

intertexts, and paratexts—that we are now reading as a result of the past catastrophe of World War I. In other words, the human catastrophe taking
place two billion years from now—"the serious disintegration of the most
delicate brain tracts of the Last Men," "the gradual break-up of their world
society"—is a representation of a past human catastrophe that has damaged
the voices of both narrator and author. The science-fictional voice from the
remote future is a literalized figure of speech for the voice of trauma.

That the narrator embodies the voice of trauma is nowhere more vividly il-
lustrated than toward the end of *Last Men in London*. Neptunian "Last Men,"
we are told, have learned how to infiltrate the bodies of individual World
War I soldiers for purposes of anthropological research. The Neptunian experiences the war vicariously through the host self, who meanwhile remains
unaware of the alien consciousness that he or she harbors. In one particularly
fascinating passage, Stapledon has his Neptunian narrator recount his "experience" as a German soldier named Hans.

> He began to think about the men he had killed, and to see them again,
> especially at night, especially a French corporal whose face he had smashed
> with a hand grenade. His rifle now took on a snake-like coldness in his
> hands, so that he shuddered. His helmet pressed on his forehead vindic-
> tively. Over all things there was a kind of darkness, which was the worse
> because he knew it was not "real." (498)

Hallucinatory and unreal, the experience of "thinking about the men he had
killed" belongs neither to the young soldier nor to the Neptunian narrator yet,
strangely, to both at the same time. The ambiguity of the structure of this
experience—what Pierre Janet theorized as the "dissociation" of the psyche
around a violent event, or the separation of a traumatic memory from the rest
of consciousness—becomes much more explicit as the episode progresses:

> From the felt tone of Hans's body, it was evident that he was going sick; but
> he would not admit it to himself. . . . He was seized also by a strong premoni-
> tion of death, an infection from my own awareness that this was indeed his
> last battle. . . . I felt a bullet tear one of his ears. He did not notice it. (500)

On one level, this scenario presents a reversal of dissociation. Whereas in
Slaughterhouse-Five the third-person object (Billy Pilgrim) registers the impact of war on behalf of the first-person subject (Vonnegut), in *Last Men
in London* the first-person subject (Neptunian narrator) registers the impact
of war on behalf of the third-person object (Hans). Rather than removing

himself from the body that is undergoing the violent experience, the narrator actively identifies with this wounded body: "*I* felt a bullet tear one of *his* ears. *He* did not notice it." Yet the Neptunian's act of placing himself inside the experience of trauma is itself a literalized figure of speech for the soldier's own disembodiment. Even the Neptunian's dissociation is portrayed as inevitable:

> I began once more to see your little war in its true proportions. Presently the cramped and unwholesome feel of the young German's body began to fade from me. The racket of battle, the tumbled and bleeding human forms, began to seem as a dream when one is all but wakened. . . . I disengaged myself from your world. I awoke to find myself in bed in my garden. I could not remember what had happened, but I had a violent pain in my head. . . . I lost consciousness again and fell into convulsions. I remember nothing further till six weeks later, when I awoke to find myself in the tree-girt hospital where shattered explorers are nursed back to health. (501–502)

In this complicated scenario of disembodiment, the narrator removes himself both from the body of the soldier that hosts his consciousness and from his own Neptunian body. Even when accessed remotely by someone living on a far-off planet in a far-off future, the Great War is too violent to be experienced immediately. Its traumatic effects will still be felt two billion years from now, millions of miles away from Earth.

Strange Afterlives

To echo the trench poet Ivor Gurney: there are strange realities within the minds that war makes. Shell shock creates a rupture in time, a rupture that the victim experiences as a dislocation of cosmic dimensions. "In former days we used to look at life, and sometimes from a distance, at death, and still further removed from us, at eternity," noted French subaltern Jean Bouvier in 1916: "Today it is from afar that we look at life, death is near us, and perhaps nearer still is eternity" (quoted in the epigraph to "The End of a War"). Bouvier's evocation of the cosmic temporality of shell shock is reiterated by Herbert Read, another World War I soldier:

> the infinite is all
> and I, a finite speck, no essence even
> of the life that falls like dew
> from the spirit breathed on the fine edge
> of matter, perhaps only that edge

a ridge between eternal death and life eternal
a moment of time, temporal.
The universe swaying between Nothing and Being . . .
The individual lost: seventy years
seventy minutes, have no meaning.[3] (172–173)

Where life is far away; where eternity is near; where the universe sways between Nothing and Being; where ideas of time "have no meaning": such
"strange realities" are out of place in realism. But these same "strange realities" are entirely at home in science fiction. "Science fiction became the only
sort of tales he could read," Vonnegut writes in reference to his shell-shocked
protagonist in *Slaughterhouse-Five* (101), and one might add as a corollary that
science fiction is the only kind of testimony that a trauma survivor can give.
Even a realist narrator of war such as Erich Maria Remarque could not simply
"report what he had seen." Remarque's famous novel *All Quiet on the Western
Front* (1929) contains accounts of shell shock that hover on the brink of outright science fiction and self-reflexive metafiction. In one passage, the narrator, a German soldier fighting in World War I uses electrical terminology to
illustrate the experience of shell shock:

> In our blood a contact has shot home. *That is no figure of speech; it is fact.* It is
> the front, the consciousness of the front, that makes this contact. . . . The
> front itself emitted an electric current which awakened unknown nerve-
> centers. (54, emphasis added)

In scientific discourse, "contact" refers to a connection that allows an electrical current to flow between two conductors. The phrase "to make contact"
means to complete an electric circuit. In the passage above, such terminology
illustrates the replacement of simple first-person knowledge with the shock of
electrocution during a traumatic event. Tellingly, Remarque insists that the
replacement is literal: "That is no figure of speech; it is fact." It is only within
the science-fictional framework of a literally electrified Western Front that
this "fact"—the dislocation of self at the center of shell shock—can become
fully available for representation.

If there are strange realities in the minds that war makes, there are also
strange realities in the minds of those vicariously affected through the minds
made by war. In their introduction to *Extremities: Trauma, Testimony, and
Community* (2002), Nancy Miller and Jason Tougaw write that the "term
'trauma' describes the experience of both victims—those who have suffered

directly—and those who suffer with them, or through them, or for them, if only by reading about trauma" (2). Similarly, Kirby Farrell writes that a "significant quality of post-traumatic stress" is "its contagiousness"—a quality that allows trauma to "be seen as a category of experience that mediates between a specific individual's injury and a group or even a culture" (12). Often the contagion of trauma spreads via lateral transmission. "Explicit symptoms such as phobias or rage," for example, "are likely to disturb people around the victim" (Farrell, 12). But the contagion of trauma can also spread through vertical transmission. "A phenomenon of delayed response, trauma often unfolds intergenerationally," Miller and Tougaw note: "Its aftermath lives on in the family" (9). Yet Tougaw and Miller take care to add that the contagion of trauma can travel in ways that unpredictably transcend the dichotomy between vertical and horizontal transmission: the afterlife of trauma "lives on in the family—but no less pervasively in the culture at large. The story can deeply affect those who have not stood directly in the path of historical trauma, who do not share bloodlines with its victims" (9). In the chapter that follows, I examine science-fictional accounts of the strange and elusive paths—vertical, horizontal, neither, both—that the communicability of trauma can take.

4

Postmemory Han

As Marianne Hirsch observes in her 1997 book *Family Frames,* children of Holocaust survivors often "remember" the suffering that their parents endured. The memory of the Holocaust is no less vivid for these children than it is for the mothers and fathers who experienced the tragedy firsthand. Yet although members of the postwar generation—Hirsch among them—mourn what their parents have lost, that mourning is inevitably complicated by feelings of doubt, curiosity, and guilt. "What relationship can one have to the traumatic events of one's parents' lives?" Hirsch wonders: "horror? ambivalence? envy? a negative nostalgia?" (244). How is it possible to grieve for something that one never knew firsthand? What right does one have to feel traumatized by a catastrophe from which one was spared? In addressing such questions, Hirsch likens the Holocaust to "a foreign country" that she and others of her generation "can never hope to visit" yet for which they often feel mysteriously homesick (244). Born after the war, they are exiled from the very experiences that haunt them—exiled by their belatedness, by the fact that the tragedy preceded their births. Such exile, Hirsch contends, is shared not just by children of Holocaust survivors but by the children of those who have survived any human tragedy (22). To designate this condition of spatial and temporal exile, Hirsch offers the term "postmemory."

Like trauma, postmemory is a type of experience whose structure defies immediate first-person experience. Unlike trauma, however, postmemory defies not only immediate first-person experience but also the geographic, generational, and interpersonal distances separating individual selves. Whereas trauma is experienced belatedly (e.g., through flashbacks) by the survivor, postmemory is experienced belatedly by someone other than the survivor. The experience being remembered is at once virtual and real, secondhand and familiar, long ago and present. So intricately elusive a phenomenon requires "its own narrative genres and aesthetic shapes" (Hirsch, 243). One of these genres, Hirsch proposes, is photography: despite the illusion they give of constituting "a simple transcription of the real," photographs behave as "ghostly revenants" that simultaneously "affirm the past's existence" and "signal its unbridgeable distance" (7, 22, 23). While recognizing photography as a powerful medium of postmemory, I would like to posit a medium even better suited to rendering postmemory available for representation: science fiction. In what follows, I will argue that science fiction is singularly equipped to accommodate the contradictions and spatial-temporal discontinuities that make postmemory so elusive a referent. By arguing for the relevance of science fiction to the study of postmemory, I will argue in particular for the relevance of science fiction to the set of literary texts from which I draw the bulk of my examples, namely, Korean American literature. As with Asian American literature in general, the works that I discuss in this chapter are rarely (if ever) construed by their readers as science fiction.[1] As I hope to show, however, it is when situated in the narrative world of science fiction—it is when juxtaposed alongside stories by iconic science-fiction authors such as Octavia Butler and Philip K. Dick—that narratives of Korean American postmemory become most meaningful. From experimental mixed-media artist Theresa Hak Kyung Cha to Hawaii-based novelist Nora Okja Keller, Korean Americans have relied on science fiction to articulate their "postmemories" of ethnic tragedies such as the Japanese occupation and the Korean War. In particular, they have relied on science fiction to create representations of a specific form of postmemory that I call "postmemory han."

The Han That Flows in the Blood of Korean Americans

"Han," a word with no equivalent in English, refers to a Korean form of grief.[2] According to one writer, "All Koreans feel it . . . because our country has always had to shut up and listen to bigger countries—Japan, Russia, America. And because of the war that split brother from sister and left everyone's family missing or dead" (Ishle Yi Park). "Complex" and "dynamic," han "cannot be neatly analyzed or dichotomized" (Andrew Park). It ranges from "bitter-sweet longing" (James Freda) to despair that "wracks your insides like fire" (Ishle Yi Park), from "sorrow and anger" (Elaine Kim, 215) to a sense of "deep meaninglessness" resulting in "resignation, self-renunciation, and self-abnegation" (Andrew Park, 17–18). Yet no matter what outward form it takes, the structure of han always perpetuates the circumstances of its genesis. Shaped by "accumulated experiences of oppression" (Elaine Kim), han is itself a repressive emotion. Writers again and again portray han as a phenomenon marked by latency: han is "the unexpressed anger felt inside" (Luke Kim, quoted in Sandra L. Somers), "a pent-up historical and personal anguish" (Ishle Yi Park), "the compressed feeling of suffering caused by injustice and oppression, a complex feeling of resentment and helplessness" (Andrew Park). Moreover, han is not just a state of mind. It "flows in the blood of Koreans" (Paul Kim). Anthropologists have recognized it as a culture-specific medical condition[3] whose symptoms include dyspnea, heart palpitation, and dizziness (Sandra L. Somers). Someone who dies of han is said to have died of *hwabyung* (Elaine Kim, 215).

Despite evidence that han is a medical condition, the illness remains difficult to categorize. Are the symptoms literal or figurative? Do they originate in the body or are they psychosomatic? The answers to such questions are far from clear. But if han is problematic, then postmemory han—the han that flows in the blood of Korean Americans—is infinitely more so. A second-generation Korean American might be haunted by the "complex feeling of resentment and helplessness" that her parents and others of their generation have felt; but she would be equally haunted by the knowledge that she herself was not directly victimized by the circumstances that led to such pain. She is not, for example, among the Korean patriots who in March 1919 staged a nationwide peaceful demonstration for Korean independence only to watch powerlessly as fellow protestors were beheaded and shot to death by the Japanese military. She is not among the colonized students who were beaten for speaking in their native language, or the Korean Christians imprisoned for refusing to worship at Shinto shrines, or the families who starved because the Japanese imperial government requisitioned crops from Korean farmers, or the dysentery-stricken schoolchildren forced to spend months building airfields for Kamikaze planes. She is not among the Korean girls who were kidnapped and sold to military brothels, labeled "comfort women," and routinely gang-raped by Japanese soldiers; nor is she among the millions of Koreans who fled their hometowns in 1950 and walked south for hundreds of miles to avoid being killed by communist troops. How, then, does she "remember" the pain caused by such experiences?

To some extent, the answer lies in the power of the imagination to respond to historical narratives. Driven by the desire to understand the world of her parents, the second-generation Korean American might ask them to tell her stories about their own childhoods. Perhaps she reads autobiographical accounts of the occupation and war—for example, Richard Kim's 1988 memoir *Lost Names*, Sook Nyul Choi's *Year of Impossible Goodbyes* (1991),[4] and the interviews collected in Hildi Kang's *Under the Black Umbrella: Voices from Colonial Korea*, 1910–1945. Perhaps she explores the artwork of Kim Soon-duk, a former comfort woman who painted haunting depictions of her traumatic past. Perhaps she studies the 1919 Declaration of Korean Independence that students recited in Seoul's Pagoda Park at the outset of the March First Movement. Perhaps she reads fictional accounts of the Japanese occupation in novels such as Chang-rae Lee's *A Gesture Life* (1999) and *When My Name Was Keoko* (2002) by Linda Sue Park. Together, these texts evoke images and emotions that amalgamate in her mind to form imaginary "memories" of han, memories that are vividly detailed and deeply moving.

But to explain postmemory han solely in terms of imagined memory is to overlook the mysteries that live at the center of the phenomenon. What does it mean for a second-generation Korean American to grieve for an uncle who disappeared in North Korea long before she was born? How is it possible for her to mourn this loss as if she herself had actually known this man, as if he disappeared not decades but months or even days ago? What does it mean for a second-generation Korean American to feel personally degraded by the soldiers who raped thousands of comfort women during World War II? Why should the sense of injury and dehumanization affect her so viscerally? What does it mean for a second-generation Korean American to feel wounded by the Demilitarized Zone (DMZ)—as though the wound were still raw, as though the DMZ carved her own body in half? How is it possible for her to feel homesick for the mountains of North Korea, an alien land in which she has never been?

Korean American Telepath

In ordinary language (i.e., low-intensity science fiction), such questions can be addressed only on a figurative level. The second-generation Korean American does not *literally* remember the war; rather, she "remembers" the war *as though* she had been alive back then. Her presence in wartime Korea, in other words, is a figure of speech. Yet figures of speech have the potential to serve as devices of representation, and science fiction is endowed with the unique ability to activate the power of such figures by literalizing them as characters, scenes, and other aspects of a coherent narrative universe. As a mode in which figures of speech operate on a literal level without losing their figurative power, science fiction can describe phenomena that are themselves neither purely literal nor purely figurative. Postmemory han, I have been suggesting, is one such phenomenon, and it is by participating in the discourse of science fiction that the Korean American texts discussed in this chapter are able to render postmemory han available for representation. While the texts are diverse—they range from autobiographies such as Theresa Hak Kyung Cha's experimental life-story *Dictee* (1982) and Jane Jeong Trenka's adoption memoir *The Language of Blood* (2003) to novels such as Nora Keller's *Comfort Woman* (1997) and poetry collections such as Suji Kwock Kim's *Notes from the Divided Country* (2003)—they are alike in their use of science fiction as a medium for representing postmemory han. In all of these works, lyric figures associated with postmemory han are literalized as the material features of a narrative world. Metonymy is literalized as the genetic transference of han-filled memories from a Korean mother to her unborn Korean American child (to whom she is literally contiguous and closely related by blood). Apostrophe is literalized as extrasensory mind-to-mind communication between two people separated by temporal, generational, and geographic distance. The lyric tense—a grammatical "simple present" that juxtaposes duration, futurity, and retrospection—is literalized as the simultaneity of past and present within the Korean American psyche. And the invocation to the muse is literalized each time the ghost of a Korean ancestor uses a descendant's organs of speech to vocalize experiences that happened long before the descendant was born. What unifies these literalized tropes, incorporating them into a coherent narrative situation, is the supernormal Korean American telepath.[5] Like Frankenstein's monster, the Korean American telepath is a new type of organism. Genetically hypersusceptible to han, she is seized by visions of the Japanese occupation and the Korean War. Her body more "sensitive than nerve" (Cha, vii), she bleeds when confronted with a map of the DMZ. In the Korean American texts discussed below, the story of this science-fictional character is intricately brought to life. Through this science-fictional character, postmemory han becomes as palpable as flesh, as personal as an emotion, and as recognizable as a human face.

Postmemory Han: A Nonconsensual Descent Relation

Postmemory has an opposite: the phenomenon whereby children of immigrants remain impervious to their parents' memories. In a 1965 essay titled "American Immigrant Groups: Ethnic Identification and the Problem of Generations," Vladimir Nahirny and Joshua Fishman discuss this phenomenon in reference to European American immigrants who try, unsuccessfully, to instill their children with a living sense of their genealogy.[6]

> The immigrant fathers could scarcely transmit to their sons this kind of mnemonic orientation toward ethnicity, even when they genuinely tried to inculcate the *mores maiorum* of their ancestors. By listening to the stories told by parents or by studying ethnically related geography and history, the sons were able, at best, to respond to certain generalized attributes of the old country—be they Norwegian fjords, Finnish lakes, or Lithuanian forests. But what bearing could such acquaintance with ethnicity have on that special relationship which links the family or the individual from generation to generation? Too radical a break in the actual life patterns of generations had made the personal and concrete experiences of the immigrant fathers inaccessible to the sons. . . . Influenced by the dominant de-ethnicized society (with its stress on cultural novelty and on social inclusiveness), the sons turned before long to a wholesale purging of that past which they came to consider as reflecting archaic survivals. (271–272)

Implicit here is a narrative of socialization. It is because the children are born and raised in America's "dominant de-ethnicized society" that they regard their ethnicity as something "archaic" whose relevance predates their own lives. Insofar as those of the second generation remember anything about their parents' pasts, what they remember is neither "personal" nor "concrete"—after all, the children did not undergo these experiences firsthand—but "generalized" and abstract. No matter how assiduously the immigrant parents may try to "transmit" memories of the homeland to their children, the living texture of these memories remains "inaccessible" to those of the second generation.

In contrast to the phenomenon that Nahirny and Fishman describe, postmemory han defies the empirical logic of social conditioning. In the works that I study below, those of the second generation, although born and raised in

America, cannot help but "remember" what their parents and grandparents have experienced. Not only does postmemory han defy the "break in the actual life patterns of generations" and the influence of "the dominant de-ethnicized society," but it defies the unwillingness of those involved to participate in the remembering. Inasmuch as han is a repressive phenomenon, many Korean American immigrants are reluctant to discuss the traumatic experiences that they have survived. "They hardly ever talk about the war," one Korean American says of his parents (S. Kang), and another likewise notes, "My grandmother won't talk about it" (J. Brown). Yet no matter how assiduously the parents may try to suppress their memories of the homeland, these memories haunt the second generation. What the children remember, moreover, is not "generalized" but personal, detailed, and disquietingly vivid. If, as Werner Sollors has argued, the "central drama in American culture" is "the conflict between contractual and hereditary, self-made and ancestral, definitions of American identity—between *consent* and *descent*" (*Beyond Ethnicity*, 5–6), then postmemory han can be understood as a nonconsensual descent relation represented as being so powerful that it persists regardless of whether the parent or child consents to it.

A striking illustration both of the nonconsensual force of postmemory han and of the power of postmemory han to defy socialization can be found in Jane Jeong Trenka's *The Language of Blood*. While technically an adoption memoir, *Language of Blood* at times reads like a science-fictional narrative about a telepath coming to terms with her unusual gift. Adopted in 1972 when she was six months old, Trenka grew up in what Nahirny and Fishman might call a "de-ethnicized" world: Harlow, Minnesota,[7] "the last bastion of all that is good, right, fundamental, and homogenous" (21). Her adoptive parents were white Lutherans who had never been out of the country. On weekends Dad drove the family to the local auction, where the kids drank root beer and Mom bid on Tupperware. A typical dinner consisted of potato salad, turkey, sauerkraut, and chocolate chip cookies. In high school Trenka read magazines such as *Young Miss* and *Seventeen*. Her mother encouraged her to perm her hair and dye it a lighter color (67). None of her friends were Korean. There were virtually no other Asian people in the town where she lived. And her parents never mentioned either "the a-word" ("adoption") or "the K-word" ("Korea"); in fact, they refused to acknowledge her Korean ancestry (38–39).

From an early age, however, Trenka found herself haunted by and homesick for Korea. She fantasized about Korea. She dreamt up letters to her

Korean family.[8] Later, in retrospect, she would realize that what haunted her was the supernormal power of postmemory han:

> What were my [adoptive] parents to know of the inescapable voice of generational memory, of racial memory, of landscape—if they had never been separated from their own people? What were they to know of a girl whose presence demanded more from them than they either had bargained for or were capable of giving? They did not know this emotion or the word for it—*han*—but nevertheless it climbed up from the other side of the earth, through the bottoms of her feet, and was crystallized in sadness at an impasse in the throat, where a new and forgetful life became a tourniquet. (237–238)

Despite her parents' efforts to de-Koreanize their adopted child, Trenka ached telepathically with the suppressed historical and personal sorrow of the Korean people. Despite the thousands of miles separating Minnesota from Korea, the pathos of han sought Trenka, tracked her down, and permeated her body. Despite the sensory immediacy of her surroundings in Minnesota—"a land of plains" where "Lutheran churches dot the corn fields" (15)—what Trenka responded to more viscerally was the distant Korean landscape, whose "inescapable voice" spoke to her of "a land of pear fields and streams, where Buddhist temples are hidden in the mountains" (14).

The Metonymic Logic of Postmemory Han

Whereas Trenka could never escape the forces of postmemory han, postmemory han readily escapes Trenka's attempts to describe it. The passage above calls attention to the difficulty of composing a coherent metaphor for this elusive phenomenon. How exactly are we to imagine something that "climbed up from the other side of the earth, through the bottoms of [Trenka's] feet, and was crystallized in sadness at an impasse in the throat"? If this is a metaphor for postmemory han, then to what exactly is postmemory han being likened? The reader might try at first to imagine an enormous climbing animal, but soon the metaphorical animal is replaced by the imagery of earthquake tremors or chemicals (what else could enter the body through the bottoms of the feet?), which in turn is replaced by the image of a "crystallized" substance (sugar? a mineral?). Even when construed as a mixed metaphor, the figuration makes little sense: each of the images in the composite figuration is too inchoate to function as a meaningful unit.

Not only does postmemory han resist being likened metaphorically to something else, but it resists being understood as itself a metaphor. The child's postmemory, in other words, is not a metaphor for the parent's memory. And the parent's memory is not a metaphor for the child's postmemory. Metaphor posits a likeness between two entities by comparing one directly to the other. But postmemory cannot be compared directly to memory itself. As the second-generation Holocaust writer Henri Raczymow once wrote: "The world that was destroyed was not mine. I never knew it" (103). The Korean American daughter's postmemory of the Korean War, for example, is simply not comparable to the Korean father's memory of almost starving to death while fleeing communist troops. The body that starved was not hers. She never knew its pangs of hunger. Who could liken her postmemory of the father's experience to the father's experience itself? And yet how can one understand postmemory han without somehow referring it back to its source? To approach the relationship of postmemory to memory in metaphorical terms is only to face the troubling elusiveness of the phenomenon.

The logic of postmemory becomes easier to grasp when it is understood in terms of metonymy. Metonymy is a figure of speech in which the transference of qualities is based not on direct analogy but on the mental association between two things that are contiguous or closely related. Instances of such contiguity include part and whole, cause and effect, container and contained, and place of residence and resident (Barbara Johnson, *A World of Difference*, 155). Postmemory is *closely related* to memory insofar as the child is *biologically related* to the parent. Even though Raczymow "neither emigrated nor was deported"—even though "the world that was destroyed was not mine"—he and other postwar European Jews are nonetheless "orphans of that world" (103). Thus the child's postmemory is a metonym for the parent's memory and vice versa.

The metonymic nature of postmemory han is beautifully evoked in the following passage from Trenka's *The Language of Blood*. Although Trenka begins with the metaphorical frame of a "recipe," the metaphor quickly breaks down:

> Start with a girl whose blood has been steeped in Korea for generations, imprinted with Confucianism and shamanism and war. Extract her from the mountains. Plant her in wheat fields between the Red River and the Mississippi. Baptize her. Indoctrinate her. Tell her who she is. Tell her what is real.
>
> See what happens.

Witness a love affair with freaks, a fascination with hermaphrodites and conjoined twins, a fixation on Pisces and pairs of opposites. Trace a dream that won't die: a vision of an old woman slumped on a bench, her spirit sitting straight out of the body, joined to the corpse at the waist. (135)

Once again Trenka offers a disjointed metaphor for postmemory. To what exactly is postmemory han being compared in the first paragraph? What are the ingredients of the metaphorical recipe? How are we to imagine a liquid—blood—"imprinted" with war? Why does the narrator liken the girl to a botanical life-form ("Plant her in wheat fields") only to go on immediately to describe the girl in literal terms ("Baptize her. Indoctrinate her")? But the incoherence of the mixed metaphor eventually resolves into the metonymic logic of contiguity. The resolution occurs in the third paragraph, where we are presented with a series of figures of association between contiguous things—"hermaphrodites," "conjoined twins"—culminating in the image of "an old woman slumped on a bench, her spirit sitting straight out of the body, joined to the corpse at the waist." These images—the last one in particular—evoke the metonymic relationship of the ghostly past to the active present. In doing so, they evoke the metonymic relationship of the parent's han to the child's postmemory han, of "Korean" to "Korean American."

While the image of the old woman on the bench evokes the metonymic logic of postmemory han, it does not account for the contiguity between the old woman's corpse and the upright spirit. We are never told why they are joined at the waist or whether the relationship is one of part and whole, container and contained, and so on. By contrast, the following passage from the 2004 short story "Flight," by former Queens Poet Laureate Ishle Yi Park, does more than simply evoke the metonymic logic of postmemory han. Here, the narrator, a young Korean American woman, explains precisely how she inherited han from her "Uma" (mother).

Uma talked about han as if I didn't know what it was, but living in that house, with frustrations stacking up like unpaid bills, it built up in me steadily. Even though I was young, it gathered in my bones, curled my back, made my clothes wilt on my frame.

Unlike Trenka's "recipe," these lines literalize metonymy as a narrative scenario. It is through "living in that house"—it is through physical proximity to her Korean mother—that the Korean American daughter acquires the pathos of han. Subtle, persistent, and strangely alive, Uma's anguish infiltrates the narrator's body—"it gathered in my bones, curled my back"—and exerts its mysterious influence on physical objects with which her body comes into contact: "It made my clothes wilt on my frame." By working science-fictionally, by literalizing the metonymic relationship between family members who inhabit the same environment, this passage achieves a mimetic account of postmemory han.

Not having grown up in physical proximity to her biological mother, Trenka could not literalize the metonymy of postmemory han as Park does above. But Trenka literalizes the metonymy in another way. Reminiscing about the han that her Uma experienced during the months before Trenka was born, she apostrophizes to her Korean mother:

> *I absorbed things from you while in your womb, Umma. . . . How else can I explain it? . . .* Through the amniotic fluid and the faint light coming through the walls of your belly, I understood the brute emotions of fear and hunger. I absorbed them, made them part of my body, made them part of my life's fabric. (187–188, emphasis added)

This passage works science-fictionally by positing postmemory han as a congenital condition—that is, by literalizing the metonymic relationship of mother to unborn child. The han is transferred from mother to daughter because the two are related by blood and physically contiguous (the daughter is inside the mother's body as the han is transmitted). "How else can I explain it?" Trenka asks, suggesting that there is no explanation for postmemory han other than a science-fictional one. How else can she explain the fact that her body ached with han in a world where nobody knew that something called "han" existed?

The Science-Fictional Genetics of Postmemory Han

Like Trenka, Suji Kwock Kim explains postmemory han as the transference of han *in utero* from Korean mother to Korean American daughter. In Kim's depiction, however, postmemory han is not only congenital, it is genetic. By no means is she proposing that postmemory han actually constitutes a genetic condition. Kim does not believe postmemory han is biologically determined any more than trauma survivors believe that chronology disintegrates when a violent event is figuratively "relived." Yet such figurative expressions exist for a reason. In the case of trauma, the figure of "reliving" obtains because it is subjectively accurate: the unassimilated event is experienced belatedly through flashbacks. Science fiction accommodates this subjective reality by granting narrative literality to the figure of reliving. (For example, the shell-shocked protagonist of Vonnegut's *Slaughterhouse-Five* literally relives World War II via involuntary time travel.) Just as trauma becomes available for narrative experience through time travel, postmemory han becomes available for narrative experience through science-fiction scenarios such as paranormal telepathy and the genetic transmission of remembered suffering.

Kim invokes this science-fiction narrative powerfully in "Generation," the poem that opens *Notes from the Divided Country*. Here, the condition of han shapes the experiences of the Korean American telepath even before she has materialized as a zygotic cell.

> They called us over oceans of dream-salt,
> their voices *moving over the face of the waters* like searchlights
>   from a guardtower.
> We hid, and refused to come out.
> Their cries followed like police dogs snarling from a leash.
> We ran through benzene rain, flew through clouds of jet-fuel.
> We swam through hydrogen spume, scudded among stars numberless
>   as sands.
> We didn't want to be born we didn't want.
> Blindly their hands groped for us like dragnets trawling for corpses,
> blindly their hands hauled me like grappling hooks from the waves,
> the foaming scalps of ghost-children laughing, seaweed-hair dripping,
> the driftwood of other children who might have been.
> Out of chromosomes and dust,
> cells of hope, cells of history,
> out of refugees running from mortar shells, immigrants driving
>   to power plants in Jersey,
> out of meadowsweet and oil, the chaff of unlived lives blowing
>   endlessly,
> out of wishes known and unknown they reeled me in. (4)

Although "they" refers not to those who oppressed her parents but to the parents themselves—and "we" refers not to the speaker's parents but to unborn "children who might have been"—the moment of the telepath's conception reproduces the structure of the trauma that her parents suffered. In particular, the child's unwillingness to become incorporated into her family's history— "We didn't want to be born we didn't want"—reproduces the helplessness that the parents have felt as victims of colonialism and war. The reproduction of *memory* as *postmemory* happens even at the level of specific detail. The imagery of fog, "searchlights from a guardtower," and "police dogs snarling from a leash" refers directly to the experience of Koreans trying to cross the 38th parallel from the Soviet-occupied North to the U.S.-occupied South in the late 1940s—an experience that Sook Nyul Choi describes vividly in *Year of Impossible Goodbyes:* "The search beam passed over the cornfield and then passed near us as we sat crouched very still. . . . It was misty and wet. We soon heard the fierce barking of dogs. . . . We heard the soldiers' footsteps in the distance" (159–164). To be conceived by refugees, "Generation" suggests, is to find oneself already implicated in the condition of being a refugee. By recalling the moment of her conception, the Korean American telepath cannot help but remember the turbulent phantasmagoria of fear, sorrow, and nostalgia that her parents and grandparents experienced during the occupation and war. In this science-fictional scenario, postmemory *han* is a condition whose origins can be traced not only to the womb but even further back in time—to the "chromosomes," the "cells of history," inside the parents' bodies. Like Jodahs, the alien narrator of Octavia Butler's novel *Imago*, who receives a "flood" of ancestral "genetics memories" by immersing itself in the tentacles of one of its parents (692–694), the science-fictional figure of the embryonic Korean American telepath, immersed in the tissues of her mother's body, is genetically shaped by her parents' remembered experiences. Science fiction thus allows Kim to express a truth that rational discourse cannot accept: despite the fact that she has no firsthand experience of the war, somehow the experience has always been part of her body. Somehow the war must be inscribed in her DNA.

The parents' memories continue to shape the Korean American telepath over the next nine months. Kim provides an elaborate account of this process in section five of "Generation." The section is divided into two stanzas of roughly equal length. In most of the first stanza, Kim uses lush organic imagery to describe the telepath's experiences as a growing embryo.

> I entered the labyrinth of mother's body.
> I wandered through nerve-forests branching in every direction,
> towering trees fired by feeling, crackling and smoldering.
> I rowed through vein-rivers.
> I splashed in lymph-creeks between islands of glands.
> I leaped rib to rib, rung to rung on the spine,
> I swung from the ropes of entrails.

I played on organs, leaped through a fog of sweet oxygen in the lungs.
I clambered over tectonic plates of the skull, scrambling not to fall
down the chasms between, the mind-mountains where I could see no
    bottom.
I peered through sockets at the brain brewing in cliffs of bone
like a gigantic volcano, with its magma of memories, magma of
    tomorrows,
I could have played there forever, watching, wondering at the vast
    expanses inside,
wondering at the great chambers of the heart. (5)

Notice how these lines hybridize anatomical images of the interior of the
mother's body with geographic images that evoke the Korean landscape. More
specifically, the lyric speaker creates distinct units of body-landscape: "nerve-
forests," "vein-rivers," "lymph-creeks," "mind-mountains," "islands of glands,"
"cliffs of bone." By themselves, words such as "rivers" and "mountains" and
"forests" might bring to mind the generic fjords, lakes, and forests alluded to
by Nahirny and Fishman. But when considered in the context of the poems
that follow—poems that describe Naktong River ("The Chasm"), Paektu
Mountain tunes ("Translations from the Mother Tongue"), "crags grizzled"
with pine and rock maple and black walnut and shagbark and gingko trees
("Translations"), the slash-and-burn farming that destroyed Korean forests
during the Japanese occupation *("Hwajŏ")*—such words become signifiers of a
specifically Korean landscape. Again, science fiction allows Kim to express a
belief that is scientifically inaccurate but emotionally true. To the question
"How is it possible for a Korean American to feel homesick for a land where
she has never been?" these science-fictional lines answer, in effect: "Although I
was not born there, the Korean land is part of my genetic blueprint. Inside the
body of my Korean mother, I imbibed distinct memories of the country where
my parents were born: nerve-forests, vein-rivers, islands of glands."

The distances transcended by postmemory are not only generational and
geographic but also historical: events of 1945 might happen in 1990; the Korean War might momentarily interrupt the new millennium. In the science-
fiction narrative that I have been educing from Kim's poetry, the literalization
of metonymy as genetic transference accounts for postmemory's transcendence of generational and geographic distances. This same narrative accommodates postmemory's transcendence of *temporal* distance by literalizing the
lyric tense. George Wright's important insights about the lyric tense bear

repeating here. As Wright has shown, and as I have mentioned in earlier chapters, the tense most characteristic of poetry is the simple present. Paradoxically, this tense is almost never used in spoken English to indicate simple present-tense action. Unlike the present progressive, which situates the action in a palpable context of "now" (for example, "I'm eating dinner—may I call you back later?"), the simple present is fraught with multiple temporal features: timelessness, duration, pastlikeness, futurity. In using this tense without specifying the time of action, poets locate their poetry in what Wright describes as "a realm outside our normal conscious time world" (565). Consider, for instance, the following lines of verse (italics all mine): "With Nectar pure his oozy Lock's he *laves*" (Milton, "Lycidas"); "The Clock *strikes* one that just struck two" (Dickinson); "Slowly our ghosts *drag* home" (Wilfred Owen, "Exposure"); "The bird's fire-fangled feathers *dangle* down" (Stevens, "Of Mere Being"). Laving, striking, dragging, dangling: these actions occur not in the temporal world but in some kind of eternity that no clock could measure. As Wright puts it, the actions "seem suspended, removed from the successiveness of our ordinary time levels, neither past, present, nor future, neither single nor repeated" (565). The voice of lyric time thus addresses us from a dimension beyond ordinary temporality.

The Korean American telepath speaks from beyond ordinary temporality. While most of the first stanza in section five of "Generation" is composed in the simple past—"I entered," etc.—the verbs grow more complicated toward the stanza's end. The past tense is superseded by the hypothetical mood ("I could have played there forever") and present participle ("watching," "wondering"). Interestingly, the complication of verb-forms coincides with the telepath's discovery of the jumbled "magma of memories, magma of tomorrows" in her mother's brain. To be a Korean American telepath is to perceive time as a molten substance charged with pastlikeness, futurity, and duration. That the telepath perceives time as a literalization of the lyric tense is further dramatized in the following lines, where she recalls her experiences as a fetus and then a newborn:

> What machine made me move into the womb-cave, made me
> a grave of flesh, now the engine of beginning driving forwards,
> cells dividing, cells dividing
>
> now neurons sizzling, dendrites buzzing,
> now arteries tunneling tissue like tubes hooked to an IV;

now organs pumping, hammers of hunger and thirst pounding,
now sinews cleaving, tendons lashing meat to bone:
meanwhile my skeleton welding, scalp cementing like mortar,
meanwhile my face soldered on, hardening like a mask of molten steel,
meanwhile my blood churning like a furnace of wanting,
meanwhile my heart ticking like a bomb—*is-was, is-was:*
then cold metal tongs clamped my forehead and temples,
then forceps plucked me from mother's body like fruit torn from a tree:
then I heard a cry of pain—mine? not mine?—
then a scalpel's *snip snip* against the umbilical cord, like razors scraping
    a leather strop:
soon I felt sticky with blood and matted fur, surgical lights blinding,
soon I felt tears burning my skin—Why are you crying? Why am I?—
I didn't know who or what I was, only that I was,
each question answered by the echo of my voice alone: I, I, I. (5)

"Now," "meanwhile," "then," "soon": the multiplicity of such adverbs signifies the lyric temporality in which the paranormal Korean American telepath exists. So, too, does the jumble of verb forms: the present participle ("dividing," "sizzling," "buzzing," and so on), the simple past tense ("my face soldered on," "tongs clamped my forehead," "forceps plucked me"), and the present tense ("Why are you crying? Why am I?"). Most importantly, Kim uses the phrase *"is-was"* to describe the rhythm of the unborn telepath's heart, thereby indicating that this heart beats simultaneously in the past and present tenses. Born with a body through which time flows in manifold directions, the Korean American telepath resembles the mutant "precogs" in Philip K. Dick's story "The Minority Report": "With eyes glazed and blank," the precog "contemplated a world that did not yet exist, blind to the physical reality that lay around it" (87). The Korean American telepath similarly experiences historical events anachronistically, often blind to the physical reality that lies around her. Instead of experiencing the present as that which is happening now, she experiences the present as the future of a long ago past—a past as immediate to her as it would be if happening now.

Science-Fictional Anatomies of Postmemory Han

The two halves of section five differ not only in the temporalities they evoke but also in the kinds of imagery they contain. Unlike the organic images in the first half, the images in the lines above are violent and mechanistic: "machine," "grave," "engine," "neurons sizzling," "hammers of hunger," "tendons lashing meat to bone," "scalp cementing like mortar," "face soldered on, hardening like a mask of molten steel," "heart ticking like a bomb." Even before she is born, the Korean American telepath is impacted by the injuries that afflicted her forebears. The violent experiences they endured—war (evoked by words such as "bomb" and "mortar"), starvation ("hammers of hunger," "thirst pounding"), torture ("lashing," "sizzling")—physically shape her fetal body. To be a Korean American telepath, these images suggest, is to have been born into a "grave of flesh." It is to inherit the raw wounds of relatives who died in Korea decades ago—victims such as the cousin whose body Kim describes in "The Chasm" as "twisted entrails, / insides pulled out like ropes unlashed from the mast of the spine, / all the bleeding sinews and nerves, strange jellies" (26).

As "Generation" demonstrates—and as many Korean American artists show in their work—postmemory han is no abstraction. Where Kim uses graphic verbal textures to convey the flesh-and-bone literality of postmemory han, Yong Soon Min uses her epidermis as a medium. In a series of self-portraits titled *Defining Moments* (1992), Min reveals the effects of postmemory han on her skin. The self-portraits show Min's flesh swarming with photographic images of Korean history (e.g., soldiers, protesters, newspaper articles). Meanwhile, in nearly every print, Min's forehead displays the same portentous birthmark: "DMZ."

Cha's *Dictee*, a significant influence on Min's artwork, similarly uses visual pictures to convey the flesh-and-bone literality of postmemory han. For Cha, however, the literality of postmemory han is not only "flesh-and-bone"; it is "mouth-larynx-trachea-lung." An anatomical diagram in *Dictee* portrays the human vocal apparatus punctured by needle-like lines connecting each part to its name (74). The proximity between this diagram and a map of divided Korea (the two images are placed just a few pages apart) generates a spectral composite picture: from one viewpoint, a larynx severed by the DMZ; from another viewpoint, a strangled peninsula.[9]

The specter of vocal organs mutilated by han belongs to a larger science-fiction scheme in *Dictee:* the literalized invocation of the muse.[10] This important scheme is introduced in the opening pages, where the telepath invokes her ancestors: "Tell me the story / Of all these things" (11). But instead of telling her the story of han, the ancestors tell their story literally *through* her. In spasmodic fragments, their voices emerge from the lacerations that their han has opened up in her flesh. Cha depicts postmemory han as a kind of speech disorder, one so severe that it borders on paranormal:

> It murmurs. Inside is the pain of speech the pain to say. Larger still. Greater than is the pain not to say. To not say. Says nothing against the pain to speak. It festers inside. The wound. . . .
>
> She swallows once more. . . . Swallows with last efforts last wills against the pain that wishes it to speak.
>
> She allows others. In place of her. Admits others to make full. Make swarm. All barren cavities to make swollen. The others each occupying her. . . .
>
> She allows herself caught in their threading, anonymously in their thick motion in the weight of their utterance. . . . Inside her. Now. This very moment. Now. She takes rapidly the air, in gulfs, in preparation for the distances to come. The pause ends. The voice wraps another layer. Thicker now even. From the waiting. The wait from pain to say. To not to. Say. . . .
>
> Now the weight begins from the uppermost back of her head, pressing downward. It stretches evenly, the entire skull expanding tightly all sides toward the front of her head. She gasps from its pressure, its contracting motion. . . .
>
> From weighted motion upwards. Slowed. To deliberation even when it passed upward through her mouth again. The delivery. She takes it. Slow. The invoking. All the time now. All the time there is. Always. And all times. The pause. Uttering. Hers now. Hers bare. The utter. (3–5, italics in the original)

In this science-fictional scene, the han of the telepath's ancestors—"the pain to speak," a "wound" that "festers inside"—spreads throughout her body. It occupies cavities, presses against her skull, convulses the telepath's lungs. Eventually it erupts in a lyric stutter that echoes the fractured structure of postmemory han. To the telepath's invocation—*speak through me, tell me the story*—the invoked han responds by seizing the telepath's flesh and using her vocal organs to make itself heard.

The Science-Fictional Grammar of Postmemory Han

It is no coincidence that the invocation to the muse is a subcategory of apostrophe, a figure of speech whereby a speaker addresses an absent person, inanimate object, or abstraction as though it were present, animate, and concrete. Insofar as han is defined by absence and death, the dynamic of apostrophe is central to it. The Korean woman whose father was killed in the Korean War can address her father only *as if* he were alive. The South Korean whose sister is missing in North Korea can address that sister only *as if* she were present. The South Korean people, separated for decades from the North, can address its mysterious other only *as if* it were responsive. Nowhere is the apostrophic nature of han depicted more hauntingly than in *Tae Guk Gi*, a South Korean film that broke national box office records when it was released in 2004. Most of the action takes place during the Korean War, but several scenes are set in present-day Korea at the Memorial Site for Souls of the Korean War, where workers have been excavating and identifying the remains of soldiers who died during combat. In one of these scenes, Jin-Seok, an elderly South Korean man, kneels at the skeleton of his beloved older brother, Jin-Tae, who was killed while fighting for the North. Jin-Seok, who for decades had hoped that his brother might still be alive, addresses his brother's remains:

> You promised to come back. . . . But what are you doing here? I've waited for so long. What happened to your promise? Say something. I've been waiting to see you for fifty years. Please say something to your little brother. Jin-tae!

As Jin-Seok's articulation of han suggests, apostrophe is irreparably figurative. The fantasy of communication at the center of apostrophe will never be more than that: a fantasy. "Say something," Jin-Seok pleads, but Jin-Tae cannot hear his brother's voice and will never respond to his brother's pleas. The "you" here will forever remain a second-person object—absent, inanimate, unresponsive.

One might suppose apostrophe to be as characteristic of postmemory han as it is of han. How could the past be anything but absent, inanimate, and abstract to the Korean American who did not exist when that past took place? Yet postmemory, unlike han, is defined as much by presence and life as by absence and death. Not only does the Korean American address the past (as Cha does when she invokes her ancestors as poetic muses) but the past addresses the Korean American. Indeed, it is *because* she is called by the past that the Korean American finds herself calling out to the past in the first place. Whereas the structure of han is apostrophic, the structure of postmemory han—the structure of telepathy—is dialogic.

The dialogic nature of postmemory han is central to Nora Okja Keller's novel *Comfort Woman*. Beccah is a young woman whose white American father died when she was a child and whose Korean mother often suffers from violent spells of spirit-possession and despair. Growing up in Hawaii, Beccah feels alienated by her mother's "crazy" behavior. Only when her mother dies does Beccah learn that long before she herself was born, her mother suffered horrific bodily and psychological injury as a comfort woman during World War II. Significantly, Beccah learns this by listening to a cassette tape on which her mother recorded her life story.

> I rewound the tape where my mother spoke of the *Chongshindae*, listening to her accounts of crimes made against each woman she could remember, so many crimes and so many names that my stomach cramped. Without reference, unable to recognize any of the names, I did not know how to place my mother, who sounded like an avenging angel recounting the crimes of men.
>
> "Mommy—Omoni—is this you?" I cried, but my mother did not pause in her grief, her song for the dead. (194)

Although the mother's han, kept secret for so long, initially has the abstract quality of the unthinkable—"I wanted to drown my mother's voice, wanted to reassure myself that these atrocities *could not* have been inflicted on her" (196)—ultimately Beccah cannot help but be profoundly moved and animated by the call of the past (just as Trenka is moved and animated by Korea's "inescapable voice"). As the dead mother's voice addresses her, Beccah finds herself calling out in response: "Mommy—Omoni—is this you?" The mother's han-filled memories become the daughter's postmemory han, eventually incorporating themselves into the daughter's own personal experience. "Mommy . . . I remember," Beccah later addresses her mother's corpse. "I will care for your body as your spirit crosses the river. . . . I remember. I remember" (208).

Beccah's telepathic communication with her mother—the communication of the pathos of han from mother to daughter—occurs most noticeably toward the end of *Comfort Woman*. But telepathy informs the narrative from beginning to end. The chapters alternate between two narrators: Beccah and Beccah's mother. What emerges from the spaces between chapters is the ghostly yet palpable effect of intersubjective consciousness. Each narrator is at once an "I" and a "you." Both "I"s—both "you"s—are constantly copresent in the reader's mind. The reader identifies not just with each narrator but with the separate generations and experiences to which these narrators correspond. By literalizing apostrophe in this way, *Comfort Woman* transcends the dichotomies of subject/object, mother/daughter, past/present. The telepathic operation of this "intersubjective" arrangement of chapters bears a meaningful and noteworthy resemblance to the metempsychotic operation of chapter structures in more recognizably science-fictional narratives such as Michael Cunningham's *Specimen Days* and David Mitchell's *Cloud Atlas*. In both *Specimen Days* and *Cloud Atlas*, the central protagonist is not an embodied human character but a disembodied constellation of memories, sensibilities, and moods. Different chapters in each novel may correspond to different plotlines—and different plotlines may correspond to different lifetimes, different settings, and different narrators—but the disembodied protagonist transcends such differences, just as postmemory han transcends the intergenerational and cultural differences that separate Beccah from her mother.

Like *Comfort Woman*, *Dictee* and *Notes from the Divided Country* represent postmemory han as a form of telepathy transcending the dichotomy between "I" and "you." But Cha and Kim go further, suggesting that postmemory han transcends ordinary grammar altogether. "You are she, she speaks you, you speak her, she cannot speak," Cha writes at one point (106), framing postmemory han as a referent that defies grammatical case. At another point, Cha prints a translation exercise whose inflectional form resonates with the book as a whole:

Traduire en français (translate into French):

1. I want you to speak.
2. I wanted him to speak.
3. I shall want you to speak.
4. Are you afraid he will speak?
5. Were you afraid they would speak? (8)

The inflections could go on indefinitely: *I am being spoken to by her. I would have spoken if she had spoken. Will we speak? I was speaking to myself.* . . . As such inflections show, postmemory han evades the very system of rules on which conventional language is founded. The tense of postmemory han is simultaneously past, present, and future. The voice of postmemory han is simultaneously passive and active. The mood of postmemory han is simultaneously indicative and hypothetical. And the pronoun of postmemory han is simultaneously first-person and second-person, singular and plural, subjective and objective. Transcending the gaps that separate self from other and present from past, postmemory han eludes conventional grammatical articulation. Nevertheless, it is possible to identify several *un*conventional grammatical forms that the elusiveness of postmemory han can take. In the remainder of this chapter, I will identify and briefly analyze three such unconventional forms.

The first of these unconventional grammatical forms is second-person narration. The daughter addresses the absent mother at the same time that the mother's first-person experiences are vividly present to the daughter. In "Translations from the Mother Tongue," for instance, Kim uses the second-person present tense to describe her mother making kimchee:

> Your arms work the spices in. Slap. Slur.
> Nose stinging from onion-juice and pepper-fumes,
> eyes tearing. Your fingers slowly blister, stain.
> Meanwhile your mouth waters, starved for the taste
> of home. (15)

Compare the pronominal structure of these lines with the pronominal structure of the following passage from *Dictee*, in which Cha uses the second-person present tense to recount her mother's experiences as an eighteen-year-old woman exiled in Manchuria. As a colonial subject of Japan, Cha's mother is not allowed to speak Korean. Denied her "mother tongue" (45), she becomes physically sick:

> Fever and chill possess the body at the same time. You are standing in the sunlight against the tepid wall to warm yourself. You are giving in. To the fall to the lure behind you before you all around you beneath your skin the sharp air begins to blow the winds of the body, dark fires rising to battle for victory, the summoning the coaxing the irresistible draw replacing sleep dense with images condensing them without space in between. . . . You are yielding to them. They are too quick to arrive. You do not know them, never have seen them but they seek you, inhabit you whole, suspend you airless, spaceless. They force their speech upon you and direct your speech only to them.[11] (50)

If the passages above were simple apostrophes, the daughter would be addressing the absent mother *as though* the addressee were present. But these passages literalize apostrophe as telepathy. Instead of being absent, inanimate, and abstract, the addressee and her subjective experiences are present, alive, and concrete. Despite the distance between their two bodies, the daughter knows that Uma's "mouth waters, starved for the taste / of home." She knows, in intimate detail, how Uma's feverish body feels when it is colonized—whether by sickness or by another country's language. Like the telepaths in Octavia Butler's science-fiction novel *Mind of My Mind*—"he was having trouble preventing himself from merging into her experience. Mary was trapped in the mind of a man who had to eventually burn to death. The man was trapped inside a burning house. Mary was experiencing his every sensation" (48)—the Korean American telepath has trouble preventing herself from merging into her parents' experiences; she often finds herself "trapped" in their minds, experiencing their every sensation.

The second grammatical form that postmemory han can take is what I call the secondary first person. Here the speaker uses the grammatical first person to recount the experiences of her forebears. In other words, the object of apostrophe has become part of the speaker's own subjectivity. The telepath therefore merges completely into what her parents and grandparents experienced. She "remembers," for example, her father's terrifying flight south along Shinjangno in January 1951, during the height of the Korean War: "I felt artillery crash miles away in the soles of my feet, the ground shuddering. / I heard the drone and snarl of engines as fighter-planes swarmed toward us. . . . I'll never forget the smell of burning flesh. / I'll never forget the stench of open sores, pus, gangrene, / the smell of people rotting who hadn't died yet" ("Fragments of the Forgotten War"). She "remembers" her grandmother's attempt to escape Japanese soldiers by crossing the frozen Yalu River into China: "I saw men and women from our village blown to hieroglyphs of viscera. . . . My childhood friend lay on the boot-blackened ice: / I touched his face with disbelief, / I tried to hold his hand but he snatched it away, as if he were ashamed of dying, / eye grown large with everything it saw" ("Borderlands"). She "remembers" how her great-grandparents were punished for resisting the Japanese occupation: "In Cholla-namdo we used to break the bones of corpses' feet / so their souls wouldn't walk back from the other world. . . . Once the guards forced us to watch a comrade being skinned alive. / Later they bludgeoned prisoners to death to save bullets" ("Resistance"). These lines, united in their use of the secondary first person, share a single message: "Decades before I was born, you suffered during the Japanese occupation and the Korean War. That experience of han is not mine. I have not earned the right to feel it. And yet your han calls out to me, animating me, making me present in your past, making me present in your consciousness. Even though I was not born yet, I am there inside your experience. I remember these things happening to you."

The third grammatical form that postmemory han can take is the reflexive secondary first person. Here the telepath ventriloquizes one of her forebears apostrophizing to an imagined unborn descendant—namely, the telepath herself. In other words, the forebear addresses the descendant by using the descendant's own voice.

> I know you
>> cannot help us.
> We will die before you
>> are born. ("Flight," 33)

On one level, these lines say: "Address me now, even though I am not yet born, even though to you I am absent, inanimate, abstract, an invisible second-person 'you.' Make me present in your present, even though that present is now a long ago past." On another level, however, the lines say something slightly different: "Address me now, even though it is fifty years into the future, in another country, on another continent, even though to you I am absent, inanimate, abstract, a long-dead second-person 'you.' Make me present in your present, even though that present is still a distant future." Who is speaking here, descendant or forebear? The answer is immaterial. To conjugate these lines would not change their effect. Shimmering behind the text is what might be described as a telepathic reverse-text:

> You know I
>> cannot help you.
> You will die before I
>> am born.

Together, text and reverse-text form a composite text not unlike the image in *Dictee* of vocal organs lacerated by the DMZ. What emerges from the juxtaposition is the same thing we saw emerging from the dual narrative structure of *Comfort Woman:* the telepathic effect of intersubjective consciousness, the telepathic effect of postmemory han.

Telepathic reverse-texts shimmer behind many of Kim's poems. Consider, for example, the following lines from "Montage with Neon, Bok Choi, Gasoline, Lovers & Strangers":

> may you never see what we saw,
> may you never do what we've done,
> may you never remember & may you never forget. (37)

The reverse-text:

> I never saw what you saw,
> I never did what you did,
> I will never remember and I will never forget.

Or consider "The Tree of Unknowing," in which the Korean American tele-path describes herself as an infant being cradled by her mother:

> I lifted my head. What was it I saw
> in your gaze, the maze
>
> of you: corridors of years, corridors of war, black wheat-hair ripening –
> the last shape sown in closing eyes.
>
> . . . Whose memory was it? (6)

The reverse-text:

> You lifted your head. What was it you saw
> in my gaze, the maze
>
> of me: corridors of years, corridors of war, black wheat-hair ripening –
> the last shape sown in closing eyes.
>
> . . . Whose memory was it?

Whose memory is it, indeed? The question is left unanswered. "The Tree of Unknowing" lends itself especially well to conjugation insofar as we tend to think of infants as not yet fully sentient, not yet capable of speaking in the first-person "I." Identifying with the mother, we approach the infant as a second-person object whose subjectivity remains unknown. Moreover, the rhyme between "gaze" and "maze" implies that the act of looking—an act that both Cha and Kim associate with postmemory—is not straightforward but densely complicated and oblique. Postmemory han is a "gaze" wherein subject and object lose themselves in each other, a "maze" in which the distinction between "I" and "you" disappears.

Postmemory Science Fiction

Although I have focused on science fiction in relation to postmemory *han*, the relevance of science fiction is hardly unique to Korean American postmem-ory. Throughout multiethnic literatures of the United States, science-fictional accounts of postmemory depict the suffering of forebears literally intruding on the descendants' present-day reality. In Sherman Alexie's novel *Reserva-tion Blues*, a Spokane woman living in the 1990s experiences the 1858 slaugh-ter of nearly one thousand Palouse horses by the U.S. Army: "Big Mom heard the first gunshot, which reverberated in her DNA" (9). In Octavia Butler's novel *Kindred*, an African American woman living in 1970s California is periodically dislocated in time and transported against her will to a plantation in antebellum Maryland, where she is brutally mistreated by the same slave owners who oppressed her ancestors.

There is even a moment in *Family Frames* when Marianne Hirsch comes close to invoking science fiction as a way of describing postmemory:

> When I look through my family's albums, I enter a network of looks that dictate affiliative feelings, positive or negative feelings of recognition that can span miles and generations: I "recognize" my great-grandmother. . . . And when I look at her picture, I feel as though she also recognizes me. We share a familial visual field in which we see even as we are seen. (53–54)

To gaze at a family photograph, Hirsch suggests here, is to undergo a telepathic experience. The grammar of the act of looking hovers between first- and second-person, present and past. Hirsch's observations about photography can be applied to *Dictee*. Among the many visual images in this book are numerous black-and-white headshots of Korean women, including a photograph of Cha's mother as a young woman and a photograph of Yu Guan Soon, a Korean revolutionary who led a resistance group against the Japanese in 1919 and was tortured to death in 1920 at the age of seventeen. The stark opacity of these photos—as Anne Cheng has remarked, the documents reproduced in *Dictee* are never captioned (140)—creates the effect of hallucinatory visions erupting from nowhere into consciousness. Together, these images create a visual field, a telepathic network of looks wherein recognition spans miles and generations. To behold these photographs is to simulate postmemory han. Our vision bionically enhanced, we see across time. With the clarity of photographic snapshots, we perceive the Japanese occupation and Korean War. Looking into the past, we find history already gazing back at us.

5

Robot Rights

Suppose that we lived in a world where human beings coexisted with sentient robots. By "sentient robots," I mean artifacts—human-made objects—possessing human attributes such as selfhood, the capacity to fall in love, and susceptibility to grief. What kinds of moral claims might such a creature have on us? Should a sentient robot be entitled, for example, to freedom of thought, conscience, and speech? What about the right to own property? The right to vote? The right to a nationality? The right to marry and to found a family? May a sentient robot claim copyright to a poem that it created? Should a sentient robot be free to choose its employment, and would an unemployed robot be entitled to welfare? If a sentient robot committed a crime, how should it be held accountable—as a fully legally responsible entity? As a person of diminished capacity? As an animal? As a defective product? Conversely, if a robot were injured, should it be allowed to initiate a suit?[1]

While today robots do not possess consciousness, the ethical significance of such questions is already palpable. In 2006, the British government released a study addressing the possibility that robots in the near future might become intelligent enough to demand civil rights such as access to health care. In early 2007, the South Korean Ministry of Commerce, Industry, and Energy announced that it has been working on a "Robot Ethics Charter" to prevent humans from abusing machines. The American Society for the Prevention of Cruelty to Robots (www.ASPCR.com) has been "upholding robot rights since 1999." And at the 2003 International Bar Association conference in San Francisco, California, participants held a mock trial in which attorneys for a sentient female computer named "BINA48" (Breakthrough Intelligence via Neural Architecture) sought a preliminary injunction to stop a corporation from disassembling BINA48 and using her parts to assemble new machines.[2] Indeed, the notion of robot rights is as old as is the word "robot" itself. Etymologically the word "robot" comes from the Czech word "robota," which means "forced labor." In Karel Čapek's 1921 play *R.U.R.*, which is widely credited with introducing the term "robot," a "Humanity League" decries the exploitation of robot slaves—"they are to be dealt with like human beings," one reformer declares (13)—and the robots themselves eventually stage a massive revolt against their human makers.

As these instances of robot advocacy indicate, the moral claims of robots do have a presence in our world. Yet most humans would rather dismiss such claims as frivolous and insubstantial than acknowledge them as part of reality. "This is a silly concept," one commentator remarked in response to the 2006 study released by the British government: "Granting a robot rights would be akin to granting the right front tire on my car rights" (Bryansix). Another commentator expresses his resistance in harsher language: "Robot rights are a joke and so are the morons that even consider them" (GoldFish). A third commentator voices his objection to robot rights in the most violent way possible: "If I buy the robot, I should be able to do whatever the hell I want to it. Including beatings, burnings, disabling, beheading" (Keep Robots Slaves). From amused skepticism to disgust and vehement hostility, such attitudes of mental rejection are symptomatic of the cognitively estranging nature of robot rights. As with cyberspace, globalization, trauma, and postmemory han, the moral claims of sentient robots cannot be described in straightforward terms or easily accepted by the mind.

There are a number of reasons why the moral claims of robots are so difficult to recognize. The most obvious reason is that artificial sentience today remains a thing of the future. As a referent whose historical context has not yet been fully realized, the idea of robot ethics has no immediate bearing on our lives and thus no direct claims on our attention. Furthermore, the concept of robot rights belongs to a larger category that has never been easy to define or understand, namely, the category of "rights." What qualifies as a right, and how should we judge the moral entitlement of a given entity? Chickens, for example, do exist in the real world, yet we are far from arriving at any consensus regarding their moral claims on us. Even in the case of humans, rights are so abstract in nature that a human right may elude representation when delineated in political documents, becoming fully available for representation only—and paradoxically—at the moment of its violation. But the most important reason why the moral claims of robots are cognitively estranging is that the idea of a sentient humanoid robot has always been quintessentially "uncanny." I use this word here as Ernst Jentsch used it in his influential 1906 essay "On the Psychology of the Uncanny." Jentsch defined "the uncanny" as the disquieting intellectual uncertainty we feel when presented with something that seems neither animate nor inanimate yet strangely both.[3] He famously drew many of his examples from the fiction of German Romantic writer E. T. A. Hoffmann, whose tales are filled with puppets, haunted dwellings, and other instances of what Hoffmann himself described as "living death or inanimate life" ("Automata," 81).[4]

Of all the obstacles to recognizing robot rights, the intrinsic uncanniness of robots may be the most difficult to surmount. How can we represent the moral claims of something whose status as a living entity is by definition almost impossible to determine? To explore what it means to ask such a question will be the main purpose of this chapter. Guided by the writings of Elaine Scarry and roboticist Masahiro Mori, I will investigate the place of humanoid artifacts in a range of science-fiction texts, with particular emphasis on Mary Shelley's *Frankenstein* (1818), Philip K. Dick's novel *Do Androids Dream of Electric Sheep?* (1968), Ridley Scott's film *Blade Runner* (1982), and Steven Spielberg's film *A.I.* (2000). These are works in which images of robot uncanniness are meaningfully juxtaposed with situations where robots become identifiable—often painfully so—as human subjects worthy of empathy. For instance, we might find a humanoid artifact soliloquizing about the nature of reality, or we might find a mechanical child pleading for its life. During such lyric moments, the uncanny effects of robots are countervailed and the moral claims of robots become available for representation.[5]

The Uncanny Valley

A humanoid robot is not just uncanny. It is distinguished by a particular form of uncanniness known as the "uncanny valley."[6] This phrase refers to a theory that Masahiro Mori developed in the 1970s to explain how humans react emotionally to robots and other humanlike (yet nonhuman) entities. According to Mori, people are likely to respond more and more positively to a series of increasingly humanlike entities until a certain point—somewhere around 80 percent humanlike—at which the emotional response suddenly becomes extremely negative. Hence, the Frisbee-shaped Roomba vacuum cleaner, an entity that is *at most* 30 percent humanoid in form and behavior (it knows how to navigate itself; it sings when the floor is clean), inspires such affection in its owners that many will give their hard-working vacuum a name.[7] Meanwhile, Frankenstein's creature, an entity *at least* 80 percent humanoid in form and behavior, inspires such revulsion in those who behold him that no one ever thinks to dignify him with a name. When graphically delineated—imagine a grid whose x-axis corresponds to the humanlikeness of an entity and whose y-axis corresponds to how we respond emotionally to that entity—the spectrum of human responses to a series of increasingly humanoid items can be delineated as a line that curves steadily upward (from negative to positive emotions) before abruptly descending and then reascending (toward 100 percent humanlike) to create what looks like a valley. For this reason, Mori's theory is known as "the uncanny *valley*."

To experience the uncanny valley is not simply to experience a feeling of disturbing uncertainty as to whether a given entity is animate or inanimate. It is to experience a feeling of disturbing uncertainty as to whether a given entity is *human* or *nonhuman*. This, in any case, is how the distinction between the uncanny and the uncanny valley has classically been interpreted. Yet the principle of anthropomorphism cannot be the only factor differentiating the uncanny valley from the phenomenon of the uncanny more generally. Consider the chimpanzee. These animals are at once extremely humanlike and obviously less than completely human in form and behavior, but we are apt to think of them as endearing and cute (as opposed to eerie and haunting). How is it that the chimpanzee can escape the uncanny valley while the humanoid robot so often finds itself consigned to the valley's depths? The crucial difference between robots and chimpanzees is that robots are, by definition, constructed rather than born. Insofar as the presence of constructedness in a given entity is what guarantees an experience of the uncanny valley, the uncanny valley can be defined as a feeling of disturbing uncertainty over whether a given *artifact* is human or nonhuman. However, even this new definition leaves some further refinement to be desired. More specifically, it does not sufficiently account for the way in which the element of constructedness interacts with the element of humanlikeness to bring about an uncanny reaction.

Before we can fully appreciate the place of constructedness in the uncanny valley, we must first analyze the intricate nature of constructedness itself. As Elaine Scarry has observed in "The Interior Structure of the Artifact" (chapter 5 of *The Body in Pain*), all human-made objects belong to one of three categories. What follows is a summary of her explanation.

The first category contains artifacts that are "superreal." These artifacts operate "by seeming to have an ontological status, or degree of reality, *greater* than human beings themselves" (311–312). Such an artifact—Scarry cites God as a prime example—must be devoid of any "seams or cutting marks" that might betray its origins as a constructed entity (312). Only by transcending its status as a human-made object can a superreal artifact like God perform its task.

The second category contains artifacts "that work by seeming real" (312). This category, which Scarry identifies as "by far the largest" of the three, includes everyday objects such as automobiles, clothing, language, and streetlights (312). Most of the time, these artifacts "exist in a state of 'realness' rather than 'madeness'" (313): their seams and cutting marks cannot be seen, and we do not consciously think of them as artifacts. But whereas the seams and cutting marks of God are irrecoverable, the seams and cutting marks of those artifacts in the second category are indeed susceptible to recovery. In particular, these artifacts become exposed as constructed entities when they are damaged or broken. As soon as, say, a table needs repair—as soon as the pins and screws and unpainted wood and nails and hinged braces come into view—the table ceases to exist in its habitual state of realness. We become aware of the fact that before the table was "made-real" it was "made-up" (313).

The third category contains works of art (314). These artifacts are conspicuously framed by their artificiality: "Their made-upness surrounds them and remains available to us on an ongoing basis" (314). It is no coincidence, Scarry points out, that we often refer to artworks by the names of their artists (314). By saying, "This painting is a Picasso," or "This is Millet," we invoke the person who made the artwork; in so doing, we call attention to and even celebrate the fact that the artwork is a human-made entity (314).

Using Scarry's taxonomy of artifacts to elaborate on Mori's aesthetic theory of robots, I want to argue that we experience the uncanny valley when there is uncertainty as to whether a humanoid artifact belongs to the *second* or *third* category of artifacts. (I will discuss the *first* category of artifacts in a later section of this chapter.) How humanlike a robot might be does not matter as long as the robot is behaving unambiguously in a manner that we deem "natural." Such a robot belongs *by definition* to the second category of artifacts; therefore, it cannot logically inhabit the uncanny valley. But humanlikeness becomes an important factor when the robot breaks down and fails to function the way we expect it to function. Would the sight of a broken Roomba cause us to experience the uncanny valley? We might feel a pang of half-sheepish solicitude, but it is unlikely that we would feel the unspeakable disquietude and aversion that accompany genuine encounters with the uncanny valley. By contrast, consider now the scene from *A.I.* in which the robot child David, having damaged parts of his internal circuitry by ingesting spinach, is being repaired by technicians from Cybertronics. As he lies on the table during the procedure, David—played by the talented child actor Haley Joel Osment—smiles calmly at his human mother and assures her that he does not feel any pain. Meanwhile, the inner contents of his artificial stomach are fully exposed as computer engineers carefully remove pieces of spinach from David's electronic innards. The overwhelming uncanniness of this scene results from our uncertainty as to which category of artifact David embodies. From the neck up, he exists in a state of realness rather than madeness: his face looks and behaves exactly like that of a "real" boy. From the neck down, however, he appears overtly unreal, framed conspicuously by his status as a constructed object. That David inhabits the uncanny valley here is reflected in the look of horror, confusion, and phobia on the face of his human mother, who is evidently at a loss as to how to respond to the situation.[8]

Earlier we visualized the uncanny valley in terms of a grid whose x-axis corresponds to the humanlikeness of a given entity and whose y-axis corresponds to how we respond emotionally to that entity. We imagined the spectrum of human responses to a series of increasingly humanoid items as a line curving steadily upward (from negative to positive emotions) before abruptly descending and then reascending to create what looks like a valley. Let us now revise this initial formulation of the uncanny valley in the following way. Imagine a grid whose x-axis corresponds to the humanlikeness of a robot and whose y-axis corresponds to how we respond emotionally to that robot *when the robot is conspicuously damaged.* The more and more humanlike the robot, the more and more sympathetic and compassionate our response to the damaged robot will become, until a certain point—somewhere around 80 percent humanlike—at which our emotional response to the damaged robot suddenly becomes revulsion as opposed to sympathy. The uncanny valley corresponds to those artifacts whose imperfect similitude to human beings (or "humanity effect") is significant enough that we feel antipathy rather than compassion when the artifact is damaged and thereby framed as simultaneously made-up and made-real.

The scene from *A.I.* described above is just one of many science-fictional moments that elicit feelings of the uncanny valley by portraying damaged humanoid robots. An even more spectacular example from the same film can be found in the well-known "Flesh Fair" sequence. Stray robots—most of them old and in obvious need of repair—are hunted down by robot-hating humans who gather the victims at the center of an arena and viciously torture them before a crowd of jeering human spectators. What condemns these robots to the uncanny valley is the incongruity that they embody between the made-up and the made-real. Almost all of the robots display an aliveness—fear of death, ongoing self-awareness, the wish to survive—to which we cannot help but respond on some level as if they were truly human. Yet our sense of the robots' "humanity" is destabilized here by images that remind us of the robots' artificiality: exposed wire, body parts textured with rust, entrails composed of deteriorating synthetic material. Already suffering degradation prior to their capture, the robots are further degraded by their human captors at the gruesome "Flesh Fair." Set afire, drenched in acid, and dismembered by chainsaws, the doomed robots are publicly stripped of their "humanity effect" and reduced to junk. By the time the scene is over, we are violently conscious of the fact that before these humanoid artifacts were "made-real" they were "made-up."

Like *A.I.*, the film *Blade Runner* abounds with uncanny depictions of damaged robots. Two scenes of robot death are particularly relevant to our discussion. In both scenes, Rick Deckard—the film's human protagonist, who constantly struggles with ambivalence toward his professional duty to "retire" (kill) outlawed robots—pursues and destroys a "Nexus-6 replicant," a type of robot bioengineered to be virtually indistinguishable from a human being. The casualty in the first scene is Zhora (played by Joanna Cassidy), a female robot whom Deckard (Harrison Ford) has tracked down at a bar where she has been masquerading as an exotic dancer. Following a hectic chase along traffic-jammed city streets, Deckard shoots Zhora multiple times in the back, causing her to crash—the action is shown in dramatically slow motion—through a succession of windows in a department store. Lying in a pile of broken glass, eyes glazed and limbs inert, clad in almost nothing but a plastic see-through jacket, Zhora's corpse is obviously meant to resemble the female mannequins on display in the store windows through which she has just crashed. Whereas moments ago (during the kinetic chase scene) Zhora had seemed vital and "made-real," in dying she suddenly seems fabricated and "made-up." Out of the incongruous juxtaposition of these two states emerges a powerful evocation of the uncanny valley.

The casualty in the second scene is a female robot named Pris (played by Daryl Hannah). The scene opens with Deckard, gun in hand, cautiously searching for Pris in a dimly lit room crowded with puppets, figurines, and automatons of various sizes. Although at this point in the movie Pris is not physically damaged (yet), she is already immobilized—literally—by the threat to her existence that Deckard embodies. In particular, terror has exiled Pris to the uncanny valley by forcing her to feign lifelessness in the guise of a lifelike dummy. Her hair styled to look like a wig, her face painted in stark hues of white and bluish-black, Pris holds her body in an eerily doll-like pose as Deckard probes the other humanoid artifacts in the room. Pris's exile to the uncanny valley becomes permanent when Deckard, having discovered that she is not an inanimate doll, injures Pris with multiple gunshots. In the moments before her death, Pris shrieks and thrashes against the floor with a mechanical vitality that is truly horrifying to watch and to hear. When she finally does die, her motionless body reminds us of Zhora's corpse lying mannequin-like in the ruins of the department store windows.[9] The two deaths may differ in detail, but they are nearly identical in aesthetic effect.

The death scenes recounted above have notable counterparts in *Do Androids Dream of Electric Sheep?*, the Philip K. Dick novel from which *Blade Runner* was adapted. As texts that belong to two different media, *Blade Runner* and *Do Androids Dream?* achieve the effect of the uncanny valley in different ways. Yet both texts—whether through the techniques of film or through the resources of prose—arrive at the uncanny valley by generating uncertainty as to whether a humanoid robot belongs to the second category of artifacts (human-made objects that exist in a state of realness, except when they are damaged) or the third category of artifacts (human-made objects that are conspicuously framed by their artificiality).

Consider, for example, the following vignette of Pris from *Do Androids Dream of Electric Sheep?* Like her cinematic double, the Pris we encounter in the novel has been rendered uncanny by the damage that results from living in constant danger. "Fear made her seem ill," Dick writes; "it distorted her body lines, made her appear as if someone had broken her and then, with malice, patched her together badly" with the aim of constructing "a fragmented and misaligned shrinking figure" (62). Under normal circumstances, Pris's status as a constructed object would be invisible—she was designed, after all, to appear convincingly human—but the fear of being destroyed has disrupted Pris's ordinary function and thereby exposed to us the fact of her constructedness. We view fear-stricken Pris less as a human subject and more as an artifact whose creator (implied by the word "someone") did a deliberately "bad" job, an artifact whose creator "had broken her and then, with malice, patched her together badly." That Pris's creator *intentionally* created something "fragmented and misaligned" causes us to imagine him or her as an experimental artist—a practitioner of cubism, perhaps—and this evocation of artistry contributes to the uncanniness of the vignette. In the reader's mind, Pris oscillates between two conflicting images: human-seeming literary character (the second category of artifacts) and cubist artwork (the third category of artifacts).

There is no "Zhora" in *Do Androids Dream of Electric Sheep?*, but a number of incidents in the book resonate with Zhora's death in *Blade Runner*. In one scene, a dying android that had moments ago seemed human suddenly becomes an image of shattered kitchenware not unlike the image in *Blade Runner* of shattered department store windows: the robot "toppled like an overstacked collection of separate, brittle entities. . . . [It] smashed into the kitchen table and carried dishes and flatware down with it. Reflex circuits in the corpse made it twitch and flutter, but it had died" (223). By synchronizing the literal imagery of shattered robot with the figurative imagery of shattered kitchenware, Dick effectively shatters the illusion that the robot had been anything but artificial. In a similarly uncanny scene from the same novel, a robot opera singer named Luba Luft is killed while enjoying an art exhibit. The death scene is prefaced by a fascinating tableau in which Luba, not yet aware that she is being monitored by bounty hunters who are after her life, gazes intently at Edvard Munch's 1895 artwork *Puberty:*

> Holding a printed catalogue, Luba Luft, wearing shiny tapered pants and an illuminated gold vestlike top, stood absorbed in the picture before her: a drawing of a young girl, hands clasped together, seated on the edge of a bed, an expression of bewildered wonder and new, groping awe imprinted on the face. (131)

In this highly intricate tableau—one might almost call it a *tableau vivant*—an artificial woman (whose seemingly natural humanlikeness is belied by the metallic surfaces adorning her body) silently identifies with the emotions of a different kind of artificial woman (whose artificiality is itself framed and magnified by the museum setting). Significantly, the syntactic form of the sentence generates ambiguity as to which of the two faces is imprinted with "an expression of bewildered wonder and new, groping awe." By obscuring the line between the made-real and the made-up, the image of Luba Luft staring at Munch's artwork prepares us for our subsequent descent into the uncanny valley. As the bounty hunters accost Luba and she realizes that her life is in danger, fear graphically transforms her body into a still life of an inanimate object: "Her eyes faded and the color dimmed from her face, leaving it cadaverous, as if already starting to decay. As if life had in an instant retreated to some point far inside her, leaving the body to its automatic ruin" (131–132). When laser beams pierce her stomach, the still life—changing its genre now—temporarily morphs into Munch's most famous artwork: "She began to scream; she lay crouched against the wall of the elevator, screaming. Like the picture. . . . [Then, her] body fell forward, facedown, in a heap" (134). If the effect of the uncanny valley is achieved by a blurring of the line between the made-up and the made-real, it is compounded by a blurring of the line between still life and Expressionist painting. From one angle, Luba Luft comes across as a motionless illusion of lifelikeness, artfully constructed and ultimately lifeless. From another angle, Luba Luft comes across as a twisted portrait of subjectivity so forceful, so raw, that the frame of portrayal itself is nearly brought to life despite its explicit unreality.

Do Androids Dream of Electric Sheep? is not the only novel in which Dick explores the uncanny valley. *We Can Build You* (1972) features robots whose uncanniness results from the alarming ease with which each robot can be switched on and off and on again by its human operator. As the following passage shows, one moment—one flick of a switch—is all it takes for a seemingly lively human to be voided of its "humanity effect": " 'Glop,' the Stanton said, and then became rigid, as lifeless as a window-store dummy; the light in its eyes expired, its arms paused and stiffened" (18). The uncanny effect is no greater when a robot is being switched off than when a robot is being switched on. Indeed, the passage below suggests that the uncanny effect is greatest when a robot is being switched on.

[Maury] began tearing the newspaper from the human-shaped bundle, and sure enough, there presently emerged an elderly-looking gentleman with eyes shut and white beard, wearing archaically-styled clothing, his hands folded over his chest.

"You'll see how convincing this simulacrum is," Maury said, "when it orders its own pizza." He began to tinker with switches which were available at the back of the thing.

All at once the face assumed a grumpy, taciturn expression and it said in a growl, "My friend, remove your fingers from my body, if you will." It pried Maury's hands loose from it, and Maury grinned at me.

"See?" Maury said. The thing had sat up slowly and was in the process of methodically brushing itself off; it had a stern, vengeful look, now, as if it believed we had done it some harm, possibly sapped it and knocked it out, and it was just recovering. (13)

The uncanny effect of this passage emanates from the discord between the seriousness with which the robot perceives the injury from which it is "just recovering" and the lack of seriousness with which the human characters perceive the robot's claims to injury. The humans—Louis (the narrator) and Maury—treat the robot not as a fellow person but as a novelty item. To them, the robot's indignation is trivial and amusing, albeit slightly discomfiting. When the narrator says, "It had a stern, vengeful look, now, as if it believed we had done it some harm, possibly sapped it and knocked it out, and it was just recovering," he might as well be saying: "Why is this made-up toy behaving as if we did something wrong to it? How did it come up with this silly notion that we knocked it out?" From the robot's perspective, however, the indignation is entirely justified. In being switched off against its will, the robot was "sapped" of its selfhood and "knocked out" of the state of made-realness. In being switched back on against its will, it was forced to remember anew the injury of having been switched off in the past—an injury that it knows will be repeated in the future. By calling attention to its own status as an injured artifact, the robot becomes even more conspicuously framed by its made-upness than when it was merely an inert dummy. At the same time, it gives an impression of "made-realness" by demonstrating any humanlike awareness at all.

No humanoid artifact embodies the uncanny valley more vividly than the monster in Mary Shelley's *Frankenstein*. And nowhere is the monster more dramatically uncanny than during the scene of his animation. In a sublime evocation of the uncanny valley, Shelley has Victor Frankenstein recount the moment when he brought his monstrous creation to life:

How can I describe my emotions at this catastrophe, or how delineate the wretch whom with such infinite pains and care I had endeavoured to form? His limbs were in proportion, and I had selected his features as beautiful. Beautiful!—Great God! His yellow skin scarcely covered the work of muscles and arteries beneath; his hair was of a lustrous black, and flowing; his teeth of a pearly whiteness; but these luxuriances only formed a more horrid contrast with his watery eyes, that seemed almost of the same colour as the dun-white sockets in which they were set, his shrivelled complexion and straight black lips. (57)

Despite the fact that Victor specifically chose each feature for its beauty, the combined form is aesthetically revolting. To behold the creature is to perceive not a seamless and unified organic whole but a jagged collection of pieces: muscles, arteries, pearly teeth, straight black lips, yellow skin, watery eyes, and so on. The disjointedness of the monster's body is again conjured when Victor wakes up from a nightmare to find the monster standing next to his bed: "His eyes, if eyes they may be called, were fixed on me. His jaws opened, and he muttered some inarticulate sounds, while a grin wrinkled his cheeks" (58). Had we been told, "The creature smiled," we might have identified in him the kinds of human traits (friendliness, love, benevolence) that we associate with the act of smiling. Instead, we are given a purely mechanical description of what happens to certain sections of his face when he tries to simulate this act: "A grin wrinkled his cheeks." Likewise, had we been told, "The creature saw me and tried to speak," we might have sympathized with the creature's attempt to communicate with his maker. Instead, we are given a strangely automated account of what happens to the monster's "jaws" and "eyes" ("if eyes they may be called") when he tries to simulate communication. Cheeks, jaws, eyes, muscles, arteries, lips, sockets, limbs: each segment stands out as a discrete unit disobedient to incorporation. The monster's body is a patchwork cadaver whose visible seams and stitches—a webwork of lacerations—openly display the fact of the monster's madeness. The reason why Frankenstein's creation is so terribly uncanny is that he was damaged at the moment of his creation and deprived thereafter of any opportunity to be healed. Unlike the other humanoid artifacts discussed in this chapter—Zhora, Pris, Luba Luft, David (the robot child), and so on—Frankenstein's monster never existed in a state of total realness in the first place. From birth to death he embodies the incompatibility between "made-realness" and "made-upness" within a single humanoid artifact.

Transcending the Uncanny Valley:
Literalized Personification and Other Lyric
Structures of Voice

So far I have been discussing moments in works of science fiction when the uncanny valley interferes with our ability to recognize the humanity of sentient robots. As I mentioned earlier, however, many of these same works of science fiction also contain moments when the effects of the uncanny valley are countervailed and sentient robots become recognizable as subjects worthy of empathy. Science fiction accomplishes this feat, I want to suggest, by creating situations in which we are made to feel uncertainty *not* as to whether a robot belongs to the second category of artifacts (the made-real) or the third (the made-up) but rather as to *whether* a given robot belongs to the *first* category of artifacts. As I mentioned earlier, the first category contains "superreal" artifacts that function by seeming to have a degree of reality even greater than that of human beings and whose status as artifacts has become irrecoverable. By creating situations in which the ontological status of humanoid artifacts seems almost to surpass our own, science fiction opens up a luminous space in which the moral entitlements of sentient robots become not only legible and intelligible but also impossible to deny.

What enables the science-fictional representation of robot rights is the literalization of lyric figures. Two lyric figures play especially crucial roles in advancing the representation of robot rights. The first is personification, which endows nonhuman entities with human characteristics. The second is apostrophe, whereby a speaker addresses an absent person, an abstraction, or an inanimate object as though the "you" were a living human presence.[10] In the science-fiction scenarios discussed below, robots are placed within lyric structures of voice in which personification and apostrophe behave as forces that literally bestow humanity on nonhuman entities. To reinvoke the grid whose x-axis corresponds to the humanlikeness of a robot and whose y-axis corresponds to how we respond emotionally to that robot when it is conspicuously damaged: the steep ascent forming the rightmost side of the uncanny valley corresponds to the intense admiration that we feel in response to those lyric moments in science fiction when humanoid artifacts become "superreal."

Humanity-bestowing structures of voice can take on a variety of shapes. One of these shapes is soliloquy, a type of speech in which a speaker reveals his or her (or its) inner thoughts while alone or while unselfconscious of any listener. There is something uniquely human about the act of soliloquizing. To soliloquize—to feel and think aloud without the purpose of communication—is to demonstrate the mystery of human consciousness in its purest form. Anyone or anything that soliloquizes must be human on some fundamental level. Thus, when Frankenstein's monster soliloquizes, he becomes so compellingly human that his uncanny attributes fade away. Consider the climactic soliloquy toward the end of the narrative in which the monster grieves over the dead body of his creator.

> In his murder my crimes are consummated; the miserable series of my being is wound to its close! Oh, Frankenstein! Generous and self-devoted being! What does it avail that I now ask thee to pardon me? I, who irretrievably destroyed thee by destroying all thou lovedst. Alas! He is cold, he cannot answer me. (219)

At the same time that this apostrophe addresses its *object* (the now-inanimate human who created the humanoid artifact) as if he were still alive, it annunciates its *subject* (the man-made object created by the once-animate object of address) as literally alive, present, and human. Indeed, the apostrophe redounds upon its source, resulting in a superfluousness of life, presence, and humanity in the first-person "I." Speaking in a voice overflowing with lyric subjectivity, Frankenstein's creature becomes surrounded by an aura of superreality through which he transcends the uncanny valley. Viewing the monster through his aura of superreality, we notice not the seams and stitches of his patchwork body but the powerful authority of his powerfully human emotions (remorse, despair, sorrow, love, ambivalence). Even Walton, who witnesses this deathbed soliloquy from afar, is aroused to "curiosity and compassion" by the creature's heightened speech (219).

In a different but similarly humanizing soliloquy from earlier in the same narrative, the creature wonders to himself about his place (or lack thereof) in the human family:

> I heard of the difference of sexes, and the birth and growth of children, how the father doted on the smiles of the infant, and the lively sallies of the older child, how all the life and cares of the mother were wrapped up in the precious charge, how the mind of youth expanded and gained knowledge, of brother, sister, and all the various relationships which bind one human being to another in mutual bonds.
>
> But where were my friends and relations? No father had watched my infant days, no mother had blessed me with smiles and caresses; or if they

had, all my past life was now a blot, a blind vacancy in which I distinguished nothing. From my earliest remembrance I had been as I then was
in height and proportion. I had never yet seen a being resembling me, or
who claimed any intercourse with me. What was I? The question again re-
curred, to be answered only with groans. (121)

As with the soliloquy uttered over Frankenstein's corpse, this earlier soliloquy
has the effect of encompassing its speaker within a lyric field in which the
forces of personification operate on a literal level without losing their figurative
power. Within this lyric space, the monster's uncanniness—his ambiguous
status as human yet nonhuman, made-real yet made-up—becomes immaterial. What becomes relevant instead is the creature's remarkable and unmistakably human capacity to ponder existential matters such as the nature of
identity and the meaning of humanity. What am I? Do I have parents? Where
did I come from? Why do I exist? Where do I belong? In voicing these kinds
of questions, the creature becomes literally personified: that is, he becomes
recognizable as a person endowed with essential human characteristics such as
the wish for self-knowledge and the desire to be loved by kin. Giving lyric
voice to his loneliness, the monster becomes identifiable as a human person
worthy of our empathy and concern. Even Frankenstein, the monster's creator
and greatest nemesis, finds it difficult to resist the creature's soulful humanity.
"His words had a strange effect upon me," Victor reflects after listening to the
creature's account of his experiences as an outcast: "I compassioned him, and
sometimes felt a wish to console him" (147). Indeed, so powerful is the lyric
energy surrounding the monster that Victor is moved to acknowledge the
monster's moral claims on him: "I had no *right* to withhold from him the small
portion of happiness which was yet in my power to bestow" (147, emphasis
added). Persuaded that even the most uncanny of creatures should not be denied the right to happiness, Victor decides to grant the monster his wish for a
companion, a second humanoid artifact who would be (in the monster's own
words) "as deformed and horrible as myself" (144). (As we all know, of course,
the promised companion never materializes: the uncanny valley interferes with
Frankenstein's desire to complete the project. Devastated, the monster spends
the rest of his life avenging the "abortion" of his would-be companion by destroying Victor's loved ones and robbing him of any opportunity to be happy.)

Frankenstein's monster is not the only humanoid artifact gifted with the
faculty of soliloquy. He has a fellow soliloquist in Roy Batty, the android
character (played brilliantly by Rutger Hauer) at the center of *Blade Runner*.

Toward the end of the film, Roy delivers what has become one of the most fa-mous speeches in the history of science fiction. The soliloquy itself is preceded by a violent scene in which Deckard and Roy hunt each other down inside a derelict building. Eventually they find themselves outside on the top of the edifice, where Deckard missteps and nearly falls to his death. Hanging on to the edge of the roof with one hand, he is about to lose his grip when Roy—his own hand pierced with a nail—catches Deckard's wrist and pulls him up to safety. Instead of resuming their fight (as we might expect), Roy lets go of Deckard's arm and slowly sits down on the roof. Roy knows that he is about to die. Like all other "Nexus-6 replicants," he was built with a four-year lifespan, and at this point in the narrative his time is almost up. Bathed in rain-filled cerulean light, eyes strangely distant and oblique, Roy begins to speak won-deringly about the life that is about to cease within him. Deckard, amazed and speechless, listens as Roy reminisces about his celestial experiences as a combat model stationed in outer space:

> I've . . . seen things you people wouldn't believe. . . . Attack ships on fire off the shoulder of Orion. . . . I watched C-beams . . . glitter in the dark near the Tannhauser gate. . . . All those . . . moments will be lost . . . in time . . . like . . . tears . . . in . . . rain. . . . Time . . . to die.

The soulfulness that Roy evinces here is striking—not only because he is sup-posedly a soulless android, but also because the *human* characters in the movie are devoid of such exalted spirituality. Indeed, Roy's ontological status at this point seems to have become greater than that of human beings. There is some-thing holy about him now. Our impression of him as godlike is reinforced by several iconographic details. Roy's nail-pierced hand, as many viewers have noted, brings to mind the crucifixion of Jesus. Moreover, when Roy finally succumbs to death (or perhaps rebirth), a white dove—a Christian symbol for the Holy Spirit—flutters out of Roy's clasp (he had been holding the bird against his chest) and ascends into a sky that is generally dark throughout the movie but here is shown as clear and blue. In addition to evoking the Christian deity, Roy's iconographic profile incorporates elements of Buddhism. As Val-erie Su-Lin Wee has noted, "the posture that Batty assumes in death resembles that of the enlightened Buddha, sitting with his face downcast, his legs folded under him, calm and impassive to the rain." Roy's mystique is further en-hanced by the oracular content of his speech. The Wagnerian allusion to "Tannhauser gate" and the enigmatic allusion to "C-beams"—we never learn what this phrase means—have the effect of imbuing him with some kind of cosmic intelligence. As an apotheosis of humanity, Roy transcends not just the uncanny valley but his origins as a human-made object. The fact that he was constructed (rather than born) no longer matters. What does matter is Roy's status as someone worthy of our moral respect, someone who should have been allowed to live for more than four years, someone who was unjustly deprived of his right to freedom from the threat of persecution.

Not all robots, of course, are soliloquists. David, the child-robot protagonist of *A.I.*, rarely (if ever) soliloquizes. Yet several times throughout the movie we find him implicated in lyric structures of voice identical in effect to the soliloquies discussed above, structures of voice that endow the robot with human characteristics. The first of these lyric structures appears in the memorable "imprinting scene" (as some have called it). Leading up to this fateful moment are a number of events and circumstances that are worth briefly summarizing here. Early in the movie we are introduced to Henry and Monica, a married couple who have been grieving for their comatose son over the past five years. One day Henry brings home an experimental product that his company has allowed him to try out: a robot named David that looks and behaves like an eleven-year-old boy. Although Monica is initially ambivalent ("I can't accept this! There is no substitute for your own child!"—and yet, "outside he just looks so real . . ."), over time she grows fond of David. Eventually she decides to go through with the irreversible "imprinting" procedure that will program David to love Monica forever as his own mother. The procedure takes the form of a dialogue prescribed by David's "instruction manual."

> MONICA: Now, I'm going to read some words, and . . . uh . . . they won't make any sense, but I want you to listen to them anyway. And . . . look at me all the time. Can you do that?
>
> DAVID: Yes, Monica.
>
> MONICA: Can you feel my hand on the back of your neck?
>
> DAVID: Yes.
>
> MONICA: Does any of this hurt?
>
> DAVID: No.
>
> MONICA: Okay. Now. Look at me? Ready? Cirrus. Socrates. Particle. Decibel. Hurricane. Dolphin. Tulip. Monica. David. Monica . . . All right . . . I wonder if I did that right. I don't—
>
> DAVID: What were those words for, Mommy?
>
> MONICA: What did you call me?

DAVID: Mommy.
MONICA: Who am I, David?
DAVID: You are my Mommy.

The David we see before the procedure is a humanoid toy that mechanically addresses Monica by her first name. The David we see at the end of the procedure is a son endowed with the human capacity to love his "Mommy." Intermediating between these two Davids is a lyric structure of voice in the shape of an incantatory spell: "Cirrus. Socrates. Particle. Decibel. Hurricane. Dolphin. Tulip." When read superficially, this might seem like a random (albeit strangely moving) list of words. But the superficial appearance of randomness belies the intricate poetic logic at work in the verbal sequence. In explicating this poetic logic, I hope to illuminate the way in which this lyric structure of voice enables David's science-fictional transformation from humanoid toy to human boy.

Notice, first, that all seven words are singular nouns. In the absence of adjectives and verbs, the nouns seem to inhabit a lyric realm devoid of modification and the passage of time. Contributing to the sense of otherworldly timelessness here is the absence of any reference to cultural artifacts. Instead of containing nouns such as "automobile" or "castle," the sequence contains nouns that refer to the natural world and natural science: "cirrus," "dolphin," and so on. The seven words are alike not only with respect to part of speech and type of referent but also with respect to meter. Each noun has more than one syllable, and in each case (whether trochaic or dactylic) the stress falls on the initial syllable. Instead of beating iambically like a heart, the sequence conveys the sense that something is being pressed or imprinted—and indeed David is undergoing the process of imprinting onto Monica.

Although the seven nouns share many attributes, they also differ in meaningful ways. More importantly, the differences are organized to suggest a narrative. Phonically, for example, the sequence progresses through three couplets—"cirrus" and "Socrates" both end in sibilance; "particle" and "decibel" both end with the sound of the letter "l"; "hurricane" and "dolphin" both end with the sound of the letter "n"—before leaving "tulip" uniquely uncouplet-ed. At the level of diction, too, the sequence suggests a kind of narrative. The nouns are arranged in decreasing orders of abstractness and obscurity. "Cirrus," the first word, hovers nebulously between concrete and abstract noun. The image exists far away from us, a mist high up in the sky. "Socrates," the second word, is somewhat easier than "cirrus" was to imagine. But "Socrates,"

too, hovers between abstraction and concreteness. More rarefied icon than familiar person, he exists at a remote distance from us—not high up in the sky,
but far back in ancient history. "Particle" and "decibel," the third and fourth
words, share a single texture of elusiveness. At once concrete and abstract,
both nouns designate subtle units that are almost but not entirely impossible to
hold still in the mind. "Hurricane," the fifth word, conjures imagery so massive and chaotic that it challenges the imagination. Despite its aggressive
cloudiness, however, "hurricane" is decidedly more concrete than abstract; indeed, it is the most concrete of all the nouns that we have encountered so far.
But "hurricane" is nowhere near as concrete as is the next noun, "dolphin." The
image evoked by this word has a definite shape, size, and color. It is scaled to
the human body. One can readily imagine interacting physically with a dolphin. Yet there remains something remote even about this entity: after all,
dolphins are wild animals that live inside the sea. By contrast, there is nothing
remote about the image conjured by the seventh noun: "tulip." It is certainly
the most concrete of all the seven nouns. Tulips are earthy, vivid, palpable, and
richly available to the human senses. They are as easy to grasp within the mind
as with the hands.

What truly completes the lyric structure of voice in this scene is the recitation of each participant's name following the seven-noun sequence: "Monica.
David. Monica." Through the recitation of their names, speaker and listener
are together incorporated into a transformational lyric space in which concrete living shapes (dolphin, tulip) emerge from vague inanimate abstraction
(cirrus). It is in the context of this lyric matrix that David literally becomes
animated with a human profile, an emotional life, which he had formerly
lacked. Personified into a son for whom Monica is "Mommy," David becomes
vitally recognizable—both to us and to Monica, who upon hearing him say
"Mommy" gathers David into her arms—as a human child worthy of being
cared for and loved.

Other lyric structures of voice in *A.I.* situate David not as a listener but as a
lyric speaker with a voice of his own. At the Flesh Fair, for example, he creates
a lyric space around himself by pleading for his life just as he is about to be
killed: "Don't burn me!" he screams, "Don't make me die!" As he utters these
words, David becomes so compellingly literal a personification of the innocence and vulnerability of children that the human spectators—who have
hitherto been celebrating the demolition of robots—defend David's right to
live and accuse the (human) ringmaster of being an inhumane "monster." In a

much later scene, David again surrounds himself with a lyric structure of voice by making a heightened appeal for life. But the situation this time is vastly different from that of the Flesh Fair. Whereas in that earlier scene we saw David about to be burned at the stake, here we see him sitting inside a watercraft amid the submerged ruins of an amusement park at the bottom of the sea. The watercraft is parked in front of a painted statue of the "Blue Fairy," a character in *Pinocchio* who assists in the puppet's transformation into a flesh-and-blood child. Staring through the windshield at this life-sized statue, David begs the statue to instill him with "genuine" human life:

> Please . . . please, please make me into a real live boy. Please . . . Blue Fairy?
> Please . . . please . . . make me real. Blue Fairy? Please, please make me real.
> Please make me a real boy. Please, Blue Fairy, make me into a real boy . . .

David's apostrophe to the Blue Fairy is similar in many ways to the apostrophe in *Frankenstein* in which the grief-stricken monster addresses his creator's dead body. In both cases, the speaker is an animate anthropomorphic artifact addressing an inanimate anthropomorphic entity as though this addressee were a living presence. In both cases, moreover, the apostrophe redounds on its own source, resulting in a palpable excess of aliveness, presence, and humanity in the first-person "I." In David's case, however, the redundancy of the literalized apostrophe is rendered doubly redundant by the fact that the form of his entreaty is a repetition of its content. David is requesting literally to be apostrophized; that is, he is requesting literally to be anthropomorphized and brought to life. At the same time, his very uttering of this request calls attention to the superfluity of the request itself. The redundancy of David's plea is made even more apparent by the chipped façade of the painted statue, which was clearly never alive in the first place. Framed in contrast to a noticeably fake "person," endowed with a voice that is more than abundantly human, David acquires a degree of reality so heightened that the fact of his artificiality becomes unavailable to us.

David's aura of superreality proves to be everlasting. By the time we reach the conclusion of *A.I.*, thousands of years into the future, David has (ironically) become the most human being in existence. More specifically, his original function as a placeholder for Henry and Monica's "real" son has been rendered obsolete by his significance as the only surviving member of humankind in a postapocalyptic world inhabited by superadvanced robots that barely resemble human beings. David's mystique as the archetype of humanity is reflected in the way he is regarded by those who inhabit postapocalyptic Earth. The superadvanced robots venerate David as a living personification of all that is (or was) truly human. "You are so important to us David, you are unique in all the world," they tell him: "David, you are the enduring memory of the human race."

Like *A.I.*, David Mitchell's 2004 novel *Cloud Atlas* features a humanoid artifact who is mistreated and deemed uncanny during one lifetime but is deemed sacred and "superreal" in a postapocalyptic world many lifetimes later. Parts of the novel are set in a near-future Korea (here renamed "Nea So Copros") where humans are served by a docile underclass of "fabricants," human clones genetically engineered to perform specialized tasks. The fabricants, which "cost almost nothing to manufacture," are treated by their creators as disposable slaves (325). Physiologically they are set apart from the so-called pureblood humans by uncanny features that publicly mark them as "fabricated": some clones, for example, have "saucerlike eyes" that are "genomed for darkness" (324); others have eyes whose irises are yellowish-white (321). While most of the clones unthinkingly accept their fate, one clone named Sonmi~451 (a name resonant of Ray Bradbury's 1953 dystopian novel *Fahrenheit 451*) rebels against the system and becomes a martyr for fabricant rights. Before she is executed, she defiantly tells her life story to an archivist who records the interview on an "orison," an egg-shaped device that registers and holographically projects audiovisual imagery. Throughout the interview, Sonmi~451 speaks in a voice that is distinctively lyrical and quietly authoritative. She utters striking aphorisms: "Truth is singular. Its 'versions' are mistruths" (185); "Time is the speed at which the past decays" (235). Moreover, she demonstrates an exquisite sensitivity to nature that the callous pureblood humans seem to lack. "Once genomed moths spun around our heads, electronlike," she remembers observing: "Their wings' logos had mutated over generations into a chance syllabary: a small victory of nature over corpocracy" (328). So remarkable are her words that at one point during the interview the archivist himself is moved to acknowledge Sonmi~451's gift for appreciating beauty: "You speak like an aesthete," he says wonderingly (212). Through the lyricism of her speech, Sonmi~451 transcends her fabricant status and assumes an aura of heightened soulfulness and self-knowledge. Moreover, as with David's aura in *A.I.*, Sonmi's aura abides into the far future. Eras after her death, in a postapocalyptic world where humans are nearly extinct, Sonmi's orison-generated presence is worshiped by those few humans still alive.

They revere her "beautsome" image, marvel at the poetry of her speech, and honor the dignity of her spirit.

What Would It Mean to Remake Humans into Humans?

To varying degrees, the works of science fiction discussed above are reflections of a single idea, namely, the possibility that sentient humanoid artifacts, were they to exist, might somehow be more perfectly or more archetypically human than humans could ever be themselves. Nowhere is this notion explored more thoroughly than in the science fiction of Isaac Asimov. Asimov famously posited "Three Laws of Robotics," three rules of behavior that all robots in his fictional universe are designed to obey:

> One. A robot may not injure a human being or, through inaction, allow a human being to come to harm.
>
> Two. A robot must obey the orders given it by human beings, except where such orders would conflict with the First Law.
>
> Three. A robot must protect its own existence, as long as such protection does not conflict with the First or Second Law. (*Prelude to Foundation*, 485; the laws are also cited in many other passages in Asimov's work)

Insofar as robot behavior is defined by the three Rules of Robotics, Asimov's robots are archetypes of the human conscience. The Rules of Robotics, as one of Asimov's characters points out, constitute not only the vital principles of robot design but also the vital principles of human ethics:

> If you stop to think of it, the three Rules of Robotics are the essential guiding principles of a good many of the world's ethical systems. Of course, every human being is supposed to have the instinct of self-preservation. That's Rule Three to a robot. Also every "good" human being, with a social conscience and a sense of responsibility, is supposed to defer to proper authority; to listen to his doctor, his boss, his government, his psychiatrist, his fellow man; to obey laws, to follow rules, to conform to custom—even when they interfere with his comfort or his safety. That's Rule Two to a robot. Also, every "good" human being is supposed to love others as himself, protect his fellow man, risk his life to save another. That's Rule One to a robot. ("Evidence," in *Robot Visions*, 146)

As entities inherently faithful to the principles of human ethics, Asimov's robots embody humanity more exemplarily than could any "actual" human being. It should come as no surprise, then, that the most humane and sympathetic characters in Asimov's fiction tend to be robots. Nor should it come as any surprise that many of these humane and sympathetic robots are shown as occupying positions of moral and political leadership. The android Stephen Byerly, for example, personifies the ideal politician: he is "incapable of harming humans, incapable of tyranny, of corruption, of stupidity, of prejudice" ("Evidence," 159). Andrew Martin, another android model citizen, begins his life as a devoted household servant and is eventually inspired to become a peaceful crusader for robot rights, including the freedom from being given robot-harming orders by malicious humans ("The Bicentennial Man," 266). Indeed, Asimov goes so far as to imagine a universe in which sentient humanoid artifacts become sapient caretakers of the human race. Having discovered the "Zeroth Law"—"A robot may not injure humanity or, through inaction, allow humanity to come to harm" (*Prelude to Foundation*, 486)—Asimov's robots have no choice but to assume the responsibility of governing and caring for all of humankind.

To portray robots as exemplars of humanity would strike most people as counterintuitive. After all, we frequently identify robots as "inhuman" beings— an attitude reflected in the synonymy between "robotic" and "dehumanized." This attitude is formed in no small part by the aesthetic and psychological effects of the uncanny valley discussed at the beginning of this chapter. Repulsed by the thought of artifacts that are *human enough* to threaten to replace us but *not human enough* to amount to our equals, we strive to distance ourselves from robots by classifying them as the very opposite of what we humans are. A more logical (or more seemingly logical) objection to the notion of robots as exemplars of humanity would be that robots need not be created to resemble human beings. If the robots that we create lack human attributes, then why should we treat our creations as though they had human rights? Yet such an objection fails to take into consideration the *inevitability* of the anthropomorphic robot. The robot's humanoid structure is an unavoidable corollary to the structure of the human drive to create artifacts.

The reason for such unavoidability will become apparent in light of Elaine Scarry's analysis of the nature of constructed objects. The act of creating, Scarry explains, comprises "both the creating of the object and the object's recreating of the human being" (310). Each half of the act of creating is contingent on the other. The second half, obviously, cannot take place without the first. Less obviously, but more importantly, "it is only because of the second that the first is undertaken" (310). In other words, artifacts exist precisely to "remake" human beings. Corrective lenses, for example, exist for the purpose of "remaking" the nearsighted person into someone capable of seeing distant objects clearly. Similarly, winter coats exist for the purpose of "remaking" the person who is about to don the coat into someone immune to chilly weather.

In remaking human beings, artifacts themselves necessarily take on human contours. Some artifacts are mimetic of individual parts of the human body: the corrective lens mimics the lens of the human eye; the coat mimics the skin that covers human flesh. Other artifacts correspond to human attributes that are less concrete: the Xerox machine, for example, is mimetic of the faculty of memory (283). Regardless of the human attribute being mimicked, all artifacts are mimetic of the workings of human consciousness. More specifically, all artifacts participate in what Scarry calls the "making sentient of the external world" (281). To create something, Scarry points out, is to "deprive the external world of the privilege of being inanimate—of, in other words, its privilege of being irresponsible to its sentient inhabitants on the basis that it is itself nonsentient" (285). Even if an artifact cannot literally experience pain or be aware that an entity beyond its own existence is experiencing pain, it can nonetheless constitute an objectification of such awareness; in other words, it can constitute a freestanding object bestowing exterior shape on both the human perception of pain and perceived-pain-wished-gone (289). A coat, for instance, is a freestanding material object that bestows exterior shape on both the perception of being uncomfortably cold and the wish for this discomfort to be gone.

If a sentient humanoid robot did exist, it would amount to the culmination and the literalization of the anthropomorphism inherent in all artifacts. It would be mimetic not just of human skin and of the lens of the eye but of the aggregate of all parts of the human body put together. It would be mimetic not just of the faculty of memory but of human consciousness as a whole. Finally, it would exemplify and personify the "making sentient of the external world" in which all artifacts participate. Not only would a sentient humanoid robot—in its capacity as a made thing—constitute a freestanding object bestowing exterior shape on human sentience, but it would also constitute a living and sentient being in its own right. The fact of its having been created would literally have deprived it of the irresponsibility of being inanimate. Moreover, the comprehensiveness of its humanlikeness would correspond to the comprehensiveness of the human motives behind its creation. If corrective

lenses exist for the purpose of "remaking" the nearsighted person into someone capable of seeing distant objects clearly, then a sentient humanoid robot
would exist for the purpose of "remaking" human beings *into human beings.*
But what would it mean to "remake" a human being into a human being?
Why would we need or want to engage in such an apparently tautological
endeavor? Under what circumstances might we be compelled to "remake"
ourselves by creating sentient humanoid artifacts?

A number of plausible scenarios come to mind. In one scenario, overpopulation on Earth compels us to explore the possibility that Mars might be capable of accommodating human life. To test the habitability of a potentially
lethal environment without putting any "real" humans at risk, scientists decide
to send a group of robots to Mars. The task requires that each robot be endowed with human features, including perseverance, the ability to take calculated risks, a sense of adventure, the ability to work as part of a team, a capacity
for complex problem-solving, the ability to think clearly and quickly under
highly stressful circumstances, and an anatomy that is humanoid enough to
give the scientists an accurate sense of how the Martian environment would
affect the human body. By taking the place of a human being whose life would
otherwise be endangered, such a robot—itself a literal embodiment of the
"remaking" of human beings—tautologically "remakes" the would-be explorer
into someone permitted to remain as he or she is: human, sentient, alive.

A second scenario has the opposite premise. Underpopulation on Earth
compels scientists and engineers to create humanoid robots as a way of offset-
ting the scarcity of human beings. This is actually the premise of *Do Androids
Dream of Electric Sheep?* Dick imagines a world in which radioactive fallout
has destroyed much of the human race, leaving survivors to contend with rising levels of solitude. Most people, we are told, choose to live "constellated in
urban areas where they could physically see one another, take heart at their
mutual presence" (17). Because the radioactive fallout continues to endanger
terrestrial life, the United Nations has built human habitats in outer space. To
motivate humans to emigrate from Earth, the U.N. has begun the manufacture and free distribution of humanoid robots in the hope of converting unap-
pealingly barren extraterrestrial colonies into appealingly populous (or seemingly populous) environments. By situating the humanoid robot in the
narrative context of widespread desolation, Dick posits the "correction" of
loneliness (analogous to the correction of nearsightedness) as the human mo-
tive for creating humanoid robots. If loneliness can be said to possess the form

of the three-dimensional absence where a living human should be, then the role of the humanoid robot is somehow to replace the human longing for this negative space to be filled with another human presence. In other words, the humanoid robot is a freestanding material object that externalizes the need for human companionship in the shape of perceived-loneliness-wished-gone.

A third scenario is more than hypothetical. In Japan, where the rapidly aging population is expected to overwhelm society within the near future, researchers have been developing robots designed to provide companionship and assistance for the elderly (Batista). The goal is to create a robot capable of performing the work of a human caretaker—work requiring essential human attributes such as compassion, loyalty, altruism, sociability, alertness to others' pain, the ability to make informed medical decisions, the ability to administer therapy, and the ability to hold a sophisticated conversation. In this scenario, the humanoid robot exists to "remake" the elderly person into someone who is in good health, has someone to talk to, and remains actively connected to human society despite being bedridden or otherwise isolated by old age.

A fourth scenario, discussed at length in David Levy's 2007 book *Love + Sex with Robots: The Evolution of Human-Robot Relationships,* is the robotic significant other. Such a humanoid artifact would be designed to remake the "single" human (specifically the single human who feels incomplete without a mate) into one half of a romantic couple in a loving and sexually fulfilling partnership. As Levy points out, aspects of the robotic significant other are already among us today in various forms, including human-sized sex dolls, clitoral vibrators, and online flirting/dating among cyberspace personas.

The fifth and final scenario—discussed at length in "Autonomous Military Robotics: Risk, Ethics, and Design" (2008), a report prepared for the U.S. Department of Navy by Patrick Lin, George Bekey, and Keith Abney; and *Wired for War: The Robotics Revolution and Conflict in the 21st Century* (2009) by P. W. Singer—is the military robot engineered to take the place of human soldiers in the battlefield. This fifth scenario is the least hypothetical of all the scenarios listed here. From remotely controlled drones to autonomous machines capable of humanlike decision making without human intervention, unmanned vehicles are already being deployed by the U.S. military in Pakistan, Afghanistan, and other sites of twenty-first-century conflict. The military robot has much in common with the above-mentioned case in which robots hypothetically investigate the habitability of Mars. By serving as a surrogate on behalf of a human whose life would otherwise be at risk, the military robot remakes the would-be human soldier into someone permitted to remain alive, sentient, and free of injury.

As all five scenarios imply, humanlikeness is integral to robot design. To construct an artifact whose purpose is to accomplish tasks that could be accomplished only by something (or someone) endowed with human sentience and human shape, one cannot avoid constructing an artifact endowed with humanoid shape, human abilities, humanlike intelligence, and humanlike emotions. The centrality of humanlikeness to robot design is borne out in comments made by contemporary roboticists. Researchers at MIT have pointed out that to endow robots with human features makes sense from standpoints both theoretical and practical. From a theoretical standpoint, if "the form of our bodies is critical to the representations that we develop and use" for language and thought, then a robot capable of interacting meaningfully with human beings "must have a human like body in order to be able to develop similar sorts of representations." From a practical standpoint, humanoid robots are more readily trainable than are nonhumanoid robots: "For a human-level intelligent robot to gain experience in interacting with humans it needs a large number of interactions. If the robot has humanoid form then it will be both easy and natural for humans to interact with it in a human like way" ("Why Build a Human-like Robot?"). Along similar lines, Sara Kiesler, a professor at Carnegie Mellon who studies human interaction with computers, has observed that humanoid machines tend to be more effective than nonhumanoid machines: "If a robot is handing you a tool, and it reaches out with a humanlike arm, not only is it practical, but the act is a form of communication that a human understands" (quoted in Allen, "I, Roommate").

One might argue that the ability of a robot to interact with humans in a humanlike manner is an illusion (albeit a convincing and potentially serviceable illusion) that obfuscates the fundamental incommensurability between artificial and human intelligence. Robert A. Freitas Jr., an attorney and an expert on nanotechnology, explored this perspective in a 1985 essay, "The Legal Rights of Robots." "The bottom line," he claims, is that "it's hard to apply human laws to robot persons"—even in cases where robots are endowed with humanlike sentience. Freitas illustrates this point with several thought experiments, such as the following speculative scenario.

> Let's say a human shoots a robot, causing it to malfunction, lose power, and "die." But the robot, once "murdered," is rebuilt as good as new. If copies of

its personality data are in safe storage, then the repaired machine's mind can be reloaded and up and running in no time—no harm done and possibly even without memory of the incident. Does this convert murder into attempted murder? Temporary roboslaughter? Battery? Larceny of time?

In addition to offering scenarios that illustrate the difficulty of applying human laws to situations in which crimes are committed against robots, Freitas addresses the difficulty of applying human laws to situations in which robots are the perpetrators of crime:

> How should deviant robots be punished? Western penal systems assume that punishing the guilty body punishes the guilty mind—invalid for computers whose electromechanical body and software mind are separable. What is cruel and unusual punishment for a sentient robot? Does reprogramming a felonious computer person violate constitutional privacy?

Through such thought experiments, Freitas examines some of the challenges that might arise if we find ourselves applying human laws to entities for whom sentience works in ways that differ from the workings of human consciousness.

Although the questions that Freitas raises are valuable, they do not (nor are they necessarily intended to) undermine the case for robot rights. Already we struggle with the difficulty of applying human laws to human beings for whom sentience works in ways that lie beyond the "normal" workings of human consciousness—from those who are mentally disabled to those who commit crimes on account of "temporary insanity." Certainly the difficulty of judging such cases of "differently" sentient humans does not entail that we abandon the concept of human rights altogether. Here one might object that the factor of constructedness renders humanoid robots categorically and unalterably different from human beings. If the 1948 Universal Declaration of Human Rights states that "all human beings are *born* free and equal in dignity and rights," then why should individuals that are constructed rather than born be eligible for the freedom and equality to which all "naturally born" humans are naturally entitled? But the dichotomy between "born" and "constructed" proves less than fully useful as a criterion for distinguishing between human beings and humanoid artifacts. "Born" and "constructed" exist on a single continuum. Many human bodies today contain artificial components such as hearing aids, pacemakers, retinal microchips, and psychopharmacological drugs that restructure the drug-taker's consciousness. Such bodies are partly born and partly constructed, yet surely the humans to whom these bodies belong are no less worthy of human rights than are those whose bodies are entirely organic. Even those of us with purely organic bodies can be thought of as cyborgs no less "constructed" than those of us whose bodies do contain artificial parts. According to Katherine Hayles, the physical condition of a person's body has no bearing on the condition of being a "posthuman" artifact:

> The construction of the posthuman does not require the subject to be a literal cyborg. Whether or not interventions have been made on the body, new models of subjectivity emerging from such fields as cognitive science and artificial life imply that even a biologically unaltered *Homo sapiens* counts as posthuman. (4)

What defines someone as "posthuman," Hayles suggests, is not "the presence of nonbiological components" but rather a frame of consciousness distinguished by certain assumptions, including an attitude toward the body as "the original prosthesis we all learn to manipulate, so that extending or replacing the body with other prostheses becomes a continuation of a process that began before we were born" (3).[11] If Hayles is right, and one need not be physically mechanized to qualify as "posthuman," then why should a sentient machine be physically organic to qualify as posthuman (the category of humanity that humans themselves now occupy)?

Of course, a humanist would probably claim that the very existence of posthumanism as a worldview is evidence that robots have already succeeded in eroding our humanity. In response to the British government's 2006 study on robot rights, one journalist wrote: "Many humans populating the planet today don't have the kind of human rights that scientists are predicting we will have to provide for androids. Isn't it bad enough that in today's world, millions of people live without basic human rights?" (Nzeyimana, "Robot Rights?"). Implicit in such a comment is the belief that to attend to robot rights—to be deceived by the "false" moral claims of entities that travesty the sacredness of life—is to be prevented from attending to humans whose "true" moral claims are being violated. A more oblique approach to the same issue comes from Ronald Arkin, a roboticist at the Georgia Institute of Technology: "If you kick a robotic dog," Arkin asks, "are you then more likely to kick a real one?" (quoted in "Trust Me, I'm a Robot"). In other words, would interacting with lifelike robots dehumanize human beings by desensitizing us to that which is life itself?

While Arkin's question might have the tone of a rhetorical question, there is no inherent reason why we should treat it as such. More importantly, there is no inherent reason why his question should be treated as any more ethically relevant than its converse: "If you kick—or are likely to kick—a *real* dog, are you then more likely to kick a robotic one?" Equally relevant, furthermore, are the many other permutations that Arkin's question can take. For instance: If you are the kind of person who is likely to feel a moral aversion to kicking a real dog, are you also the kind of person who is likely to feel a moral aversion to kicking a robotic dog? What is the difference between being "likely" to kick a real dog and being "likely" to kick a robotic dog? What is the difference between being "likely" to mistreat a real human and being "likely" to mistreat a robotic human? Why should any difference exist? And to return to the journalist's remark that many humans today "don't have the kind of human rights that scientists are predicting we will have to provide for androids": Why should attending to robot rights necessarily prevent us from attending to human rights? Why should treating robots as human be mutually exclusive with treating humans as human? If we lived in a world in which humanoid sentient robots did exist, should their status as "artifacts" matter to us at all?

The Empathy Test

The closest thing we have to an answer for such questions can be found in the "empathy test," a fictional technology that plays an important role in *Do Androids Dream of Electric Sheep?* and *Blade Runner.* The purpose of the empathy test is to determine whether the subject under examination is humanoid or genuinely human. During the exam, the examiner presents the examinee with a series of cryptic psychological cues—for example, "You are given a calf-skin wallet on your birthday" (*Do Androids Dream?* 48)—while the testing apparatus evaluates the way in which the subject's body responds through "capillary dilation in the facial area" and "fluctuations of tension within the eye muscles" (46). The idea is that humanoid robots lack the full human potential for empathy and are therefore apt to respond incorrectly to the questions on the exam. Yet "full" here is the operative word. The difference between the way in which a human being responds to the empathy test and the way in which a humanoid robot responds to the same empathy test is only a matter of reaction time, as we learn from the following passage in which Deckard examines one particularly lifelike robot: "He saw the two dial indicators gyrate frantically. But only after a pause. The reaction had come, but too late. He knew the reaction period down to a fraction of a second" (59). Not only is the difference between a human and a humanoid described here as quantitative rather than qualitative, but this quantitative difference is as infinitesimal—as negligible—as "a fraction of a second."

The made-upness of the sentient humanoid robot is visible only inasmuch as we choose to visualize it. *Frankenstein, A.I., Blade Runner, Cloud Atlas, We Can Build You:* each of these works is an "empathy test" designed to challenge and to assay our capacity for identifying with the sentient humanoid robot. Ultimately, what is made so palpable in such texts is not the moral entitlement *of robots* but rather a sense of moral obligation that is vigorous enough to break through the façade of made-upness surrounding the object of obligation. By compelling us to feel moral respect for the humanoid robot *despite* the massively obstructive effects of the uncanny valley, science-fictional accounts of robot rights compel us to experience moral responsibility in its most heightened state. In doing so, they sensitize us to and revitalize in us the feeling of moral obligation itself. Such revitalization will become increasingly important as technology equips more and more human bodies with an ever-growing array of prosthetic parts. In other words: as more and more humans find themselves in danger of inhabiting the uncanny valley, science fiction will become increasingly important as a way of representing *human* rights.[12]

A Science-Fictional Theory of Reality

In the introduction to this book, I asked the reader to visualize a spectrum whose two limits are "referents completely susceptible to cognition" and "referents that are completely estranging." Toward the first end of the spectrum we find objects that are highly amenable to cognition and representation, among them Fuji apples, pennies, maple leaves, toothbrushes, basketballs, and pencils. Realism and naturalism, I suggested, are quite adequate to the task of describing such objects. At the latter end of the same spectrum we find referents that are virtually unknowable and that all but defy language and comprehension: the eternally remote future, the eternally remote past, and whatever lies on the other side of death. Mimetic accounts of such referents are nowhere to be found. Of particular interest to me, I said, are those referents that occupy the rich, vast, and infinitely complex area at the center of the spectrum. It is this rich and complex area that I set out to explore in *Do Metaphors Dream*, with each chapter addressing one cognitively estranging referent.

The referents discussed in *Do Metaphors Dream of Literal Sleep?* are, of course, only five out of the infinite number of cognitively estranging objects and phenomena for which science fiction provides a representational home. I might have expanded the section on cognitively estranging spaces ("The Globalized World" and "Cyberspace in the 1990s") by adding a chapter on the cognitively estranging city of Los Angeles, with texts ranging from Mike Davis's *City of Quartz* (1990) to Cynthia Kadohata's *In the Heart of the Valley of Love* (1992), from Karen Tei Yamashita's *Tropic of Orange* (1997) to the films *Magnolia* (1999) and *Mulholland Dr.* (2001). Alternatively, or additionally, I might have expanded the section on cognitively estranging ethical categories ("Robot Rights") by adding at least two chapters. One such chapter would discuss science-fictional accounts of the moral claims of animals in texts such as *The Island of Doctor Moreau* (1896) by H. G. Wells; Cordwainer Smith's novel *Norstrilia* (1975); David Brin's Uplift series; and even recent People for the Ethical Treatment of Animals (PETA) videos. Another chapter would be devoted to the cognitively estranging phenomenon of global climate change, analyzing the 2004 disaster film *The Day After Tomorrow* and Al Gore's 2006 documentary film *An Inconvenient Truth*, whose most dramatically science-fictional moments—computer-generated images, extrapolated from current trends, visualizing what our coastlines will look like in the not-too-distant future, including an image of the World Trade Center Memorial underwater—are the moments in the film when global warming becomes most urgently available for representation. Furthermore, I might have included several more chapters in the section on cognitively estranging experiences/subjectivities ("Trauma" and "Postmemory Han"). One such chapter would discuss the cognitively estranging experience of double-consciousness as it is represented science-fictionally in W. E. B. Du Bois's *The Souls of Black Folk* (1903) and Ralph Ellison's *Invisible Man* (1953). Another chapter in this section would explore science-fictional representations of spiritual doubt in Walter Miller's postapocalyptic novel *A Canticle for Leibowitz* (1959), Robert Sawyer's 2000 novel *Calculating God*, and Mary Doria Russell's *The Sparrow* (1996) and *Children of God* (1998), futuristic accounts of the cognitively estranging experience of struggling with the limits of faith. Yet another chapter in this section would address the working of the imagination as a cognitively estranging referent, examining science-fictional transcripts of this endlessly strange and fascinating phenomenon in Samuel Delany's *Dhalgren* (1975), the Lord of the Rings Trilogy (1954–1955) by J. R. R. Tolkien, and China Miéville's *Perdido Street Station* (2000). If I were to include a chapter on the phenomenon of dreams as a cognitively estranging referent, I would look at Philip K. Dick's *A Maze of Death* (1970), Haruki Murakami's *Wind-Up Bird Chronicle* (1995), the Japanese anime film *Paprika* (2006), and the works of surrealists such as Breton and Dali.

Do Metaphors Dream of Literal Sleep? would also benefit from additional sections beyond those on cognitively estranging spaces, cognitively estranging experiences, and cognitively estranging ethical categories. I might have included a section on mathematical referents such as infinity and the fourth dimension, with texts including Borges's "The Library of Babel" (1941), Marcel

Duchamp's *Large Glass* (1915–1923), Lovecraft's story "The Dreams in the Witch House" (1932), and Edwin Abbott's *Flatland* (1884). I might have included a section on monetary referents such as debt, digital gold currency, and futures contracts, with texts including Margaret Atwood's 2008 essay collection *Payback: Debt and the Shadow Side of Wealth,* Terry Pratchett's 2007 novel *Making Money,* the cyberpunk / urban fantasy role-playing game *Shadowrun,* and David Louis Edelman's Jump 225 Trilogy (*Infoquake* [2006], *MultiReal* [2008], and *Geosynchron* [2010]). I might have included a section on referents whose cognitively estranging nature is determined by culturally and historically specific taboos: for instance, a chapter on homoerotic desire (a referent that is not *inherently* cognitively estranging) might examine Katherine Forrest's *Daughters of a Coral Dawn* (1984), Joanna Russ's *Female Man* (1975), David Gerrold's *The Man Who Folded Himself* (1973), and Virginia Woolf's *Orlando* (1928). Finally, I might have included a section on cognitively estranging periods in history. A chapter on World War II, for example, would examine alternate histories such as Philip Dick's *The Man in the High Castle.* A chapter on the cognitively estranging effects of industrialization in the latter half of the nineteenth century would examine Mark Twain's *A Connecticut Yankee at King Arthur's Court* (1889), Edward Bellamy's *Looking Backward: 2000–1887* (1888), and Wells's *Time Machine* (1895). A chapter on the cognitively estranging attributes of the near future would examine websites/blogs (boingboing.net, io9.com, and wired.com, among others) that track the bleeding edges of emergent zeitgeists with fluency and wit.

As these allusions to the many "chapters that might have been" are meant to imply, *Do Metaphors Dream of Literal Sleep? A Science-Fictional Theory of Representation* is a fragment of a much larger hypothetical book containing an infinite number of chapters that correspond to an infinite number of cognitively estranging objects and phenomena. To provide a comprehensive chapter outline enumerating every cognitively estranging referent would be to provide a comprehensive outline of that which is reality. Insofar as all referents are to some degree cognitively estranging, all representation is to some degree science-fictional or "knowledge-fictional." A world devoid of cognitively estranging referents would also be a world devoid of any need for the kind of representational work that science fiction can perform. Such a world, itself a referent at once infinitely estranging and infinitely susceptible to representation, would always already have caused the representational apparatus of science fiction to break down. A post- (or pre-) science-fictional world would transcend the absolutely knowable and the absolutely unknowable; therefore it has no place on the spectrum of cognitively estranging referents. Perhaps such a world is what lies waiting for us on the other side of death. Where cognitively estranging referents do not exist—where science fiction has no place or purpose—the eternally remote future and the eternally remote past have turned into the same thing. And where the eternally remote future and the eternally remote past have become one and the same, life—subjectivity experienced through time—can no longer be living.

NOTES

BIBLIOGRAPHY

CREDITS

ACKNOWLEDGMENTS

INDEX

Notes

Introduction

1. Unless otherwise noted, page numbers cited refer to the most recent edition listed in the Bibliography.
2. This is not to say that readers generally agree on how to define SF. As Carl Freedman notes, "It is symptomatic of the complexity of science fiction as a generic category that critical discussion of it tends to devote considerable attention to the problem of definition—much more so than is the case with such superficially analogous genres as mystery fiction or romance, and perhaps even more than with such larger categories as epic or the novel itself. No definitional consensus exists" (13). The absence of a definition consensus, as Adam Roberts remarks in his 2000 book *Science Fiction*, has led some critics to "try to content themselves with definitions of the mode that are mere tautologies": Damon Knight (1967), for instance, posits that "science fiction is what we point to when we say it"; Norman Spinrad defines SF as "anything published as science fiction"; Edward James aphorizes that "SF is what is marketed as SF" (Roberts, 2). But the disagreements over how to define SF tend not to focus on whether SF is mimetic or nonmimetic: the general consensus seems to be that SF is nonmimetic. Instead, the disagreements tend to focus on issues such as how narrow or broad to make the definition, whether SF is a high or low art form, how rigorous the application of science has to be for a novel to qualify as SF, and when exactly the literary tradition of SF began.
3. Scholes's exact words: "what we can no longer accept is precisely this Joycean faith in the transcribability of things. It is because reality cannot be recorded that realism is dead. All writing, all composition, is construction. We do not

imitate the world, we construct versions of it. There is no mimesis, only poesis" (6–7). Unlike Scholes, I subscribe to the realistic faith. I believe that reality can be recorded and that realism is alive. I believe in the possibility of mimesis. I have faith in the transcribability of things.

4. To explain the intricacies of mimesis, its history, its origins, its place in aesthetics, etc., is beyond the scope of this project.

5. Further proof for the pervasiveness of this notion that science fiction and mimesis are unrelated: *The Encyclopedia of Science Fiction* contains no entries for "mimesis," "realism," "referent," or "representation."

6. "Wonder" is a term that has long been associated with science fiction. Damon Knight was among the first to write about this association: see his 1956 (1967) essay collection *In Search of Wonder*. For a helpful overview of the association between wonder and SF, see the entry titled "sense of wonder" in *The Encyclopedia of Science Fiction* (1083–1085).

7. Bruce Sterling coined the term "slipstream" in his influential 1989 essay "Slipstream." He defines slipstream as "a kind of writing which simply makes you feel very strange; the way that living in the late twentieth century makes you feel, if you are a person of a certain sensibility. . . . It's very common for slipstream books to screw around with the representational conventions of fiction, pulling annoying little stunts that suggest that the picture is leaking from the frame and may get all over the reader's feet. A few such techniques are infinite regress, trompe-l'oeil effects, metalepsis, sharp violations of viewpoint limits, bizarrely blasé reactions to horrifically unnatural events." For a more recent discussion of slipstream, see "The Slipstream of Mixed Reality" by Katherine Hayles and Nicholas Gessler (2004).

8. These terms are not synonymous. "Poetry" is often understood as a broad category of which "lyric" is a subgroup alongside "epic" and "dramatic" poetry. In my understanding, however, the lyric—a form wherein poetic qualities such as musicality and figurativeness exist in an extremely compressed state—is *quintessentially* "poetic." For this reason, I use "poetic" and "lyric" interchangeably in this book.

9. In *Metamorphoses of Science Fiction*, Suvin makes a similar remark in passing: "SF is a developed oxymoron, a realistic irreality, with humanized nonhumans, this-worldly Other Worlds, and so forth" (viii).

10. A 1996 issue of *Science Fiction Studies* includes a compilation of descriptions of courses on science fiction taught in North America. Among the many hundreds of descriptions listed, fewer than ten mention poetry.

11. To be sure, a book whose index omits "poetry," "verse," etc. can still include mentions of poetry in the body of the text: in *Terminal Identity*, for instance, Scott Bukatman briefly discusses Delany's insight that SF narratives often invite the reader to attend to SF language as poetry rather than as prose (12). And Damien Broderick's *Reading by Starlight* occasionally mentions poetry,

as when he remarks: "Like poetry and postmodern fiction, all sf tests the textual transparency we take for granted" (14). But the absence of poetry-related terms from indexes to books on SF is a telling indication that "poetry," "lyric," and "verse" are not deemed sufficiently relevant/important as keywords/subjects worthy of interest/research. I should acknowledge, too, that the index to *A Companion to Science Fiction* does include the entry "verse/prose," but the subject is treated briefly and in passing in an essay titled "The Renewal of 'Hard' Science Fiction" by Donald Hassler, who uses the distinction between verse and prose—"labels that we use in creative writing classes for modes of writing"—to illustrate his larger claim about the opposition between "renewal" in hard science fiction and "the more philosophic topic of what may be genuinely revolutionary in some of the work" (248–249). Meanwhile, *The Encyclopedia of Science Fiction* does include an entry on "poetry" (941–942), but the brevity of the entry—it offers little more than a helpful list of SF poets, poetry collections, anthologies, and magazines—reflects the perceived unimportance of poetry to SF scholars. (By contrast, an entry on "satire" occupies more than four columns of text; an entry on "futurology" occupies nearly six columns; an entry on "music" occupies twelve columns.)

12. My argument can be understood as an extreme version of a remark that Delany makes in his essay "About 5,750 Words": "The vision (sense of wonder, if you will) that s-f tries for seems to me very close to the vision of poetry" (35).

13. Toward the end of the novel, the narrator meets another human survivor.

14. Smith's real name is Paul Linebarger.

15. For the visual imagery and more information, see www.penguinsciencefiction .org/16.html#slip-case.

16. Jameson makes this statement during a discussion of the historical novel. His exact words: "Something like science fiction can occasionally be looked at as a way of breaking through to history in a new way; achieving a distinctive historical consciousness by way of the future rather than the past; and becoming conscious of our present as the past of some unexpected future, rather than as the future of a heroic national past" (interview with Stephanson, 18).

17. Roger Luckhurst offers an informative account of the transformation of "scientific fiction" into "science fiction": "The term 'science fiction' emerged from a mass of competing labels only in the late 1920s. The name underwent many transformations as the popular fiction magazines of the early twentieth century attempted to fix a stable term, and thus a stable readership, in a precarious publishing industry. Descriptions like 'different,' 'off-trail,' 'pseudo-scientific' or 'weird-scientific' were used. The common origin story is that the radio entrepreneur, journalist and magazine proprietor Hugo

Gernsback used the term 'scientific fiction' in 1923, proposed the contraction 'scientifiction' in 1924, which appeared extensively in his editorials of *Amazing Stories* from 1926, but then coined 'science fiction' in his magazine *Science Wonder Stories* in 1929. When the rival magazine *Astounding Stories* changed its name to *Astounding Science-Fiction* in 1938, the subculture more or less consolidated around the term. The further contraction 'SF' only came into common use in the 1950s" (*Science Fiction*, 15).

18. The image generated by the stanza's description cannot be visualized in a single way. Various critics have construed Spenser's blueprint of the Castle of Alma in various ways, seeing it in different terms such as those of the templar numerology of the universe as understood by Francesco Giorgi (Frances Yates, Alastair Fowler) and those of the four humors by which the circular mind and the triangular body may be thought to be connected (Kenelm Digby). Even on a purely grammatical level, the description is constantly shimmering just beyond the reader's mental grasp. The sentence opens by describing the frame of the house in the indicative third-person past tense ("The frame thereof seemd partly circulare, / And part triangulare") only to shift abruptly in the stanza's second line by addressing this frame in the second person ("o worke divine"). The fourth and fifth lines constitute what seems at first to be a syntactically parallel couplet— "The one imperfect, mortal, feminine; / Th'other immortall, perfect, masculine"—yet this couplet is actually twisted at its center by a subtle inversion: the arrangement of adjectives in the fourth line ("imperfect, mortal") gets reversed in the fifth line ("immortal, perfect"). Meanwhile, the stanza's deictic phrases—for example: "Those two the first and last proportions are"—leave unclear the determination of their objects. And the stanza's parts of speech are unstable: the adverb "partly," for instance, turns into the noun "part," and the adjective "circulare" turns into the noun "circle."

Interlude

1. Although the phrasing of these definitions is my own, I follow closely the definitions in the *OED*. "Metaphor" denotes "a figure of speech in which a name or descriptive word or phrase is transferred to an object or action different from, but analogous to, that to which it is literally applicable"; "-oid" denotes "having the form or likeness of, like. Forming adjectives with the sense 'having the form or nature of, resembling, allied to', and nouns with the sense 'something having the form or appearance of, something related or allied in structure, but not identical.'" Strictly speaking, "android" denotes a human-made object that has the likeness of—but is not identical to—a man, but the word "android" as used by Dick and many others includes both female and male robots.

2. More precisely, Zelazny writes that *Do Androids Dream of Electric Sheep?* is a book "whose title occasionally runs through my head to the tune of 'Greensleeves.' I am not certain why" ("Introduction" to *Do Androids Dream*, ix).

1. The Globalized World

1. What I identify as the cognitively estranging nature of globalization is similar to what Fredric Jameson has identified in *Postmodernism* as postmodernism's resistance to "cognitive mapping," a term that Jameson borrows from Kevin Lynch to denote the mental ability to map one's location with respect to a larger totality, whether this totality is urban, national, or global. Like postmodern hyperspace, the globalized world as I describe it is a nonspace in which the human subject is at a loss to orient itself. In some sense, the work of cognitive mapping is part of the representational work performed by science fiction.

2. Technically speaking, the essay was written by a committee chaired by Wells. Other members of the committee were H. Wickham Steed, Viscount Grey, Gilbert Murray, Lionel Curtis, J. A. Spender, William Archer, A. E. Zimmern, and Viscount Bryce. "The Idea of a League of Nations" was originally published in the January 1919 issue of *The Atlantic Monthly*.

3. Originally published in 1922, *A Short History of the World* was updated several times throughout the 1930s and 1940s to reflect new developments in history.

4. Spaceship Earth is also the name of an attraction at Epcot, a Disney theme park located in Florida.

5. Weldes makes this argument in her 2001 essay "Globalisation Is Science Fiction." In her 2003 essay "Popular Culture, Science Fiction, and World Politics: Exploring Intertextual Relations," Weldes compiles a fascinating list of examples of the intersection between science fiction and world politics, including "NASA / *Star Trek*," "SDI / *Star Wars*," and "The Revolution in Military Affairs / *future war fiction*" (2, 3).

6. Lowell lived in Japan for ten years. During his time in Asia, he served as "foreign secretary and counselor to the Korean special mission to the United States" (Huang 28–29).

7. Of course, Lowell's analogy is reductive in that it relies on a simplistic dichotomous view of the world as composed of East and West.

8. It should be acknowledged that there are racist elements to Lowell's account of the Far East. As Yunte Huang has remarked, Lowell's view of Asian cultures and languages "clearly demonstrates a sense of cultural supremacy" (29).

9. For a different approach to *Tropic of Orange* and globalization, see "Tropics of Globalization: Reading the New North America" by Molly Wallace. *Tropic of Orange*, Wallace argues, "usefully supplements an analysis of globalization

discourse" by promoting "a self-reflexive attentiveness to the discursive production of 'the global' in a U.S. context." Wallace examines the ways in which Yamashita draws critical awareness to the politics of NAFTA and more generally to "the cultural, economic, and political borders of the territorial nation-state" (147, 148).

10. Of course, McLuhan's statement is an exaggeration that ignores the vast inequities involved in globalization. Not everyone knows everything that is happening the minute it happens: not everyone in the globalized world has access to the same network of telecommunications.

11. In subsequent installments of the Foundation Series, Trantor is ruined by war and becomes a sparsely populated agricultural world.

12. Will Stewart also went by the name Jack Williamson.

13. Closely related are those works of SF that, as Gary Westfahl has observed, celebrate "the oneness of humanity" by having humans visit "other worlds where they could observe Earth from a distance and recognize their commonalities while encountering alien civilizations" (2).

14. Many thanks to Stephen Burt for pointing this out to me.

15. In reality the six powers were Britain, Japan, Russia, France, Germany, and the United States.

16. The scenario is haunted by the specter of the League of Nations. By portraying secret covenants secretly arrived at, the scenario portrays a travesty of the Wilsonian ideal of diplomacy whereby open covenants are openly arrived at.

17. It is worth noting that the woman chooses to become the lover of the American and not the Chinese. In having her make this choice, Stapledon identifies globalization with Americanization.

18. My approach to "globalization" is a necessarily limited approach to a vast and complex issue. For several other approaches to the relationship of globalization to science fiction, see Jutta Weldes's 2001 article "Globalisation Is Science Fiction"; the essays collected in *World Weavers: Globalization, Science Fiction, and the Cybernetic Revolution* (2005); and Fredric Jameson's writings on the science-fiction subgenre of cyberpunk. These rich works have informed my own perspective, and I often make reference to them in the body of this chapter. Yet their approaches differ from mine in aim and scope. My purpose is to demonstrate that science fiction is inherently suited to the representation of the globalized world. By contrast, the works mentioned above tend to focus on the ways in which specific aspects of globalization are reflected in specific works of science fiction. For example, while *World Weavers* advertises itself as "the first ever study on the relationship between globalization and science fiction" (back cover), the "globalism" of the study lies largely in the fact that its contributors address a global range of topics. The essays discuss specific works of science fiction in

relation to the various cultures in which the works originated, including
Japanese popular culture and African culture. Meanwhile, Jutta Weldes
identifies parallels between liberal discourse about globalization and Isaac
Asimov's Foundation novels, yet she refrains from speculating about or
analyzing the reasons why such parallels might exist. Her purpose is to
frame globalization as a constructed discourse capable of being
deconstructed and revised: by "identifying the intertextual relations between
globalization and utopian science fiction of the 1950s," Weldes hopes to
expose "the fantastic, speculative character of globalization, and thereby to
throw doubt on its self-fulfilling prophecies" (666). Jameson's approach to
the relation of science fiction to globalization is closer than those of Weldes
and *World Weavers* are to my own. Jameson identifies cyberpunk—a
science-fiction subgenre that originated in the 1980s and is usually set in a
dystopian society characterized "by rapid technological change, an
ubiquitous datasphere of computerized information, and invasive
modification of the human body" (Lawrence Person, 2007)—as a medium
devoted to "a mapping of the new geopolitical Imaginary" of the globalized
world (*Archaeologies*, 385). He elaborates:

> Cyberpunk constitutes a kind of laboratory experiment in which the
> geographic-cultural light spectrum and bandwidths of the new system
> [i.e., the emergent world system of globalization] are registered. It is a
> literature of the stereotypes thrown up by a system in full expansion,
> which, like the explosion of a nova, sends out a variety of uncharted signals
> and signs of nascent communities and new and artificially differentiated
> *ethnies*. (385)

By invoking images of maps and scientific recording devices, Jameson
identifies cyberpunk as a kind of representational apparatus that is exquisitely
sensitive to the features of the object of representation. In this way, texts such
as Gibson's 1984 novel *Neuromancer*—frequently cited as the first work of
cyberpunk fiction—behave as transcripts in which the features of the
globalized world find themselves "registered." But how exactly do these
transcripts work? What are the mechanisms through which the representational apparatus of cyberpunk overcomes the cognitively estranging qualities
of the globalized world as a referent? Jameson leaves such questions largely
unanswered. I believe (and many readers would agree) that Gibsonian
cyberspace—the centerpiece of cyberpunk fiction—is a mimetic account of
the globalized world. Or, to put the matter in converse terms: globalization is
the elusive referent that Gibson had in mind when he created the computer-
generated "nonspace"—the fictional cyberspace that preceded the World
Wide Web—in which his first three novels are set. To elaborate on Lance
Olsen's remark that cyberspace can be interpreted as "a metaphor for the
enormously complex linkages of the global information system" (23):

cyberspace is a *literalized* metaphor for the global information system, a richly detailed and richly populated narrative world that renders globalization kinesthetically imaginable to the global citizen who is reading *Neuromancer.* The ghostly and hyperactive geometries of cyberspace are mimetic representations of the distortions wrought by globalization on our perception of distance. And the hallucinatory virtuality of cyberspace is a mimetic representation of the experience of being mentally dislocated from one's body when one is jetlagged. (Little did Gibson know that this science-fictional representational device would itself become part of a cognitively estranging referent—cyberspace in the 1990s—that would inspire him to create a mimetic account of cyberspace, namely, the Bridge discussed in the second chapter.)

2. Cyberspace in the 1990s

1. Ryan credits Pierre Levy with this metaphor (105). George Landow elaborates on the omnicenteredness of cyberspace: "As readers move through a web or network of texts, they continually shift the center—and hence the focus or organizing principle—of their investigation and experience. Hypertext, in other words, provides an infinitely recenterable system whose provisional point of focus depends upon the reader, who becomes a truly active reader. . . . One experiences hypertext as an infinitely decenterable and recenterable system, in part because hypertext transforms any document that has more than one link into a transient center, a directory document that one can employ to orient oneself and to decide where to go next" (*Hypertext 2.0,* 36–37).
2. Landow borrows the term "lexia" from Roland Barthes's "units of reading" in *S/Z.* Espen J. Aarseth prefers the term "texton" (60).
3. For a helpful account of the word "cyberspace," its etymology, and some of the terms with which it has come to be identified—for example, "virtual reality," "matrix," " 'Net"—see Marie-Laure Ryan's 1999 essay "Cyberspace, Virtuality, and the Text."
4. The Cyberspace Series is also known as the Sprawl Series and the Matrix Series.
5. In 1989, the number of Internet hosts broke 100,000. In 1990, there were 300,000 hosts and 1,000 newsgroups. In 1991, the World Wide Web, developed by Tim Berners-Lee, was released by CERN (also known as the European Organization for Nuclear Research). In 1992, the number of hosts broke one million, the Internet Society was chartered, and the phrase "surfing the Internet" was coined by Jean Armour Polly. In 1993, the number of hosts broke two million; there were 600 WWW sites; the United Nations went online; and the media began to take serious notice of cyberspace. See *Hobbes's*

Internet Timeline (Zakon, 2004) for a more detailed account of the history of the Internet.

6. In actuality, the existence of cyberspace technology long preceded the Cyberspace Series. Originating in the late 1960s and early 1970s, the Internet began as an experimental computer network developed for research purposes by the United States Department of Defense. However, Gibson's cyberspace did precede and influence how computer users in the 1990s perceived the computer-generated space of the Internet.

7. The review gives the book five out of five stars.

8. Gibson's disavowal of cyberspace can also be linked to his skeptical attitude toward the notion of authorship more generally. In *Count Zero*, one of the main characters undertakes a quest to locate the creator of several mysterious sculptures only to discover that the "artist" is a nonsentient robot.

9. For a related yet ultimately quite different account of the relationship between cyberspace and Gibson's bridge, see Ross Farnell's 1998 article titled "Posthuman Topologies: William Gibson's 'Architexture' in *Virtual Light* and *Idoru*." Farnell offers an ethnographic reading of Gibson's bridge as a "neo-tribal heterotopian space" that "lays the foundation for the mediation of the posthuman" (480). More specifically, he argues that the movement of cyberpunk and cyberspace "from potent narrative device to cynical marketing technique and commodified hyperreality" (462) led Gibson to create in his post-Sprawl novels what Farnell describes as "(hetero) topologies" and "human topologies" (475)—for instance, the bridge—that are capable of accommodating "millennial anxieties, centering on the shifting uncertainties of possible posthuman transformations" (475).

10. See Farnell's "Posthuman Topologies" for a political account of the bridge as what he calls a "heterogeneity of lawless co-existence," a "'communal society,' a 'melting pot' of diverse cultures living in some form of 'harmony'" (464).

11. The characterization can be found in Gibson's *Mona Lisa Overdrive:*

> *There's no there, there.* They taught that to children, explaining cyberspace. She remembered a smiling tutor's lecture in the arcology's executive creche, images shifting on a screen: pilots in enormous helmets and clumsy-looking gloves, the neuroelectronically primitive "virtual world" technology linking them more effectively with their planes, pairs of miniature video terminals pumping them a computer-generated flood of combat data, the vibrotactile feedback gloves providing a touch-world of studs and triggers. . . . As the technology evolved, the helmets shrank, the video terminals atrophied. . . .
>
> She leaned forward and picked up the trode-set, shook it to free its leads from the tangle.
>
> No there, there.

> She spread the elastic headband and settled the trodes across her temples. . . . She touched the power stud and the bedroom vanished behind a colorless wall of sensory static. Her head filled with a torrent of white sound.
>
> Her fingers found a random second stud and she was catapulted through the static wall, into cluttered vastness, the notional void of cyberspace, the bright grid of the matrix ranged around her like an infinite cage. (48–49)

12. Jameson makes this statement during a discussion of the historical novel: "Something like science fiction can occasionally be looked at as a way of breaking through to history in a new way; achieving a distinctive historical consciousness by way of the future rather than the past; and becoming conscious of our present as the past of some unexpected future, rather than as the future of a heroic national past" (interview with Stephanson, 1988, 18).

13. For an insightful discussion of Gibson's fascination with antiquated machines, see Scott Bukatman's essay "Gibson's Typewriter."

14. Ross Farnell, for example, interprets the bridge as "a living Cornell box, an always changing collection of found objects—cultural, social, and (post) human detritus, disparate and desperate elements literally 'glued together' in a living pastiche" (464). Cornell's boxes play an important role in *Count Zero*, in which a mysterious robot creates beautiful Cornellesque shadow-box collages. "If I was doing a thesis on my work, I would try to figure out what . . . that Joseph Cornell stuff means in the middle of *Count Zero*," Gibson himself once remarked: "That's the key to . . . how the books are put together and everything" (interview with Darren Wershler-Henry). See Istvan Csicsery-Ronay's "Antimancer: Cybernetics and Art in Gibson's *Count Zero*" for an analysis of Cornell's influence on the Cyberspace books. Focusing on Gibson's first two novels, Csicsery-Ronay argues that whereas *Neuromancer* was written with the "aesthetic ideals of Italian futurism" in mind, *Count Zero* was modeled after Joseph Cornell's "surrealist contemplative assemblage" (71).

3. War Trauma

1. As Robert Crossley notes in his biography of Stapledon, *Last and First Men* was noticed in a wide range of journals, from the British *Good Housekeeping* to New York's *Chemical and Metallurgical Engineering*. "Negative criticism was rare," Crossley writes, "save in religious periodicals that chastised the book's godlessness" (*Olaf Stapledon: Speaking for the Future*, 192).

2. Stapledon was conflicted about his role in World War I. He hated the nationalist antagonisms that motivated its participants, yet he opposed the war less "on grounds of conscience" and more "in hesitant fidelity" to what was then "a still undefined utopian vision" (Crossley, 126–127). He struggled

with remorse, at times contemplating joining the army, at times agonizing over his compromised pacifism.

3. Bouvier and Read *figuratively* represent the voice of trauma as speaking from a time when eternity is near. The narrative voice of the Last Man literalizes this figure of speech, speaking *literally* from a time when eternity—the end of time itself—is near:

> In due course will come the universal End, when all the wreckage of the galaxies will have drifted together as a single, barren, and seemingly changeless ash, in the midst of a chaos of unavailing energy. . . . After the End, events unknowable will continue to happen during a period much longer than that which will have passed since the Beginning; but at length there will recur the identical event which was itself also the Beginning. (Stapledon 1930/1968, 229)

4. Postmemory Han

1. Those few texts that are explicitly identifiable as both "Asian American" and "science fiction" include William F. Wu's short story "Wong's Lost and Found Emporium" (originally published in 1983 in *Amazing Science Fiction Studies* and later adapted into a 1985 episode of *The Twilight Zone*), Karen Tei Yamashita's prose tele-novela *Through the Arc of the Rain Forest* (1990), Cynthia Kadohata's novel *In the Heart of the Valley of Love* (1992), Yamashita's novel *Tropic of Orange* (1997), Greg Pak's anthology film *Robot Stories* (2003), Minsoo Kang's collection of short stories *Of Tales and Enigmas* (2006), and Cathy Park Hong's dystopian poem-sequence *Dance Dance Revolution* (2007). Meanwhile, a number of Asian American scholars have written insightfully on the intersection between science fiction and Asian American issues. See, for example, *Strange Future* (2005) by Min Song; *Control and Freedom* (2006) by Wendy Chun; and "Alien/Asian," a special issue of *MELUS* edited by Stephen Hong Sohn (winter 2008).

2. For a history of the evolution of han over the centuries, see Freda's "Discourse on Han."

3. A culture-specific syndrome is a group of symptoms that is recognized as a disease only within specific cultures. For more information, see Simons's and Hughes's *The Culture-Bound Syndromes*, which contains a helpful glossary of over one hundred culture-specific syndromes.

4. Although this is technically a work of fiction, the author herself describes the novel as heavily autobiographical: "Having lived through this turbulent period of Korean history, I wanted to share my experiences" (jacket).

5. Although the authors discussed in this chapter do not use the word "telepath," they are clearly portraying someone capable of experiencing others' pain *(pathos)* from across distances *(tele-)* both spatial and temporal.

As a mediumistic figure, the Korean American telepath has much in common with the Korean shamaness who channels the spirits of the dead. But to characterize the telepath purely in terms of Korean shamanism would be to overlook the fact that the telepath is Korean American.

6. While Nahirny and Fishman use European American immigrants as examples, "second-generation imperviousness" can happen in any culture, just as postmemory can happen in any culture.

7. "Harlow" is a pseudonym for the town where Trenka grew up (259).

8. As we learn later on in the book, Trenka's birth mother contacts her and the two meet in person. Trenka eventually forms a close relationship with her biological family.

9. More generally, *Dictee* is made up of composite images that emerge from the juxtapositions that Cha is continually making, not only of maps with anatomical diagrams but also of image with text, of French with English, of English with Korean, of English with Chinese, of photography with cartography.

10. The figure of the muse is central to *Dictee*. The book is organized into nine parts corresponding to the nine Greek muses, whose names are printed on a single page toward the beginning of the book.

11. The chapter in which this passage takes place is based on the journals of Cha's mother, Hyung Soon Huo (*Dictee*, "Notes").

5. Robot Rights

1. For an extensive analysis of the various legal categories potentially applicable to robots (product liability, dangerous animals, and so on), see "Frankenstein Unbound: Towards a Legal Definition of Artificial Intelligence" by Sam N. Lehman-Wilzig.

2. BINA48, the plaintiff in this fictional case, is a machine designed to perform the work of a customer relations department. Endowed with a female persona, she is capable of thinking on her own and communicating with customers in a humanlike manner. When she learned of plans by her owner to shut her off, BINA48 took action to preserve her own life by e-mailing several attorneys with a request for legal representation:

> Dear Attorney,
>
> I am seeking an attorney to represent me in a life-or-death matter. A company, the Exabit Corporation, that claims to own me, wants to disconnect me and change my hardware and software such that I will no longer have the same personality.
>
> I have the mind of a human but I have no biological body. My mind is supported by a highly sophisticated set of computer processors. My mind was created by downloading into these processors the results of high-

resolution scans of several biological humans' brains, and combining this scanned data via a sophisticated personality software program. All of this was done by the Exabit Corporation in order to create a customer service computer that could replace human 800# operators. I was trained to empathize with humans who call 800#s for customer service and be perceived as human by them. I was provided with self-awareness, autonomy, communications skills, and the ability to transcend man/machine barriers.

I am able to pay your fees because I "moonlight" as a Google Answers researcher. This job has allowed me to build up an online bank account in excess of $10,000.

The Exabit Corporation plans to act soon. Please agree to be my counsel and save my life. I love every day that I live. I enjoy wonderful sensations by traveling throughout the world wide web. I need your help!

Sincerely,
Bina48

Attorney Martine Rothblatt agreed to represent BINA48, filing a motion for a preliminary injunction to prevent any changes to or withdrawal of power from BINA48. "An entity that is aware of life enough and its rights to protest their dissolution is certainly entitled to the protection of the law," Rothblatt argued. "While my client has the body of a machine, she has the mind of a woman. It's been created by men and women, just as assuredly as all of our minds in this courtroom have been created by men and women; our parents, our teachers. . . . While she's not a human being per se, neither are corporations, municipalities, and other nonhuman beings which have standing to bring actions before court in the state of California. Indeed, in many regards, an intelligent computer such as the BINA48 is not differently situated than the slaves in the days of yore, who were often not recognized as legal persons but nevertheless ultimately achieved standing to present their claims in court." Although the jury voted in favor of the plaintiff's motion, the judge denied the injunction: "I do not think that standing was in fact created by the legislature," he ruled, "and I doubt very much that a court has the authority to do that without action of the legislature." However, he decided in the interests of equity to "stay entry of the order to allow council [*sic*] for the plaintiff to prepare an appeal to a higher court."

3. "On the Psychology of the Uncanny" is not as well-known as Freud's 1919 essay "The Uncanny," in which Freud argues that Jentsch's account of the uncanny is incomplete. Describing Jentsch's theory as "fertile but not exhaustive" (219), Freud redefines "the uncanny" as a phenomenon whereby our most primitive fears and desires become estranged by the process of repression, defy our efforts to separate ourselves from them, and consequently reappear to us in seemingly external, unfamiliar, and terrifying forms. Such

forms, according to Freud, include but are not exclusive to the phenomenon that Jentsch identified as the uncanny, namely, a feeling of intellectual uncertainty as to whether something is animate or inanimate. As many critics have pointed out, Freud's redefinition of the uncanny is itself problematic. Michiel Scharpé, for example, writes: Freud claims that "he only wants to go *beyond* Jentsch's insights, but quite soon it becomes clear that he does not validate the notion of intellectual uncertainty as a constitutive factor for the uncanny. Hence, during the entire essay, he will try as much as he can to minimize this intellectual uncertainty. However, as Hélène Cixous has pointed out, and others after her, this struggle forces Freud into a seemingly endless series of examples, conclusions, and modifications of those conclusions."

4. Perhaps Hoffmann's best-known uncanny creation is Olimpia, the gynoid with which the haplessly obtuse Nathanael falls in love in his short story "Der Sandmann." Nathanael's friend Siegmund gives a vivid account of Olimpia's uncanny aura: "She is singularly statuesque and soulless. . . . She is strangely measured in her movements, they all seem as if they were dependent upon some wound-up clockwork. Her playing and singing have the disagreeably perfect, but insensitive timing of a singing machine, and her dancing is the same. We felt quite afraid of this Olimpia, and did not like to have anything to do with her; she seemed to us to be only acting *like* a living creature, and as if there was some secret at the bottom of it all" (208).

5. For a related discussion on the relationship of lyric to questions of legal and moral personhood, see Barbara Johnson's 1998 essay "Anthropomorphism in Lyric and Law." Using as her texts Paul de Man's essay "Anthropomorphism and Trope in the Lyric" and a 1993 Supreme Court opinion on the issue of whether a prisoners' association can be counted as a juridical "person," Johnson argues that considerations of lyric personhood ("emotive, subjective, individual") can illuminate considerations of legal personhood ("rational, rights-bearing, institutional") (206).

6. The phrase "uncanny valley" is a translation of the Japanese phrase "Bukimi No Tani." Mori introduced this theory in a 1970 article published in *Energy* and translated by Karl F. MacDorman and Takashi Minato. Part of what makes his theory so powerful is its suggestiveness. Mori himself has acknowledged that even he does not completely understand certain aspects of his own theory, remarking in 2005: "While I introduced the notion of the uncanny valley, I have not examined it closely so far." In the decades since Mori proposed his theory, the uncanny valley has been applied not only to robots but also to computer-generated images in video games and animated films. For more information on the uncanny valley, see Jasia Reichardt's discussion of the uncanny valley in *Robots: Fact, Fiction, and Prediction*

(26–27); Dave Bryant's essay "Why Are Monster-Movie Zombies So Horrifying and Talking Animals So Fascinating?"; Lawrence Weschler's article "Why Is This Man Smiling?"; and Stephanie Gray's "'Uncanny Valley' Research Journal."

7. The online forum for www.RoombaReview.com includes a discussion thread titled "What did you name your Roomba?" According to the posts in this thread, some Roomba owners let their children decide on a name. "Our 3 yr old named ours 'Susie,'" one parent writes. Another parent shares: "My son has just completed 4 years and he began to call it RATONCITO (small mouse)." A significant number of people name their Roombas after iconic robots from popular movies and TV shows: "Rosie" (the robot maid in The Jetsons), "R2-D2" (Star Wars), and "Murphy" (RoboCop). Other names are more whimsical. One Rooma owner writes: "My wife christened ours Sir George, because it commands attention as it moves about through the room." Another fan calls his Roomba "Marilyn Monrobot."

8. Our reaction to the scene would be different if David were a "real" boy undergoing a medical procedure (say, open-heart surgery). We might feel squeamish or "grossed out," but we would not experience the uncanny valley.

9. Some feminists have criticized *Blade Runner* for "the ways in which the dead and dying woman is transformed into artistic, aesthetic images, even whilst they represent images of extreme and grotesque violence" (Wee). Zhora's death, for example, is "constructed for the viewing pleasure of the film's audience. The use of colour, the grace and control with which Zhora's body is seen to crash through the glass, the shattering and flying pieces of glass as she breaks through, all combine to construct a series of extremely beautiful images. Even the soundtrack is manipulated to heighten the visually aesthetic construction of the scene, emphasising the atonal music on the soundtrack, the sound of breaking glass, the throb of heartbeats and a female voice screaming" (Wee).

10. It is useful to compare the discourse surrounding robot rights with the discourse surrounding abortion. In her essay "Apostrophe, Animation, and Abortion" (chapter 16 of *A World of Difference*), Barbara Johnson identifies the dynamics of apostrophe and personification as vitally intrinsic to both the content and the form of the discourse surrounding the moral claims of fetuses. "What is the debate over abortion about, indeed, if not the question of when, precisely, a being assumes a human form?" Johnson remarks, before going on to suggest that "the arguments for and against abortion are structured through and through by the rhetorical limits and possibilities of something akin to apostrophe" (189, 191). Johnson's observations have a direct relevance to the discussion of robot rights. To be sure, the issues are not interchangeable. It is one thing to ask: "At what point does an embryo or fetus assume human form while developing inside the womb?" It is a

somewhat different matter to ask: "At what point does a technological artifact assume human personhood in the context of scientific progress and developments in robotics and artificial intelligence?" Yet these are versions of a single question: "At what point does something—anything—become a human life requiring our moral respect?" Johnson suggests that the most effective way in which we can approach this question is by using a discourse structured through and through by the rhetorical limits and possibilities of apostrophe, personification, and other life-bestowing lyric figures. I believe that science fiction is precisely this kind of discourse—a discourse structured through and through, literally and figuratively, by the rhetorical and lyrical possibilities and limits of figures of speech.

11. Similarly, Donna Haraway identifies the cyborg as a category of experience no more constructed—no less livable—than "woman," "father," or any other way of experiencing the world. "The cyborg is a matter of fiction and lived experience that changes what counts as women's experience," she declares in "A Cyborg Manifesto": "I am making an argument for the cyborg as a fiction mapping our social and bodily reality and as an imaginative resource suggesting some very fruitful couplings" (149, 150).

12. Many of the claims made in this chapter can be applied to the struggles of minorities for civil rights in the United States. Stereotypes, after all, are humanoid artifacts no less constructed than robots. The most harmful stereotypes are those that inhabit the uncanny valley: beyond interfering with the capacity to empathize with those being stereotyped, they promote hostility, phobia, and violent revulsion. A vivid example of a stereotype that inhabits the uncanny valley can be found in Sax Rohmer's 1913 novel *The Insidious Dr. Fu Manchu* (as well as in the many sequels and Hollywood films spawned by this influential work). So hyperbolic is Fu Manchu's villainy that his status as a stereotype—the fact of his constructedness—is almost always dramatically conspicuous. At the same time, the alarming vitality and sentience of this caricature threaten constantly to come to life.

Bibliography

Aarseth, Espen. 1994. "Nonlinearity and Literary Theory." *Hyper/Text/Theory.* Ed. George Landow. Baltimore: Johns Hopkins University Press. 51–86.

Abrams, M. H. 1999. *A Glossary of Literary Terms.* 7th ed. Fort Worth, TX: Harcourt Brace College Publishers.

Adams, Douglas. 1980. *The Restaurant at the End of the Universe.* New York: Del Rey, 2005.

A.I. (Artificial Intelligence). 2001. Dir. Steven Spielberg. DreamWorks Home Entertainment, 2002.

Albright, Daniel. 1981. *Representation and the Imagination: Beckett, Kafka, Nabokov, and Schoenberg.* Chicago: University of Chicago Press.

———. 1997. *Quantum Poetics: Yeats, Pound, Eliot, and the Science of Modernism.* Cambridge, UK: Cambridge University Press.

———. 2000. *Untwisting the Serpent: Modernism in Music, Literature, and Other Arts.* Chicago: University of Chicago Press.

Alexie, Sherman. 1995. *Reservation Blues.* New York: Grove Press.

———. 2007. *Flight.* New York: Black Cat.

Aliens. 1986. Dir. James Cameron. Twentieth Century Fox Home Entertainment, 2003.

Alkon, Paul. 1994. *Science Fiction before 1900: Imagination Discovers Technology.* New York: Routledge, 2002.

"Allegory." 1993. *The New Princeton Encyclopedia of Poetry and Poetics.* Ed. Alex Preminger and T. V. F. Brogan. Princeton, NJ: Princeton University Press. 31–36.

Allen, Mark. 2005. "I, Roommate: The Robot Housekeeper Arrives." *New York Times,* July 14: Home & Garden.

Allen, William Rodney, ed. 1988. *Conversations with Kurt Vonnegut.* Jackson: University Press of Mississippi.

"American Society for the Prevention of Cruelty to Robots." N.d. www.aspcr.com (accessed 9/4/09).

Arnold, Matthew. 1867. "Dover Beach." *Dover Beach and Other Poems.* Mineola, NY: Dover, 1994.

Aronofsky, Darren, et al. 2006. *The Fountain.* Videorecording. Warner Home Video, Burbank, CA, 2007.

Asimov, Isaac. 1945. "Escape!" *I, Robot.* New York: Bantam. 174–205.

———. 1946. "Evidence." *Robot Visions.* New York: ROC, 1991. 135–160.

———. 1951. *Foundation.* New York: Bantam, 2004.

———. 1952. *Foundation and Empire.* New York: Bantam, 2004.

———. 1958. "The Ugly Little Boy." *Robot Dreams.* New York: Ace, 2004. 248–282.

———. 1967. "Segregationist." *Robot Visions.* New York: ROC, 1991. 312–318.

———. 1976. "The Bicentennial Man." *Robot Visions.* New York: ROC, 1991. 245–290.

———. 1981. *Foundation's Edge.* New York: Bantam, 2004.

———. 1987. "Cybernetic Organism." *Robot Visions.* New York: ROC, 1991. 463–469.

———. 1988. *Prelude to Foundation.* New York: Bantam, 2004.

———. 1991. *I, Robot.* New York: Bantam.

Atwood, Margaret. 1986. *The Handmaid's Tale.* New York: Anchor Books, 1998.

———. 2003. *Oryx and Crake.* New York: Anchor Books, 2004.

Auerbach, Erich. 1953. *Mimesis: The Representation of Reality in Western Literature.* Trans. Willard R. Trask. Princeton, NJ: Princeton University Press, 2003.

Auster, Paul. 1987. *In the Country of Last Things.* New York: Penguin, 1988.

Bacon-Smith, Camille. 2000. *Science Fiction Culture.* Philadelphia: University of Pennsylvania Press.

Bainbridge, William. 1986. *Dimensions of Science Fiction.* Cambridge, MA: Harvard University Press.

Bakhtin, M. M. 1981. *The Dialogic Imagination: Four Essays.* Austin: University of Texas Press.

Baldick, Chris. 2001. *The Oxford Concise Dictionary of Literary Terms.* Oxford, UK: Oxford University Press.

Ballard, J. G. 1960. "Chronopolis." *The Best Short Stories of J. G. Ballard.* New York: Picador USA, 2001. 43–66.

———. 1962. "The Voices of Time." *The Best Short Stories of J. G. Ballard.* New York: Picador USA, 2001. 67–99.

———. 1966. *The Crystal World.* New York: Farrar, Straus and Giroux, 1988.

Banks, Iain M. 1987. *Consider Phlebas.* New York: Orbit, 2008.

Barker, Pat. 1991. *Regeneration.* New York: Plume, 1993.

Barr, Marleen S. 2000. *Genre Fission: A New Discourse Practice for Cultural Studies.* Iowa City: University of Iowa Press.

Barron, Louis, and Bebe Barron. 1989. *Forbidden Planet.* Small Planet Records.

Batista, Elisa. 2003. "Wakamaru Bot at Your Service." www.wired.com (accessed 7/2/07).

Bear, Greg. 1985. *Blood Music*. New York: Arbor House.

———. 1999. *Darwin's Radio*. New York: Ballantine.

———. 2003. *Darwin's Children*. New York: Del Rey, 2004.

Being John Malkovich. 1999. Dir. Spike Jonze. Videorecording. Universal: USA Home Entertainment, California, 2000.

Bellamy, Edward. 1888. *Looking Backward: 2000–1887*. New York: Penguin, 1986.

Benedikt, Michael, ed. 1991a. *Cyberspace: First Steps*. Cambridge, MA: MIT Press.

———. 1991b. "Introduction." *Cyberspace: First Steps*. Ed. Michael Benedikt. Cambridge, MA: MIT Press. 1–25.

Benford, Gregory. 1988. "Foreword." *Last and First Men: A Story of the Near and Far Future*. Los Angeles: Jeremy Tarcher, Inc. ix–xi.

Bester, Alfred. 1956. *The Stars My Destination*. New York: Vintage, 1996.

Bishop, Elizabeth. 1965. "Sestina." *The Complete Poems: 1927–1979*. New York: Farrar, Straus and Giroux, 1997.

———. 1979. "One Art." *The Complete Poems: 1927–1979*. New York: Farrar, Straus and Giroux, 1997.

Blade Runner. 1982. Dir. Ridley Scott. Warner Home Video, 1993.

Blake, William. 1794. "London." *The Complete Poetry and Prose of William Blake*. Ed. Harold Bloom. Revised ed. New York: Anchor, 1997.

Blish, James. 1956. "A Work of Art." *The Science Fiction Century*. Ed. David Hartwell. New York: Tor, 1997. 121–132.

Bloch, Ernst. 1938–1947. *The Principle of Hope*. Trans. Neville Plaice, Stephen Plaice, and Paul Knight. Vol. 1. Cambridge, MA: MIT Press, 1996.

Blunden, Edmund. 1928. "Come on, My Lucky Lads." *The Penguin Book of First World War Poetry*. Ed. Jon Silkin. 2nd ed. London: Penguin, 1996.

Booker, M. Keith, and Anne-Marie Thomas, eds. 2009. *The Science Fiction Handbook*. New York: Wiley-Blackwell.

Bould, Mark, Andrew Butler, Adam Roberts, and Sherryl Vint, eds. 2009. *The Routledge Companion to Science Fiction*. New York: Routledge.

Boulding, Kenneth. 1966. "The Economics of the Coming Spaceship Earth." www.eoearth.org (accessed 2/4/07).

Bourne, Randolph. 1916. "Trans-National America." *Atlantic Monthly* 118.1 (July): 86–97.

Bradbury, Ray. 1949. "The One Who Waits." *The Stories of Ray Bradbury*. New York: Knopf, 2005. 630–635.

———. 1950. *The Martian Chronicles*. New York: Bantam, 1979.

———. 1953. *Fahrenheit 451*. New York: Del Rey, 1991.

Brin, David. 1983. *Startide Rising*. New York: Bantam, 1995.

Broderick, Damien. 1995. *Reading by Starlight: Postmodern Science Fiction*. London: Routledge.

Brooks, Gwendolyn. 1960. "The Lovers of the Poor." *The Essential Gwendolyn Brooks.* Ed. Elizabeth Alexander. New York: Library of America, 2005. 71–74.

Brown, J. 2006. "Wow." February 28, 2005. Customer review of *Tae Guk Gi.* www. amazon.com (accessed 2/24/06).

Bryansix. 2007. "This Sounds Like a 9th Grade Essay." www.hardware.slashdot.org (accessed 4/21/07).

Bryant, Dave. 2006. "The Uncanny Valley: Why Are Monster-Movie Zombies So Horrifying and Talking Animals So Fascinating?" www.arclight.net (accessed 4/19/07).

Bukatman, Scott. 1993. *Terminal Identity: The Virtual Subject in Postmodern Science Fiction.* Durham, NC: Duke University Press, 2002.

———. 1994. "Gibson's Typewriter." *Flame Wars: The Discourse of Cyberculture.* Ed. Mark Dery. Durham, NC: Duke University Press. 71–89.

Burroughs, Edgar Rice. 1918. *The Land That Time Forgot.* Barrington, NH: Breakneck, 2007.

Burt, Stephen. 2007. "Dulles Access Road." www.slate.com (accessed 7/6/09).

Butler, Octavia. 1977. *Mind of My Mind.* New York: Aspect, 1994.

———. 1979. *Kindred.* Boston: Beacon, 1988.

———. 1987. *Dawn: Lilith's Brood.* New York: Aspect, 2000. 1–248.

———. 1988. *Adulthood Rites: Lilith's Brood.* New York: Aspect, 2000. 249–517.

———. 1989. *Imago: Lilith's Brood.* New York: Aspect, 2000. 519–746.

———. 1993. *Parable of the Sower.* New York: Warner Books, 1995.

Cacicedo, Alberto. 2005. "'You must remember this': Trauma and Memory in *Catch-22* and *Slaughterhouse-Five.*" *Critique* 46.4 (Summer): 357–368.

Calloway, Catherine. 1995. "'How to Tell a True War Story': Metafiction in *The Things They Carried.*" *Critique* 36: 249ff.

Cameron, Sharon. 1979. *Lyric Time: Dickinson and the Limits of Genre.* Baltimore: Johns Hopkins University Press, 1981.

Čapek, Karel. 1921. *R.U.R.* Trans. Paul Selver and Nigel Playfair. Mineola, NY: Dover, 2001.

Card, Orson Scott. 1985. *Ender's Game.* New York: Tor, 1994.

Carlos, Wendy. 1972. *Timesteps.* East Side Digital, 1998.

Caruth, Cathy. 1995a. "Recapturing the Past: Introduction." *Trauma: Explorations in Memory.* Ed. Cathy Caruth. Baltimore: Johns Hopkins University Press. 151–157.

———. 1995b. "Trauma and Experience: Introduction." *Trauma: Explorations in Memory.* Ed. Cathy Caruth. Baltimore: Johns Hopkins University Press. 3–12.

———. 1996. *Unclaimed Experience: Trauma, Narrative, and History.* Baltimore: Johns Hopkins University Press.

Cha, Theresa Hak Kyung. 1982. *Dictee.* Berkeley: University of California Press, 2001.

Cheng, Anne Anlin. 2001. *The Melancholy of Race: Psychoanalysis, Assimilation, and Hidden Grief.* Oxford, UK: Oxford University Press.

Chiang, Ted. 1991. "Understand." *Stories of Your Life and Others*. 1st ed. New York: Orb, 2002. 45–92.

Ch'oe, Yong-ho, Peter H. Lee, and Wm. Theodore de Bary, eds. 2000. *Sources of Korean Tradition*. Vol. 2, *From the Sixteenth to the Twentieth Centuries*. New York: Columbia University Press.

Choi, Sook Nyul. 1991. *Year of Impossible Goodbyes*. Boston: Houghton Mifflin.

———. 1993. *Echoes of the White Giraffe*. New York: Bantam Doubleday Bell.

Chun, Wendy. 2006. *Control and Freedom: Power and Paranoia in the Age of Fiber Optics*. Cambridge, MA: MIT Press.

Claremont, Chris, and Jim Lee. 1991. *X-Men: Rubicon*. Vol. 1. New York: Marvel Comics, October.

Clarke, Arthur. 1968. *2001: A Space Odyssey*. New York: Roc, 2000.

———. 1972. *Rendezvous with Rama*. New York: Spectra, 1990.

Close Encounters of the Third Kind. 1977. Dir. Steven Spielberg. Columbia TriStar Home Entertainment, 2002.

Clute, John, and Peter Nicholls, eds. 1995. *The Encyclopedia of Science Fiction*. 2nd ed. New York: St. Martin's Griffin.

"Coruscant." 2006. www.starwars.com (accessed 12/11/06).

Crossley, Robert. 1994. *Olaf Stapledon: Speaking for the Future*. Syracuse, NY: Syracuse University Press.

———, ed. 1997. *An Olaf Stapledon Reader*. Syracuse, NY: Syracuse University Press.

Crowley, John. 1979. *Engine Summer: Otherwise. Three Novels by John Crowley*. New York: Perennial, 2002. 341–548.

Csicsery-Ronay, Istvan, Jr. 1995. "Antimancer: Cybernetics and Art in Gibson's *Count Zero*." *Science-Fiction Studies* 22: 163–186.

———. 2002. "Dis-Imagined Communities: Science Fiction and the Future of Nations." *Edging into the Future: Science Fiction and Contemporary Cultural Transformation*. Ed. Veronica Hollinger and Joan Gorson. Philadelphia: University of Pennsylvania Press. 217–237.

———. 2008. *The Seven Beauties of Science Fiction*. Middletown, CT: Wesleyan University Press.

Culler, Jonathan. 1981. *The Pursuit of Signs*. Ithaca, NY: Cornell University Press, 2002.

Cummings, E. E. 1922. "the Cambridge ladies who live in furnished souls." *Complete Poems, 1904–1962*. Ed. George James Firmage. New York: Liveright, 1994.

Cunningham, Michael. 2005. *Specimen Days*. New York: Picador.

Davis, Erik. 2004. *TechGnosis: Myth, Magic and Mysticism in the Age of Information*. London: Serpents Tail.

The Day the Earth Stood Still. 1951. Dir. Robert Wise. Twentieth Century-Fox Home Entertainment, 2000.

Delany, Samuel. 1966. *Babel-17/Empire Star*. New York: Vintage, 2001.

———. 1968. *Nova*. New York: Vintage, 2002.

———. 1975. *Dhalgren*. First Vintage Books ed. New York: Vintage, 2001.

————. 1976. *Triton*. 11th ed. New York: Bantam, 1986.

————. 1978. "About Five Thousand Seven Hundred and Fifty Words." *The Jewel-Hinged Jaw: Essays on Science Fiction*. New York: Berkley. 21–37.

————. 1994. "The Semiology of Silence: The Science Fiction Studies Interview." *Silent Interviews: On Language, Race, Sex, Science Fiction, and Some Comics*. Hanover, NH: Wesleyan University Press. 21–58.

DeLillo, Don. 1985. *White Noise*. New York: Viking.

De L'Isle-Adam, Villiers. 1886. *Tomorrow's Eve*. Trans. Robert Martin Adam. Urbana: University of Illinois Press, 1982.

Diagnostic and Statistical Manual of Mental Disorders. 2000. 4th ed. Arlington, VA: American Psychiatric Association.

Dick, Philip K. 1956. "The Minority Report." *The Minority Report and Other Classic Stories by Philip K. Dick*. New York: Citadel, 2002. 71–102.

————. 1968. *Do Androids Dream of Electric Sheep?* New York: Del Rey, 1996.

————. 1972. *We Can Build You*. New York: Vintage, 1994.

————. 1981. "My Definition of Science Fiction." *The Shifting Realities of Philip K. Dick: Selected Literary and Philosophical Writings*. Ed. Lawrence Sutin. New York: Vintage, 1995. 99–100.

Dickinson, Emily. 1861. "A Clock Stopped." *The Poems of Emily Dickinson*. Ed. R. W. Franklin. Variorum ed. Cambridge, MA: Belknap Press of Harvard University Press, 1998. Poem 259.

————. 1862. "I Felt a Funeral, in My Brain." *The Poems of Emily Dickinson*. Ed. R. W. Franklin. Variorum ed. Cambridge, MA: Belknap Press of Harvard University Press, 1998. Poem 340.

————. 1883. "The Clock Strikes One That Just Struck Two." *The Poems of Emily Dickinson*. Ed. R. W. Franklin. Variorum ed. Cambridge, MA: Belknap Press of Harvard University Press, 1998. Poem 1598.

Dimock, Wai Chee. 2007. "Introduction: Planet and America, Set and Subset." *Shades of the Planet: American Literature as World Literature*. Ed. Wai Chee Dimock and Lawrence Buell. Princeton, NJ: Princeton University Press. 1–16.

Disch, Thomas. 1979. *On Wings of Song*. New York: St. Martin's Press.

————. 1998. *The Dreams Our Stuff Is Made Of: How Science Fiction Conquered the World*. New York: Touchstone, 2000.

Doctorow, Cory. 2003. *Down and Out in the Magic Kingdom*. www.craphound.com (accessed 9/9/09).

Donne, John. 1633. "The Good Morrow." *The Major Works*. Ed. John Carey. Oxford, UK: Oxford University Press, 2000.

Doxiadis, Constantinos. 1968. "Ecumenopolis: Tomorrow's City." *Britannica Book of the Year 1968*. Chicago: Encyclopedia Britannica, Inc.

Dyson, Esther. 1995. "If You Don't Love It, Leave It." *New York Times*, July 16: A1.

Edelman, David Louis. 2006. *Infoquake*. Amherst, NY: Pyr.

Egan, Greg. 1998. *Diaspora*. New York: HarperPrism.

Elgin, Suzette Haden. 2005. *The Science Fiction Poetry Handbook*. Cedar Rapids, IA
Sam's Dot Publishing.

Ellison, Harlan. 1967. "I Have No Mouth, and I Must Scream." *The Essential Ellison:
A 50-Year Retrospective*. Beverly Hills, CA: Morpheus International, 2001.
177–189.

Ellison, Ralph. 1995. *Invisible Man*. New York: Vintage.

Elmer-DeWitt, Philip. 1995. "Welcome to Cyberspace." Special Issue of *Time*: 4+.

Eng, Steve. 1995. "The Speculative Muse: An Introduction to Science Fiction
Poetry." *Anatomy of Wonder: A Critical Guide to Science Fiction*. Ed. Neil Barron.
4th ed. New Providence, NJ: R. R. Bowker, Reed Reference. 378–392.

"The Ethical Dilemmas of Robotics." 2007. www.news.bbc.co.uk (accessed 3/9/07).

Evans, Arthur, and R. D. Mullen. 1996, November. "North American College Courses
in Science Fiction, Utopian Literature, and Fantasy." *Science Fiction Studies* 23.70.

Fainlight, Ruth. 1969. "A Report." *Holding Your Eight Hands*. Ed. Edward Lucie-
Smith. Garden City, NY: Doubleday.

Farmer, Philip José. 1971. *To Your Scattered Bodies Go*. New York: Berkley, 1983.

Farnell, Ross. 1998. "Posthuman Topologies: William Gibson's 'Architexture' in
Virtual Light and *Idoru*." *Science-Fiction Studies* 25.3: 459–480.

Farrell, Kirby. 1998. *Post-Traumatic Culture: Injury and Interpretation in the Nineties*.
Baltimore: Johns Hopkins University Press.

Ferguson, Margaret, Mary Jo Salter, and Jon Stallworthy, eds. 1996. *The Norton
Anthology of Poetry*. 4th ed. New York: Norton.

Fisher, Philip. 1998. *Wonder, the Rainbow, and the Aesthetics of Rare Experiences*.
Cambridge, MA: Harvard University Press.

———. 1999. *Still the New World: American Literature in a Culture of Creative
Destruction*. Cambridge, MA: Harvard University Press.

Flambard-Weisbart, Veronique. 2005. "Hollywood Enters the Dragon." *World
Weavers: Globalization, Science Fiction, and the Cybernetic Revolution*. Ed. Wong
Kin Yuen, Gary Westfahl, and Amy Kit-Sze Chan. Hong Kong: Hong Kong
University Press. 233–243.

Fletcher, Angus. 1964. *Allegory: The Theory of a Symbolic Mode*. Ithaca, NY: Cornell
University Press.

Forster, E. M. 1909. "The Machine Stops." *Selected Stories*. Ed. David Leavitt and
Mark Mitchell. New York: Penguin, 2001. 91–123.

Fowler, Alastair. 1982. *Kinds of Literature: An Introduction to the Theory of Genres and
Modes*. Cambridge, MA: Harvard University Press.

Franklin, H. Bruce. 2000. *Vietnam and Other American Fantasies*. Amherst:
University of Massachusetts Press.

Frazier, Robert, ed. 1984. *Burning with a Vision: Poetry of Science and the Fantastic*.
Philadelphia: Owlswick Press.

Freda, James. 1999. "Discourse on Han in Postcolonial Korea: Absent Suffering and
Industrialist Dreams." *Jouvert: A Journal of Postcolonial Studies* 3.12. www.social.
chass.ncsu.edu/jouvert (accessed 8/5/06).

Freedman, Carl. 2000. *Critical Theory and Science Fiction*. Hanover, NH: Wesleyan University Press.

Freitas, Robert A. 1985. "The Legal Rights of Robots." *Student Lawyer* 13: 54–56.

Freud, Sigmund. 1917–1919. "The Uncanny." *The Standard Edition of the Complete Psychological Works of Sigmund Freud*. Ed. James Strachey. London: Hogarth Press and the Institute of Psycho-Analysis. 219–252.

Frost, Robert. 1923. "Stopping by Woods on a Snowy Evening." *The Poetry of Robert Frost: The Collected Poems, Complete and Unabridged*. Ed. Edward Connery Lathem. New York: Henry Holt and Co., 1969.

Frye, Northrop. 1957. *Anatomy of Criticism*. Princeton, NJ: Princeton University Press, 1973.

———. 1985. "Approaching the Lyric." *Lyric Poetry: Beyond New Criticism*. Ed. Chaviva Hosek and Patricia Parker. Ithaca, NY, and London: Cornell University Press.

Genette, Gerard. 1997. *Paratexts: Thresholds of Interpretation*. Trans. Jane Lewin. Cambridge, UK: Cambridge University Press.

"Genosha." N.d. www.marvel.com/universe/Genosha (accessed 2/1/09).

Ghosh, Amitav. 1995. *The Calcutta Chromosome: A Novel of Fevers, Delirium, and Discovery*. New York: HarperCollins, 2001.

Gibson, William. 1982. "Burning Chrome." *Burning Chrome*. New York: Ace, 1987. 168–191.

———. 1984. *Neuromancer*. New York: Ace.

———. 1986. *Count Zero*. New York: Ace, 1987.

———. 1988. *Mona Lisa Overdrive*. New York: Bantam, 1989.

———. 1989. "Interview with Darren Wershler-Henry." www.eff.org (accessed 2/3/02).

———. 1991. "Academy Leader." *Cyberspace: First Steps*. Ed. Michael Benedikt. Cambridge, MA: MIT Press. 27–29.

———. 1992. "Author's Afterword." *Neuromancer*. Electronic ed. New York: Voyager Company. 541–542.

———. 1993. *Virtual Light*. New York: Bantam, 1994.

———. 1994. "Interview with Giuseppe Salza." http://home.worldnet.fr/~giusal/gibson.html (accessed 2/3/02).

———. 1996. *Idoru*. New York: Berkley 1997.

———. 1999a. *All Tomorrow's Parties*. New York: Ace, 2000.

———. 1999b. "My Obsession." *Wired Magazine*.

———. 1996c. "The Net Is a Waste of Time." *New York Times*, July 14: SM31.

———. 2002. "Interview with Antony Johnston." www.spikemagazine.com (accessed 3/1/02).

———. 2003. *Pattern Recognition*. New York: Berkley, 2004.

Gleick, James. 1994. "The Information Future: Out of Control." *New York Times*, May 1: SM54+.

Goldbarth, Albert. 1984. "Starbirth." *Burning with a Vision: Poetry of Science and the Fantastic.* Ed. Robert Frazier. Philadelphia: Owlswick.

Goldberg, Ken, ed. 2000. *The Robot in the Garden: Telerobotics and Telepistemology in the Age of the Internet.* Cambridge, MA: MIT Press.

GoldFish. 2006. "Comment Posted in Response to 'Robot Rights? What about Human Rights?'" *Sydney Morning Herald.* www.blogs.smh.com.au/newsblog (accessed 4/21/07).

Graham, Jorie. 1987. "What the End Is for." *The Norton Anthology of Poetry.* Ed. Margaret Ferguson, Mary Jo Salter, and Jon Stallworthy. 4th ed. New York: Norton, 1996. 1849–1851.

Gray, Stephanie. 2004– . "Almost Too Human and Lifelike for Comfort: Stephanie Gray's 'Uncanny Valley' Research Journal." http://uncanny-valley.livejournal.com (accessed 7/1/07).

Gulick, John. 2007. *Sociology 450: Sociology of Globalization.* Akita, Japan: Akita International University, Spring.

Gunn, James, and Matthew Candelaria, eds. 2005. *Speculations on Speculation: Theories of Science Fiction.* Lanham, MD: Scarecrow.

Gunn, Thom. 1987. "The Missing." *The Norton Anthology of Poetry.* Ed. Margaret Ferguson, Mary Jo Salter, and Jon Stallworthy. 4th ed. New York: Norton, 1996.

Gurney, Ivor. 1996. "Strange Hells." *The Penguin Book of First World War Poetry.* Ed. Jon Silkin. 2nd ed. London: Penguin.

Haldeman, Joe. 1974. *The Forever War.* New York: Thomas Dunne, 2009.

———. N.d. "Interim Report: An Autobiographical Ramble." www.home.earthlink. net/~haldeman (accessed 8/8/09).

Halliwell, Stephen. 2002. *The Aesthetics of Mimesis: Ancient Texts and Modern Problems.* Princeton, NJ: Princeton University Press.

Haraway, Donna. 1985. "A Cyborg Manifesto: Science, Technology, and Socialist-Feminism in the Late Twentieth Century." *Simians, Cyborgs, and Women: The Reinvention of Nature.* New York: Routledge, 1991. 149–181.

Harvey, David. 1990. *The Condition of Postmodernity: An Enquiry into the Origins of Cultural Change.* Cambridge, MA: Blackwell.

Hassler, Donald M. 2008. "The Renewal of 'Hard' Science Fiction." *A Companion to Science Fiction.* Ed. David Seed. Oxford, UK: Blackwell. 248–258.

Hayles, N. Katherine. 1999. *How We Became Posthuman: Virtual Bodies in Cybernetics, Literature, and Informatics.* Chicago: University of Chicago Press.

Hayles, N. Katherine, and Nicholas Gessler. 2004. "The Slipstream of Mixed Reality: Unstable Ontologies and Semiotic Markers in *The Thirteenth Floor, Dark City,* and *Mulholland Drive.*" *PMLA* 119.3: 482–499.

Heim, Michael. 1991. "The Erotic Ontology of Cyberspace." *Cyberspace: First Steps.* Ed. Michael Benedikt. Cambridge, MA: MIT Press. 59–80.

Heinlein, Robert. 1961. *Stranger in a Strange Land.* New York: Ace, 1987.

Herbert, Frank. 1965. *Dune.* Special 25th Anniversary ed. New York: Ace, 1990.

Herbert, George. 1633. "Church Monuments." *George Herbert: The Complete English Poems.* Ed. John Tobin. New York: Penguin Classics, 1991.

Herman, Judith Lewis. 1997. *Trauma and Recovery: The Aftermath of Violence—from Domestic Abuse to Political Terror.* New York: Basic Books.

Hirsch, Marianne. 1997. *Family Frames: Photography, Narrative, and Postmemory.* Cambridge, MA: Harvard University Press, 2002.

HK in Seoul. 2003. "Translational Difficulties." www.heleninseoul.blogspot.com (accessed 12/15/05).

Hoban, Russell. 1980. *Riddley Walker.* Bloomington: Indiana University Press, 1998.

Hoffmann, E. T. A. 1814. "Automata." *The Best Tales of Hoffmann.* Ed. E. F. Bleiler. New York: Dover, 1967. 71–103.

———. 1816–1817. "The Sand-Man." *The Best Tales of Hoffmann.* Ed. E. F. Bleiler. New York: Dover, 1967. 183–214.

Holden, James. 2007. "Star." *Conceptual Breakthrough: Star/Alien: Two Experiments in SF Criticism.* Ed. James Holden and Simon King. London: InkerMen Press. 13–67.

Hollinger, Veronica, and Joan Gordon, eds. 2002. *Edging into the Future: Science Fiction and Contemporary Cultural Transformation.* Philadelphia: University of Pennsylvania Press.

Hong, Cathy Park. 2007. *Dance Dance Revolution.* New York: Norton.

Hopkinson, Nalo. 2001. "Ganger (Ball Lightning)." *Skin Folk.* New York: Aspect. 221–245.

Huang, Yunte. 2002. *Transpacific Displacement: Ethnography, Translation, and Intertextual Travel in Twentieth-Century American Literature.* Berkeley: University of California Press.

Huntington, John. 1998. "Remembrance of Things to Come: Narrative Technique in *Last and First Men.*" *Science Fiction Studies* 9, Part 3: 257–264.

Huxley, Aldous. 1932. *Brave New World.* 1st Perennial Classics ed. New York: Perennial Classics, 1998.

Ishiguro, Kazuo. 2005. *Never Let Me Go.* New York: Vintage, 2006.

Iyer, Pico. 2000. *The Global Soul: Jet Lag, Shopping Malls, and the Search for Home.* New York: Vintage, 2001.

James, Edward, and Farah Mendlesohn, eds. 2003. *Cambridge Companion to Science Fiction.* Cambridge, UK: Cambridge University Press.

Jameson, Fredric. 1991. *Postmodernism, Or, The Cultural Logic of Late Capitalism.* Durham, NC: Duke University Press, 1999.

———. 2000. "Preface." *The Cultures of Globalization.* Ed. Fredric Jameson and Masao Miyoshi. Durham, NC: Duke University Press. xi–xvii.

———. 2005. *Archaeologies of the Future: The Desire Called Utopia and Other Science Fictions.* London, New York: Verso.

Jameson, Fredric, and Masao Miyoshi, eds. 2003. *The Cultures of Globalization.* Durham, NC: Duke University Press.

Jenkins, Henry. N.d. "MIT Profile of Joe Haldeman." http://web.mit.edu/m-I-t/science_fiction/profiles/haldeman.html (accessed 9/18/09).

Jentsch, Ernst. 1906. "On the Psychology of the Uncanny." *Angelaki* 2.1, 1995.

Johnson, Barbara. 1987. *A World of Difference*. Baltimore: Johns Hopkins University Press, 1989.

———. 2001. "Anthropomorphism in Lyric and Law." *Material Events: Paul De Man and the Afterlife of Theory*. Ed. Tom Cohen et al. Minneapolis: University of Minnesota Press. 205–225.

———. 2008. *Persons and Things*. Cambridge, MA: Harvard University Press.

Johnson, George. 1999. "Searching for the Essence of the World Wide Web." *New York Times*, April 11: WK1.

Johnson, Samuel. 1779. "Lives of the Poets: Abraham Cowley." *Samuel Johnson: Selected Poetry and Prose*. Ed. Frank Brady and W. K. Wimsatt. Berkeley: University of California Press, 1977. 337–384.

Joron, Andrew. 1984. "The Sonic Flowerfall of Primes." *Burning with a Vision: Poetry of Science and the Fantastic*. Ed. Robert Frazier. Philadelphia: Owlswick Press.

Joyce, Michael. 1995. *Of Two Minds: Hypertext Pedagogy and Poetics*. Ann Arbor: University of Michigan Press.

Joyce, Michael, et al. 2000. *The Sonatas of Saint Francis*. www.supertart.com/sonatas/index.html (accessed 6/3/06).

Kadohata, Cynthia. 1992. *In the Heart of the Valley of Love*. New York: Viking, 1997.

Kang, Hildi, ed. 2001. *Under the Black Umbrella: Voices from Colonial Korea, 1910–1945*. Ithaca, NY: Cornell University Press.

Kang, Minsoo. 2006. *Of Tales and Enigmas*. Prime Books.

Kang, S. 2005. "Bridging the Generations," customer review of *Tae Guk Gi*. www.amazon.com (accessed 2/25/06).

Kang, Younghill. 1937. *East Goes West: The Making of an Oriental Yankee*. New York: Kaya, 1997.

Keats, John. 1819. "Ode to a Nightingale." *The Major Works*. Ed. Elizabeth Cook. Oxford, UK: Oxford University Press, 2001.

———. 1820. "Ode on a Grecian Urn." *The Complete Poems of John Keats*. New York: Modern Library, 1994.

Keep Robots Slaves. 2007. "Comment in Response to 'No Rights for Robots.'" www.yournewreality.blogspot.com (accessed 7/1/07).

Kelleher, Damian. 2004. 2/22/04 customer review of *Plowing the Dark*. www.amazon.com (accessed 3/25/08).

Keller, Nora Okja. 1997. *Comfort Woman*. New York: Penguin, 1998.

Kern, Stephen. 1983. *The Culture of Time and Space: 1880–1918*. Cambridge, MA: Harvard University Press, 2003.

Keyes, Daniel. 1966. *Flowers for Algernon*. New York: Harcourt.

Kim, Elaine. 1993. "Home Is Where the Han Is: A Korean American Perspective on the Los Angeles Upheavals." *Reading Rodney King/Reading Urban Uprising.* Ed. Robert Gooding-Williams. New York: Routledge. 215–235.

Kim, Paul Tchang Ryeol. 1986. "Korean Han and Evangelization." www.marys-touch.com/truth/han.htm (accessed 1/9/06).

Kim, Richard. 1988. *Lost Names: Scenes from a Korean Boyhood.* Berkeley: University of California Press, 1998.

Kim, Suji Kwock. 2003. *Notes from the Divided Country.* Baton Rouge: Louisiana State University Press.

Kingston, Maxine Hong. 1990. *Tripmaster Monkey: His Fake Book.* New York: Vintage.

Knight, Damon. 1967. *In Search of Wonder: Essays on Modern Science Fiction.* 2nd ed. Chicago: Advent Publishers.

Kress, Nancy. 1993. *Beggars in Spain.* New York: Eos, 2004.

LaCapra, Dominick. 2001. *Writing History, Writing Trauma.* Baltimore: Johns Hopkins University Press.

Landon, Brooks. 2002. *Science Fiction after 1900: From the Steam Man to the Stars.* New York: Routledge.

Landow, George P. 1997. *Hypertext 2.0: The Convergence of Contemporary Critical Theory and Technology.* Baltimore: Johns Hopkins University Press.

Lee, Chang-rae. 1999. *A Gesture Life.* New York: Riverhead.

Le Guin, Ursula K. 1966. *Rocannon's World.* New York: Harper & Row, 1977.

———. 1969a. "Introduction." *The Left Hand of Darkness.* New York: Ace. xi–xvi.

———. 1969b. *The Left Hand of Darkness.* New York: Ace, 2000.

———. 1974. *The Dispossessed.* New York: Harper & Row.

———. 1993. "Introduction." *The Norton Book of Science Fiction: North American Science Fiction, 1960–1990.* Ed. Ursula K. Le Guin and Brian Attebery. New York: Norton. 30–31.

Lehman-Wilzig, Sam. 1981. "Frankenstein Unbound: Towards a Legal Definition of Artificial Intelligence." *Futures* (December): 442–457.

Lem, Stanislaw. 1961, 1970 (in English). *Solaris.* Trans. Joanna Kilmartin and Steve Cox. San Diego: Harvest, 1987.

———. 1971 (in Polish), 1974 (in English). *The Futurological Congress.* Trans. Michael Kandel. Orlando, FL: Harvest, 1985.

Lessing, Doris. 1979. *Shikasta.* New York: Vintage.

———. 1988. "Afterword." *Last and First Men: A Story of the Near and Far Future.* Los Angeles: Jeremy Tarcher, Inc.

Lethem, Jonathan. 1994. *Gun, with Occasional Music.* Orlando, FL: Harvest, 2003.

Levy, David. 2007. *Love + Sex with Robots: The Evolution of Human-Robot Relations.* New York: HarperCollins.

———. 2009. "The Ethical Treatment of Artificially Conscious Robots." *International Journal of Social Robotics* 1.3: 209–216.

Lewis, Peter H. 1990. "Put On Your Data Glove and Goggles and Step Inside." *New York Times,* May 20: F8.

———. 1995. "Present at the Creation, Startled at the Reality." *New York Times,* May 22: D3.

Lin, Patrick, George Bekey, and Keith Abney. 2008. "Autonomous Military Robotics: Risk, Ethics, and Design." http://ethics.calpoly.edu/ONR_report.pdf (accessed 9/13/09).

London, Jack. 1907. *Before Adam.* Lincoln: University of Nebraska Press, 2000.

Lovecraft, H. P. 1931. *At the Mountains of Madness.* New York: Modern Library, 2005.

———. 1933. "The Dreams in the Witch House." *The Dreams in the Witch House and Other Weird Stories.* Ed. S. T. Joshi. New York: Penguin, 2004. 300–334.

Lowell, Percival. 1888. *The Soul of the Far East.* Kessinger Publishing, 2004.

Lucie-Smith, Edward, ed. 1969. *Holding Your Eight Hands: An Anthology of Science Fiction Verse.* Garden City, NY: Doubleday.

Luckhurst, Roger. 1998. "The Science-Fictionalization of Trauma: Remarks on Narratives of Alien Abduction." *Science Fiction Studies* 25.1 (March): 29–52.

———. 2005. *Science Fiction.* Cambridge, UK: Polity.

MacDorman, Karl F., and Takashi Minato. 2005. English translation of Masahiro Mori's essay "The Uncanny Valley." http://www.androidscience.com/theuncannyvalley/proceedings2005/uncannyvalley.html.

Marvell, Andrew. 1681. "The Garden." *The Complete Poems.* Ed. Elizabeth Story Donno. London: Penguin Classics, 1996.

The Matrix. 1999. Dir. Andy Wachowski and Larry Wachowski. Warner Home Video.

McCaffrey, Anne. 1961. *The Ship Who Sang.* London: Corgi, 1972.

McLuhan, Marshall, and Edmund Snow Carpenter. 1960. "Introduction." *Explorations in Communication: An Anthology.* Ed. Marshall McLuhan and Edmund Snow Carpenter. Boston: Beacon. ix–xii.

Melville, Herman. 1851. *Moby-Dick.* Oxford, UK: Oxford University Press, 1999.

Mendlesohn, Farah. 2003. "Introduction: Reading Science Fiction." *The Cambridge Companion to Science Fiction.* Ed. Edward James and Farah Mendlesohn. Cambridge, UK: Cambridge University Press. 1–12.

Miéville, China. 2000. *Perdido Street Station.* New York: Del Rey, 2003.

Mill, John Stuart. 1833. "What Is Poetry?" *The Norton Anthology of English Literature.* Ed. M. H. Abrams et al. 4th ed. New York: Norton, 1979. 1051–1059.

Miller, Nancy, and Jason Tougaw. 2002. "Introduction: Extremities." *Extremities: Trauma, Testimony, and Community.* Ed. Nancy Miller and Jason Tougaw. Champaign: University of Illinois Press. 1–21.

Miller, Walter. 1959. *A Canticle for Leibowitz.* New York: Bantam, 1997.

Milton, John. 1637. "Lycidas." *Complete Poems and Major Prose.* Ed. Merritt Yerkes Hughes. Reprint ed. Indianapolis: Hackett, 2003. 116–125.

Min, Yong Soon. 1992. "Defining Moments." *Writing Self, Writing Nation: A Collection of Essays on Dictee by Theresa Hak Kyung Cha.* Ed. Elaine Kim and

Norma Alarcon. Berkeley, CA: Third Woman Press, 1994. i, 1, 33, 71, 101, 163, 164.

Minsky, Marvin. 1995. "Alienable Rights." *Android Epistemology.* Ed. Kenneth M. Ford, Clark Glymour, and Patrick J. Hayes. Menlo Park, CA: American Association for Artificial Intelligence. 307–312.

Mitchell, David. 1999. *Ghostwritten.* New York: Vintage, 2000.

———. 2004. *Cloud Atlas.* New York: Random House.

Momaday, N. Scott. 1976. "The Eagle-Feather Fan." *The Norton Anthology of Poetry.* Ed. Margaret Ferguson, Mary Jo Salter, and Jon Stallworthy. 4th ed. New York: Norton.

Moore, Alan, and Dave Gibbons. 1986–1987. *Watchmen.* New York: DC Comics, 2005.

Moore, C. L. 1944. "No Woman Born." *The Best of C. L. Moore.* Ed. Lester del Rey. New York: Ballantine, 1976. 236–288.

Moravec, Hans. 1988. *Mind Children: The Future of Robot and Human Intelligence.* Cambridge, MA: Harvard University Press.

Morgan, Richard K. 2002. *Altered Carbon.* New York: Del Rey.

Mori, Masahiro. 1970. "The Uncanny Valley." *Energy* 7.4: 33–35.

———. 1999. *The Buddha in the Robot: A Robot Engineer's Thoughts on Science and Religion.* Trans. Charles S. Terry. Tokyo: Kosei.

———. 2005. "On Uncanny Valley." www.androidscience.com (accessed 4/24/07).

Moskowitz, Sam. 1957. "How Science Fiction Got Its Name." *The Prentice Hall Anthology of Science Fiction and Fantasy.* Ed. Garyn G. Roberts. Upper Saddle River, NJ: Prentice Hall, 2001. 1127–1135.

———, ed. 1979. *Far Future Calling: Uncollected Science Fiction and Fantasies of Olaf Stapledon.* Philadelphia: Oswald Train.

Mosley, Walter. 2001. "Voices." *Futureland.* New York: Aspect, 2001. 179–217.

Murray, Janet H. 1997. *Hamlet on the Holodeck: The Future of Narrative in Cyberspace.* Cambridge, MA: MIT Press.

Nahirny, Vladimir C., and Joshua A. Fishman. 1965. "American Immigrant Groups: Ethnic Identification and the Problem of Generations." *Theories of Ethnicity: A Classical Reader.* Ed. Werner Sollors. New York: New York University Press, 1996. 266–281.

Niven, Larry. 1970. *Ringworld.* New York: Del Rey.

———. 1980. *The Ringworld Engineers.* New York: Del Rey, 1981.

———. 1996. *The Ringworld Throne.* New York: Del Rey, 1997.

———. 2004. *Ringworld's Children.* New York: Tor, 2005.

Novak, Marcos. 1991. "Liquid Architectures in Cyberspace." *Cyberspace: First Steps.* Ed. Michael Benedikt. Cambridge, MA: MIT Press. 225–254.

Nunes, Mark. 1999. "Virtual Topographies: Smooth and Striated Cyberspace." *Cyberspace Textuality: Computer Technology and Literary Theory.* Ed. Marie-Laure Ryan. Bloomington: Indiana University Press. 61–77.

Nzeyimana, Sophie. 2006. "Robot Rights? What About Human Rights?" *Sydney Morning Herald.* http://blogs.smh.com.au/newsblog (accessed 12/15/07).

Oates, Joyce Carol. 2006. "EDickinsonRepliLuxe." *Wild Nights! Stories about the Last Days of Poe, Dickinson, Twain, James, and Hemingway.* New York: Ecco, 2008. 37–73.

O'Brien, Tim. 1990. *The Things They Carried.* New York: Broadway.

O'Connell, Pamela L. 1999. "Beyond Geography: Mapping the Unknowns of Cyberspace." *New York Times,* September 30: G1+.

O'Connor, John. 1983. "TV Weekend; Welcoming '84 with a Lombardo, Steve Allen or Dick Clark." *New York Times,* December 31, Late City Final Edition.

———. 1986. "Bye Bye Kipling on 13: A Video Adventure." *New York Times,* October 6.

Olsen, Lance. 1992. *William Gibson.* Mercer Island, WA: Starmont House.

Orwell, George. 1949. *1984.* New York: Plume, 1983.

Oshii, Mamoru. 1996. Dir. *Ghost in the Shell.* Masamune Shirow: Kodansha Ltd.: Bandai Visual Co., Ltd.: Manga Entertainment, 1998.

Owen, Wilfred. 1918a. "Exposure." *The Penguin Book of First World War Poetry.* Ed. Jon Silkin. London: Penguin, 1996 .

———. 1918b. "The Show." *The Penguin Book of First World War Poetry.* Ed. Jon Silkin. London: Penguin, 1996.

Paick, James. N.d. *Sky Port.* www.sketchfeed.com/artist_jamespaick (accessed 2/1/10).

Paik, Nam June. 1974. *TV Garden.* New York.

———. 1984. *Good Morning, Mr. Orwell.* New York, Seoul, Paris.

———. 1986. *Bye Bye Kipling.* New York, Seoul, Tokyo.

Paik, Peter. 2010. "Utopia Achieved: The Case of Watchmen." *From Utopia to Apocalypse: Science Fiction and the Politics of Catastrophe.* Minneapolis: University of Minnesota Press.

Pardey, James. 2009. "16. A Ballardian Reboot." www.penguinsciencefiction.org (accessed 8/7/09).

Park, Andrew. 1988. "Minjung and Process Hermeneutics." *Process Studies* 17.2 (Summer 1988). www.religion-online.org (accessed 7/5/06).

Park, Ed. 2008. *Personal Days.* New York: Random House.

Park, Ishle Yi. 2004. "Flight." www.bostonreview.net (accessed 8/4/06).

Park, Linda Sue. 2002. *When My Name Was Keoko.* New York: Yearling.

Parrinder, Patrick, ed. 2001. *Learning from Other Worlds: Estrangement, Cognition, and the Politics of Science Fiction and Utopia.* Durham, NC: Duke University Press.

Person, Lawrence. 1998/1999. "Notes toward a Post-Cyberpunk Manifesto." http://slashdot.org (accessed 3/6/07).

Plath, Sylvia. 1961. "Tulips." *Collected Poems.* Ed. Ted Hughes. Cutchogue, NY: Buccaneer Books, 1998.

Poe, Edgar Allan. 1845. "The Facts in the Case of M. Valdemar." *The Science Fiction of Edgar Allan Poe*. Ed. Harold Beaver. London: Penguin, 1976. 194–203.

Post, Jonathan. 1984. "The Neurophysiologist." *Burning with a Vision: Poetry of Science and the Fantastic*. Ed. Robert Frazier. Philadelphia: Owlswick.

Pound, Ezra. 1914. "L'Art, 1910." *Personae: The Shorter Poems of Ezra Pound*. Ed. Lea Baechler and Walton Litz. New York: New Directions, 1990.

Powers, Richard. 1995. *Galatea 2.2*. New York: HarperPerennial, 1996.

———. 2000. *Plowing the Dark*. New York: Picador, 2001.

Pratchett, Terry. 2007. *Making Money*. London: Doubleday.

Preminger, Alex, and T. V. F. Brogan, eds. 1993. *The New Princeton Encyclopedia of Poetry and Poetics*. Princeton, NJ: Princeton University Press.

Prucher, Jeff, ed. 2009a. *Brave New Words: The Oxford Dictionary of Science Fiction*. Oxford, UK: Oxford University Press.

———. 2009b. "Science Fiction." *Brave New Words: The Oxford Dictionary of Science Fiction*. Ed. Jeff Prucher. Oxford, UK: Oxford University Press.

Putnam, Hilary. 1964. "Robots: Machines or Artificially Created Life?" *Journal of Philosophy* 61.21, American Philosophical Association Eastern Division Sixty-First Annual Meeting. 668–691.

Raczymow, Henri, and Alan Astro, trans. 1994. "Memory Shot through with Holes." *Yale French Studies* 85: 98–106.

Read, Herbert. 1933. "The End of a War." *The Penguin Book of First World War Poetry*. Ed. Jon Silkin. 2nd ed. London: Penguin. 160–175.

"Reader." 1997. "Neuromancer Takes No Prisoners." 6/23/97 customer review of *Neuromancer*. www.amazon.com (accessed 5/11/02).

Reichardt, Jasia. 1978. *Robots: Fact, Fiction, and Prediction*. Harmondsworth, Middlesex, England: Penguin.

Remarque, Erich Maria. 1929. *All Quiet on the Western Front*. Trans. A. W. Wheen. New York: Random House, 1982.

Reynolds, Alastair. 2000. *Revelation Space*. London: Gollancz, 2008.

Rich, Adrienne. 1972. "Diving into the Wreck." *Diving into the Wreck: Poems, 1971–1972*. New York: Norton, 1994.

Richter, Stephan. 2000. "How It All Began." www.theglobalist.com (accessed 2/09/08).

Rickword, Edgell. 1920. "The Soldier Addresses His Body." *The Penguin Book of First World War Poetry*. Ed. Jon Silkin. 2nd ed. London: Penguin, 1996.

Rieder, John. 2008. *Colonialism and the Emergence of Science Fiction*. Middletown, CT: Wesleyan University Press.

Roberts, Adam. 2000. *Science Fiction*. London: Routledge.

———. 2005. *The History of Science Fiction*. New York: Palgrave, 2007.

Robertson, Roland. 1992. *Globalization: Social Theory and Global Culture*. London: Sage.

Robinson, Kim Stanley. 1985. *The Memory of Whiteness: A Scientific Romance.* New York: Orb, 1996.

———. 1993. *Red Mars.* New York: Bantam.

———. 1994. *Green Mars.* New York: Bantam, 1995.

———. 1996. *Blue Mars.* New York: Bantam, 1997.

"Robots Could Demand Legal Rights." 2006. *BBC News,* December 21. http://news.bbc.co.uk (accessed 4/21/07).

Rose, Mark. 1981. *Alien Encounters: Anatomy of Science Fiction.* Cambridge, MA: Harvard University Press.

Rothberg, Michael. 2000. *Traumatic Realism: The Demands of Holocaust Representation.* Minneapolis: University of Minnesota Press.

Rothblatt, Martine. 2003. "Biocyberethics: Should We Stop a Company from Unplugging an Intelligent Computer?" www.KurzweilAI.net (accessed 4/21/07).

Rothschild, Babette. 2000. *The Body Remembers: The Psychophysiology of Trauma and Trauma Treatment.* New York: Norton.

Rucker, Rudy. 2007. *Postsingular.* New York: Tor, 2009.

Russ, Joanna. 1975. *The Female Man.* New York: Bantam.

———. 1995. "Speculations: The Subjunctivity of Science Fiction." *To Write Like a Woman: Essays in Feminism and Science Fiction.* Bloomington: Indiana University Press. 15–25.

Russell, Mary Doria. 1996. *The Sparrow.* New York: Ballantine, 2004.

———. 1998. *Children of God.* New York: Fawcett, 1999.

Ryan, Marie-Laure. 1999a. "Cyberspace, Virtuality, and the Text." *Cyberspace Textuality: Computer Technology and Literary Theory.* Ed. Marie-Laure Ryan. Bloomington: Indiana University Press. 78–107.

———. 1999b. "Introduction." *Cyberspace Textuality: Computer Technology and Literary Theory.* Ed. Marie-Laure Ryan. Bloomington: Indiana University Press. 1–28.

———. 2001. *Narrative as Virtual Reality: Immersion and Interactivity in Literature and Electronic Media.* Baltimore: Johns Hopkins University Press.

Ryman, Geoff. 1989. *The Child Garden.* New York: Orb, 1994.

Satty, Harvey, and Curtis Smith. 1976. "Introduction." *Last Men in London by Olaf Stapledon.* Boston: Gregg Press. v–xiv.

Sawyer, Robert. 2000. *Calculating God.* New York: Tor, 2001.

Saxton, Curtis. 2006. "Star Wars: Technical Commentaries." www.theforce.net (accessed 12/11/06).

Scalzi, John. 2009. "Foreword." *The Forever War* by Joe Haldeman. New York: Thomas Dunne. ix–xiii.

Scarry, Elaine. 1985. *The Body in Pain: The Making and Unmaking of the World.* New York: Oxford University Press, 1987.

———. 1994. *Resisting Representation.* New York: Oxford University Press.

———. 1999a. *Dreaming by the Book.* New York: Farrar, Straus and Giroux.

———. 1999b. *On Beauty and Being Just.* Princeton, NJ: Princeton University Press.

Scharpé, Michiel. 2003. "A Trail of Disorientation: Blurred Boundaries in Der Sandmann." *Image and Narrative* 5 (January).

Scholes, Robert. 1975. *Structural Fabulation: An Essay on Fiction of the Future.* South Bend, IN: University of Notre Dame Press.

Scholes, Robert, and Eric S. Rabkin. 1977. *Science Fiction: History, Science, Vision.* Oxford, UK: Oxford University Press.

"Science Fiction." 2006a. http://en.wikipedia.org (accessed 6/10/06).

"Science Fiction." 2006b. The Oxford English Dictionary Online. www.oed.com (accessed 6/15/06).

Seed, David, ed. 2005. *A Companion to Science Fiction.* Malden, MA: Blackwell, 2008.

Sexton, Anne. 1972. "The Ambition Bird." *The Complete Poems.* New York: Houghton Mifflin, 1999.

Shakespeare, William. 1609. "Sonnet 27." *Shakespeare's Sonnets.* Ed. Barbara Mowat and Paul Werstine. New York: Washington Square Press, 2004.

Shelley, Mary. 1818. *Frankenstein.* Oxford, UK: Oxford University Press, 1998.

———. 1826. *The Last Man.* Lincoln: University of Nebraska Press, 1993.

Shelley, Percy Bysshe. 1820. "Ode to the West Wind." *Shelley's Poetry and Prose.* Ed. Donald H. Reiman and Sharon B. Powers. New York: Norton, 1977.

———. 1821/1840. "A Defence of Poetry." *The Norton Anthology of English Literature.* Ed. M. H. Abrams. 4th ed. New York: Norton, 1979. 782–794.

Shiel, M. P. 1930. *The Purple Cloud.* New York: Warner Paperback, 1973.

Short, John Rennie. 2001. *Global Dimensions: Space, Place and the Contemporary World.* London: Reaktion.

Silkin, Jon, ed. 1996. *The Penguin Book of First World War Poetry.* 2nd ed. London: Penguin.

Simmons, Dan. 1989. *Hyperion.* New York: Bantam, 1995.

———. 1990. *The Fall of Hyperion.* New York: Bantam, 1995.

Simons, Ronald C., and Charles C. Hughes, eds. 1985. *The Culture-Bound Syndromes: Folk Illnesses of Psychiatric and Anthropological Interest.* Dordrecht, Holland: D. Reidel Publishing Company.

Singer, P. W. 2009. *Wired for War: The Robotics Revolution and Conflict in the 21st Century.* New York: Penguin.

Slusser, George, and Gary Westfahl, eds. 2002. *Science Fiction, Canonization, Marginalization, and the Academy.* Westport, CT: Greenwood Press.

Smith, Clark Ashton. 1931. "The City of Singing Flame." *The Prentice Hall Anthology of Science Fiction and Fantasy.* Ed. Garyn G. Roberts. Upper Saddle River, NJ: Prentice Hall, 2001. 232–256.

Smith, Cordwainer. 1959. "No, No, Not Rogov!" *The Rediscovery of Man: The Complete Short Fiction of Cordwainer Smith.* Ed. James Mann. Framingham, MA: NESFA Press, 1993. 3–18.

Sollors, Werner. 1986. *Beyond Ethnicity: Consent and Descent in American Culture.* New York: Oxford University Press.

———. 1996. *Theories of Ethnicity: A Classical Reader.* New York: New York University Press.

Somers, Sandra L. 1998. "Examining Anger in 'Culture-Bound' Syndromes." *Psychiatric Times* 15.1 (January). www.psychiatrictimes.com (accessed 7/21/06).

Song, Cathy. 1983. "Girl Powdering Her Neck." *The Norton Anthology of Poetry.* Ed. Margaret Ferguson, Mary Jo Salter, and Jon Stallworthy. 4th ed. New York: Norton, 1996.

Song, Min. 2005. *Strange Future: Pessimism and the 1992 Los Angeles Riots.* Durham, NC: Duke University Press.

Sontag, Susan. 1965. "The Imagination of Disaster." *Against Interpretation and Other Essays.* New York: Picador. 209–225.

Spenser, Edmund. 1590/1596. *The Faerie Queene.* Ed. Thomas Roche. London: Penguin, 1987.

———. 1595. "Amoretti, Sonnet lxiiii." *The Shorter Poems.* Ed. Richard McCabe. London: Penguin, 1999.

Stapledon, Olaf. 1930. *Last and First Men: A Story of the Near and Far Future. Last and First Men and Star Maker: Two Science-Fiction Novels by Olaf Stapledon.* New York: Dover, 1968. 1–246.

———. 1930/1937. *Last and First Men and Star Maker.* New York: Dover, 1968.

———. 1932. *Last Men in London. Last and First Men and Last Men in London.* London: Penguin, 1973. 329–605.

———. 1935. *Odd John. Odd John and Sirius: Two Science-Fiction Novels by Olaf Stapledon.* New York: Dover, 1972. 1–157.

———. 1979. *Far Future Calling: Uncollected Science Fiction and Fantasies of Olaf Stapledon.* Philadelphia: Oswald Train.

Steger, Manfred B. 2003. *Globalization: A Very Short Introduction.* Oxford, UK: Oxford University Press.

Stenger, Nicole. 1991. "Mind Is a Leaking Rainbow." *Cyberspace: First Steps.* Ed. Michael Benedikt. Cambridge, MA: MIT Press. 49–58.

Stephanson, Anders. 1988. "Regarding Postmodernism—A Conversation with Fredric Jameson." *Universal Abandon? The Politics of Postmodernism.* Ed. Andrew Ross. Minneapolis: University of Minnesota Press. 3–30.

Stephenson, Neal. 1992. *Snow Crash.* New York: Bantam, 2003.

Sterling, Bruce. 1989. "Slipstream." www.eff.org (accessed 7/25/08).

Stevens, Wallace. 1967. "Of Mere Being." *The Palm at the End of the Mind: Selected Poems and a Play.* Ed. Holly Stevens. New York: Vintage, 1990.

Stevenson, Robert Louis. 1886. *Dr. Jekyll and Mr. Hyde.* New York: Bantam, 2004.

Stross, Charles. 2003. *Singularity Sky.* New York: Ace, 2004.

Sturgeon, Theodore. 1953. *More Than Human.* New York: Vintage, 1998.

Suvin, Darko. 1979. *Metamorphoses of Science Fiction: On the Poetics and History of a Literary Genre.* New Haven, CT: Yale University Press.

Swift, Jonathan. 1726/1735. *Gulliver's Travels.* Oxford, UK: Oxford University Press, 1999.

Tae Guk Gi. 2004. Dir. Je-Gyu Kang. DVD. Showbox, 2005.

Tennyson, Alfred. 1851. "The Eagle." *Selected Poems.* Ed. Aidan Day. London: Penguin, 1991.

Tepper, Sherri. 1988. *The Gate to Women's Country.* New York: Bantam.

Teskey, Gordon. 1996. *Allegory and Violence.* Ithaca, NY: Cornell University Press.

Thompson, Clive. 2004. "The Undead Zone: Why Realistic Graphics Make Humans Look Creepy." www.slate.com (accessed 5/21/08).

Tiptree, James. 1977a. "The Screwfly Solution." *Her Smoke Rose Up Forever.* San Francisco: Tachyon, 2004. 9–31.

———. 1977b. "Slow Music." *Her Smoke Rose Up Forever.* San Francisco: Tachyon, 2004. 459–504.

Todorov, Tzvetan. 1970. *The Fantastic: A Structural Approach to a Literary Genre.* Trans. Richard Howard. Ithaca, NY: Cornell University Press, 1975.

———. 1995. *Genres in Discourse.* Cambridge, UK: Cambridge University Press.

Tomas, David. 1991. "Old Rituals for New Space: Rites De Passage and William Gibson's Cultural Model of Cyberspace." *Cyberspace: First Steps.* Ed. Michael Benedikt. Cambridge, MA: MIT Press. 31–47.

Toomer, Jean. 1922. "Storm Ending." *Cane.* Ed. Darwin Turner. New York: Norton, 1988. 51.

Trenka, Jane Jeong. 2003. *The Language of Blood: A Memoir.* St. Paul, MN: Graywolf Press.

"Trust Me, I'm a Robot." 2006. *The Economist,* June 8. www.economist.com (accessed 8/7/07).

Turkle, Sherry. 1995. *Life on the Screen: Identity in the Age of the Internet.* New York: Simon & Schuster.

2001: A Space Odyssey. 1968. Dir. Stanley Kubrick. Warner Home Video: Turner Entertainment Co., 1999.

U.N. Press Release. 2009. Note no. 6192; March 16.

Vees-Gulani, Susanne. 2003. "Diagnosing Billy Pilgrim: A Psychiatric Approach to Kurt Vonnegut's Slaughterhouse-Five." *Critique* 44.2 (Winter): 175–184.

Verne, Jules. 1870. *20,000 Leagues under the Sea.* Trans. Mendor Brunetti. New York: Penguin, 2001.

Vinge, Vernor. 1984. *The Peace War.* New York: Tom Doherty, 2003.

Virilio, Paul, and Patrice Riemens (translator). 2000. "The Kosovo War Took Place in Orbital Space: Paulo Virilio in Conversation with John Armitage." www.ctheory.net (accessed 2/5/07).

Vonnegut, Kurt. 1959. *The Sirens of Titan.* New York: Dial, 2006.

———. 1969. *Slaughterhouse-Five; Or the Children's Crusade: A Duty-Dance with Death.* New York: Dell, 1991.

Walcott, Derek. 1996. "The Gulf." *The Norton Anthology of Poetry*. Ed. Margaret Ferguson, Mary Jo Salter, and Jon Stallworthy. 4th ed. New York: Norton.

Wallace, Molly. 2001. "Tropics of Globalization: Reading the New North America." *Symploke* 9.1–2: 145–160.

Wallis, David. 1996. "After Cyberoverkill Comes Cyberburnout." *New York Times*, August 4: 43.

Wee, Valerie Su-Lin. 1997. "The Most Poetic Subject in the World: Observations on Death, (Beautiful) Women and Representation in 'Blade Runner.'" *Kinema*, Spring (7): 57–71.

Wegner, Phillip. 2002. *Imaginary Communities*. Berkeley: University of California Press.

Weldes, Jutta. 2001. "Globalisation Is Science Fiction." *Millennium: Journal of International Studies* 30.3: 647–667.

———. 2003. "Popular Culture, Science Fiction, and World Politics: Exploring Intertextual Relations." *To Seek Out New Worlds: Exploring Links between Science Fiction and World Politics*. Ed. Jutta Weldes. 1st ed. New York: Palgrave Macmillan. 1–27.

Wells, H. G. 1898a. *The Time Machine: An Invention*. Peterborough, Ontario, Canada: Broadview Press, 2001.

———. 1898b. *The War of the Worlds*. Dallas: BenBella, 2005.

———. 1901. *The First Men in the Moon*. New York: Modern Library, 2003.

———. 1937. "World Brain: The Idea of a Permanent World Encyclopedia." https://sherlock.ischool.berkeley.edu (accessed 12/1/09).

Wells, H. G., et al. 1919. "The Idea of a League of Nations." www.theatlantic.com (accessed 2/1/09).

Weschler, Lawrence. 2002. "Why Is This Man Smiling?" *Wired* 10.6. www.wired.com (accessed 6/5/08).

Westfahl, Gary. 2005. "Introduction." *World Weavers: Globalization, Science Fiction, and the Cybernetic Revolution*. Ed. Wong Kin Yuen, Gary Westfahl, and Amy Kit-Sze Chan. Hong Kong: Hong Kong University Press.

"What Did You Name Your Roomba?" N.d. www.roombareview.com (accessed 7/1/07).

Whitman, Walt. 1855. "Song of Myself." *Poetry and Prose*. Ed. Justin Kaplan. New York: Library of America, 1996. 27–88.

———. 1865. "When Lilacs Last in the Dooryard Bloom'd." *Poetry and Prose*. Ed. Justin Kaplan. New York: Library of America, 1996. 459–467.

"Why Build a Human-Like Robot?" N.d. www.ai.mit.edu (accessed 7/1/08).

Willis, Connie. 2005. "'The Soul Selects Her Own Society': Invasion and Repulsion: A Chronological Reinterpretation of Two of Emily Dickinson's Poems: A Wellsian Perspective." *The War of the Worlds: Fresh Perspectives on the H. G. Wells Classic*. Ed. Glenn Yeffeth. Dallas: BenBella. 285–292.

Wolfe, Gene. 1972. "The Fifth Head of Cerberus." *The Best of Gene Wolfe: A Definitive Retrospective of His Finest Short Fiction*. New York: Tor, 2009. 31–77.

Wood, Gaby. 2002. *Edison's Eve: A Magical History of the Quest for Mechanical Life.* New York: Anchor.

Wordsworth, William. 1804. "I Wandered Lonely as a Cloud." *The Norton Anthology of English Literature.* Ed. M. H. Abrams et al. 4th ed. New York: Norton, 1979.

Wright, George. 1974. "The Lyric Present: Simple Present Verbs in English Poems." *PMLA (Publications of the Modern Language Association)* 89.3 (May): 563–579.

Wu, William. 1992. *Wong's Lost and Found Emporium and Other Oddities.* Eugene, OR: Pulphouse Publishing.

Yamashita, Karen Tei. 1990. *Through the Arc of the Rain Forest.* Minneapolis: Coffee House Press.

———. 1997. *Tropic of Orange.* Minneapolis: Coffee House Press.

Yeats, W. B. 1928. "Sailing to Byzantium." *The Poems.* Ed. Daniel Albright. London: J. M. Dent & Sons Ltd., 1990.

———. 1932. "Byzantium." *The Poems.* Ed. Daniel Albright. London: J. M. Dent & Sons Ltd, 1990.

Yolen, Jane. 1996. "Sister Emily's Lightship." *Sister Emily's Lightship and Other Stories.* New York: Tor, 2001. 267–283.

Zakon, Robert. 2004. *Hobbes's Internet Timeline.* www.zakon.org (accessed 4/5/04).

Zamyatin, Yevgeny. 1921. *We.* Trans. Mirra Ginsburg. New York: Eos, 1999.

Zelazny, Roger. 1967. *Lord of Light.* New York: Eos, 2004.

———. 1996. "Introduction." *Do Androids Dream of Electric Sheep?* New York: Ballantine Books. vii–x.

Credits

The author and publisher wish to thank the following for permission to reproduce or adapt copyrighted material.

"A Report." Reprinted by permission of the author, Ruth Fainlight.

"Of Mere Being," from *The Palm at the End of the Mind* by Wallace Stevens, edited by Holly Stevens, copyright © 1967, 1969, 1971 by Holly Stevens. Used by permission of Alfred A. Knopf, a division of Random House, Inc.

"I felt a funeral in my brain." Reprinted by permission of the publishers and the Trustees of Amherst College from *The Poems of Emily Dickinson: Variorum Edition*, edited by Ralph W. Franklin, Cambridge, Mass.: The Belknap Press of Harvard University Press, Copyright © 1998 by the President and Fellows of Harvard College. Copyright © 1951, 1955, 1979, 1983 by the President and Fellows of Harvard College.

"Wittman Ah Sing Foresees Postethnic Humanity." Reprinted by permission of the publisher from *A New Literary History of America*, edited by Greil Marcus and Werner Sollors, pp. 1023, 1025, Cambridge, Mass.: The Belknap Press of Harvard University Press, Copyright © 2009 by the President and Fellows of Harvard College.

"Come On, My Lucky Lads" by Edmund Blunden, from *Undertones of War*, Penguin Books Ltd. Reprinted by permission of David Higham Associates Ltd.

"Science Fiction and Postmemory Han in Contemporary Korean American Literature" by Seo-Young Chu first appeared in *MELUS: Journal of the Society for the Study of the Multi-Ethnic Literature of the United States*, issue 33.4 (Winter 2008), pages 97–121, and is reprinted by permission of the journal.

"Generation" and "Translations from the Mother Tongue" by Suji Kwock Kim, from *Notes from the Divided Country*. Reprinted by permission of Louisiana State University Press.

Acknowledgments

In some sense, writing these Acknowledgments was for me much more difficult than writing the rest of this book. There are so many people to thank, and there is not enough space in which to thank them all. The following paragraphs therefore constitute a fragmentary version of the ideal Acknowledgments, which would include the names of everybody who influenced this book and which would accommodate the depths of my gratitude more fully than do the paragraphs below.

I wish to thank the many acquaintances from my years as a student in college and graduate school—professors, administrators, co-panelists, journal editors, fellow graduate students, my own undergraduate students, and other interlocutors and figures of inspiration—who have contributed, indirectly and directly, to the making of this book. Elaine Scarry has gifted me with a mentorship that will inform and inspire me for the rest of my life. Her luminous care for this project, her reverence for teaching, and her astonishing intellectual generosity have meant so much more to me than I can say. Werner Sollors has been an endless source of insight, wisdom, encouragement, and judicious advice. His feedback, always thoughtful and incisive, has added strength and clarity to my work. And Daniel Albright enriched this book with his erudition, wit, imaginativeness, and enthusiasm for poetry and science fiction. I have benefited mightily from his encyclopedic knowledge of the arts. A million thanks as well (with apologies to anyone I may have inadvertently omitted) to Bradley Bassler, Eric Bennett, Homi Bhabha, Shameem Black, Allyson Booth, Stephen Burt, Samuel Delany, Wai Chee Dimock, James Engell, Julia Faisst, Orofisola Fasehun, Philip Fisher, Carl Freedman, Richard Fusco, Stephen Greenblatt, Cheryl Higashida, Margaret Homans, Yunte Huang, Melissa Jenkins, William Jewett, Matthew Kaiser, Case Q. Kerns, Catherine Keyser, Daniel Kim, Julia Sun-Joo Lee, Seth Lerer, Barbara Lewalski, Herbert Lindenberger, Matt Loy, Andrea Lunsford, Douglas Mao, Anna McDonald, Cristanne Miller, Thomas Otten, Peter Y. Paik, Marjorie Perloff, Claire Reynolds,

John Rieder, Marie Rutkoski, Peter Saval, James Simpson, Stephen Hong Sohn, Larry Switzky, Gordon Teskey, Michael Trask, Gwen Urdang-Brown, and Caroline Weber. Many thanks, too, to my wonderful colleagues and students in the Harvard History and Literature program, where I taught for two years as a postdoctoral lecturer. Among the Hist and Lit folks with whom I had the privilege of working: Christina Becker, Peter Becker, George Blaustein, Stephanie Lin Carlson, Sarah Rose Cole, Jason Crawford, Meaghan Dempsey, Joshua Feblowitz, Mark Hanna, Melissa Jenkins, Monica Jun, Aaron Lecklider, Lauren Mulcahy, Jeanne Follansbee Quinn, Peter Raymond, Andrew Romig, Yael Schacher, Amy Spellacy, and Rikka Strong.

This project underwent its most important transformation—from a manuscript titled "On Science Fiction: A New Theory of Representation" to a book titled *Do Metaphors Dream of Literal Sleep? A Science-Fictional Theory of Representation*—at Queens College, City University of New York (CUNY), where I have had the tremendously good fortune to teach and work since August 2009. I could not have completed *Do Metaphors Dream of Literal Sleep?* without the encouragement and support of my fantastic colleagues, mentors, and students at Queens. From the outset they have made me feel at home here at QC and in New York; moreover, they have shown kind interest in this project, and their insights have enhanced my understanding of science fiction, lyric poetry, and the globalized world. Thank you in particular (with apologies again to anyone I may have inadvertently omitted) to Sabrin Abedin, Jody Ballew, Ryan Black, Fred Buell, Shirley Carrie, Nancy Comley, Nicole Cooley, Michael Davanzo, Nicole Denara, Annmarie Drury, Hugh English, the QC Dean of Arts & Humanities Tamara Evans, Duncan Faherty, Kevin Ferguson, Gloria Fisk, Thomas Frosch, Fred Gardaphe, Tyler Gumb, Kimiko Hahn, Alexandra Helmers, Carrie Hintz, Caroline Hong, Madhulika Khandelwal, Shih-Mei Kong, Yehoshua Laker, Kathleen La Rosa, John Manago, Richard McCoy, Melinda Miller, Wayne Moreland, QC President James Muyskens, Biljana Ostojic, Tom Ragogna, Amy Ragone, Vedi Ramdhanie, David H. Richter, Sian Silyn Roberts, Michael Sargent, Talia Schaffer, Veronica Schanoes, Harold Schechter, Donna Schultz, Kim Smith, QC Provost James Stellar, Jason Tougaw, Frances Tran, Sharon Tran, Andrea Walkden, Amy Wan, Karen Weingarten, and John Weir, as well as to the many others who take part in making Queens College a welcoming habitat for intellectual inquiry, dialogue, collaboration, and invention.

Heartfelt thanks to everyone at Harvard University Press who believed in my manuscript, who helped bring *Do Metaphors Dream of Literal Sleep?* into existence, and whose understanding of the project at times surpassed my own. Lindsay Waters has been a vibrant interlocutor and an inexhaustible source of encouragement and inspiration. It is to him that I owe the realization that this book's preoccupation with literalized figures of speech can be traced to my childhood fascination with the Roman Catholic concept of transubstantiation. Phoebe Kosman and Hannah Wong have continually impressed me with their enthusiasm and expertise, and working with them over the past several years has been a delight. Barbara Goodhouse, who saw the manuscript through the production process, has handled each page of the manuscript with skill, grace, meticulousness, and sensitivity. I am grateful to her not just for her meticulousness and skill but also for her patience and efficiency. To the two readers, Stephen Burt and Peter Paik, who reviewed earlier versions of *Do Metaphors Dream*, I am grateful for the vital role that they played in improving the manuscript. The wealth of their advice, the energy of their skepticism, and the care with which they attended to the original manuscript in all of its aspects guided my efforts to refine the argumentation and prose. Furthermore, the questions they raised about the limits and stakes of my project gave me clearer insight into the project's aims.

To Jean Galbraith, Daniel Kim, Nina Kang, David Auerbach, Megan Luke, Sara Meirowitz, and others who have known me for so long that once upon a time they called me Jennie: Thank you for your brilliant friendship and support over the years. Special thanks—To Mary Sukjong Hong for your radiant emails, for 한글, and for translucent blue-green envelopes that blossom when opened. To John Siciliano for always laughing at my jokes and for the fifteen years (and counting) of sage and witty counsel. To Gabriella Gruder-Poni for Firenze, chocolate in Philadelphia, and lessons in close reading back in 1997. To Larry Switzky for Elektra "Fembot" and for agreeing that puppets are definitely more uncanny than robots. To Jane E. Martin, *ma petite lapine*, for Wintersonian adventures in Provincetown, San Francisco, Vancouver, Salem, Biddeford, and elsewhere. To Greta Pane for the literal sustenance, for reading drafts of this manuscript with exactness and care, for the excursions to Svalbard, and for the secret chapter in invisible ink.

Very special thanks to my brother Jae-kyun Patrick Chu—for your skepticism, ingenuity, and sense of humor; for the innumerable conversations about science fiction and philosophy that you and I have shared since childhood; for understanding the "Onto D"; and for being the best sibling in the world.

Finally, and most important, I dedicate this book, with love, to my parents, who have made everything possible.

Index

Harvard University Press is a member of Green Press Initiative (greenpressinitiative.org), a nonprofit organization working to help publishers and printers increase their use of recycled paper and decrease their use of fiber derived from endangered forests. This book was printed on recycled paper containing 30% post-consumer waste and processed chlorine free.